Wildest Dreams

*A History of the Moody Blues, Rock Band Extraordinaire
of the Fabulous Sixties and Beyond*

Christie Grayson

Wildest Dreams History of the Moody Blues Copyright 2012 Christie Grayson All rights reserved. This book may not be photocopied or used in any way (electronic or otherwise) without written permission.

Cover art by Rhonda Conley

Every reasonable effort has been made to verify the facts and events described herein, and the author can bear no responsibility for source-driven errors.

Cedar Chest Publishing Bremerton WA
Tech support by Stephanwurks
Printed in the United States of America
Fourth Edition, April 2018

ISBN: 9781980746676

Table of Contents

I) Prelude: Are You Sitting Comfortably? (Pg.9)
II) In the Beginning back unto World War II: (Pg.13)
III) Mists of Time: 1955-1966 (Pg. 17)
IV) Step Back Out: ..... (Pg 47)
V) I Think I Am: Fall 1966 (Pg. 51)
VI) Crystal White Sands (A call to arms): Fall 1966—November 11, 1967 (Pg. 71)
VII) Heroes' Journey (They set forth on a Quest): March 1968-July 1969 (Pg.97)
VIII) Across the Threshold: 1969-1970 (Pg.124)
IX) Land of Make Believe: 1971-February 4, 1974 (Pg. 153)
X) Middle Eight (Further from the Shore): 1974-1977 (Pg. 168)
XI) A Higher Octave: 1978-1980 (Pg. 191)
XII) Veteran Cosmic Rockin' 1980-1982 (Pg.206)

XIII) No Time Like the Present: 1983-1986 (Pg. 218)
XIV) On the Sea: 1987-1990 (Pg. 229)
XV) Keys of the Kingdom: 1990-September 1991 (Pg. 251)
XVI) The Other Side of Being Moody: March 1991-April 1994 (Pg. 265)
XVII) Red Rocks, Moody Blues: Fall 1992-March 2000 (Pg. 277)
XVIII) A View from a Certain Hill: September 1991-1999 (Pg. 292)
XIX) Step into the Light (Mike follows his Bliss): (Pg. 309)
XX) Strange Times (unto the New Millennium): (Pg. 320)
XXI) Winter's Tale: the Christmas album: (Pg. 332)
XXII) Twenty-first Century Moodies: (Pg. 335)
XXIII) Absolute Final Word: (Pg. 351)

Appendices

A) Standing in a Tour Zone: the view from the footlights (Pg.355)
B) Blue World: the view from the House (Pg.375)
C) Who Are You Now? (Pg.405)
D) Moody Art: The Beggars' Opera meets the Veteran Cosmic Rocker (Pg. 433)
E) Say Again? Odd phrases and words: (Pg.446)

Bibliography: (Pg.475)

Yet to Come..
Wildest Dreams Vol. II: Blue Timeline
A listing of articles and performance dates, as well as other significant dates in Moody Blues history. Published under separate cover.

For Lorna, Ross and John, who were all there at the beginning of this.

"Whatever these words are all about, they were all written for you."

I) Prelude: Are you Sitting Comfortably?

My beta readers skidded off the original Introduction (a manifesto), so a good deal of *that* was moved to the end. Nonetheless, a few things should be outlined prior to reading.

If they write a biography about us, it could never be complete because they'd have to leave out the naughty parts! -- Hayward, Storyteller interviews, 2010

This is not an authorized biography. In no way has the band given their input, other than to sit still for a lot of media interviews (with other people than me!) over the past fifty plus years. It is a compilation of a massive amount of published articles and various media outlets; take a look at all the primary source data at
https://www.tapatalk.com/groups/moodybluesattitude/
Hopefully this biography is positive exposure in a commercial sense, and thus shall enrich all artists mentioned. This is a fourth edition, with many updates since initial publication in 2012. All writers should have the utmost respect for intellectual property; every effort has been made to avoid violating the copyrights of other artists. As a researcher I continually ran across website owners or those selling articles on-line, who put their OWN watermark over scans of vintage articles, as if this gave them some sort of ownership. I'd recommend looking up the concept of "fair use" in case this keeps you awake at night. (In America, after fifty years, copyrights expire unless renewed.)

When the legend becomes fact, print the legend. -- apocryphal

Titles and subtitles of this book are of course, clever reflections of Moody Blues lyrics (which often are quite "generic.") For example the phrase "living in strange times" comes from Marcia Clarke's biography (and she was a huge Doors fan, ref *Strange Days*.) Graeme claims he coined the phrase "senior citizens" indeed he may have. Did Justin coin the phrase "In your wildest dreams"? It's part of the English lexicon now; I found at least eight books with the title "Wildest Dreams" in print.

There are many opinions in the book, especially the Red Rocks chapter. This book (written over twenty years) was quite a journey through the learning curve, and I found the writing broke into three types of narrative: informational (a bit dry), opinion (everyone has one), and storytelling. You can take this book either as a poorly referenced rock history tome, an attempt at mythic fiction, OR as entertainment. My objective has been to entertain by telling a *story*. Maybe it would help to think of the Moodies as being a slightly "mythological." Think of Oliver Stone doing *The Doors*, or *Alexander*. The myth, the stories, the legends, all belong to shifting realities. The Moody Blues Story is already part of Dreamtime.

The Moody Blues are a commercial band. They are not mystics, they are just professionals making money. Fans take it far too seriously. -- the Unknown Roadie

Without a doubt, someone somewhere isn't going to like something in this book, probably a hard-core fan. On November 11, 2012, I posted an Internet notice to let those mentioned in the book know that they were being mentioned (to be polite, and also for legal purposes; I don't know where some of them are anymore, you can only do what you can, in good faith, and go forth.)

What is history but a fable agreed upon? – Napoleon.

One on-line detractor DID bring up a good point, that I was writing from "a biased perspective." There is worth to this, as all of us write and speak through our personal filters. In no way is this intended as "the ultimate authority on the Moody Blues." I do urge all readers to continue with your own further research if you love the band like I do. Start with *https://www.tapatalk.com/groups/moodybluesattitude/* as the ultimate repository of source material; I started collecting about the same time Taran did, and she's done a great job with the archives.

You take what you can get and make a decision --June 2009, overheard on the news report.

My biggest problem was keeping track of all the references. This was a lot of work, it's the best I could do with the data given. It's a historical, "secondary source" tome, intended for pleasure reading. Everything in this book, unless in italics (some of those are personal experiences and "out takes") is backed up by documentation. Remember, even the primary sources are suspect! Of course, there will be inaccuracies in it (reality check here! There are inaccuracies in every history book!) Hopefully the booboos are few, but there are a lot of truths too. None of it is deliberate misinformation. Bad karma comes back on those who intentionally spread lies about the Moodies.

Those who know their Shakespeare will remember a cute little "play within a play" at the end of *A Midsummer Night's Dream* wherein the gentle-ladies in the audience are warned of the lion's roar "do not be a-feared." Well, this book has a few lion roars, notably during my description of fan behavior in Appendix B, and the discussion of legal matters. Justin certainly regales us to "Say it With Love" in concert. But there is no light without darkness, and to avoid unpleasant situations in our future, sometimes a good honest look at the past is helpful. I tried to be as factual and fair as I could in each situation. Commentary (fair or foul) doesn't define the Moody Blues. Their music does.

Four band lawsuit references are included in the interests of being complete. Everyone makes bone-headed decisions once in a while, even rock heroes; I tried to be fair to all and stick to "just the facts." Fans of the band want to know what happened as a matter of history, so this is the most clinical portrayal I can make of those happenings.

In December, 2013, an academic paper entitled "Band Name Protection: What's in a Name?" was discovered, dated February 14, 2012 (and the author didn't put his name on it either.) This paper is a secondary source document, referencing primary document *Pinder v. Decca Record Co. Ltd. and Another* (May 15, 1981.) We are only as good as our sources: the information in this was an important missing puzzle piece to the events around the formal separation of Pinder and Clarke from the band.

Much was rewritten and updated, as was the annotated bibliography. Many typos were corrected. The author wishes to apologize for any misconceptions which may have arisen from the erroneous narrative of the first edition More information on legal matters for the band may be accessed at *travellingeternityroad.yuku.com/topic/10906/Pinder-vs-Decca-moraz-mentioned-as-well#.UsR5PrSWRdd*

A companion "website" of graphics for this book, may be found at *www.wildestdreamsthebook.yuku.com*. Most of the items on this site are "freeware" found readily on the Internet. It was developed to expand and enhance this story.

So get comfortable. Here we go.

II) In The Beginning

The first radio broadcast was opera, Jan 13, 1910.--Old Farmer's Almanac

Without a song, the day would never end; without a song, a man ain't got a friend, without a song, the road would never bend, so I keep singing a song --Elvis Presley

Where did rock n' roll come from anyway?? Seems a redundant sort of question, if you think about it. It's so much a part of our lives, those of us born after World War II, that we rarely stop to think about it. It's folk music, it's soul; "Rhythm and blues married soul and the result was rock n' roll" a guitarist once quipped. Certainly American folk music, honky-tonk blues, and otherwise, ALL traces its roots back to Irish and Scots immigrants, who brought the songs across the pond to America some 400 years ago. But that's a little bit too far to go back.

What I know about the deepest beginnings is this: during the Depression and World War II (1928-1946), radio became a very important thing. People wanted to stay in touch with the rest of the world, which was suddenly coming apart at the seams. People wanted information. In between the bits of information, they wanted something to make them feel better, and into this vacuum came that international language, music. Sometimes it was big band, or classical music, which up until the invention of radio, only people in the big cities had heard. Radio music knows no boundaries, and crosses political borders. It needs no language to understand. Tokyo Rose kept American sailors "in touch" all over the Pacific. A young American G.I. in Germany listening to Marlena Dietrich singing "Lili Marlene" was just as moved as a young German soldier, hearing the same radio broadcast. Even girls in Italy squealed over Frank Sinatra, I have no doubt.

Dietrich and Sinatra were obviously not alone in the super stardom of radio; World War II spawned an entire spectrum of popular music, the music loved by the parents of the baby boomers. If you will pardon my academics: I would say there are at least three or four factors that went into development of rock n' roll in the English-speaking world.

First Factor: One of the first popular (non-orchestral, and non-big band) music groups to take advantage of the radio was Bob Wills and the Texas Playboys, coming out of the honky-tonks and the swamps of Oklahoma (and the Deep South of course, as did the lyrics to "Johnny B. Goode"!) During the Great Depression, Bob Wills (and friends) filled the airwaves on KVOO Tulsa during the noon hour. What went on in the American heartland, around the Playboys, was a somewhat underground, grassroots entourage of boxcar musicians such as Woody Guthrie, his friend Ledbetter ("Leadbelly"), and Pete Seeger, all leaders of the modern American folk moment.

My uncle (who grew up in Oklahoma) was one of these boxcar musicians, along with countless other poor American country boys. They couldn't buy guitars, so they made them out of old cigar boxes. When Uncle Ross went to England during World War II, he picked up a guitar in his travels, and apparently became quite a hit in the nightclubs near the airbase he worked at in Essex; I think he picked up some gigs in London pubs, too. His act consisted of singing songs he knew from Okie honky-tonks and telling stories about "cowboys and Indians" in between. My grandma (a nice little old lady from Oklahoma) treasured for years a letter written to her by an enthusiastic British fan who referred to her son as "Godfry."

Perhaps it was not only my Uncle's doing; I like to think that many American G.I.s took their honky-tonk "soul" music to the U.K. with them, to share with British cousins. This is some of what people like Mike Pinder, and Mick Jagger grew up with, in pubs, sleeping in the arms of their parents, listening to American G.I.'s and their guitars, singing songs like "Irene Good-Night" and "San Antonio

Rose." During the terrible years of World War II, America must have seemed like a beautiful, rich fairyland full of singing cowboys, to the troubled and brave people of England.

    Second Factor: Oddly enough this comes from John Steinbeck [what, you've never read a Steinbeck novel? SHAME ON YOU! Go down to the library right now, and check out *Cannery Row*!] One of the most moving articles I've ever read about English children comes from Steinbeck, in his war correspondence book *Once There Was a War*. With a reporter's eye, this genius American novelist spent time in London finding out what the War was about; he then reported it back to America. He was most moved by the children, who literally followed American G.I.s around like hungry dogs, starving. In his later book *Travels with Charley* (1960) Steinbeck made this mind-blowing statement: *The Cockney children in London were restless when the bombing stopped and disturbed a pattern in which they had grown accustomed.*

    Mein Gott in Himmel!!!! Did they all start banging on trash can lids (skiffle) to relieve their restlessness???? And does it explain why Justin Hayward, younger and born the year after VE Day, tends more toward ballads, rather than rocker songs???? To validate my point, at the Storyteller gig (Washington DC, Spring 2010) Justin said very clearly British drums had more thump to them than American drums, but Americans rapidly picked that up. [You should have seen me dive for my notebooks and scribble when he said that!] It makes sense. Ginger Baker alluded to the same effect in his documentary *Beware of Mr. Baker*.

    A third factor: which I think applies to ALL British Invasion groups. The early '60s were deeply traumatic for the American people for two reasons; Baby Boomers went through public school, learning how to dive under our desks in case of atomic attack. (I know this from personal experience, I was in first grade during the Cuban Missile Crisis.) This was followed closely by the assassination (televised over and over again) of our president. When the Beatles landed in New York, young American girls had a very good reason to scream at the top of their lungs. Rock n' roll was the relief they were looking for. Big Time.

Then there's a FOURTH factor: and not the least of the factors at all. Enter a style of music with African roots, called rhythm and blues. The '50s and '60s were a time of deep unrest and friction between the white and black races of America. The friendship that blossomed between Lead Belly and Woody Guthrie was going to grow into a bridge between the two races. That bridge of music had to work, for America, and our British cousins, to heal, survive and grow.

III) Mists of Time: 1955-1966

"The album didn't work? It's not supposed to "work"! What do you think it is, a bloody motorcar?"-Mike Pinder

We get into slippery "definition" territory when we talk about rhythm and blues. It's probably the most abused term in the music world! Those of us with an ear for music (that is, people who like music with more than three chords) don't make the distinction that pedantics might. Honky-tonk music suddenly became "jazz" when Gershwin did it. It was dubbed "Country Swing" as done by Bob Wills. Ray Thomas called the style "rockabilly." It became rock n' roll when Chuck Berry and Buddy Holly did it. It's "folk" if it has an acoustic guitar behind it, but can be the same music. If you do a simple trick, take the beat and slow it down, suddenly you have a ballad. So who is to say what style of music is what style???. The only way I can sort it out, is when Denny Laine tried to sing blues, he sounded like a banshee, and when Billie Holiday did it, it sounded wonderful, soft and mellow. But both sound like good blues!

While the seminal Birmingham and London bands were developing rhythm and blues, the REAL thing was going on in the USA. Never underestimate a story from Seattle. At the Experience Music Project (The EMP, a thinly veiled front for a very fine museum of modern rock) we are educated regarding what black performers called "The Chitlin Circuit" in the late '50s and early '60s. There, genius musician Jimi Hendrix was also getting his feet wet on stage with a guitar. The original R&B is where it began, and we can only hope in today's less racist world, that the stars of the black music scene come to full recognition as true founders of modern rock n' roll. It's WONDERFUL music!!! So many times it's been said by the British bands that they just gave us back our own American sound....it's very very true.

Sherman, take the Way Back Machine to the year 1955. America is being swept by Cowboy fever; *Davy Crockett* and *The Lone Ranger* are captivating television audiences far and wide. Disneyland was also born in 1955, bringing us right back to that Western romanticism exploited by Uncle Walt, and centered in the conservative heart of Orange County, California. (Knott's Berry Farm was just over that thar hill, after all. Well, just down the freeway anyway!)

    The Cowboy Blitz was so strong it oozed over the Atlantic to England, where it was embraced whole-heartedly. The Baby Boom was on: English kids loved cowboy boots and *The Lone Ranger*, just like their American counterparts did. Ray Thomas was later to enter the stage flying "on his knees" and wearing a sombrero and leather-tooled boots, in a frightening burlesque of American cowboy movies. Banjo and guitar music was going to surface from Brum to Merseyside in the form of songs like "Down the Line" by El Riot, very like Bob Wills w/ steel guitar; the flip side is "Blue Moon." Or "Lose Your Money" with a Banjo-n-Harmonica beat. Flamenco surfaced in "Day is Done."

    "Who's That Knockin'" (Wilde Three) is called (by country singer Mac Davis) "hambone," a style of back-hills music in America. And if you pay attention, you will understand it's sometimes nothing more than Irish spoon-playing and washboard thumping.

    In reviewing tapes for writing this, I was struck by how much Marty Wilde sounded like Roy Orbison, and how much the Brum rhythm sounds like steel guitar country swing, or banjo music. Harmonicas were everywhere. Plainly the English kids were "fishing" for any bit of American music mythology they could grasp, and the result was sometimes chaotic, but beautiful and fun at the same time. *A rose by any other name would smell as sweet.* The young English kids called this musical movement skiffle.

    Mike Pinder always claims his biggest musical influences were Frank Sinatra, Nat King Cole, big band (Glenn Miller), and "big piano" sounds. When he saw the Shadows on tour in the U.K. Mike's destiny was forever bound to the noble path of rhythm and blues, and rock n' roll.

Likewise were all young musicians in England influenced. Mike's early music speaks for itself: some of the items on his resume include playing with a Brum band called the Dakotas, doing some sort of "stomp dance" impression of Johnny Preston's "Running Bear": an American cowboy-and-Indian influence again. John Lodge claims it was seeing the movie *Blackboard Jungle* with Bill Haley and the Comets, doing "Shake Rattle and Roll" and "Rock around the Clock" in 1954, which turned on the youth of Brum. But no one can remember how long it took for that movie to make it from America to England! Maybe it got there in 1955?

Then Chuck Berry did "Johnny B. Goode" in America and everything changed. Chuck not being a white guy (and times as they unfairly were, exclusionary), it was left to a young fellow from the American heartland with a pair of horn-rimmed glasses, to take up the role of rock n' roll king: Buddy Holly. I can hear the shrieks: Elvis was cool too, but the Beach Boys and the Moody Blues always cite Buddy Holly as their inspiration).

Where DID all that hip wiggling come from anyway? (*From the Man himself, Bo Diddly!*) I think the hep "lean back" hip wiggling bent knee, finger snapping, limbo step that Holly and Elvis both did, came from the soul-music performers in the "Chitlin Circuit" honky-tonks [*and they got it from church revival meetings. At wild parties during the '50s, while dancing, people used to fall over backward in ecstasy fits, flopping....we called it Dead Bug when I was in the Navy. Fighter pilots love doing it at parties. I digress.*]

It was so outrageous and subliminally erotic, that repressed white people *lapped* it up! And while Elvis was wowing the Hollywood moguls, there was Buddy Holly in his nerdy horn-rimmed glasses, putting out the most rocking, happy songs in rock n' roll. It's no wonder that so many teenagers, soon to be rockers in their own right, were fond of Holly. In Justin's words, "He was a nerd like the rest of us. There was hope after all!"

The Brum Beat--While post-war American society in the '50s was listening to classical music and Gershwin

(Gershwin also had roots in honky tonk R&B); over in England, there was a whole 'nother musical movement that we Americans had swept under the cultural rug. Honky-tonk music resurfaced as rock n' roll. At this point, I need to acknowledge an incredible body of work, the book *Brum Rocked* (AND *Brum Rocked On*), by Hornsby. On page 23, beyond all doubt, there is picture of Buddy Holly, playing Town Hall in Brum, March 1958. John Lodge even claims he was at this concert.

Rock had come to stay in the fair hamlet of Birmingham. To the dedicated music historian, the books *Brum Rocked*, and *Brum Rocked On*, together are a true treasure trove, a delightful ramble through the history of every Brum band to tread the boards. For instance, did you know that the Electric Light Orchestra (ELO) came originally from Birmingham??? And that they got their start as The Move doing naughty post cards of the Prime Minister and spreading them about Brum in secret? (And they do such pretty music too.) Ozzie Osbourne is from Brum too, which explains a lot. More can be found out about Brum in *Higher and Higher* #7/8. As well, a wonderful article about the Moody Blues during the Brum Beat era can be found in *Goldmine*, October 28, 1994 (Bruce Eder). And in *Brum Rocked On*, find a lovely photo of the very early Beatles with El Riot, who must have opened for them one night.

Around the same time Buddy Holly was in England, rocker Gene Vincent (a lively American lad from Norfolk, VA) also played in Brum, and German (Hamburg) cabaret, so we cannot discount his leather-driven, hard-bitten approach to music. Picture Jim Morrison in leather if you will, only during the '50s. Young Marlon Brando on a motorcycle fits the image. Gene Vincent was a prototype for a LOT of Rock and Roll in the '50s. According to Hornsby, the Beatles actually backed Gene Vincent at the Hamburg Star Club during their early formative years. It was early grunge and punk if you will. Gene Vincent pioneered the "modern" rock star persona by wearing a black leather jacket and knocking down microphone stands and writhing on the ground. Sadly he burned up and died young; Vincent has a biography in print should anyone be interested in this.

During the late '50s in America, Buddy Holly and the Cricketts followed a parallel development to English kids, who were getting their R&B ready to invade the States. Take a good close look at the Cricketts, and their clones, the Champs; they wear cowboy outfits, like on the cover to the hit single "Tequila". Obviously the Bob Wills influence was part of the Champs, and the Cricketts were from Texas, how could they miss that country influence? We will never know where the innovation of Buddy Holly was going to take the music world, because on Feb 3, 1959, he died in a plane crash, along with the Big Bopper and Richie Valens. The music only "died" for a few years, because (Buddy Holly having toured the UK in 1958 and left his mark) the Beatles brought the rock n' roll sound right back to American shores again. Buddy Holly lives on in the music of many '60s rockers, Jim Croce, the Beach Boys, the Stonies, Beatles and yes the Moody Blues, just to mention a few.

Liverpool today, Birmingham tomorrow: that's the forecast for the beat business.... yes, the Brum Beat is all set to take over from the booming Merseyside market -- TV Times, 1965 (England)

So, we will say that, for the purposes of our tale, in the early '60s, the Moody Blues and the Wilde Three, and all their ancestral musical groups (the Avengers, the Diplomats, El Riot and the Rebels), started out as rhythm and blues bands, mostly centered in the industrial area of Birmingham (Brum), England. Brum would come to be known as "the Other Motown," industrial, and full of poor kids trying to reach stardom. Just as Justin was doing in Swindon, the original Moody Blues started out in skiffle bands in and around Brum. In one of these groups (The Lawmen) was a fellow by the name of Nicky James, who was to later join Ray Thomas in his solo efforts (mid '70s). Then, there was this older guy, Mike Pinder, who was into electronics, and also was a wizard on the keyboards.

Mike the Moonboy --Michael Thomas "Mike" or "Mick" Pinder was also called "Moonboy" due to his taste for science fiction. He is the most senior member and original guru-leader of the Moody Blues; a talented lad from Wheelwright Road, Erdington. Mike also has a lovely West Country accent (like Justin's), so I suspect he has roots there. Mike began his music career by playing the piano in pubs, and was supported by his parents, which is not always common for musicians. Many parents want their children to choose more substantial careers, nine to five!! His first band is recorded as the Checkers. Later he played with a band called the Rocking Tuxedos, at places like the Bielefeld Youth Club, and Carlton Ballroom (Erdingham) songs like "Wipe Out" and various Beatles, Chuck Berry and Bo Diddly songs.

As Mike's dad (and grandfather too) had been in the English Army in India, it was expected that Mike do the same. So for a while, Mike dropped his musical aspirations, and went into the Army, stationed in Germany (1962). He wasn't wild about the military career path, spent time jamming with his own band whilst serving his country, and then came back to Birmingham to make his way.

Mike's skills are in the combined realm of music and electronics; at various times during the early '60s, he worked for Streetly Electronics of Birmingham (development and repair), which was then building a music synthesizer they called a Mellotron. The technology for this apparently came from the Chamberlain synthesizer, an American instrument. A quick side note: in the post WWII era, the U.K. boycotted American technology in music (some embargo deal) but still some ideas cross-pollinated. Mellotrons and Chamberlains were cutting edge music technology at the time, and Mike claims to have sold each of the Beatles a Mellotron in their early years.

Pinder refers to himself as "a poor English boy singing the blues, which is why we related to poor black kids in America, singing the blues." Though his main band was the Rocking Tuxedos, he was a welcome addition on the keyboards to many different Brum bands before he settled in with the Moody Blues. Even though Mike opted out of the Moodies in the early '80s, he cannot be overlooked as the godfather of their spiritual approach to music. Mike grew up in England during the Blitz & WWII, when, to put it mildly, things were not nice. Few of the Moodies will talk about this time, nor will many other rock stars their age, because they are times best forgotten. So Mike, that wizard of the keyboards, met up with this good-looking Welsh cat who had a big bushy moustache, and a great voice….

Take It Away, Bunny Boy --Ray Thomas can be counted as the second most senior member of the Moody Blues. Ray speaks a little (Welsh) Gaelic, has those strikingly good looks (and Roman nose) common to Celts and Capricorns; as far as music is concerned, he's the guy to call on when you want something to be "blown."

Ray was born right after America entered WWII, on December 29, 1941 in Stourport-on-Severn, England, which used to be part of Wales. He is very *very* proud of his Welsh ancestry. His family moved to Erdington later. Ray was born in Lickhorn Manor, as that is where expectant mothers from Birmingham were being housed while Brum was being bombed. I REALLY recommend checking Ray's website *www.raythomas.me* for many more stories and history. Ray twittered a curious blurb on 11-23-10, saying he could remember as a small child, the ladies around him, when they were all diving into bomb shelters, they'd say "Hark listen here they come….." They could actually hear the buzz bombs clicking as they armed over English soil. What a thing to have come out in song lyrics ("Eternity Road") twenty years later.

All of Ray's paternal family are Welsh (many coal miners), and he lived into retirement near his relatives in Wales. Ray's grandfather and great-grandfather both were carpenters, and carved the Bard's chairs for the Welsh Eisteddfodau (music festival), the chairs were awarded to the "poet of the year." His great-grandfather made the pews in the little church where Ray and his second wife, Lee were married.

Ray put glitter and confetti in his black wavy hair back in the early days, he was quite foxy, with a sexy baritone to go with the good looks! He started out singing in the Birmingham Youth Choir as a youngster (and met Graeme there), and played skiffle with a teen band "Saints and Sinners" in 1956, at age 15 where he put in time on a "washtub bass." Ray claims to have been raised on music, as his dad taught him how to play the harmonica early on; Ray then picked up the flute later. He's a bit self-deprecating about his abilities on the harmonica, wrongfully so; he picked the harmonica back up in the mid '90s for live performances of "Never Comes the Day" and did a wonderful gig. He has even played sax on stage a few times, and in recordings.

Ray has a good set of lungs, despite his naughty habit of smoking like a chimney (I actually saw him light up in the '90s on stage, in the dark where he thought no one could see him!) He was the power house singer of the Moody Blues, and was a valued singing member in all of the groups he was in prior to joining the Moody Blues.

For the record, Ray's flute music is first to be heard on "From the Bottom of my Heart." That was penned by Mike Pinder in 1966, which pre-dates King Crimson (*The Court of the Crimson King*, 1969) and also predates Ian Anderson's fine flute work as lead for the rock band Jethro Tull. Lots of information can be found on Ray in *Higher and Higher* #6.

Ray apprenticed in engineering at George Hughs Ltd. of Erdington, but could not get the performing bug out of his system! Besides the Saints and Sinners, he was briefly in another skiffle group the Ramblers. Ray said he was 15, and John 14 (1956?) when they met on that railcar, both of them lugging amplifiers. They hit it off, and with their friends, formed El Riot and the Rebels. El Riot was skiffle at first, and then graduated to real guitars. Without a doubt,

John Lodge was a solid part of El Riot, and is seen as the most cheerful of young men, smiling ear to ear in all their photos in *Brum Rocked*. Ray was "El Riot" himself, and the lead singer, doing an acceptable impression of Gene Vincent in "Be Boppa Luma," "Say Mama," and "Blue Moon." John worked into the bass position, playing a guitar altered with just the bottom four strings to simulate a bass guitar.

Their first performance is alleged to have been at the Birlec Club on Cheston Road, where John Lodge Sr. worked. Brian "Bunny Boy" Bettridge, lead guitar for the Rebels, was no slouch himself, and was apparently a devil on the strings, doing a ripping version of "Tequila" as part of their repertoire. Mike Pinder, originally an electronics roadie, filled in on piano for El Riot; reports have it that he did a very good version of "Telestar."

Mike claims he started out as a manager for Ray and John, when they were with El Riot (they really WERE a riot, as they wore huge sombreros, "dagger" boots, and tight pachuco pants!) They recorded one single, and as offers to tour started pouring in, the band was on the upswing, without a doubt. They were even on the telly on *Lunchbox* a few times and opened for the Beatles in Tenbury Wells on April 15, 1963 (The Riverside Dancing Club.) Brum was apparently a pretty tough town. "Viva Ned Flanders", the Simpson's cartoon with the Moody Blues, is not too far from reality; fisticuffs were a desirable trait in surviving the various youth hotspots and nightclubs. Ray and Mike were all for moving upward and taking El Riot to the "big time" in London.

With all this in mind, John's parents (being rational people, and wanting a good life for their son) convinced him to go to school. So he opted out of the touring offer to apprentice as a draftsman at Parkinson Cowan (he had his heart set on being a car designer!) Brian had family issues and could not tour either. On top of that, they lost their sombreros, which set the band back considerably. When they failed an EMI audition, El Riot broke up in May 1963, setting Ray Thomas and Mike Pinder on the streets once more, looking for action.

What fellow El Riot band member "Take it Away, Bunny Boy" Brian Bettridge did for his dosh after the break-up is unknown, and he fades from our tale at this time; he was next sighted at a Moodies concert in Brum in year 2000, some thirty-seven years later. He also popped up selling a lot of vintage Moody Blue photos. Thank goodness someone saved that sort of thing!

The waters between England and Hamburg must have been thick with migrating English rockers. Not just the Beatles, but ALL British groups played in that former German submarine town, trying to get their break by playing nightclubs which are best left to your wildest cabaret-Kit-Kat club nightmares. Probably the closest American analog we could have today would be something like the movie *The Blues Brothers*. Ray told one story (Anne Nightingale interviews) that sounded like something right out of the wild wild west, having to dive for the ground in a Hamburg pub one night, as some nasties entered the bar they were in, and opened fire.

Mike borrowed thirty quid off Bunny Boy, and bought himself a "clavoline," a sort of early electronic organ. Thus armed, Ray and Mike went to Hamburg and Hanover (Germany), with a group called the Krew Cats. At least one German cabaret they played was the Weybridge.

In listening to the Anne Nightingale interviews, I can understand why Ray and Graeme so seldom interview for the Moodies: Ray's vocabulary is rather gutter bucket.....but very funny. Between the miserable bootleg, and Ray's thick accent (and laughing so hard), I had to run it back a few times with a "did I REALLY hear him say that?" Ray said Germany was *full of madness* and referred to the living conditions as "diabolical." Graeme babbled a lot about the money (or lack of it) but Ray comes out in interviews with comments like "got really raunchy—sitting there naked" whanging on a guitar "nobody had haircuts" and muttering about putting a bowl on one's head for a trim.

Ray also mentioned Graeme getting hit with a brass club while playing, and delicacy forbids I repeat where Ray said it struck.

Intense Beatles fans will recognize this era. It's probable they ALL went back and forth between Germany and the UK more than we can imagine (Beatles, Krew Cats, John Bull Breed, etc). In an interview with *Jonesy's Jukebox* (2018) Denny Laine said he met "two of them in Germany" and I presume he meant Ray and Mike. Like I say, they all knew each other, and that explains their later connection May 2, 1964 at the Moathouse.

While Mike was in the background, checking out the wiring, Ray distinguished himself in this time period by wearing very weird things on stage (or maybe nothing at all!) And Ray started ruining his knees by sliding onto the stage bent legged....it must have been impressive to see.

When they ran out of money and the Krew Cats broke up (shortly before Christmas, 1963) Ray and Mike started walking north, in the snow. *Shudder.* After seven days (cold, short on food and sleep) they staggered into a British consulate, severely hypothermic. Ray alleges the consulate "...give us a rubber duck and said 'There's the Channel.'" British humor is cruel, I agree; Ray said they had to threaten criminal acts to get deported back to England (he mentioned a brick and a window.) The consulate finally gave them ferry fare, and back they went to Jolly Old. (Nightbird interview, and *www.raythomas.me*)

As per apocryphal news reports, a relative of George Harrison's (living in Benton, Illinois) is unaccredited, but responsible for getting the British Invasion started: in September 1963, she convinced a DJ in Frankfort, Illinois to play Beatles music over American airways. It mushroomed. "I Wanna Hold Your Hand" was released in the States on December 26, 1963. The Beatles took their U.K. success on the road and landed in New York on February 7, 1964.

When Ray and Mike made it back to the shores of Albion in very early 1964, they found Brum hideously glutted by R&B bands on every corner, each one eager to be the next "Beatles." Stripped of their assets, Mike and Ray had no choice but to get day jobs. Ray (having an engineering background) went back into tool and die. Mike went back to Streetly Mellotronics, which was developing a new machine that did sound effects.

Dr. Feelgood --Graeme Edge was born in Rochester March 30, 1941; his family moved to Brum when he was six months old, they lived on Coventry Road, Small Heath. Graeme always claimed he started out as a band manager; his parents' house was the only one big enough to store their gear, so he got elected, and they rehearsed in his garage.

Graeme is the son and only child of a former cabaret singer and a pianist (his dad and mum respectively.) I believe he has also said his Mum rode bareback in the circus and played piano for silent films: a talented lady, obviously! His father and grandfather were both stage singers; from Graeme's description, the duo were a bit like a Scottish version of Gallagher and Sheen, wearing kilts, doing stand-up comedy and singing songs. By his account, Graeme is fifth in a long line of stage/circus performers. Graeme is apparently the original free spirit; in one of the early interviews, he proclaimed that he "only wore clothing because he didn't want to be arrested!"

Graeme is alleged to have first met Ray when they both sang in the Boys Youth Choir in Brum. The future drummer started writing poetry at age eight, and first played snare drum at the same age in Boys Brigade (the U.K. version the Boy Scouts). Somehow Graeme wound up on the entertainment council at Aston University (where he was studying structural engineering) and had to throw together an act at the last minute for a student body show. From there he drifted into playing with local bands. Those bands were the Silhouettes, and the Blue Rhythm Band. According to Hornsby, Graeme was taken on by Gerry Levene and the Avengers when their "wheels" dropped out for a while; little known fact: many of these rockers weren't old enough to drive, or didn't have cars. Graeme actually had a van!

He picked up the drumsticks for a gig with his first band, the Blue Rhythm Band, then later he joined "Jerry Levene and the Four Avengers", as a desperation measure. In one early interview, Graeme thought the band was a bit too "bubblegum" for his taste, but he gave it a try anyway. He sometimes refers to the band as "Cherry Latrine and the Four Flushers," perhaps having something to do with an apocryphal tale of Ray Thomas singing with a commode seat about his neck.

The Avengers did a vigorous show, "stomp" dances in places like the West End Ballroom, and they got to play on *Thank Your Lucky Stars* T.V. show. They did at least one single, "Dr. Feelgood," recorded on Decca Records, was popular with musicians, but barely made the charts back then. The Avengers played a lot of music from the Beatles in Liverpool, and the Beatles (hot from their first hit), played at gigs in Brum, while the Avengers backed them up. John Lennon mentioned "Dr. Feelgood" in one interview, as an inspiration for "Dr. Robert." The Avengers also played in The Battle of the Bands against the Beatles in 1962.

Even MORE intriguing, Graeme came out with a story (second Storyteller event) on the fourth "Moody Cruise" about "playing back up for Sister Rosetta Tharp" by which I think he meant the Avengers backed her up, when she came to England for a Blues festival. What a great connection, as the Moodies and Sister Tharp were inducted in the same "class" at the Rock and Roll Hall of Fame. Sister Tharp is awesome (godmother of modern rock) look her up on the 'nets.

So the bands all stole from each other. The competition was tight, and only a super group could hope to get gigs in the race for the spotlight.

A curious note from modern times needs to be inserted here. After consulting two of my younger relatives, it seems that Motley Crue actually did a song "Dr. Feelgood" which they have performed and recorded with success! Dr. Feelgood also was an R&B group in the early '80s, according to my research. The song is a bit rude, but obviously has a lot of appeal, cutting across several generations.

Go Now --Denny Laine and the Diplomats would be the third super group to fall into the scope of our tale. Denny (born Brian Hines, Oct 29, 1941, in Birmingham) is from Holcombe Road, Tyseley. Hornsby says of Denny that "every lyric hit home" a fine tribute to the performing talents of the original lead singer of the Moody Blues. Brian Hines was with a band called the Deltas briefly, then became "Johnny Dean" of the Dominators. He then tried working for Rackham's Department store for a while, as the Dominators weren't very ambitious. Then came "Denny Laine and the Diplomats," the entire title apparently pulled from the air, and no I don't know what year "Penny Lane" was written by the Beatles. Brian put on the name of "Denny Laine."

They apparently put on a helluva show, Denny occasionally breaking into back-flips, the entire band peroxiding, or dying their hair orange. There is even one wonderful report of Denny playing "The Sabre Dance" with the guitar balanced on the back of his neck…..while their co-band The Beatles (fresh from their first American tour) stood and applauded, egging him on! The Diplomats tried their stuff in London's Tin Pan Alley, and didn't make much progress, but did pick up a new talent while there: Nicky James. Laine described James as being a pretty good English version of Elvis. Good story, it's in *Brum Rocked*.

We must presume at this time that all the lads in all the bands had day jobs, but they gloss over what those were in interviews. Graeme claims he was a design estimator. Any performer will tell you that it's hell in the early days; money is tight, jobs are scarce, and when you get a job, you don't let go of it. England had it ten times worse than any job shortage in America in the recession days of the early '60s; the generation of Baby Boomers all wanting the same entry level positions made things grim indeed. Justin has said that hehung-out a lot at music stores, hoping for jobs (and fingering guitars he couldn't afford). John also mentioned a place called Jackal Drums, where agents and promoters would arrive in the morning, looking for acts for that night.

Ray mentions another music store, Woodroffe's in Brum. As John Lodge put it about those early gigs "Sometimes they even had curtains." And if you were real lucky, the loo flushed as well! Anyway, the music stores were the congregation point for all the young musicians in that area.

Uncle Clint --The last member of the early Moody Blues to introduce is "Uncle Clint" Warwick, bassman first of the Rainbow Boys, then of the Dukes (or Danny King's Dukes). Clint's real name was Albert Eccles, born in Brum on June 25, 1940. More can be read about Clint in *Higher and Higher* #43, but I can throw in a few more things about him. Denny always said Clint was the one who put together their harmonies, he had an excellent ear for music. He also was Ray's fishing buddy. Clint was the first one to start a family. His first son was born just as Secunda picked up the band for promotion; starting a family had a lot to do with him dropping out of the band first.

Apparently the Diplomats weren't doing it for Denny either, and he had feelers out to Pye Records. Clint, Graeme and Denny all met one day at the local hangout, Alex's Pie Stand, which was a "snackery" British cross between Winchell's Doughnuts and Carl's Jr. Or better yet it was like Marie Callender's in '60s Fullerton; they ate *pot-pies* there, for you confused Americans.

That late night feeding hole is alleged to have been the place a lot of deals, break-ups and music group formations happened in '60s Brum. Another late-night feeding spot where all the bands met is mentioned as the Blue Boar, 100 miles north of London on the M1 highway. ALL the bands stopped there if they had been gigging in the north country that night. The Scotch of St. James is also mentioned as a band hangout.

Young performers are a curious lot; some are just into it for the parties. Some band members are "go-getters" and some are not. Denny, Graeme and Ray all kept bumping into each other at the bank or at the booking agents, or Woodroffe's Music store. They became friendly as it was plain that they all had brains, and all were serious about their business, wanted to go pro. Everyone knew everyone else; for example, a guy named Wood was not only in the Four Avengers along with Graeme, but also in the Falcons, along with John Lodge, and I think Nicky James, and possibly Denny Laine.

The upshot of all this was, Graeme, Clint and Denny (along with Danny King) formed a small band called the R&B Preachers. A curious backlash came out of this. When Denny and Graeme bailed on the Diplomats and the Avengers (respectively) the drummer from the Diplomats, Bev Bevan, found Roy Wood, grouped up and eventually became The Move, which then became ELO.*

An interview in *Moodymania* #22 with Mike Pinder, quotes him as saying he simply got fed up with working at the Mellotron factory one day, and walked out, drove to the factory where Ray was working, said "give notice and let's get the band back together." Ray was equally disgusted with his job, and they went looking for the rest of the band. Mike and Ray had been approached for sponsorship by Mitchell and Butler's Brewery. All the breweries had dance halls in the back, and sometimes hired bands to play.

Ray and Mike retired to the Moat House Club (quite a lively place, bookies and card sharks lurked in the back room) to drink the cheap beer and talk it over. They checked out the Diplomats who were playing there that night. Recognizing Denny from Germany, they decided to get better acquainted. Mike, the persuasive talent of the group, performed musical espionage born of desperation, and approached Denny after the show.

Bolstered by the promise of a gig with free beer, Denny mentioned some other guys he'd been sitting in with. (Sad to report, by this point in Denny's career, he was kicked out of the house by annoyed parents.** He had moved in with the free-thinking Edge family, "adopted" almost. So he and Graeme were very close by now.)

They then looped into their scheme the rest of the Preachers; Graeme claims they almost went with Ray's friend, John Lodge on bass, but John had his school to think of, so they got Clint. Some claim that Nicky James (also in the Diplomats) was originally a Moody Blue, but dropped out; amazingly, Nicky was still speaking to Ray in the mid '70s! The date is Saturday, May 2, 1964 at the Moat House; where they hatched the plot. Then they painted "The M&B Five" on the side of their van.

The Moody Blues' first gig was Monday, May 4, 1964 at the Carlton Ballroom, also known as the Erdington Ballroom and/or Brooks Brothers (since it was over a suit shop; below, the clientele apparently cringed with every whomp of the bass guitar.) Brooks Brothers was a bit notorious for harboring Teddy Boys, and the bands playing there were liable to encounter brawls, like the sorts your daddy told you to leave if you were any kind of a lady. Today it's known as Mother's, a vintage landmark in Brum. Also on the bill that night: The Reformed Diplomats (a new singer replacing Denny.)

Anne Nightingale referred to the early formation of the Moody Blues as *some pretty ruthless purloining of the other bands around Birmingham*. At least one article claims that Tony Secunda was the brains behind the reshuffling of the Preachers (M&B Five) and the Reformed Diplomats (The Move). Graeme concluded his description of this matter by saying *so we could all eat*. But it does sound like they stayed friends, even with the band reshuffles.

After their first audition, they were informed by Mitchell's and Butler's that they were not wanted as a house band. Not put off a bit, they continued to seek gigs, and hired on with the Midland Top Ten Agency, as the Moody Blues "5." Graeme said it was "Pinder and Tomo" who came up with the name, but Ray typically is modest and doesn't take credit. The name "Moody Blues" arose spontaneously to go with the initials, according to interviews with Laine and Warwick (Hornsby, pg. 120.)

According to Mike Pinder, *he* came up with it, being inspired by Elvis. Denny said in his *Higher and Higher* interview that HE had thought of the name Moody Blues! According to Nick Warburton, Denny was inspired by a Slim Harpo song "Moody Blue." Mike also claimed (*Goldmine*) that he liked a Duke Ellington song "Mood Indigo" and it was not a far leap from there to Moody Blue. All of this "I did it" stuff might lead you to believe the guys weren't what you want to call overly clear-headed in those days. Ah, the excesses of youth!

"Moody" has a slightly different connotation in the U.K. than it does in America. It seems to be like the word "shady" (American slang). I found this on a newsgroup: *The slang term "Moody" is used a lot to refer to something that is not quite as it should be. Somebody taking a "sickie," a day off work after calling in claiming false illness, is said to be doing a "moody." Also, goods of uncertain origin are "moody." "That guy is selling moody watches."* So a translation to American of "Moody Blues" would be "Shady, suspicious, sly Blues."

Tony Secunda, their unflaggingly entrepreneurial manager, sent a demo to Decca; undoubtedly the connection with former Decca recording artists, the Avengers helped. They started getting nibbles. I found an amusing quote about Secunda: *the Moodies were one of the bands that had already blasted the Birmingham sound into the Top 10 in recent months, with the Moodies' manager, Tony Secunda, already firmly established among the most audacious of the entrepreneurs who pulled the strings of the period's pop industry. (Goldmine* #618) Secunda got them a season of Monday nights at the Marquee in London, right after their initial show at Brooks Brothers, then he got them a spot on the telly, *Ready Steady Go* show.

The Moodies already had a good repertoire of Bo Diddly songs, and Tony then turned up some blues singles fresh from America, passed to them by a couple of DJs named B. Mitchell Reed (U.K.), and James Hamilton (U.S.A.) They eagerly pawed through them for new material; among the offerings, Bessie Banks doing "Go Now," which they recorded with historical success. Banks apparently had released it only about a week prior! Her recording is really good blues, too; she has a wonderful voice. The Moodies loved the piano in it, and they had a pianist who could reproduce the sound. This first song was recorded in a small studio in the back at the Marquee. Within a few months, the Moody Blues had a hit with "Go Now" (November 1964). December found them in the Top Ten in both the U.K. and America.

This first hit was not written by them, so Mike and Denny both agreed that they should start writing their own songs, and not just do covers of other people. And write they did, but still they failed to follow up their first hit. Some of the earliest songs the Moody Blues recorded are "Lose Your Money" (*and we did*, as Graeme put it) and "Time is on My Side" prior to the Rolling Stones recording it.

They did "Bye Bye Bird" which was first done by a friend of theirs, Sonny Boy Williamson. And another neat thing: they did a song called "Little Red Rooster" as a standard song in the early days! How interesting that another band on the other side of the world in Los Angeles would also do this song as a standard bit, and that L.A. band was also influenced, not only by Huxley's *Doors of Perception*, but also by an album the Moodies loved; *The Zodiac*. That band was the Doors.

Despite "Go Now" hitting the charts, and despite the major amount of touring they did, the Moody Blues still found themselves tight for cash. But they must have had fun! Vintage videos of these times are in black and white; films shot in smoky dance halls, the Carlton Ballroom, and places with dubious names like the Bag o' Nails. They opened for Sonny Boy Williamson at the Cavern in Liverpool, and also backed up Memphis Slim once. The videos show young people writhing in a dance step that was the U.K. version of the twist.

The Rank Suites are another early Moody venue, apparently a chain of dance places owned by the Rank family (Top Rank International). You ate & drank below and you danced on the open-air roof, by accounts of English fans I've talked to. Going "Top Ranking" was part of the slang in the U.K. in those days, meaning to go bar hopping or "honky Tonkin.'"

A letter in *Record Collector* dated Feb 2011 mentions one of the "Sonny Boy" gigs, Sonny was quite popular in the U.K. during this period. The Moodies were playing "Go Now" and Sonny Boy insulted them, calling them the "Muddy Boots" and said "You don't understand the Blues." The venue was the New Fender Club, in Kenton, Middlesex. Sonny Boy was nursing a bottle, and the audience was not receptive.

Something I found on line, remembrances from Moody fans: *I can remember being with them backstage and we were very impressed with their stage outfits. Double breasted dark blue suits worn with a black polo-neck sweater............ calf-length black boots....* For young men in their teens and early 20's, it must have been heaven, because frankly the women all look pretty shameless, the dancing is raunchy, and they are in very short skirts.

Some of the videos also show a *very* lively Denny and Ray, they did almost hip-hop sorts of performances. Nightclub names continually mentioned as part of the "Brum" circuit are The California, The Whisky A Go Go (YES I know there was a Whisky on Sunset in L.A. too, which came first, I wonder????), the Crystal Ballroom (there was one of those in Portland, Oregon too.) The Golden Eagle (former feared haunt of American servicemen), The Firebird, the Swan, the Wolseley, the Hens and Chickens, the Blankenhal Youth Club, The Say Mama, The Star Club (in Hamburg, where the Beatles also played) the names just go on and on. Cabaret nightclubs were big items in those days, in England and Northern Europe.

Other sources claim the early Moodies were also booked at the Butlins, which were (are?) holiday "camps," a run-down chain of teen motel hang-outs in both Wales and Scotland, according to my source. (I made her spell it out for me, at first I thought she was saying "The Butt Lands." It was a very late night conversation.) Bill Bryson described the Butlins well in *The Road to Little Dribbling*.

A cute interview from *New Music Express*, dated February 14, 1970, tells a story of these days, like something out of a Marx Brothers comedy. Tony Secunda got the band a shared flat in Kensington Church Street, and the landlady was told it would be occupied by "five Polish businessmen."

This is possibly during the same time that Sonny Boy Williamson toured the U.K. and stayed with them for two weeks. Ray said it was a great time, and he learned a lot from Sonny Boy. The suspicious landlady eventually kicked them out (obviously, Sonny Boy was not Polish!) the Moody Blues just weren't as cute and cuddly as the Beatles, though they looked a lot like them.

Other rumors persist of the Moody Blues "shared house" in Roehampton becoming a hot bed for wild parties (which included members of the Rolling Stones, Herman's Hermits, and the Beatles, among others.) The parties got so lively that their carpet, and Ray's collection of Blues and Bo Diddley records grew legs and walked off one night. John Lennon, George Harrison, and Brian Epstein had to crawl over the neighbor's fence to get in once, because fans were so thick around the front door!

[clipped off line] *Wed, 3 Dec 2003 Today in music history, December 3: In 1965, the Beatles set out on what would be their last ever UK tour at Glasgow's Odeon Cinema. Also on the Bill, The Moody Blues, The Koobas and Beryl Marsden.*

Graeme tells a very funny (and for him, terrifying) story about being attacked during the tour they did supporting the Beatles. He had his hair cut the same way, a mushroom cut...and was mugged by teeny boppers and had his clothes clipped off him, along with his hair! His knit necktie was pulled so tight that he almost strangled, and it had to be cut loose. Two beefy roadies had to rescue him, and physically tear girls off!

Another funny story, but only to a musician. Mike always wanted a "big piano" sound to the Moodies (aka "Go

Now"). Mike Pinder is one of those talented, rare people who can sit down to a piano and rip off any tune by ear, with no sheet music. In later interviews, he griped (*Goldmine*) about part of their contract requiring "...that the piano be in concert tuning." Concert tuning means the piano is tuned after EVERY performance. Most music halls couldn't even manage to get the piano in normal tuning to begin with, so it was a source of contention. The band arrived at one venue, and found a grand piano, but with one leg sawed off, in order to get it on stage.

After this traumatizing event, the Moodies took to hauling along their own upright baby grand! I'm sure Mike was happy with his concert tuning, but this probably went over like a lead balloon with the other boys, as no one likes hernias at such tender young age. No wonder the lighter Mellotron was eventually adopted.

El Fenebre--Another amusing story Mike Pinder told in the Spring of 2000 (interview with Richard Silverstein), involved Bob Zimmerman (aka Bob Dylan), John Lennon, and Pinder cruising London and bar hopping in what Mike called "an Austin limo." Lennon's biography says Lennon had a black Rolls Phantom V, dubbed El Fenebre, which is Spanish for "hearse," Lennon had the car custom rigged whilst filming *How I Won the* War in Spain.

Lennon was nearsighted and didn't drive much, so Mike was at the wheel. It not only had a fold-down bed in the back, but had an external speaker wired in under the car, and John got his jollies by telling drivers in other cars "Hey, pull over" like something out of a cheesy Beatles movie. Rather immature one has to admit, but people today cannot imagine how straight the average person on the streets was back in those days, and how unused people were to electronic trickery.

Lennon had in his car a collection of weird songs worthy of Dr. Demento, so they were having a great time, driving down the street blaring this stuff. (The story went on, that Dylan passed out in the back; and when Mike and John found some girls, said lovelies told them if they ditched the dude snoozing in the back seat, they would come along. I wonder what they did with poor Dylan after that; I still have visions of Dylan, laying on a city sidewalk snoring. Never pass out in the back-seat with John Lennon navigating, you don't know where you'll wind up!)

At one of his CD signings in the late '90s, I saw a little girl shyly go up to Mike Pinder, and tell him a confused story about him "being friends with Mr. Conductor" that is, Ringo Starr. It was very sweet, as she was obviously a *Thomas Tank Engine* fan. Mike replied very seriously, that he would call up his friend Ringo and say she was a fan. And he probably did.

Articles of the time leave a convoluted timeline trail. For example, I ran across one pop fanzine that told about the Moody Blues and the Beatles playing snooker together somewhere (photos and all). What the outcome of the game was, no one knows, as the author "Gigi" was writing it at 3 a.m.

In a Moody Blues article, *Melody Maker*, March 1975, there is a curious blurb about Paul McCartney on the ski-slope set of *Hard Day's Night,* and he's going on about a new record: "Go Now." In Ray Coleman's biography of Brian Epstein, the facts are clear: in 1965, the Moody Blues, with their hit "Go Now," were signed by Seltaeb (Beatles spelled backward) management, and the results were not pretty. The lure of the big money, and touring in America caused the Moodies to make their first professional mistakes in casting their financial lot with the managers of the Beatles, rather than staying with Tony Secunda.

The overloaded Epstein put the Moody Blues on his very back burner: little ever came of their partnership (though Epstein DID eventually get them bookings in America.) He just didn't have the time while he was handling the Beatles, and he left the Moody Blues to more junior managers.

As the Beatles' fame grew, so did the Rock business; ripples in band management went through the entire industry, the Stonies, the Beatles, the Kinks, and the

Moodies (as the big R&B bands in London) and thence waves went out to the entire industry (via friends and family.) It took a few years, but the Moodies finally got lucky by falling in with WEG. Read the Norman biography on John Lennon for the unabridged, LP version of this period's rock management industry. Interesting stuff.

In 1965, the Moody Blues were on the same marquee (different date) with the Beatles (the famous concert at Shea Stadium in New York.) The Moodies were supposed to play with the Kinks at the Academy of Music (June 19th) but apparently the work visas weren't processed (something managers are supposed to handle!) and they never made it.

I plucked this one off a newsgroup on line: *the Moody Blues did not do any of the 1965 US dates with the Kinks at all despite long-standing myth to the contrary. They were scheduled to do the whole tour but couldn't get the necessary visas at the time and the Kinks carried on without them.* The (inaccurate) *Showbiz* article under discussion in that on-line debate, says: *After touring Britain with Chuck Berry, the Moody Blues traveled to the United States as an opening band for The Kinks.*

Over the years, Mike, Graeme and Ray have commented in veiled but scathing terms about this. It did appear to "prime the pump" for greater things to come, if nothing else, by generating pure stubborn persistence.

Laine would add to this a very pithy comment, that "...no one ripped us off." (*Higher and Higher* interview with Denny.) The Moody Blues were known far and wide for the lavish multi-day rocker parties at their home, not to mention women crawling in through the bathroom window. There was a lot of spending going on; I'd say so, lugging around their own grand piano, and throwing sybaritic parties! Denny bluntly says the band had no one to blame but themselves for their financial situation in those early days.**

Pop Magazine (a UK fanzine) dated Sept 11, 1965 shows that the Moodies were concerned (unto disenchanted) about what was happening to them. Their managers were changing their image (perhaps not for the best) and even though their album was charting in the Top Ten, they weren't getting media coverage. There is also evidence that Epstein wanted the Moodies to cover Beatles songs, but the Moodies wanted to find their own identity, and write their own stuff. The Moodies weren't anyone's clone band, they wanted to do things their own way.

Their first album, *The Magnificent Moodies* was redone and released in America (under the title of *Go Now*). Four of the original songs were replaced with fresh material, and the tracks were rearranged. Released in America in 1965, it went to #5 in the charts.

Whatever the facts were, the Moodies were not reading the account books very well. Ray claimed that he "only got 13 quid" for their first album, *The Magnificent Moodies*. The rest was gobbled up by taxes and curious accounting practices… and fees for piano movers. In those days, the venues signed the contract with the manager, not the band, so that the musicians were last in line for any money hand-outs. Of course, the managers have to pay the bills with something. When asked about MP3 in the year 2000, Justin and Graeme would allude to this. MP3 isn't hurting the artists: it's hurting the middle-men.

Many have tried but none have succeeded in tracking all the early tour dates reliably; lists do pop up on the Internet. [As of this writing, I recommend the Blue Pages.] No one can figure out if some dates really happened or not, the dates from play bills tend to be unreliable, because sometimes bands cancelled at the last minute. But there is no doubt that the Moody Blues were in demand, and were kept very, very busy playing live gigs all over England.

"Go Now" was a hit January 13, 1965, eventually going to #1 in the U.K. and #10 in the US. Their nightly fee multiplied by ten-fold. They filled in for the Rolling Stones at the Crawdaddy, they toured Europe (Paris), and cut a commercial for Coca Cola; they interviewed on *Hullabaloo*. BUT, despite "Go Now" being a hit in the States, despite bookings with the Kinks, Chuck Berry and Sonny Boy Williamson, and despite playing with the fabulous Beatles, the Moody Blues were not making money at it. They failed to follow up "Go Now" with another hit.

The Moodies finally made it to America, and there are fading memories of them playing on Ed Sullivan (*Billboard*) and it was not reported as a good night. Though *Murray the K*, according to Wikipedia, was off the air in early 1965, other evidence says that the Moody Blues played a grueling series of shows Dec 1965-Jan 1966 on that New York show. Their contract was four shows a day, for nine days straight, and included not only "Go Now" but "Barbara Ann."

"Barbara Ann" was a spectacular song to pick up, it had been turned down by (Los Angeles) Capitol executive Ken Mansfield in November, but the Beach Boys persisted, and finally released it as a single Dec 20, 1965. The Moodies must have picked up that single steaming off the press and immediately put it in their show. "Barbara Ann" eventually went to #13 on the *Billboard* charts. Pretty good for a funky little song named after a brand of American white bread!!!

There's a very weird tidbit that needs to be inserted here, and you can take it for what it's worth. In *Higher and Higher* #18/19 they quote from a pulp sci-fi magazine that the Moody Blues encountered a UFO during this period (early 1966), while driving between gigs in their van. (Mike Pinder radio interview, Spring 2009 "Cara's Basement").

Further development of this theme is probably call for serious therapy session in Post Traumatic Stress Syndrome, but be that as it may, it's an indication that things got too hectic for the band, while they tried to maintain the level of success that "Go Now" had handed them.

It wore on Clint apparently. In *Brum Rocked*, I found this interesting comment by Clint Warwick: "I left the Moodies straight after our season with Wilson Pickett in New York. That was on the Friday evening. By the Monday morning I was at a bus stop in Brum with a bag of tools under my arm." So yes, the early Moodies did indeed play in New York, in early 1966. But not with the Kinks. And after reading *Blue Timeline*, you might figure that Clint's memory is probably a bit off, but that's the information I found.

As Clint was married and had a family to think about (and tended to fall asleep at the parties), he dropped out in early to mid 1966, apprenticed as a carpenter/cabinet maker, and vanished from the music circuits. He resurfaced in the year 2000 at some Moody Blues shows, and was warmly received by all, band and fans alike. In fact Marie Hayward tried to get in the car with her husband after the Brum show, and apparently was shocked to find her seat occupied by Clint, who was chatting with the band. As of fall, 2000 (source: *Higher and Higher*) Clint had joined Birmingham neighbors, Danny and Jerry, from The Avengers. Object: to play more Rock and Roll!

The Moodies briefly picked up (July 14, 1966) Rod Clarke to replace Clint on bass, and they tried again to record. Rod Clarke was from Los Garcons and played his first date with the group at the Locarno, Coventry, Warks. It's difficult to tell whether or not they toured a little bit in northern Europe too, during the summer of 1966: a brief blurb in *Disc and Music Echo*, dated July 2, 1966 has a blurb about the Moodies *To do Denmark, France, Belgium, and Television shows.*

From Denny's interviews, I don't think they did this, or if they did, it was brief! By most documentation, Denny Laine departed from the Moody Blues in late Summer 1966. Ray sang more when Denny left, doing "Go Now" in Spring 1967, before the band phased that song out of their line-up. There are photos of Denny with the band published in September 1966, but as with all publicity shots, there is a time delay between members actually leaving bands, and having their photos pulled from publicity releases.

In Denny's words, that Summer of 1966, they had good paying offers to tour in Germany, and he didn't want to go, feeling that they really needed to do some more recording at home in the studio. A new album, *Lookout* was in the works, and Denny thought that needed their attention, saying "We're going to lose this three album deal we have if we tour!" (*Gibson* interview, July 2010)

Mike Pinder claimed in a 1968 European interview that, while Denny had really been the driving force and leader in these days, it finally came down to Denny having different ideas than the rest of them about how the band should proceed. Denny liked a more active approach to their stage act, a type of performing that would be called hip-hop today (R&B). Graeme called Denny "a talented and crazy guy" and their leader, as well as a close friend of Graeme's. "The wild [stuff] wasn't well received anymore, we wanted to calm down, that didn't fit Denny's plans." The rest of the band was leaning toward a ballad format. It also fit with what Epstein was nudging the Beatles toward at the time.

So, with visions of the Kit Kat Club dancing in his head, Denny told them they could go on without him, and bailed; and Rod left too. Denny for a while had his own band and later surfaced in Wings, Paul McCartney's group that he formed after the Beatles split up. (That is all in other books and falls outside the scope of this tome.) Tony Visconti*** (of all people!) roomed briefly with Denny after he left the Moodies, and Tony tells some great stories about Denny having to roll a joint in between each string when he re-strung a guitar (*Higher and Higher* # 25). No wonder they were seeing UFOs. In 1970 Denny is mentioned in one article as being briefly in Ginger Baker's Air Force. (Ginger Baker is a pretty wild drummer from Cream and Blind Faith, who later hooked up with Graeme and the Gurvitz Brothers.)

After Denny left Wings, a rather nasty "kiss and tell" article surfaced that left the reader with the feeling Denny was not too thrilled with the McCartneys' hippie housekeeping arrangements, something about living in a shack on Sir Paul's property with no electricity or running water. It was a British tabloid, so you can take that for what it's worth. Denny said in his *Higher and Higher* interview that Paul and Linda treated him like family, and he used to go up to their farm not only to sit around and record, but to help them shear their sheep! As of 2017, Denny and McCartney have teamed up for a few shows, but this falls outside the scope of this book.

According to Warburton, Denny's Electric String Band (which included Move members), formed soon after he left the Moodies and would influence the later Electric Light Orchestra.

Back to the Moodies, where the general feeling from promoters was, when Denny left, the band was finished. The rest of the band waited for Brian Epstein to tell them what to do, but help was not forthcoming from that quarter.**** . The band asserts that Epstein was a gentleman about them wanting out, and gave them back their contract, so they were free to seek other management (this after the junior accountants handling the Moodies evaporated into thin air.)

By mid to late 1966, Ray, Mike and Graeme, the flotsam and jetsam of the original Moody Blues, were left holding whatever bag the band had left to their name, and some of the debt, too. Songs were recorded with Decca during the Clint and Denny years; these recordings cost the young, naive musicians money. They had not gleaned enough cash return to dig out of their "one hit wonder" status.

There was something (a lot actually) to be said for Ray's voice, and for the new sound of the Mellotron that Mike was developing (little known factoid: mellotron technology led into VCR development, with pinch rollers and such.)

The Moody Blues did not want to let go of what they had. They put an ad in *Melody Maker* for a songwriter/guitarist, telling themselves they needed "younger blood" as most of them were "getting too old for the pop music scene." Ray called up his friend, John Lodge, and said "Let's get the old band back together."

And so they did.

* I clipped this off the ELO website, isn't this interesting? *ELO began from much humbler beginnings - as an experimental offshoot of sixties hit English band The Move. Legendary singer-songwriter Roy Wood had the initial idea for the Electric Light Orchestra during Tony Visconti's orchestral arrangements for his early Move songs, but it was Jeff Lynne who composed "10538 Overture," the track that became the first ELO song on 12 July 1970.* And of course, ELO went on to make a lush orchestrated movie soundtrack (in the '80s) with Olivia Newton John, called *Xanadu*. And of course, Tony Visconti worked with the Moodies in the late '80s too.

**According to the article "Denny Laine Saves the World" (Raoul Hernandez: 4-26-2018) Denny was very firm about saying his parents supported him in his musical career, so again… remember they all do a bit of storytelling in interviews. From other articles, Denny seems nice enough, a "follow the money" kind of guy, a canny Scorpio; Denny Laine has very good interviews in *Higher and Higher* # 36-#37, from whence came much information for this chapter. He claimed to have gotten into lawsuit with Tony Secunda himself after he left the Moodies (and went back to Secunda as an agent). Laine was not born in a sailboat as so many interviews have it; in fact, when questioned about this, Laine was very frank about "what we used to say for the PR thing." In other words, just because you read it in a Moody Blue interview (or anyone else for that matter) doesn't mean it's true. Anyway, Denny said he was born, not in a sailboat, but in Brum, right after an air raid. When Ray passed away, Denny was still coming up with good stories about this era, he and Ray roomed together during this time, and Ray kept pet squirrels in a cage! Denny also said, when they came back after their summer tour in Europe, fall of 1966, not only had their manager-accountants disappeared, but their apartments had been stripped too. That was the REAL "skint."

*** In March, 2013 the Strawbs happened to be along on the Moody Blues Cruise, and did some of their OWN story telling. It seems they were produced by Tony Visconti during this time period, so that tells us what Visconti was doing for bread at the time, and also explains his later connection with the Moodies. The Strawbs also said their engineer was Gus Dugan (engineer for "Fly Me High"), and they also spoke with fondness of Sir Edward Lewis. So I count (just from casual research) the Moodies, The Move (ELO), the Strawbs and the Stonies as four Decca bands; times were indeed good and they are all connected technically. For those who don't know the Strawbs, they do MOST excellent music, a bit Irish/Celtic, and they remind me of the Incredible String Band. Less thump than the Moodies, more melody.

****Historical note: Brian Epstein overdosed about a year later, Aug 1967

IV) Step back out......

"I dig a pony, I roll a Stoney"-- Lennon and McCartney

People are probably going to be writing about the birth of rock n' roll, and the British Invasion for centuries to come. How do the Moody Blues fit into the big picture? The Beatles (Columbia) are pretty well documented; they led the invasion in February, 1964, coming from a very solid performance base in the U.K. They took American by storm, without a doubt. They had natural charm, but it's also a fact that they also had very enlightened promotion. Rumor is that Decca execs actually turned down the Beatles, so they went over to Columbia, and the rest is history. This later had bearing on (remembering their mistake) the Moodies NOT being passed over by Decca execs. There was a maniac demand for Beatles, but only so many Teddy Boy bands to go around.

The Stonies and the early Moodies slid into that "need" niche. But they WEREN'T the Beatles, and inevitably developed their own distinct signature sound. The Rolling Stones (Decca) followed hot on the heels of the Beatles, but of course, not all British bands are born equal... some are more equal than others. While the Beatles managed to convey a sense of "wholesomeness" the Stonies heartily embraced Raunch and Roll. Thinking America would too, landed in New York with a bang and a wail of rhythm and blues. White America didn't buy it the first time around, a-tall. The Stones' promoters went back to the drawing boards, cleaned up their act; and during the next 1964 tour, the Stonies did quite well. Even the most sarcastic of male teens found identity with the rough-edged Stonies, an identity that they didn't share with jellybean-tossing females who swooned for the Beatles.

Despite the band shuffling in Brum, all was not lost. Creativity, color popping art and wild ideas, spawned by the spreading use of hallucinogens like marijuana and LSD (not to mention color TV, brand new on the market), flew about London like cosmic butterflies. A major focal point undoubtedly was the Bag o' Nails where the Moodies played frequently, as house band. I'm sure it wasn't just beer they were sucking, behind those smoky pub doors.

Like all people faced suddenly with overwhelming success, the high-profile Stones and Beatles (Donovan, the Doors, etc.) suddenly were being targeted by police out to make a name for themselves, by busting "these wild kids" for various illegal substances…. and riotous behavior. While the Moody Blues might have been the deprived second sons of the British Invasion, they also had the luxury of "laying low" and learning from the mistakes of others. In all their years of touring, the Moodies were never caught with drugs on them (or in their road show), and to date, only have one known DUI to their collective credit (and that was dismissed.)

Every yin has a yang. While the Stonies were the wicked side of the British Invasion, the Moody Blues would go on to become the "gentlemen's band" of early rock n' roll. This image has served them very very well. Trailing along like kid brothers in their older siblings' footsteps, the Moody Blues' promoters kept telling them the Brum Beat was going to be the next big sound, and they were on top of that coming wave. But, they underestimated the American people. There was already quite enough "British" on the airwaves, and California bands started to form a solid musical rebuttal to the Invasion. Groups like the Beach Boys, Buffalo Springfield, the Doors, and Jefferson Airplane took over American airwaves. The Brum Beat went flat like last night's champagne. Brum bands imploded, and split into new groups.

- **The Avengers** (1963 to 1964) Gerry Levene Roy Wood Mike Hopkins (later with Reformed Diplomats) Jim Onslow (later with Reformed Diplomats) Graeme Edge (drums)
- **El Riot** (1959-1963) Ray Thomas, Mike Pinder (he sat in with other bands on keyboards too) John Lodge, Micky Herd, Brian Betteridge, Bobby Shure

- **Crew Kats** (various spellings, broke up in Germany Dec 1963) Ray Thomas, Mike Pinder
- **The Falcons** (duration unknown) Roy Wood, John Lodge
- **The Lawmen** (duration unknown) Roy Wood, Dave Green, Nicky James, Mike Pinder
- **John Bull Breed** (exact dates of existence unknown) Mark Stuart, Terry Guy, Trevor Griffin, Graham Green, Gene Rose, Mike Heard (of El Riot??? Did someone screw up the spelling?) Johnny C. Storme (John Lodge)
- **The Diplomats** (1962-1964) Bev Bevan, Phil Ackrill, Steve Horton, Denny Laine, Nicky Jame,s (joined later, found him in Denmark Street and took him home)
- **Wilde Three (Bunch)** (1964(?)-Summer 1966(?) Marty Wilde Joyce Wilde (formerly of the Vernon Girls) Justin Hayward

A Quickie Time-line:
>Feb 1964: the Beatles land in New York.
>Early 1964, Denny, Graeme and Clint (and maybe Nicky James) formed the R&B Preachers "on the side" and began jamming together informally.
>John Lodge joined various groups, The Carpetbaggers, John Bull Breed (a large group!) and the Falcons, and toured Germany in 1964-65. He used the stage name "Johnny C. Storme." John claims one of the groups he was in was supposed to replace or merge with the Blue Caps.
>In May 1964, Mike and Ray joined the R&B Preachers, and renamed their group The M&B Five, and later, the Moody Blues. Nicky James and John Lodge are both mentioned as being part of the original line-up, but had to drop out due to other obligations. The Moodies were managed in their early years by Tony Secunda, and later by Brian Epstein's junior partners, and toured as opening act to many big stars, including the Beatles.

>Bev Bevan and Roy Wood formed The Move shortly thereafter and were managed by Tony Secunda until late 1967.
>Fall, 1965: Justin (under the auspices of Lonnie Donegan) went to Denmark Street, began songwriting and recording, and formed a band made up of high school friends, variously named All Things Bright, The Shot, or the Whispers.
>The Wilde Bunch/Three did a tour to the Middle East (Beirut) as military entertainment during their time together (Easter 1965 or 1966 as per Justin's biography *www.commonwealarts.co.uk*)
>Mid 1966: Clint leaves the Moody Blues. Denny leaves in late summer. Ray recruits his friend John Lodge, and Justin is recruited from a newspaper ad. Denny forms the Electric String Band, allegedly with Klaus Voormann on bass.
>Early 1967: Tony Clarke becomes the 6th Moody, and takes over production duties. In 1967, Denny works with some members of The Move, is managed by Secunda. That doesn't work out, Denny meets Tony Visconti (they room together), then Denny eventually joins (after the Beatles break up) Paul and Linda McCartney in Wings.
>1968: The Move tours with the Moody Blues in America, as does Led Zeppelin (Zep in Seattle, the Move in Detroit.)
>In the '80s, members of The Move form Electric Light Orchestra, work with Tony Visconti, and have a hit sound track to the movie *Xanadu*. Visconti hooks up with the Moodies later in the '80s. In 1986, Bev Bevan (who left the Diplomats, and eventually joined ELO and probably The Move prior to that) shows up as the cameraman for George Harrison's *Heartbeat* benefit concert, which Moody Blues are part of.

V) I think I am: Fall 1966

Therefore I am. I think -- Justin Hayward

That which we survive makes us stronger -- Nietzsche

John Lodge (bassman for the Moody Blues) was born unto parents Charles and Olive Lodge, July 20, 1943: more than one birthdate has been found, but I take the date off the John Bull Breed single. His official fan club birthdate is in 1945. He recalls his childhood little publicly, but did say in one interview he could remember, when very small, food coming to England from South Africa during the ration years following World War II. He remembered reading the packages that said "Outspan," a place in South Africa; the crates were full of oranges, syrup and other goodies.

He attended Birches Green Junior High School and Central Grammar School, in Birmingham, England. John says he had violin lessons at age 11, though in later years during the recording of his hit song "Ride My See-Saw," he would find out that he tuned the cello all wrong!

John also was in the Boys Brigade, the British equivalent of the Boy Scouts, as was Graeme. I read somewhere John made equivalent of Eagle Scout. John also claims he won a Scottish dance competition at age 11. (Now I'd like to see that, John dancing in a kilt! As an adult of course.)

In a rather tongue-in-cheek biography on the OFC website, John claims he was moved from music class to woodworking class in school, due to not knowing Beethoven's birth date. In a cheeky exchange, John asked the teacher BACK if he knew "Whole Lot of Shakin'" by Jerry Lee Lewis. John said in later interviews "Well, I really wanted to know how the song was put together!" Among other things, John says he is a great fan of American movies, which did their own "invasion" of England when he was thirteen, in the late '50s, movies like *Blackboard Jungle,* and *Rock Around the Clock.*

For those (like me) who have fond memories of bucolic visits to the movie house as a youngster, you might be shocked to hear that, according to John, in Birmingham they threw Coke bottles at the screen and tore up the seats! Good heavens, what a mad town to grow up in.

Ray and John claim to have met on a bus at age fourteen or fifteen, both lugging musical gear, and the friendship formed. Both worked in the tool and die industry of Brum. It is said that when Ray and Mike first put the Moodies together, they originally picked up John as their bass (having all done El Riot together) and he was at their first "band" meetings. But when they joined with the R&B Preachers, THAT group brought along their own bassman, Clint, and for a while had Nicky James too, it depends on who is telling the story. John had aspirations to be a car designer, and with the thought of a real job in mind, finished up his schooling at Birmingham College (he focused on metallurgy) before venturing into the professional music world in London. Those flying Coke bottles maybe had him thinking twice as well.

While John was studying to be an engineer, Mike and Ray were at the German Top Ten club, and/or floundering about in Hamburg cesspools. Later, while the Moodies formed and did a year of work, John joined a band called the Carpetbaggers. During his interview with his mate Mike Smith on the Brooklands radio (Swindon, April 27, 2009, really good interview too) John said his hero at this time was Gene Vincent, and John had been with a band called the Blue Caps, backing up Gene. Mark that with a question mark, read on. John wrote a song "Blues in the Night" intended for Gene. The song finally turned up on a fan generated album *In Search of the Lost Song*. I *think* I got that right, I couldn't tell if the Carpetbaggers or the Blue Caps were backing up Vincent, further research has not turned up John's name listed with the Blue Caps.

John was nineteen at the time. By his account, the Carpetbaggers never practiced, which must have been interesting. After the lack of rehearsal caught up with that band, John joined a band called either Jungle Breed, John Bull Breed, or Bulldog Breed (I found all three names in the articles); and he began calling himself "Johnny C. Storme." John Bull Breed cut at least one single: "Can't Chance a Breakup" / "I'm a Man." John Storme (aka Lodge) listed his favourite band as the Moody Blues; no surprise as his mate Ray Thomas was in the Moodies at the time.

According to *Higher and Higher* #44, JBB also recorded on Pye Records. The article about John Bull Breed in *Higher and Higher* has some very funny stories in it; the best has to be their mode of transport. When in the U.K. they drove an old ambulance, painted up in psychedelic colors. John was reported to have complained when he joined "I'm not traveling in that!" I don't know what he had to gripe about, I've heard of some rock bands who travel in a hearse! The bad news is they apparently terrorized the good citizens of Brum and "red lighted" it when they were going places in town. People actually got out of their way.

Under the stage name "Johnny C. Storme," John also (having finished his engineering apprenticeship) went to Germany for a stint of cabaret. Hornsby turned up a great story in *Brum Rocked!* about John during the Germany tours. A thoughtless manager awoke them at 4 am to play a gig, either the Top Ten, or the Star Club in Hamburg. John "ever cool" proceeded to don his sunglasses, and still wearing his pyjamas, did the gig.

John was, like Ray and Graeme, an engineering student, and old enough by summer 1966 to move out on his own, so he did so with his buddy Ray. I bumped into a curious comment in *Moodymania* October, 1995, alluding to "They played places John's parents weren't fond of, but they felt better if he was with Ray."

John's and Ray's mums were actually very good friends, and remained so throughout the band's career, so it's probably true. Various accounts say that John generously sold his bike (a Vespa motor-scooter??) and/or his amplifier to pay the Moodies' grocery bills. My, that IS friendship!!!

More about John can be read in the wonderful issue dedicated to him, *Higher and Higher* #11/12.

But as of August 1966, the Moody Blues still came up short a lead guitar. Even more important, they really needed to support budding composer Mike Pinder with another talented songwriter, to fill in the gaps they had in the repertoire; "Go Now" was not going to get them very far with Denny gone. The music scene was rapidly changing from the Mersey Beat/Brum Beat, to the new rock n' roll sound that the Beatles were spreading across the seas. They needed to surf that British Invasion tsunami.

Enter Justin --Whether all that consciously crossed their minds at the time is debatable, but what is certain is that Justin Hayward answered a blind ad in a music magazine (which had been placed there by Eric Burdon of the Animals) for a songwriter. Eric had his man by the time all the letters from musical hopefuls started accumulating in his office. He and Ray were talking about it in a bar, having a drink, and Eric mentioned the huge sack of letters; by reports, Ray stood in Eric's office, poking through the mail bag. It was pure chance that Justin's letter came out first, possibly because it was attached to Justin's "resume," a single he had recorded with Pye Records.

Graeme tells the story just a little differently (*LA Herald Examiner,* Aug 26, 1988) and claims the Moodies, Manfred Mann, and the Animals all chipped in on the *Melody Maker* ad. Klaus Voormann (bass) went to Manfred Mann (since the Moodies already had John) and Justin was plucked out of the fray (they auditioned a couple of guys) for the Moodies.

Mike had seen Justin play with the Wilde Three earlier on and called him up (found him hanging out at the Swindon music store!) to come meet the rest of the band. The band was still based in London, because Justin hopped on the Great Western, and met Mike in Paddington Station. John was summoned and came down from Brum. In Justin's words, "I had a guitar and an amp, so I was in." It may have been just that simple. John's comments on first meeting

Justin is pretty amusing, but probably had something to do with passing the audition. John claimed he asked Justin if he liked girls. I leave it to you to figure that one out.

Justin's approach to music was out of the Brum Beat loop, and definitely changed their sound. I found an excellent post on a guitar forum about Justin's guitar work, the poster called it "a very fat, warm sound." Of course, professionals know this is a combination of both amp and guitar. Fans of post WWII country music will recognize some of this in Bob Wills music, apparently a "Les Paul" sound is part of the secret. While with the Wilde Three, Justin grew attached to his 335 Gibson, and during his first tour of America, had a black Les Paul he played on stage.

Summer of 2010, Justin did a lovely video backstage interview, explaining his amps, so the discerning Moody historian would do well to look that one up, because the amp discussion went off my music map technology-wise, can be found on *www.moodybluestoday.com*. Justin says he self-taught himself on the guitar; this isn't difficult if you have a little theory behind you, Justin's mum taught piano.

Justin cites the Shadows as his earliest inspiration, at age fourteen. He began experimenting with chords when the sound track to *Hard Day's Night* hit the airwaves, moving away from the "three chord" approach to more sophisticated sequences. If anyone wants more biography on Justin, you can check out *Higher and Higher* #21/22.

And check his website out too, it has lots and lots of nice vintage photos, and a wonderful blog written by Justin that he has done for many years (as of this writing.) This is what I have managed to put together on him from bits and pieces and many, many articles and interviews:

Justin was born October 14, 1946, at 109 Dean Street in Swindon, Wiltshire; his grandparents lived at 110 Dean. Justin tends to talk about his childhood and early days a bit more than the other band members. It could be that he is younger, a country boy, and has more pleasant memories; he was born the year after VE Day, so he missed the horrible times during WWII. He grew up in the country around Oxford (Wiltshire) with middle class parents who were both teachers; Mum taught at Grove Road and Dad at Sanford Street. Justin went to public school at Swindon's Commonweal School and is still a patron of the school.

Hayward has said that his family came from "navigators," and his mum's people were seafarers. I think his dad (Frederick) worked on planes during the War, and Justin lived near an airstrip as a child. The Haywards worked for and around the railways for generations. He was heavily influenced by his religiously-oriented, and talented family. In a 2011 interview on Utah PBS, Justin said his father studied for the priesthood; then when WWII came along, put that on hold, and after the war taught English and Latin. His mum taught "home economics."

Justin got his start singing in the choir at St. Saviour's Church (Swindon) in the 1950s. Mum Gwenda played the piano, and taught music on the side. Mike Pinder said Mrs. Hayward reminded him "of a favourite aunt" and she was a very nice lady. Justin says in his website journals (June 2002) that he spent a good deal of his childhood in Bourton in England. It's wonderful journal entry, he describes midsummer as a sort of "country fair" time. Justin is a very capable writer, his articles and on-line journal *justinhayward.com*, are among the most enjoyable I found during this research, lots of biographical notes.

Justin was apparently recognized early as gifted in music and was encouraged in this. He listened to his grandfather's 78 records on a wind-up gramophone, much of it oriental music like "In a Persian Market" which, in Justin's words "opened an entire fantasy world of music." By his account, he was given music lessons at a very early age (like six) and didn't like it at all; Justin apparently clashed with several music teachers in his youth. Someone gave him a ukulele at age eight, he heckled his parents for a guitar by age ten, and with the aid of a guitar chord book, taught himself how to play. Justin said during interviews, about his 2011 recording, that he reads music slowly; he and John both play keyboards but that doesn't require music reading skills.

Legend has it Justin made his first amplifier on his own, from an old radio, and we must presume with a lot of help from *Popular Electronics* at the local library. Justin is also a self-proclaimed bibliophile; no distinction, ALL the Moodies seem to be good readers and well informed. One of Justin's classmates mentioned on-line that Justin was one of those guys at school who is always sitting around at lunch, picking on a guitar.

In what we Americans would call junior high, Justin was working up skiffle bands, which turned into real bands as soon as they could afford guitars.

The bands were the Riversiders (skiffle, age ten), the Rebels Rock Group, the Off Beats, The Satellites, the Woodpeckers (research conflict, this might have been John Lodge's first skiffle band), then the Whispers, the Shots, All Things Bright. They did covers of songs by Buddy Holly, the Everly Brothers, and the Four Seasons. They played at school assemblies; various accounts say Justin wore fake glasses like Buddy Holly. All Things Bright was on the telly show "Looking for a Star."

According to Justin, the very first song he sang on stage in front of an audience was "Charlie Brown" ... *fee fee fi fi fo fo fum...I smell smoke in auditorium.*

I turned up a VERY wacky post on Twitter that said, "Justin used to play 'Hava Nagila' at school assemblies with his guitar behind his head!" That's gotta make you smile!

All Things Bright (the Whispers?) apparently backed the Hollies on one tour, so they had something going for them. Justin was twelve when Buddy Holly crashed, and was devastated (like so many others) by the loss of his hero. Justin said in later interviews, "Everybody worshiped Buddy Holly. He played guitar, wrote his own songs, he was a bit nerdy. He was someone we could all associate with." Contrast Buddy Holly and most '60s bands, with later top-pop male groups, the Backstreet Boys and N'Sync; they don't play their own instruments, and don't write many (if any) of their own songs.

Various interviews say that the brown Telecaster Justin plays "Ride My See Saw" with in their Moody Blues' curtain call, is a guitar he has owned since he was in school. That might be another myth. Fender sold a very inexpensive guitar back in the '60s, the early ones are collectible now of course. I've seen Justin's guitar up very close a few times; he uses it in their encore "Ride My See Saw" as well as their live version of "Peak Hour," and it's very vintage. He used it for "Question" on their 1970 *Isle of Wight* DVD, in open tuning. I can't match the guitar up with his pre-Moodie photos (Justin went through a few guitars when he was younger!) and the "identification" thing is made more difficult probably by Justin altering them a bit, changing pick guards and so forth. Yes he worked (still works) on his own guitars. The crew doesn't touch Justin's red 335, they just lay it out for him (still in its case) backstage and he tunes it himself.

Hayward claims to have learned how to drive, much as young country people in America do too, sitting behind the wheel on combine harvesters in the rural Swindon area.

Sometime in 1960, the Hayward family went for a holiday to Lyme Regis, where Justin noticed the theatre troupe was short a guitarist. He auditioned and landed a guitar part in *Boy in Blue Jeans*. The Haywards, being enlightened (and very brave) parents, allowed their second son to finish the season with the troupe. At the Storyteller event in Portland, June 3, 2011, Justin explained that his Mum knew people in the theatre troupe, and he and his Mum BOTH played for them. Next summer, he landed the part of the butler (at age fourteen) in *Peg o' My Heart*; and continued to get cast in older roles due to being so tall.

Justin and some of the guys from his earlier groups formed a musical group called (first) the Rebels, later the Offbeats, and played the summer of 1961 in Lyme Regis, and the summer of 1962, Isle of Jersey. Justin appears to know a bit about theater, probably from these days. If other naughty interviews Justin has given are any indication, he got a real good taste of life during these years!

He also says he worked after leaving public school, answering phones "as a tea boy" apprentice salesman, for "Bradley's Builders on Okus Road" for a year and a half, apparently a landmark in Swindon. This undoubtedly gave him his excellent customer service skills he still has. In school he excelled at track, being tall and lanky, and able to run well with his long legs. He apparently "medaled", won the South West County Championships for the 440 yards, while still in high school.

Here, alas, I show my ignorance about British schools, but I think Justin has what we would call a "GED" (5 "O" levels) which in England probably shows a higher proficiency than most American high school graduates could manage today. He claims to have taken these levels tests at age sixteen. At the Santa Barbara solo shows in the '90s, he commented about his marks in school; saying he "would show promise if he paid more attention."

He also said his music teacher gave him horrible marks! As Justin has over the years, shown the enviable talent of falling asleep at a moment's notice, especially when bored, like in courtrooms and right before shows;* we can only surmise what his public school years must have been like. Justin has often said that his lyrics are like a diary, and I can think of no better words than the lyrics to "London is Behind Me," which he wrote describing where he was at as a teenager. He left school in 1963, at age sixteen. He whimsically says he was "run out of town" in '64! (BBC Radio Swindon, fall 2005).

Justin's eye was *always* on "going pro" as a musician.** He and his friends played in 1962 at a pub called McIlroy's in Swindon, as a house band, opening for the likes of early Rolling Stones and Beatles. Even though he plays in a band full of college boys; over the years in interviews, Justin has distinguished himself by having an excellent command of the Queen's English, and a highly developed vocabulary.

Even before being picked up by Marty Wilde, Justin and his band (the Whispers at this point I think) were getting some attention. They recorded six songs (written by Justin) which hopefully will be released at some point; said songs surfaced on the Internet in 2009. ALL of them are quite good, even listening around the ragged condition that the files are in. Justin was also interviewed for the newspaper just prior to joining the Moodies, and discussed of all things, his collection of walking sticks! So he was making a name for himself even before being found by Marty Wilde, Donegan or the Moodies.

Wilde Thang--Clipped off line: *It doesn't say "Wilde Three" but thought I'd pass this along anyway from This Day In Music History. "In 1964 [Jan 6], the Rolling Stones launched the band's first headline tour of Britain, with the Ronettes and 1950s rocker Marty Wilde opening."*

I found an obscure reference that says Justin signed a contract to perform in Germany next, but that fell apart. There are also obscure references to Justin playing folk music in pubs, much in the way guitar soloists play coffee houses in the States.

In summer 1964, Justin answered an ad in the *Melody Maker,* and joined a fellow from Blackheath by the name of Marty Wilde ("Bad Boy," "Sea of Love," "Teenager in Love"). Along with Marty's wife Joyce, Justin became back-up guitar, bass and vocal for a small R&B group called first the Wild Cats, then the Wilde Bunch, then the Wilde Three; he stayed with them about a year. Of where they played, Justin said "It was cabaret, and it was hard work." Justin fit in well with Marty's band. Marty Wilde is taller than Justin, and Justin is around 6'3"!

In 1965, the Wilde Three toured for several weeks, over the Easter holidays. They travelled the Middle East with a combined services tour, rather like U.S.O. tours for American troops (*commonwealarts.co.uk*, Justin has a biography up there as a patron.) Justin discussed this tour in his March 17, 2011 Q&A on *moodybluestoday.com*, saying the Wilde Three toured Northern Ireland, Cyprus, Libya, Beirut, across

North Africa and the Middle East, entertaining British and U.N. troops. Justin said he wore "a Bob Dylan hat and sunglasses" for the whole tour; put that together with the bluesy numbers they did, like "Who's that Knockin'" and you'll get some idea of their style.

The songs they managed to get recorded are really great, and Justin always says of these years "Marty was the one who encouraged me to write." Marty also apparently taught him how to sing right. I believe it, Marty's voice is awesome.

After the Middle East tour, the Wilde Three played at the Royal Aquarium in Yarmouth (twice nightly) from July 2 thru September in 1965, and possibly at other seaside summer venues in the U.K.

Many years later Justin would express nervousness at an ocean-going gig on a cruise ship. Experiences like "twice nightly at the Aquarium" might leave you feeling water-logged for life, and hating fish forever.

The Haywards and the Wildes have stayed friendly over the years; Justin and Marty are both members of SODS (Society of Distinguished Songwriters.) The Haywards and Wildes (as well as Cilla Black) all lived in the close-knit Cornwall community. Justin attended Ricky Wilde's wedding in 1986, and Kim was kind enough to video a few nice words for Justin's "This is Your Life" episode, even though she was on her honeymoon; very thoughtful of her. During Justin's "This is Your Life" show, Justin stopped the announcer in his tracks and took time to praise Marty lavishly and thoroughly. It's one of the few times I've known Justin Hayward be even mildly short with an interviewer, he must really admire Marty a lot.

While they were playing in Yarmouth "at the end of the pier" Justin ran into Lonnie Donegan (the king of skiffle) who was the headliner at the Aquarium. (You can almost picture this in your mind's eye, two musicians meet, eating their lunch, gazing morosely out to sea, and throwing crumbs to the birds. They fall into a conversation...) Justin was having an emotional slump, and told his sorrows to

Lonnie, Justin saying he was thinking about quitting the music business, he just wasn't making any money at it.

Whether it was natural compassion, or whether Lonnie was as slippery as he sounds, we'll never know, but certainly Justin played him some of his songs. Lonnie (knowing what he had) was delighted to take Justin under his wing, asking him if he had a contract. Justin did not say "get thee behind me," he snapped at it like a hungry fish! For a mere £50, Justin signed (against Marty's advice) a contract which would eventually give Donegan control over Justin's early work, including the yet to be written "Nights in White Satin". Tyler Music is Donegan's music company.***

According to his Commonweal biography, Justin played with the Wilde Three on April 8, 1966 (research conflict: that date is recorded as 1965 elsewhere), a televised charity event from the London Palladium. The Moodies picked him up in late summer 1966. Trying to put Justin's timeline together, I came to the conclusion that his time with "his own band" "with Marty" and "with Lonnie Donegan as manager" probably all overlapped for a couple of years. He picked up gigs here and there, where he could, and led the life of a musical gypsy, not uncommon in the profession.

Justin does Tin Pan London --Donegan was pulling top dollar at the time, and wanted Justin to write for him, but Justin insisted on doing the singing himself. Donegan conceded (reluctantly.) Then Lonnie loaned Justin a 12-string guitar (in serious need of repairs: read Justin's blog entry on his website for March 2006.) Justin says "I recorded demos in Denmark Street," the Dean/Denmark area being known as London's "Tin Pan Alley" (*Record Collector* spring 2003). Some early Hayward titles are, on Pye Records, "London is Behind Me," "Day is Done," and "Can't Face he World Without You." There is also a "hoe-down" version of "London is Behind Me" with both Lonnie and Justin singing and playing on it, the CD *Puttin' On The Style*.

Justin off-handedly claimed to have had his own group in August 1966 (2000 audio interview on his website) comprised of former members of All Things Bright. Justin also helped to cut a commercial, earned twelve pounds singing for Typhoo Tea, backed by (of all people) Jimmy Page on the guitar! Justin met a producer named Martin Wyatt at this time, who would turn out to be a life-long friend. Wyatt would not only produce *Moving Mountains* in 1985, but went along as Justin's manager in the '90s on Justin's solo tours.

Justin always remembered that Lonnie helped him out when he was struggling, and never complained (too much, and in varying degrees over the years) about Donegan controlling rights to "Nights." Now that Lonnie has passed away, his partner David Platts has the copyrights.****

But call us and say when you're passing this way, And let us still know that you care —Justin Hayward, "Stagedoor"

He of course stayed close to his family after he became successful in music and went back to his home town in 1991 to do a benefit concert. In 2005, he did a concert at his old stomping grounds, McIlroy's in Swindon, which is called The Apartment now. However, having the soul of a traveler, he always maintained that Swindon only "inspired him to leave" as quickly as possible.

Justin allegedly had releases on Pye, Decca and Parlophone prior to joining the Moodies. He says of that time in 1964-66, he had to make a lot of sacrifices and worked with people who "weren't right for him" and he knew it. With Justin's good looks one can only shudder to imagine; Justin is made of sterner stuff than many of us might suspect! The music was worth it. One listen to "Can't Face the World Without You" with the sophisticated melodies and metre shifts, and everyone should have known they had something.

Somewhere along the line Justin and his mates had gone into London and bought his first Gibson 335, but as the money failed to roll in, his payments lagged (Justinblog, Nov 2007). Justin claims he sold his original Gibson 335 the week before the Moody Blues called him up, which is how tight he was for money. He had played his first 335 when touring with the Wilde Three, loved it, but his Fender guitar cost half what the 335 had.

All this brings us up to August 1966, and Justin again looking for a gig. According to Donegan's interview in *Higher and Higher,* it was a pretty unsettled time in Justin's life. In German articles of the time, the original Moodies seemed to think they needed "a younger front man" and thought they were all too old for the rock scene! Go figure.

When they found Justin's application letter in Eric Burdon's mailbag, Mike Pinder tracked Justin down at the Swindon music store, Duck, Son and Pinker: Fleet street in Swindon. Justin's mate Brian Gregg (later of Johnny Kidd and the Pirates) drove him to the station with his Fender guitar and amp. Justin relates his meeting with the other Moodies as being picked up by Mike in his Chevy (Mike had a 45 record player installed in his car); and they played Justin's single "London is Behind Me" on the way back to meet the rest of the band in Esher. Mike asked, "When can you start?"

Meeting the rest of the band was just as auspicious, happily ever after, Justin was one and the same with the other Moodies. Graeme recalled having Justin over, and playing albums, and comparing what they liked and didn't like about various artists; Graeme said he and Justin both liked Simon and Garfunkel. Mike liked the "big sound" of the (renovated) 12-string acoustic that Justin was lugging with him. Justin also claims he was the only one with an amp left, the others having sold theirs for grocery money. So he was "in."

Justin shows a considerable sense of humor over being adopted by the Moodies. When he first was offered an audition with the band, he said "I had a few job offers all at once, one of which was as a Flower Pot Man." It is recommended that the reader seek The Flower Pot Men on *youtube.com* at this point, all will be explained, a sort of psychedelic version of the Backstreet Boys. The offer from the Moody Blues, a real name band was a considerable lure. Then Justin was shocked to find the rest of the Moodies were even more broke than HE was!

We are now up to August 1966. When Brian Epstein failed to "get back" to them about the missing lead guitarist, the Moodies regrouped on their own, and might have gone back to Secunda for management. If so, it didn't last long as the Moodies never mention him during this time period; the impression I have is the Moodies did their own promoting both in the U.K. and on the Continent, with a little help from Colin Berlin.

Secunda was at the time juggling The Move, who were "rock cousins" to the Moodies. Not only did Denny Laine wind up eventually suing Secunda, but Secunda landed The Move in court (September 1967) by a *bad move* using post cards with a lurid cartoon of the prime minister to promote them. The Moodies' money kept mysteriously vanishing, and they were in debt besides, and holding what one British source calls "red tax invoices," apparently for the flops after "Go Now."

It sounds like the Moodies *moved* away from managers, until Tony Clarke joined them in early 1967 and became producer. Other Decca-assigned managers are occasionally mentioned, none of lasting note. Put simply, Moody fortunes took a turn for the better after they parted company with stone-age managers and began being proactive about their own management and booking.

That fall of 1966, the reconstructed Moody Blues, with their new members, tried to recapture their past "Go Now" glory, but all they could get was working-man cabaret acts, and it was grueling. Justin has said in interviews he couldn't begin to remember all the places they played, it was one big hasty blur.

Some of the names of those early English cabaret spots are the Fiesta, Sheffield; the Flamingo, Sussex; the Titus, Stockton; El Dolce Vita, Newcastle; the Cromwell Inn. John came up with MORE nightclubs they did (*Birmingham Mail*, 8-6-10), mentioning the Navigation, the

Aston Chain and Hook, the Fox, the Cedar Club, Mothers, Tyburn, The Elbow Room. I'm still trying to picture the Moodies playing "Nights in White Satin" for a slow dance at the Butlins.

The chomping and smacking of diners during the shows was to leave a deep mark on all the Moodies; at Chastain Park during a 1994 concert, Justin came up and quipped, "Do you have any Grey Poupon?" to some munching diners in the front rows. As a joke of course. I personally was at one Las Vegas show in 1994, and during a blackout, saw Justin casting a jaundiced eye on a waiter in the front row in the Circus Maximus, who had about 20 glasses on his tray; I was a foot from stage, as was the waiter. Justin glared quietly (a friend of mine calls it "his cockroach glare") a long time, probably trying to hoo-doo the guy into dropping the drinks. The oblivious waiter took about 15 minutes to gather his money and deliver drinks, pretty annoying to all.

I've also seen fights between drunks break out in the front rows in nightclub shows, literally at Justin's feet; and people throwing ice (and the glass too) at John, who, bless him, ducked and kept on smiling. This was also in the '90s, at Circus Maximus shows. Some things never change. If nothing else, cabaret circuits developed character and a sense of humor.

I still haven't figured out when the Moodies first played the Bag o' Nails (zero documentation); it could have been during this late 1966 time period, if not earlier with the Denny Laine band incarnation. But play they did, and in some rough places. Tony Clarke confessed in chat that he was knocked out once in the Bag o' Nails, bar hopping with the Moodies. He said someone else started it, and he didn't duck quick enough. It must have been a lively place!

According to Graeme, this reconstruction period in the U.K. "doing Cabaret with Justin and John" only lasted a month. They kept one eye on the Beatles as the trend setters in their musical genre. "What is that stuff?" more than one of them have commented in interviews, about hearing

Beatles music developing from R&B to folk to their distinctive style we are familiar with now.

We must presume that somewhere along the line they ran across John Lennon (ever the "mad artist") spouting the usual artistic rhetoric about "being authentic" in one's pursuit of The Muse. Justin had also been around theater people, and something of method acting must have rubbed off on him. It couldn't help but come out. You have to be authentic to really make it in the creative world…..and "do what feels right." You shouldn't compromise on what you know is right, for some "popular trend."

A turning point came for the Moodies sometime in late 1966. Their act was lacking in some ways. Justin recalled once (while playing "Wild Thing") he got to bantering with Teddy Boys in the front rows, who were turned with their backs to the band, checking out the girls. It's a side we fans seldom see from mild-mannered Justin, but apparently he has a pretty lethal wit when it comes to exchanging verbal barbs with rude audience members hootin' and hollering. (I saw Justin do this once during his solo gigs, and I'm not EVEN going to tell who he aimed it at. Quite evil it was.)

Teddy Boys were certainly nothing to mess with. In *Brum Rocked*, Pat Wayne tells a story about some Teds showing up and egging the bands; music is obviously not a career path for the faint of heart. Anyway, this night the Teddy Boys (being just like the "bad asses" and punks you find in any country bar in America) threaten to beat the band up after the show 'cause Justin wiggled his eyebrows at the girls. The entire band remained huddled in the dressing room until long after closing. Presumably said Teds made off with all the hot birds in the meantime.*****

Justin was still trying to sing "Go Now," but it was without the same banshee verve that Denny Laine had wailed. In fact, Ray claims to have been singing "Go Now" in the post-Denny era.

And they were still going for the Teddy Boy look, wearing the matching serge suits with "reefer" jackets; if you are old enough to remember the early Beatles, you will see them immediately in your mind's eye. *Yeech*. There is at least one reference about their hard times doing cabaret, to "Justin blubbering." Graeme claimed to have put his arms around him, saying "Never mind, we're going home soon" and broke down himself. Those must have been very hard times for the band. (*Moodymania* #19, *Rock Family Trees* BBC2) They were soon to get their "call to arms."

By their accounts, the Moodies were in the dressing room after a show, sometime in the chilly fall, somewhere in darkest Wales; the Fiesta in Sheffield is most commonly mentioned. A customer came knocking on the door; it had been a typical "chicken in a basket" type of dinner show, small cabaret. They thought he wanted their autographs. No, he was lodging a complaint, with renown Welsh bluntness. "I pay two pound ten to take the Missus out to dinner, and I want to tell you that was the most bloody awful performance I have ever seen. I just thought you ought to know."

Hearts broken, the Moodies slunk to their van, and after fighting over who was going to sleep on the mellotron (the largest bit of solid non-moving gear in the van), they headed back home, in dead silence. After a bit, Graeme piped up from the dark in the back, where he was wedged in between some speakers. "You know, he's right, that bloke ....we do stink." John muttered something about getting some clothes that fit; he and Justin had inherited the blue reefer jackets from prior members, and the Jays are pretty big guys.

Upon those words of wisdom, Moody legend has it that they swore a solemn vow, and shook hands on it, in that dormobile, that they were going to be authentic, and do the music they loved, and only the music they loved. And they would write their own stuff, and quit trying to do what someone else did, or thought they should do. They needed a new approach, they weren't *po' folks* in the deep south of America, moaning the Delta Blues. They were middle class white guys in England, and should do songs that fit THEM.

They were going to be themselves. They were going to do what sounded RIGHT.

*Some fans actually spotted Justin running WILDLY for the elevator in Tahoe (in the '90s), from his room....apparently late for his Call. With his talent for sleeping, we figured he went up between the double shows for a cat nap, and had to be called so the show could start. I think he also fell asleep during the Moodies vs Moraz hearings on *Court TV*.

** It's amazing some of the utter lies people spread in this fan base, that sometimes will persist for years. I found legitimate notes that "Justin performed under the pseudonym of Valentine Hilton" so that bit of information is out there. From what I found out later, Valentine Hilton is the lead guitarist for the Animals, and indeed may be the dude that Eric Burdon hired when Justin applied for the same position. Clearing up this matter is just beyond the scope of my research, but it was an interesting bit of data. And, some is just plain old mistaken assumptions too.

***Notes on Lonnie Donegan: according to Hornsby, Donegan started with "train" songs, rather in the same vein as Donovan's first album. Dylan of course, went the same way, emulating Pete Seeger and Woody Guthrie. "London is Behind Me" by Hayward really fits into this genre quite well. "Nights in White Satin" has been used in perfume commercials, underwear ads, as well as evocative cinematic ballet sequences and movies about prostitutes, and Justin can do nothing about it; Donegan's estate controls the rights. The 12-string guitar Justin repaired, and recorded "Nights" with, was reclaimed by Donegan too. American music historians will tell you that Donegan is noted for his Brum-beat "skiffle" song "Does Your Chewing Gum Lose It's Flavor on the Bedpost Overnight?" No kidding. It was a major hit Stateside with the *Mad Magazine* crowd. Justin says he had fixed up the 12-string guitar, and straightened out the neck (Justin is a bit of a fix-it guy!) and had put new strings on it. Once "Nights" became a hit, Lonnie sent one of his minions to reclaim his guitar. Despite all this, Justin claimed to be on good terms with Lonnie! Donegan had been a MAJOR star during the pre-Beatle skiffle era in England, and on Oct 27, 2000 received an MBE from the Queen for "services to popular British music." Donegan was born in 1931, making him a bit older than Justin. Donegan passed away November 2002, so what happens to the rights to "Nights" is now up to lawyers and the future. Justin got the guitar back too.

****Justin is not the only one to have these contract difficulties stemming from the early years; Mike Pinder and some of the Beatles (among others) also signed bad contracts like this in their youth. Music and theatre can be a really ugly business. It also explains why Justin won't put a lot of his earlier songs on CD, because he doesn't stand to profit in the slightest from them, not owning the copyrights. A shame, because they really are good songs, but you can't blame Justin either. I personally will never forgive Donegan for his attempts at country western singing. It's painful to listen to

***** I found a very funny story in a book *The Beat Merchants* (p. 278), about the last night at The Golden Eagle, which was a notorious biker/Teddy Boy bar; they trashed the place as a final gesture to their beloved haunt. I've seen British in riot conditions whilst in the Navy; we Americans are quite tame compared to the English brawling style. The Moodies and many other British bands were very brave indeed to play in such places. Not only do they fight rough, the onlookers place side bets!

VI) Crystal White Sands: November 1966
November 11, 1967

The tick of time is not sublime, it's just Man's own invention --
Graeme Edge, alleged to have been left off the album *Days of Future Passed,* and written on a "Players" cigarette package during a three and a half hour drive from London to Carlisle.

From a historical vantage point it will probably look like the troubadour period in France. I'm sure it will look incredibly romantic. -- attributed to Jim Morrison, 1969, *No One Here Gets Out Alive.*

Hunger makes an English musician better! -- Justin Hayward, *Saturdag* April 14, 1977

    After reading about their beginning days in Birmingham, I hope by now everyone has figured that the Moodies may have been a bit skittish of Teddy Boys (a rational perspective, if you ask me) but they were anything but shrinking violets. And considering how quickly everyone shuffled from band to band in Brum, it's a tribute to them that the Moodies stayed together long enough to "make it." Who knows what oaths were sworn in smoke-filled rooms, by the light of flickering candles?
    When the Sun Goes down--Twilight Time to dream a while in veils of deepening blue......... the Moody Blues, 1967 As their gigs petered out, the jingle in their jeans vanished, their wallets got thinner and they were forced to move back in with family. It didn't set well with Ray, and he found himself buying the cheap tickets at the London Symphony, just so he could "find some place to think in peace." It rubbed off on him, and he began to acquire a taste for an orchestral sound.
    As British males are wont to do, that fall of 1966, the band began to gather in the evenings in a little town on the outskirts of London, called Cobham. There, at the sign

of the Running Mare Pub, whilst quaffing brews, they began working on "music that sounded like them." They staked out an old velour couch in the corner, and wrote poetry, composed music, and generally thought out what they were going to do as a band.

Mike then made the leap of genius to the mellotron, with which he was very familiar, having worked for that company. He first spotted the mellotron being used as a musical instrument by a guy named Graham Bond. The Moodies' original format had been a "big piano sound," as per that upright baby grand they tried to haul around. But it seems inevitable that Mike would quickly convert to the lighter mellotron for their new band (as per his aching back!) Mike had already gotten the Beatles into mellotrons in 1966 (*Goldmine*: Mike says each Beatle bought a mellotron; Lennon still had his when he and Yoko were recording *Imagine*).

While Mike had tried several keyboards for his sound, he could see that the "swooping" mellotron noise (caused by variable frequency oscillators or VFO) speeding up and slowing down the tape for weird effects, was going to give them a whole new sound, one which bore investigation.

Lest we forget, *Switched on Bach* surfaced (with a huge splash!) in 1965-1966, on BOTH sides of The Water. EVERYONE had *Switched on Bach*. Electronic synthesized music experimentation had been part of the industry since 1957, coinciding with a new market for television science fiction, and weird theme music. Synthesizer music only really became commercially feasible in the 1965 time-frame.

Mike and the other Moodies (as well as the Beatles) undoubtedly ran across the Carlos/Moog album by 1966 and wanted to incorporate electronic music into their sound. Mellotrons were cheap, available, and Mike knew how to fix them. From the *Switched on Bach* album, the implication is that the earliest music synthesizer filled up an entire room. However, the mellotron could easily be lugged to-and-from live shows, by two to four hearty young men.

Sensing a trend in the pivotal year of 1966, with that new format in mind, Mike and the band rescued a neglected mellotron from the Dunlop Social Club in Brum, where they found it laying in a very dusty attic, with the chord cut off it. I've bumped into interviews saying it cost them anywhere from £20- £300, which makes one wonder just who was watching their finances! Justin says he and Mike bought it, Graeme said they got the old machine in exchange for that night's fee.

The development of the synthesizer era is a fascinating bit of history; there exists a CD with this history, entitled *Rime of the Ancient Sampler*, released May 13, 1993. It has tracks from Patrick Moraz, Mike Pinder, and Rick Wakeman, among a host of others. The mellotron was designed to be a "sound effects" machine, and indeed a few of the notes on early Moody songs sound like eerie, musical, dreamy train whistles. In interviews, Mike (and Justin) mention a keyboard, attached to up to 35 tapes per keyboard (advanced mellotrons had two keyboards); there were eight seconds of tape each, complete with pinch rollers.....that's a lot of small delicate machinery to work with in a tight space. There is something to be said for the wheezy, spacey sound of the mellotron, *visceral* as one article put it; it was a worthy machine and a fellow band member with a heart and soul of its own.

The mellotronic aura has a lot to do with the appeal of the early "Core Seven" albums the Moodies made before 1973. Much about mellotron technical details can be read in *Higher and Higher* #11/12, and #20.* Also, check out Mike's portion of the documentary in the *Isle of Wight* DVD, released in 2009. Really cool watching him work The Beast!

Paul McCartney apparently still had his eye on the Moody Blues, for the Beatles used the mellotron themselves (1966-1967, *Magical Mystery Tour*) with some success. The Moodies certainly did better than the Beatles with only calliope "oompah" noises to show for their efforts on "Strawberry Fields" and some cartoon *gobbledigoop* on "I Am the Walrus."

Time waits for no one; fascinating as mellotron history is, by 1971 Mike was talking about getting into Moog technology. Mike claimed to have the second mini-Moog off the assembly line, Stevie Wonder got the first one! So Mike indeed stayed current and innovative in his keyboard sound. For the record, Tony Clarke was also part of the development of the Moody Mellotron, it seems to have been a joint engineering project.

On the Continent --Late 1966: even with their new mellotron sound, the Moodies still weren't showing a positive cash flow. John was running out of assets to sell to support everyone; John and Justin put it bluntly "we were skint" in a radio interview with Michael Jackson in L.A. We can only wonder where all that dosh from Justin's 335 went, sold the week before he joined the Moodies, it's best not to ask. Mike had a mediocre job offer from Ember Records, but Graeme had a girl in France. The band had some collective decisions to make.

They managed to get sponsorship from amplifier companies (Vox) around Brum, and replenished their gear. Lightening their load, they threw away the serge suits. John and Justin bought smart new red jackets, they picked up some Mod frilly shirts, and Mike added a jabot to his stage ensemble. About this time, "Boulevard de la Madeleine" flopped and probably pitched the band into heavy debt. Something drastic had to be done.

They took their bookings into their own hands. Mike called up a friend who was associated with a cabaret on the border of Belgium and France, who offered to put the band up in exchange for their musical services. When the weather turned cold, and with the Red-Tax Man threatening to lock them up, as Graeme put it, something needed to happen. There were even rumors of repo men trying to grab their amplifiers.

So, they sailed for France. Think about it, if they were a band for two years, beginning in May 1964, and had flaky managers who didn't pay the taxes, it would take about two years for the taxman to catch up with them. This must happen to young people all the time who suddenly get thrown into the limelight and have poor management. This way to fast burn out.

Shaking loose what was left of their pocket change, the band took the Dover ferry across the channel to Calais or Dunkirk and traveled bit southeast and inland to the small town of Mouscron, just inside the Belgium border. There, they based themselves in a little family-run hotel called Madame Elaine's. John pronounces the town as "Moo-cron." A U.K. newspaper clipping from Nov 5, 1966 says they are "on the Continent." There, they wrote music, did some gigs, and generally restructured the band.

Being engineers, I'm sure they used that tired old phrase "back to the drawing board" with true verve. The mellotron went with them, also to have some serious modifications, *a la Pinder*. Mike says he pulled the heavy speakers out of the mellotron at some point, and cranked the output signal through amplifiers, making it much lighter. As the band grew, he took out the heavy tubes (valves) and replaced them with solid state circuitry and "cards."

According to Justin (*Saturdag*, April 14, 1977) they spent time in Europe under the direction of a promoter who booked them in France and Belgium. They performed in Utrecht, "Holland several times, twice for the Grand Gala du Disque." Tom Jones' agent Colin Berlin was a guy Justin had met whilst recording on Dean Street before he joined the band; so Berlin also helped the Moodies to get the first bookings on the continent and in the U.K. They backed up Tom Jones at the Olympia in Paris, and on *The Tom Jones Show* during this time, as well as later after they released *Days of Future Passed*.

To this day, the Moodies have ties to Belgium and the continent; John's wife Kirsten is Danish. Even unto 1991, during the promotion of *Keys of the Kingdom*, the Moodies did promo gigs in shop windows in Belgium, and interviews on Holland radio, as well as a tour through Germany.

There is an interview that says the band considered a name change when John and Justin joined, but the promoters wanted to keep the Moody Blues name. The change was so radical with the addition of the new members and change in electronic sound, that Graeme says (*Legend of a Band*) he thinks of the old "Go Now" Moodies as a totally different band.

Probably they had to take day jobs; Mouscron (Belgium) is pretty much a shipping region; it's also known for the good beer they brew. Justin made one very funny crack on the *Late Late Show* (April 27, 1995) about the "engine room of a Belgian trawler." Now how would he know what that looks like? One can only shudder to imagine what they must have done for groceries during this time.

John got a little upset in one interview, venting hotly, about people who claimed to have been there when the band started. "Where was you when we were pooling our money on the bed, wondering who was going to eat that night?" Things must have been very rough for the band, indeed.

When you read about this time period, you have to wonder why they went on. The reason is the same for every artist: given the choice between boring lives of despair in the factories of Birmingham, or maybe getting a break in something they loved doing; the five band members felt strongly enough about their talents that they wanted go on. They believed in themselves. And too, as John would say in an interview (*Palm Beach Post*, Oct 7, 1994) "The band members realized how small they are in relationship to the Universe. [There was] more sense in working together and having fun."

Perhaps too, there was that feeling of ultimate destiny. Whatever the reason, they stubbornly refused to give up. That's still a good perspective to take, here forty-plus years later. *Never never give up*!

The years 1966-1968, and their gigs on the continent are hazy for the band, just bits and pieces of collective memories have surfaced about this time period.

"We went back for Christmas '66" someone piped up on *The Moody Blues Story*. Justin says they recorded on Dean Street. On the back of *Higher and Higher* #5 is a Coke ad with the Moodies in suits-and-ties, and it's copyrighted 1967. It also mentions that Ray can sing and tap his foot in different rhythms at the same time (it's actually a marimba beat: later cognitive psychology researchers call this "streaming," not many people can do it!)

They played "Please Don't Let Me Be Misunderstood" on the BBC January of 1967, and the tape still exists, along with a song by John called "Beautiful Dream" (found on *www.youtube.com*) and possibly "Peeping and Hiding" a bluesy number by Ray (*Higher and Higher* #4 and #5). They played a place called "Kremlin-Bicetre" near Paris in 1968 (quite radical in the Anarchist movement of the time); and they also played before 500,000 people in a Communist Rally in France in August 1969, apparently in a cleared pasture, using hay bales to put their speakers on.

The Moody Blues were indeed supposed to play at Woodstock and are on the poster. However, they were also offered the Communist gig in France the same weekend, and literally flipped a coin to decide which they would do. France won out! Justin said they didn't have any idea what they were walking into when they took the Communist gig; in many of their interviews, they skittishly say "Socialist" rally! Apparently, the show was pretty wild, with simulated bombings of Viet Nam, and a good deal of outrage regarding American foreign policy at the time.

Justin was Capitalistic in his reflection of the event, saying "It was great exposure, and our sales went up in France!" Justin also remembers the Moodies being in Prague when Soviet tanks rolled in and took over in 1968. The band spent an afternoon doing a video in the open streets of Prague (can be found with some persistence on *youtube.com*), and possibly did one gig on the television, or were slotted to anyway. After being called by the British Embassy, and told to get out of town, they were diverted from their hotel, and found the Soviet Army had taken over. Said military escorted the band to the airport (I think it was at a Storyteller on the fourth cruise, Graeme said they were MARCHED to the airport!) and they were very lucky to hitch a ride back to the U.K. with a Pakistani Red Crescent cargo plane.

Ray tells a story on his website about this gig: they had no place to change, so the local promoter (handler?) took them to a nearby state-owned comrade's home, "turfed the guy out" of his bedroom (and the poor guy had been up all night working) so the band could use it as a dressing room. Communism in action, it is. Ray concluded by saying "I haven't had much use for left wing politics ever since."

They were in France in early 1968, in time to take the place of The Supremes, the ladies didn't get their backing tape in time. This was at the Midem Festival in Cannes, which the Moodies just happened to be at, with gear. They stepped in (always be prepared) and did their stage show, forty-five minutes live on EuroTV. All the sudden, "Nights in White Satin" was a huge success on the continent. One of the first videos of "Nights" was shot right after that at Grande Briggard Castle, north of Brussels, and it also was a hit.

The act kept as hold-overs, some of the earlier songs. Easter of 1967, the Moodies played in Helsinki's Icehall, including the songs "Go Now," "Boulevard de la Madeleine" and "From the Bottom of My Heart." One of the singers wore green glasses! But the reporter couldn't figure out whom was whom, and named one of them "Justin Thomas." (*Jaahalli,* Mar 26, 1967)

Ray Coleman, Paris correspondent for *Melody Maker*, happened to go to one of their shows on the continent in early 1967, liked it a lot, called up Dave Symonds of the BBC (radio), and raved about the Moodies. Coleman incidentally became a life-long friend of the band. Symonds got them a slot on *Easybeat* in the UK. That was enough to make the taxman happy; they went home to England and played there too, concentrating on the college circuits. (That was where Graeme started out, remember?)

BBC Radio underwent major reconstruction in 1967, and was "brought out of the Dark Ages." So there was some new technology in the air, and the BBC was anxious to have cutting-edge bands play on their cutting-edge equipment.

Once the band had enough money to keep the creditors from seizing their equipment, in early 1967 they returned to their London home base. They began to get little slots of recording time: Justin's "blog" letter of November 2009 (*www.justinhayward.com*) explains how they recorded "Fly Me High" in what had to have been one of the first studio sessions for their "Mach II" incarnation. Justin claims also this is where they first met Tony Clarke, and also an engineer named Gus Dugan. It was the combined talents of these electronic wizards that made "Fly Me High" into the marvelous recording it is.

At first they lived together in a house in rural Hampton, but then (as cash flow improved) split up into various bedsitters and apartments. Justin and Graeme settled into a bedsitter on Gunterston Road, in West Kensington (Bayswater?), a rather notorious complex where many other rockers (Stonies and such) also resided.

Mike even told a story about the Beatles song "She Came in through the Bathroom Window" being about a groupie who crawled in HIS window and (finding Mike asleep or playing 'possum) went on her way to another room. Mike's Beatle friends found it hilarious. The fans would write graffiti on the walls of their apartments, and all sorts of things crawled in after hours!

White Nights --Mike Pinder, our keyboard player, had written a lovely song which he asked me to sing, which was called "Dawn is a Feeling." And I thought, Gee, I really want to write the thing - dawn, nights - and to write the other end of this stage show. He's written the beginning, I really want to write the end of it. So, that's where really "Nights" came from. Very quick song to write, and I took it into the rehearsal room the next day. -- Justin Hayward

Probably the most asked question of Justin Hayward, composer of "Nights in White Satin" (which went to #2 in America during 1972, and even charted in 2010!!!) is "What did you write 'Nights' about?" Even Justin says it's hard to remember sometimes, and certainly it was (and is) a very personal song for him; one is not exactly always open and forthcoming about personal poetry. It's a slow waltz song, in three-quarter time, unlike most of their music, which is four-four time. "Dawn is a Feeling" is also in three-quarter time; so is "Go Now."

"Nights" has heavily romantic, sad lyrics, and somehow struck a chord with everyone in America in the overloaded year of 1972. In France it was recognized much sooner (1968), and the Moodies were able to tour a good deal on the impetus from that one hit song. Of the song, Justin says he had broken up with a girlfriend. His wife Marie, in a U.K. tabloid article, piped up at this remark and said "He wrote it in the bathroom," allegedly the acoustics were better in there.

Another former girlfriend had left behind her white satin sheets, thus the title, although "White Nights" is also a phrase used in northern latitudes to describe sleepless nights and "long summer days," the title of another Justin song.

I suspect "Nights" was heavily influenced by a song, Marty Wilde's "I Cried," which mentions "your letter" over and over again. Justin's direct words about the song are "a flat in Bayswater, and an audience in Glastonbury." In later years, Justin would change this to "I wrote the song in adulation of all women" which is beautifully poetic, and rather nice if you ask me. Whatever the explanation, Justin and his lady had parted company, and he wasn't happy about it; thus the song. Haven't we ALL had these moments?

Further stories say that he played his guitar so much in the bathroom late at night, that the neighbors had a nasty habit of getting up and playing loud classical music down the pipes for HIM in the mornings (*Beethoven's Fifth*.) So "Nights in White Satin" like any good artistic creation, has a lot of both fact and myth wrapped around it. Like a rainbow, it would be foolish to analyse it overmuch. Just ENJOY it!

Justin would say later in many interviews, about this relationship that evoked such a wonderful song "It's best not to know [about your first love], it's better to have wonderful memories." Justin certainly emotes on stage every time he sings this song, but a stage performance is not real life; Justin seems a very practical person, and a happy man today, so he must have gotten over it! It's a nice song, one that means a lot, in many different ways, to different people. What does it mean to the composer? Justin tends to cast his eyes upwards after performing the song live, so perhaps he is thanking Someone, Somewhere, for all that it did for the band. *Amen* indeed.

Justin met Marie at the Bag o' Nails, and she eventually became his wife; they were married December 19, 1970, and still are. Justin and Graeme were roommates in Bayswater, and Graeme's girlfriend Carol (eventually to be the first Mrs. Edge) was a model on Carnaby Street and friends with Marie (a model, and also the hat check girl at the Bag O' Nails), and THEY were roommates.

One has to assume that between Graeme getting worried (and annoyed) at his roomie moping around, playing romantic songs in the loo; and Carol trying to get Marie and Justin out of the way so she and Graeme could socialize, all of this falls into place. Marie says she first met Justin when he came to collect Graeme, who had fallen asleep on Carol's couch. Justin claims his first date with Marie was taking her home in his blue Cortina from a gig one night and stopping for late-night coffee.

Justin says (several interviews) he was nineteen when he wrote "Nights in White Satin," but it is one of those "glitches" you find in the research. Justin turned age 20 on Oct 14, 1966. By almost EVERY piece of documentation, Justin joined the band in August or September of 1966. Mike Pinder says he wrote "Dawn is a Feeling" in January of 1967, and Justin says he wrote "Nights" after "Dawn." Mike says he had a red piano, and actually wrote "Dawn" as the Sun was coming up after a very long night of restless thought. There are also stories that "Dawn" was written on the way home from a gig at The Speakeasy in London.

Foma! A pack of Foma! (Kurt Vonnegut) Found on Wikipedia: *In the late 1990s, the U.K. magazine "Record Collector" printed a claim that "Nights In White Satin" had not been written by Justin Hayward at all, but that in fact the Moody Blues' management had simply bought the song outright in 1966 from an Italian group called The Jellyroll and taken credit for it. This spurious claim seems to have arisen from the discovery of a 7" single by The Jellyroll which allegedly carries the words "This is the original version of Nights In White Satin" on the label.*

Refutation: First off, *what* management???? Been following along? (chuckle) Justin says that "Nights" was written as a "bookend" to Mike Pinder's song "Dawn" and indeed, both are in three-quarter time (unusual for a Moody song) and the melodies are inversions of each other musically; you can listen and decide for yourself. If the Jellyroll wrote "Nights" then they wrote "Dawn" too, and I don't believe it in either case. Justin's and Mike's songwriter/composition skills have since been proven many times over. All this aside, I found that alleged "first song by the Jellyroll" and it wasn't all THAT similar to "Nights." Unless you're tone deaf. I direct your searching fingers to *youtube.com* if you have further concerns.

According to *The Apocalypse Now Book* by Peter Cowie, "Nights In White Satin" was the original song choice in the opening of the film *Apocalypse Now* before "The End" by The Doors was chosen. And aren't you glad they used "The End" instead? I just can't imagine "Nights" playing over glowing napalm. And didn't "Nights" work great for the opening of *Dark Shadows*???

A Day in a Life --Justin frequently tips his hat to Mike and Ray, who worked up the Middle 8 melody bridge of "Nights" in between verses of "Nights." After writing it on the edge of his bed that night, Justin took it in the next morning, and played it for the boys. By his account, the rest of the band sorta sat there, being very British and said "not bad."

At their urging, he played it again, and Mike began to pick up the mellotron line on it; suddenly the song had some life. (Sydney Radio, Aug 5, 2011). That was the pattern; Graeme said (Beard, *Classic Pop Examiner* Feb 18, 2012) when he took in his poems for the album, Tony Clarke asked Mike to "hit some chords and flow around, do some grand waves." As with "Nights," the songs took on shape and form, and the spoken poems became the opening and ending tracks for the entire album. They always said Mike was the "fix it" guy, and he did so, filling in gaps with his incredible keyboard skills.

By the Spring of 1967, they began performing "Nights" and "Dawn." with Lodge's rail-rocker song "Peak Hour." Graeme had written (in best Beatnik tradition) two lovely poems, "Morning Glory" and "Late Lament" about the morning and evening.

Realizing it was ALL about some "time of day", they got the idea of writing a cycle of songs that would take in each hour of the day. They already had "concept album" examples, like *The Waltz of the Hours*, *The Planets* (Horst). One of their favorite albums was *The Zodiac* by the Cosmic Sounds (on Electra) released early 1967; *The Zodiac* also used a Moog. It began to fall into place, they smoothed out the wrinkles during their stay in Mouscron, got the mellotron up and running, and began to perform for audiences on the Continent, polishing their stage act as they went.

All three of those songs "Nights," "Dawn," and "Peak Hour" being "along the same line of thought" was a concept that was to govern the Moodies for the next 5 years...."everyone on the same wavelength." In interviews, even today, the Moodies seem to anticipate the next person's words, and courteously let their band mates speak, in a fine example of a positively applied of "Group Think." It was just good teamwork, which they found applied nicely to another passion they all shared.

Take the "Way-Back Machine" forward to 1991, the Bay Area of California. I was going to school at the time and lived in some apartments not far from campus. My eight-year-old son happened to hear the British accents of my neighbors, who were hanging over their balcony, beers in hand, enjoying a day off. Being a mouthy child, he heckled them about their accents. And then he continued "Do you know who the Moody Blues are?" Yes I'm afraid his mother had been playing the records a bit too much. The bloke with the beer kept a totally straight face, and replied "That's football team, isn't it?" My son insisted they were musicians. "No, they're a football team, and a good one too!" About this time I retrieved my son with a grin of apology to the neighbors.

The funny thing is it turned out, as I found out more about the band, the bloke with the beer was absolutely right. The Moodies, and their producers, publicists, and roadies, had their own soccer "football" team in the late '60s and early '70s. And as *Rolling Stone* put it (Sept 16, 1971), *were feared in their league!* Perhaps the clue from Justin's song "Top Rank Suite" will tell us just when this team started to form, "They play a good game of football in Mouscron." The Moodies, like the good English lads they are, spent a lot of time in those days kicking a ball around, and waiting for it.....or the Muse of Inspiration....to bounce off their heads.

Eventually, they played games for various charities. John would in later interviews, comment "turned sideways, the resident orchestra conductor's booth made an ideal goal box." One can only hope these orchestra leaders had retired by 1993! Their positions (I don't play soccer, so this is possibly a bit tongue-in-cheek, it's more or less a direct quote) were Graeme: Center back; Justin: Right back behind the goal; Ray: Left Half next to John; John: next to Ray. Mike didn't play soccer, according to sources who were there. I'm getting a little ahead of the story, but other team players (1970) would eventually include Tony Clarke, and crewmembers Tony Clarkson, Gerry Hoff, and Keith Altham; AND David Rohl, who did the photography on the inside of *Question of Balance.*

I think there IS still a soccer team in the U.K. named "the Moody Blues" but I have no idea of their origin. Threshold Music certainly still sponsors youth sports. If you go to *www.raythomas.me*, you'll find photos of the Moodies playing soccer in the photo album section. Very cool stuff.

So, much of 1967 was spent playing colleges (with guitars and with a soccer ball?) in England, according to articles of March 1968. Touring colleges was probably the best thing they could have done: college is always a hot-bed for exchange of revolutionary ideas and good music. They used to rehearse in an old church, Wigan Hall in Barnes, next to a railway. According to articles, they were there for about a month, probably in 1967. John wrote "Peak Hour" and "See-Saw" coming down the M1 in the van and stomping on the floorboards for the beat. So, they toured a lot this year.

In 1967, the band was able to rekindle contacts with Decca, which was really more known for their classical music. Hornsby mentions Decca in 1967, grooming Brum bands for recording, hoping for a hit to match Capitol's success with the Beatles. The Moodies had ties to the Rolling Stones, a Decca band; and Graeme had been in the Avengers, also Decca. Technology in the recording business was rapidly closing in; record executives knew it, and realized that young, huge group of Baby Boomers was the up-coming market. At the same time, they had to tap the new stereo market.

According to one Decca executive, they gave the Moodies £5,000 "To keep them from bugging us," but at the same time, you don't just drop £5,000 on a group of long hairs; they must have trusted the band to do something eventually. There is also some thought that this sum had come from their Brum beat flops, in mid-1966. Their prowess on the continent must have preceded them, for Decca to have such confidence.

New World--It was impossible to miss the success of the Beatles. *Sergeant Pepper's Lonely Hearts Club Band* was released only three months prior to recording *Days of Future Passed*, and it was good rock n' roll interlaced with orchestral tidbits, i.e. "A Day in a Life." Sergeant Pepper blew right to the top of the charts. The trend was there. The Moodies were so good at making sound with their new mellotron, that the musician's union almost walked off due to the threat of "being replaced" by a machine! (Caroline interview, February, 2001)

Music and psychedelia exploded in year 1967. Literally overnight, music and clothing fashions changed from "straight" to "flower power." Decca needed new blood, and fast! Some executive somewhere recognized true talent when he heard it, and the mellotron got everyone's attention.

So, the Moodies caught a break and some studio time finally at Decca. In early 1967, Decca assigned junior executive staff producer Tony Clarke to the band. Justin claims some of the earliest music recorded by the Mach II incarnation of the Moody Blues was done at Regent Sound (Dean/ Denmark Street). Derek Varnals had interesting comments on this: in his Adelaide interview with Spence Davis (3-2-10) he talked about all the musicians at Decca "being very businesslike" with shirts and ties, not very relaxed in the beginning for the young struggling Moody Blues (who were just happy to have the studio time.)

One cannot believe the rancour with which rock n' roll was greeted by the older generation in those days. At my house (being the proud child of a couple of Red Necks), when the jangling loud caterwauling came on the air, it was often expletive ethnic slur deleted dirty word, followed by slamming doors and unplugged radio. There was true warfare for which pop music was going to win the hearts and minds of the Boomer generation. Folk? with the soft smiling faces and beautiful guitar strumming. Or raunchy leather hard-bitten rebellious Rock?

Deramic Sound was a new technology division for Decca. Simultaneously they were trying to incorporate pop music, as was Capitol and Sergeant Pepper just down the street. Tony Clarke was going to finish out the Moodies' expiring contract and last-ditch effort. Derek Varnals (who sounds remarkably like Graeme Edge and must have vocally confused a few folks in the studio) was assigned as engineer.

The Moodies had a reputation of being not only "a bit difficult to get along with" (Tony Clarke's exact words were "they devoured producers") but were also a very, very creative, talented group of guys. Tony says he went to the bar next door to have a drink with the band, and it was a "meeting of the minds." (Tony claimed Ray Thomas was the funniest of the group.) Tony was the same age as the band, and from the same general area in England, so that had to have helped.

It's even possible the wily Decca executives set up the ultimate expectancy effect when they told Tony Clarke, "These guys are producers," and so they indeed turned out to be. The Moody Blues had finally found someone who could handle them!

Tony said the first time he heard of the Moody Blues, he played back some raw tapes of their music, and really liked "Nights in White Satin." After the first few demos were cut, Tony, the band, and Decca's managing director had a meeting, and the director also said, "I really like that one, Knights in white helmets, or armour or something...." Being folk-oriented as a studio, the Decca execs found "Nights" more bluesy folk, rather than rock. So, in fall 1967, hearing the demo, said execs gave the go ahead for recording a sampler album, demonstrating both rock and classical music in Deramic stereo.

Clarke's interview in *Higher and Higher* #29-#30 concerning this time period is incredible; his easy-going personality oozes right off the interview page and into your lap, making friends with you, the reader. Tony, a former bass player himself, had found the management end of music to be more lucrative than the playing end, and had been "taking care" of people like Roy Orbison and Bill Haley for Decca.

According to Tony, in 1967, Decca was putting together what he called "Phase Four" demos on their new stereo technique. Lodge called them FFRR, Full Frequency Range Recordings (*Crawdaddy*, July 17, 2011.) Where Deramic sound had the technical edge, was in integrating the signals in the electronics better. The stereo sound became such that there was not a "ping-pong" effect between the right and left speakers, drums on the left, guitars on the right, but there was rather a smooth range of sound. And that nice smooth sound lent itself well to the new FM radio in America when *Days of Future Passed* broke out in Spring 1968.

"Tuesday Afternoon" not only showcases how sound could shift smoothly from one side to the other; listen to it in stereo, with headphones; hurrah, no ping pong!! Then they altered the tempo midway through, something that rock n' roll had never tried before. "Tuesday Afternoon" is a watershed track, melding rock and classical in one tight, nicely performed, lovely little song***.

With this new technology and the activity at the studios, the Moodies slid into a crack in studio time: some corporate executives weren't aware it was even going on. Even with such advanced prowess in audio filtering, legend has it that on *Days of Future Passed*, one can still hear slamming doors, ringing phones and so forth, coming through thin walls. But the whole thing has been refined so that the average ear misses it.

At the end of the album, either the studio cat or a confused percussionist knocked over a bell tree, right in time with a large crescendo. Justin says he was sitting in the studio watching, and claims the cat went up in the air with a squall; don't know how the timpanist got into it, but both stories are out there. Maybe an addled percussionist stepped on the cat!

The Moodies often praise Decca staff member Derek Varnals as being a master engineer; Varnals did an excellent technical interview in *Higher and Higher* #26-#27. Clarke also speaks highly of Varnals, and in turn, both Clarke and Varnals speak highly of Mike Pinder; there was a lot of enlightened electronic wizardry going on. Clarke even went so far as to say he was practically psychic with Varnals at times. Justin also gets mentioned as being part of the "nuts and bolts" of the albums; Mike and Justin are acknowledged by all to be the two band members who can construct musical harmonies with true genius.

If you check the photo on the back of *Days of Future Passed,* you'll see Graeme stubbing out the fag. From Graeme, clockwise around the table are Justin, (maybe Graeme is wedged in here, the photo is very dark) Ray, John, Mike, Tony Clarke. To Tony's left is Peter Knight. According to Justin (Sept 20, 2017 radio interview) the guy with his back to the camera is Michael Barkley, who was a promoter involved in album production. Notice that there is a photo of the phases of the moon on the table open. I wonder if they weren't brainstorming the cover to the album. The artist David Anstey is credited with the artwork on "Days."

Now you have to remember that the Moody Blues were performing on stage live in 1967. Their opening half of the show was a grab-bag of songs, both self-written, and covers: "Wild Thing," "Don't Let Me Be Misunderstood," "Fly Me High," "Time is on My Side." For the last half of the show, they did all the songs about "one day in a life" of one guy, just like they appear on *Days of Future Passed.* As John puts it, "this slotted in nicely" to the overall concept Decca had.

They started by recording singles with Clarke, often at night after their shows, going to bed at dawn because other artists had the studio by day. The singles were released and began to get play time here and there, sporadically. "Fly Me High" was quite popular with the pirate radio broadcasters who sat on ships off England in those days, competing with the BBC.** "Fly Me High" turned up later in a movie, *The Dish*; it was so popular, it traveled to Australia! The Moodies were gaining fame as an "underground band."

Five of these early "extra" songs outside *Days of Future Passed* were bootlegged onto a 1971 album *The Answer to the Mystery of Life,* which was produced in fair quantity in the States. It contained not only the "five," but a live performance (and it's miserable quality) in which Ray talks about Dr. Leary, on the lam at the time.

Eventually Decca would release the same five songs in a better quality album *Caught Live Plus Five,* which the Moodies were never very happy about; they didn't like "the Five" songs, and had shelved them for a reason. "Caught Live" contained a live performance of December 12, 1969 at the Royal Albert Hall. The "Five" can also be found on *Prelude,* released on early CD in the '80s.

As they had the Moodies on tap in 1967, someone at Decca had the brilliant idea to record Dvorak's *New World Symphony* and do part of it as a rock concert. "Do it with a beat" added the exec who assigned the project. It might have actually worked well; Emerson, Lake and Palmer did something similar with *Pictures at an Exhibition* in later years. Other documentation mentions Decca's plan to produce "The Young Person's Guide to the Orchestra," which should make anyone shudder to contemplate. Ray Thomas claimed (interview with Bill Kopp, 31 Aug 2017) that the Moodies were supposed to play rock classics, like Elvis and Jerry Lee Lewis, to fit between the strains of orchestrations. There is mention that the Moodies were to write lyrics to the strains of the *New World Symphony* (~~~aggghh!!!~~~)

An orchestral conductor by the name of Peter Knight was assigned to the project, he rounded up a handful of orchestra musicians (44-48 pieces, from the London Symphony and the Royal Symphony.) The "London Festival Orchestra" was nothing more than some loose musicians who came together for a little extra dosh. The Moodies, with the usual financial monster (and expiring contract) breathing down their necks, readily agreed to the entire thing.

Much better to beg forgiveness than to ask permission -- Graeme Edge, *The Saratogian,* 4-4-2012.

Decca exec Michael Barclay had the idea after he and Knight came to see the live Moody stage show prior to recording, in a "little club on Oxford Street" (*Access Atlanta,*

03-16-12.) The Moodies described Pete Knight as a "younger sort of Santa Claus." Knight had that "leap of faith" and loved their music. He might also have been rightfully revolted by the thought of lyrics "and a beat" to *The New World Symphony*, not to mention the outdated "Young People's Guide to the Orchestra." Young people were taking their music FAR beyond the normal boundaries! He helped roll the boulder over the door.

Days of Future Passed was born. It was recorded on the four-track machines of the time, but with above average recording quality, as Decca was primarily a classical music studio. Most albums in this time period are done on eight-track, but this WAS very early on. Orchestral music is recorded with full frequency, and this was the new Deramic (early Dolby) sound. So Decca treated "Days" in the same manner, which lent itself well to the digital 5.1 version that was to come later. Justin mostly did the 5.1 re-master. (WABE interview, March 19, 2012) He talked about this with Steve Goss in a neat tech interview; Justin talks about "bouncing" tracks electronically to get a fuller sound.

Peter Knight took the melodies the Moodies had written about "the day in one guy's life" and scored the orchestral leitmotifs to match. According to Hayward, in interviews 50 years after the fact, more songs were written during the process, and only a few pre-existing songs are really orchestrated in the "bits in between." For example, "The Sunset" is a grooving, spooky song, really beautiful done live with just the band, but has no orchestrated version on the album.

Though the Moodies claim it took "two weeks to make" there must have been prep time with Knight creating the scores (Justin said Knight had a little writing shed at his home.) To date, the original scores have not re-appeared and are lost. The band recorded in the studio when they could; some documentation says during days, but they used the "off" hours in the studio, like the wee hours in the middle of the night and on weekends.

"Nights in White Satin" was recorded on a Saturday morning. Then the band went out evenings and did their live gigs to keep the cash flow going.

Varnals had some interesting comments on how they recorded in those days. They would just hang a "boom" microphone over the orchestra, and they had to do things like separate woodwinds and brass to avoid "sound bleed over." Strange and wonderful, how much things will change by the time the 1992 Red Rocks concert comes along.

At the end of a two-week period of recording the band, Knight called in the orchestra, and recorded all the *Days of Future* Passed symphony parts in one day. Clarke said the studio was jammed with 44+ pieces, so much that one guy was wedged into a doorway! Other Moodies recalled actually counting off the spaces on the tape where the orchestra would fit, and then picking up and playing their songs timed just right on the tapes. The bits were spliced together; like a patchwork puzzle, the whole thing fell into a cohesive, majestic, and very solid stereo album, effectively demonstrating exactly what the executives wanted: both rock and classical music in "Deramic sound" stereo. And yes at the end, Tony Clarke said he was able to mix the rock and orchestral version of "Nights" right together on the same track, no small feat for the time, but they were able to match the rhythms together.

Tony Clarke said when they played back the final mix of "Nights" (in the dark) that everyone was a bit stunned, thinking they might actually have a hit on their hands. In fact, when Tony wandered out to his car, he had a flat tire, and said "I didn't care." The Moodies claimed it was on the way back from doing "Nights" live on a BBC show (*Ready, Steady, Go*) when they heard it on the radio, and were a little shocked, thought they might have something. When they called the station and asked for the tape, they were told it had been erased!

For the record, the first Moody Blues BBC shows live (still in existence) are dated May, 1967. "Nights in White Satin" live on the BBC was played on *The Dave Symonds Show*,

Nov 6, 1967. Allegedly that original tape they heard in the car DID show up finally and is remastered on the *Days of Future Passed* 50th anniversary issue. Radio stations in those days tended to record over shows that had already been broadcast, as tape was expensive and was reused.

John Lodge says that "Redwave" was a fictitious person they made up as the "writer" of all their music. By the second album, they dropped the idea as it "sounded silly."

The finished album was presented at the Monday meeting, Armistice Day, November 11, 1967. The first thing out of one execs' mouth was "Damn it! This isn't want we asked for!" Naturally the Dvorak lovers in the executive meeting protested the change in program, especially when this group of long hairs showed up, with their mod blonde girlfriends in tow. Some execs complained "You can't dance to it." We must presume from this that they expected young people to dance to a rock version of Dvorak. Now there's a visual image.

"What are we going to do with THIS?" one griped, acting like the album was a dead fish. A couple of the Decca execs were going to toss it, according to Graeme, saying "I have no idea who we could sell this to." Thankfully, other execs present recognized what a work of genius it was. "Give that to me, I can sell it!" replied Walt Maguire; he was the American head of Decca, who just by chance happened to be in town for the playback. Several Moodies have said Maguire physically took it out of the hands of a naysayer; oh how thin the thread of Fate!

Those in favor of the new album also included Hugh Mendl, their "folk and stage" label chief, and very influential. He is also mentioned as being A&R exec and procurement chief, the guy who watched the budgets, AND instrumental in the skiffle movement. Maguire is credited by Justin and Mike both, for really getting the album going in America, with his unstoppable enthusiasm. He must have sent out a lot of promos of the album to various rock stations; that is where we heard it first, in spring 1968, on the airwaves of Los Angeles; they played the whole album at once! The new Deramic sound worked beautifully with the new FM stereo radio systems which were flooding American airwaves (especially in Los Angeles.) Jerry Huff (of American Decca) is also mentioned as part of the promotion team.

Curious note: in a New Zealand interview (Nov 23, 2011) Justin claimed that it was "independent promoters" who were pushing the whole Dvorak idea. And they all mysteriously vanished after "Days" was released.

Needless to repeat, the album was greeted with great favor. One reviewer even referred to Graeme's "Late Lament" as Keatsian. Wow. All that from a hippy band. If I'm not mistaken, Decca made back that £5,000 with no problem; John Lodge was to say in later interviews "They didn't have much choice except to release it and try to recoup the loss!" Someone also had the brilliance to put as a cover, one of the most attractive pieces of psychedelic art imaginable. Believe me, it helped sell the album; I can remember sitting around partying with my friends, trying to figure out what those little half-finished, spacey images meant. It fit the spring of 1968 perfectly.

The Moody Blues were also lucky to be recognized by Sir Edward Lewis, head of Decca (also a supporter of the Rolling Stones. Justin and Mick Jagger both are effuse in their praise of Lewis.) The Stones were driving Sir Edward nuts in 1967; when *Days of Future Passed* started to sell, Sir Edward invited the Moodies to tea/lunch to size them up and saw how they handled themselves.

Favorably impressed, he said to Justin (sitting next to him) "Boys, I don't know exactly what it is you are doing, and I don't understand it, but people seem to like it. Keep doing it, just do the best that you can, and we will sell it. You can have the studio any time!" (Justin interviews, fall 2012) Justin said in *Goldmine* magazine: "He was the last man I knew in this business with authority, and with the confidence in his artists, to be able to stand there and say that." Sir Edward must have been quite a guy.

So, the stage was set for another British invasion of the Moody kind......and like something out of a Joseph Campbell myth, they set forth on their own Hero's Journey.........

*Mellotron history just goes on and on. Mike Pinder must be acknowledged as a leading developer in early synthesized music, in fact he remained chums with the Beatles (recording just down the street from the Moodies) 'cause he could fix their mellotrons!!! (used on *Magical Mystery Tour* quite a bit.) The first modifications he made consisted of better mechanics (refined adjustments to pinch rollers and such.) Eventually he would replace the AC motors with more efficient DC motors; remember, Mike had to switch between power requirements in America and the U.K. which were vastly different in regards to Hertz and voltage. During the *Isle of Wight* video documentary, Mike said it was pretty touchy getting the mellotron to stay up to speed, because *housewives all over the island started cooking at the same time for evening tea, and down went the amperage across the grid.* And he replaced the old valve-tube situation with the modern upcoming transistors, thereby reducing breakage, and lightening the machine. This sort of thing always comes into interviews with Graeme and Mike, they are really neat reading; if you have a bend for electronics, I urge you to look up the references on these. Those who have poked about on the inside of a VCR will notice from diagrams that mellotron technology appears to be a forerunner to the VCR. I bet everyone was glad to see the American space program develop solid state miniaturization in response to NASA's requirements for lighter payloads. 20th Century electronics exploded financially and miniaturized physically so much from 1960 to 2000, it's indescribable.

** Pirates broadcasting off the coast of England are something we Americans don't remember. If you're a fan of old '60s T.V. series, there is a *Secret Agent (Danger Man)* episode wherein John Drake is doing some spy thing on the ships off the shore. Those are the pirate radio stations, and apparently there were a lot of them. England only allowed the BBC to broadcast legally, or did then anyway. They even took the time in that episode to show the reel-to-reel tapes and electronics on the ships ..... one of the DJs was a bad guy I think. Hopefully that clears up a bit of history. Anorak heaven!

***It's been a real jigsaw puzzle figuring out what "Deramic Sound" was, but Varnals DID say in one interview that they were using Dolby sound. Later in a *Sound Board* interview (3-14-2014), Justin confirmed this, saying that Dolby's wife was chatting with him and told him this. *Days of Future Passed* was apparently the first album recorded in Dolby, the Dolby labs were in London. (Curious note, the first movie sound track ((by Wendy

Carlos, who did *Switched on Bach)*) in Dolby was *A Clockwork Orange*.) A quick turn through the Dolby Wiki is quite enlightening, and after reading it, Sir Edward Lewis moved up a good deal in my estimation. They were taking a huge risk with a new rock band and new tech BOTH, and didn't it turn out well??? Obviously, Sir Edward also thought the Moodies could keep their mouths shut, so he let them near the gear!!! Dolby tech had engineering parallels in top secret autopilots and inertial navigation systems, which were being developed and refined by the military in this same time period. The Sixties were like that technologically, with improved electrical engineering, which just kept getting better and better. It's all about the feed-back loops!!! In *Where Have All the Pop Stars Gone?* Mike Pinder claimed they were "locked down" when they recorded their songs for DOFP (all night.) So yes, the Deramic Sound technology was really really cutting edge, and closely guarded, though the Moodies probably weren't aware of it at the time.

VII) Heroes' Journey: March 1968-July 1969

Like adventurers on a quest, the Moody Blues set forth to conquer the music world. Along the way they were to find fellow travelers who were "seekers" just like they were.

By their own report, the Moodies were "spoiled" by Decca founder and chairman, Sir Edward Lewis. One of the first things they had asked for (semi in jest) when *Days of Future Passed* started making money, was for "every instrument ever made" to play. Decca obliged, and the Moodies got books to learn how to play them if they couldn't figure it out! So that's how they recorded their next album in 1968, *In Search of the Lost Chord*. "Legend of a Mind" was the last song to be recorded in the fall of 1967 (the *Days of Future Passed* sessions). It was a good beginning to the next album.

They continued to drive DJs bonkers, as the tracks all blended smoothly together, making the album a complete whole, rather than a jumble of unrelated songs. Some of the notes from the development of this album are wonderful: they scooped up and used songs they just had going, like "The Actor," which really doesn't tie into a concept, but is wonderful anyway. Overall for a theme, they thought of themselves as on a journey somewhere, like Dr. Livingston; "We're all looking for someone." Forecasting their own future, they were to find their Doctor in the wild jungles of Laguna Beach, California, but that's still in the future.

Justin tells a very good story about writing "The Actor" in his on-line journal, January 2006. He said he was still living in Bayswater, opposite Kensington Gardens. For those who don't know their British literature, Kensington Gardens is the birthplace of Peter Pan. It's a wonderful journal entry, go look up Justin's website and read it: *www.justinhayward.com*.

They must have had fun recording this time, not having to be sneaky about it like before.

Listen carefully to the "door" opening in the "House of Four Doors" sequences, it's the bow of a fiddle being dragged raggedly over some bass strings. Justin picked up a sitar, and Mike a tambora, they played both on the new album. Justin would later say in *Record Collector* (1996) "It was all fingers-widdly diddly stuff, it was great!" I found references that say they moved a old pipe organ from St. John's Chapel to their studios (*Guitar Player*, 1995).

In August 2007, Justin did an interview and explained some of the song writing process of the time. He and Ray always "had a little extra time" because they did their homework. They called Ray "Dr. One Take" because he hated doing things twice; he said re-do's were a good way to mess it up! They came in with songs prepared, while the others might still be thrashing with their songs in the studio. The big Decca One studio they recorded in had great ambiance; it also had a lot of cubby holes and practice rooms to hide in. Lest they disturb their testy band-mates, Ray and Justin found the perfect hide-out, a broom closet in the back of Studio One which held mops and an old glockenspiel, but (like Justin's bathroom) had a great resonance; better yet was sound proof. It had two doors to it, one leading to a vestibule outside, and the other door to the recording studio itself.

He and Ray would hole up there, and doodle with "just a flute and a guitar." That is where Justin claims "Visions of Paradise" was written. Another song "The Dreamer" sounds like something you'd write in a closet, which may be why they left it off the album *Threshold of a Dream*. VERY weird song, written in 2/2 time. Those who were around at the time will remember popular Gothic novelist H.P. Lovecraft, and I think "The Dreamer" is one of his short stories. Sitting in a dark closet, playing flutes, reading sci-fi and doing funny cigarettes would probably make you think Cthulhu was crawling through the walls.

A note here for the guitar people: once their first album started making money, Justin rented a Gibson 335 for the recording of *In Search of the Lost Chord*; but after the rental, he had to return it to the owner. After heckling them, Justin was finally able to buy it from the music store outright. If you ever get the chance, pick up a Gibson 335 in a music store; be prepared, you will find the shop owners watch you like the proverbial hawk! The 335 they let me finger in a Seattle music store cost $3,500.00. They may look elegant but are BIG and HEAVY (I'm used to a Martin acoustic); the metal is very sturdy pot metal, on the keys and tailpiece. The neck is very long. B.B. King and Stephen Stills (and of course, Michael J. Fox in *Back to the Future*) are the only other rockers I have seen play these guitars. Justin is over six feet tall, and the only person I have seen make it look like a small guitar. Justin describes his 335 as "a 1963 Gibson 335 with a stock Bigsby vibrato bar." He DOES use the vibrato bar in concert, but his hands are so big, you don't notice it.

Recording was apparently informal and loose under the guidance of Tony Clarke; according to Tony, they used to gather for breakfast around a drum riser for their brainstorming sessions.

As always, the business side of a band is something different. The media started getting interested (again) in the Moody Blues by March of 1968. It's likely someone in the band was racing pigeons at this time, as it's mentioned in one of the articles (*Beat Instrumental*, March 1968; the Moody Blues used a pigeon to send an invitation!) One thing is clear in these articles, the pop gurus will not support "Nights in White Satin" as a single, because it's too long and too slow for the jerky dance rhythms of English youth. *It works great for modern dance though, which I did in 1969 myself.*

Some real stuff, like the Moodies loving *Pilgrim's Progress*, comes out in these interviews. Some bogus stuff comes out too, like "playing a fall concert [1968] with an orchestra at the Hollywood Bowl."

There could have been real plans, only they couldn't dig up the money; the Moodies' Red Rocks show in September 1992 was their first live performance with an orchestra. Mention of "movie contracts for film scores" is also to be found in 1968 articles, though this may be a bit of smoke being blown by young men intent on their careers. And it could have been real ideas Bill Graham was considering too; they did indeed play the Fillmore gigs in 1968. AND it turns out that Graeme and Justin drank boiler makers at this time in their lives; they met the reporter in a bar!

They didn't let fame go to their heads. But once their albums started selling, they made a concession to comfort, and installed airplane seats in their transit van they drove around England. As John said, it was more comfortable than sleeping on the gear! As they got closer to their night's gig, they warmed up their voices in the travel van by singing bawdy songs.

I've had people tell me they saw the Moodies play in 1967 at the Fillmore, but the "second incarnation" Moody Blues weren't invited to the States until 1968. *Days of Future Passed* wasn't released in America until March 1968. In 2007, Justin claimed in an interview, that they came over to play the Fillmore in February, 1968, at the invitation of Bill Graham, see *Blue Timeline* for 1968.

Those times are hard to sort out by even those of us with good memories, or those of us who were old enough to be allowed to go to such places. Things started happening so fast for the Moodies, they can't even remember all the details themselves. It seems obvious from articles in 1968, that they played shows in the U.K. January and February, parallel to the U.K. release of *Days of Future Passed*. It makes sense that they might follow Walt Maguire to America and promote their first album release in early 1968. From 1966 and into early 1968, the band loosely based themselves in Paris, France where they frequently played the Olympia Theatre (and being young men, probably partied quite a bit.)

As they got a fairly reliable management in late 1967, they picked up more gigs in the U.K. at colleges and on the BBC, then moved gradually back to their home country (and got their bills straightened out!)

One look at their timeline will make this all clear, it's difficult to figure out EXACTLY where they were, but they did the continent as much as they did the U.K. in those really early years. France had a VERY lively anarchist movement at the time, with which the Moodies blended nicely, parallel to the American beat/hippy movement. The "leader" of the French underground, Leo Ferre, even put the Moodies into one of his lovely poems, "C'est Extra," easily found on *youtube*.

Graeme recalled one show they did in France in a park outside Paris; there were 150,000 in the crowd, and they were the only band playing! He said from his vantage up on the drum podium, he could see the crowd moving like a wave, and the stage got rushed about three or four songs into the show. People were hurt; the promoters had to stop it finally, fearing for the safety of the band and crowd alike. (Graeme on Minneapolis radio 1-27-11)

We find them in Prague in August 1968 during a Soviet invasion.* They played the Queen Elizabeth Hall June 29, 1968; they also played the Hippodrome (Brum) around this time. *In Search of the Lost Chord* was released in August, 1968, so sometime between February and August was spent in the studio. They were still in the U.K. in late Aug-Sept. Tony Clarke says they were still playing real gigs in U.K. nightclubs, as he can remember mixing the music they had just recorded, while the band packed up the van and headed out for some remote destination. Tony would stay home while they toured the States, working his wizardry on the music they had recorded during their time in England.

Days of Future Passed was released Stateside, in the second Summer of Love (1968) The Moodies were invited by Bill Graham to come play in October 1968, if not earlier (see *Blue Timeline*, 1968) at the Fillmore East and the Fillmore West. No surprise, the Fillmore in San Francisco was and is still on Fillmore Street. These were huge warehouses that Bill Graham bought and more or less repaired (fixed the leaking roofs.) Inside, a thick coat of black paint covered everything, and they were hung with every sort of wild lighting you can imagine; think of deep purple lights in the chandeliers, and rainbow strobes on the ceiling.

Then Graham invited or hired young bands to play in these psychedelic pits. He charged a cover charge, the bands got a percentage of the house take, and young people came to dance, drink, smoke and whatever else they could get away with, all night. So many classical rock n' roll bands played the Fillmore that it would be redundant to repeat them all, and it's been done elsewhere, in other books. If you like this period of time, and you haven't read it yet, find a copy of *The Electric Kool-Aid Acid Test*; all will be explained.

Justin was to say later that he was shocked to see people casually sucking joints in the audience at these venues, and recalled thinking, "My God, is someone actually smoking pot in here?" they would have been arrested had they done this openly in the Bag o' Nails in 1967.

When I went to see It's a Beautiful Day at the (restored) Fillmore Ballroom in 1997 (San Francisco), the same thing happened. People casually lit up all around me and settled in to enjoy the show. Recovering from my shock, I checked to see where the exits were in case we were busted, then forgot about it and enjoyed the show. Some old fart came up with a smoldering joint, waved it in my face and asked if I'd like to smoke weed with one of the "original hippies." I said "No, thank you," as I had a three-hour drive home that night. But it did smell rather yummy. It's nice to know some things never change.

What the Moody Blues didn't know during their first tour (and this is common to many people who have never been here) is that America is a very, very big place.

They had no idea that the two gigs they had committed to were ten weeks apart; and even further apart in mileage, New York to San Francisco. As they tell it, they arrived and played the Fillmore East. The mellotron continually gave them headaches; it was touchy, cantankerous, prone to tummy aches when damp, and spit tapes at a moment's notice. The gear was still damp from being in the belly of the plane, the mellotron burped out all of its tapes onto the stage, "like spaghetti" as John puts it.

The curtains closed and Mike (witnesses claim that Mike would roundly curse the mellotron on stage when it acted up) had to fix it with a coat hanger and a screwdriver. Everyone else apparently fired up, and watched Looney Tunes all night. John made this explanation in *Q Magazine*, April 1990: "We've only been fashionable once-for about two minutes. It was the first time we played the Fillmore East. The mellotron blew up, we had to play second fiddle to Roadrunner cartoons, and the review said 'The Moody Blues looked as though they were modeling for Carnaby Street'. That was the end of our fashionable period."

A small aside here: Carnaby Street clothing apparently arose from the wild things the rock bands in England were wearing in an attempt to gain the spotlight. Remember Denny and the Diplomats dying their hair orange? Clothing started going the same way, Mods showed up on stage wearing lime-green striped pants with orange polka dot shirts. Real men wore pink!

I think another thing that contributed to the wild colors of the time, discounting the effect of marijuana on your optical circuits, was the onset of color television. Can you imagine going from black-and-white to color TV? WOW was that a whole new world to bring into your living room! As Ed Sullivan would say about some of the more exotic hippy bands, "He was made for your color TV!"**

According to Tony Clarke (chat), a friend of Walt Maguire's, one Les Paul was backstage at the Fillmore. Seeing their plight, he told the boys to bring their mellotron to his house in New England and use his tools to fix it. Thus they happened to find the hospitality of a true guitar legend, the maker of the Gibson guitar.

They stayed all night in his home full of every Les Paul/Gibson ever issued, Paul had a catacomb cellar, where he kept his stringed hoard. He had a "guy named Igor" who lived down there, doing nothing but keeping the guitars all eternally in tune. The Moodies must have thought they had died and gone to heaven.

After a more successful show the second night at the Fillmore, they hired a U-Haul, and with a good deal of courage (and being too young to be scared), took off cross-country to look for America. After they got the hang of staying on the right side of the road (the film evidence shows they put their car engineer, John, behind the wheel), they started to pick up gigs here and there.

Now there is certainly room for a "10 week tour" of the U.S. in the Spring of '68, if you look at the Moody Blues tour schedule for that year (see *Blue Timeline*.) The way the Moodies told it, they only had two scheduled Fillmore shows on opposite coasts, and picked up the rest on their own; in fact Justin said they had to earn money so they could come back home! Tony Clarke also said in chat, that he didn't remember any planned dates for that first tour.

With this in mind, the "first American tour" as per *Higher and Higher* #24 p.19; is evidenced by a Deram tour ad dated Oct 26,1968. Pre-planned by Decca, the venues were Minneapolis, NY City (Fillmore East?), Boston, Baltimore, Philadelphia, Washington DC, Chicago, San Francisco (Fillmore West, Nov 21-24?), San Diego, Los Angeles, Portland, Seattle, Spokane.

The venues aren't listed in the ad; Justin mentioned an "ice hockey rink where boards were laid down" which matches the Key Arena (Seattle), or could refer to the Wintergarden. During the stop at Chess studios in Chicago, they recorded commercials for Coca-Cola: "Sweet Things" and "Use Your Imagination". They eventually landed in San Francisco, at the height of the Flower Power "Summer of Love."

Outside Looking In: California Dreamin-- the Cheetah is a very fond memory. I saw quite a few B and C list bands at the Cheetah. I remember seeing Buffalo Springfield, the Grass Roots, the Dave Clark Five, the Righteous Brothers (several times) and who knows who else, at the Cheetah.-- from a friend in Southern California

It was about this time (spring 1968) that my brother, home from the Navy for the weekend, burst into my room, with a "Hey

Christie, how much money do you have?" Turns out he was hustling me for money to buy a new album he had just heard on the radio, Days of Future Passed. This was going out over the Los Angeles Basin airwaves, and it sounded good; the Moody Blues were impressing DJs everywhere, it seems. Thinking back on it, the Moodies doing hippy gigs in the L.A. basin probably helped the promotion too. So I came up with half the cost (my brother was always stripped for cash) and at age thirteen, it became my first album. I got to keep it while my brother was off "defending Viet Nam." I guess there are families out there who don't listen to classical music, but we always had it around when I was a kid. "Days" was (and is) a wonderful album; even when played on the poor quality stereos my middle class family had, my parents would frequently poke their heads in my bedroom, and comment favorably on the music. That was saying something for the times, because all "right thinking" parents in those days hated rock n' roll!

The Moodies occasionally tell hilarious stories about the early years. Like the girl in the fur coat. Justin claims he went to the hotel door once after a show, hearing a knock. There stood a young woman, wearing nothing (and it was hot weather) but a fur coat, which she swept open in a lavish gesture. "Ya wanna bawll?" she said coyly to Justin.

About this time Justin's room-mate John came out of the bathroom, blow drying his hair, saying "Whaaaa????" Justin regained his composure, said "No thank you" to the furry young female, and continued politely, "....perhaps you could try the drummer, he's a few doors over?" gesturing down the hall. Graeme never finished the story, so we leave the next chapter up to the imagination of the reader.

During their first American tour, whilst traveling across the Great State of Texas, they happened to pull their van over to a diner for food, and bumped into a group of young locals dressed in Western garb, plaid shirts, Levis, cowboy hats, burred hair, etc. The Moodies were dressed in Carnaby Street garb, with long hair! Graeme said, "We just laughed at each other," they had such different looks. "I think they figured we were harmless." (*VC Star*, 5-13-11)

So many of the West Coast venues the '60s bands used to play either burned down due to flaky wiring or have been torn down by people who hate rats. This is part of the problem with nailing down dates, as the records all burned up too. Some of these places were the Crystal Ballroom (Portland OR, restored and owned now by McMenamin's Pubs); and the Emporium Club in Portland too, the Blue Unicorn (Berkeley? the Bay Area at least), Shriner's Hall in Southern California, the Troubadour (West Hollywood, yes, a hippy nightclub, and it's still there), and the Psychedelic Grocery Store in Hollywood. I ran into a hippy, Tom Kelly, who helped put together the love-ins in Los Angeles. He claimed the Psychedelic Grocery Stores were in Boston, and in Hollywood on a corner of Las Palmas.

Also of note, the Cheetah in Venice, CA, which I know for a fact burned down, but was once the Venice Ballroom. My big brothers used to (enthusiastically) hang out there. It was a REAL animal pit by their accounts, and they claim the Moodies played there too. I don't think the Moodies ever played the Whiskey on Sunset during the '60s, though I could be wrong. Memory fades.

According to Justin, the Moodies hooked up with Jefferson Airplane on the West Coast, and shared their chataqua truck. This had one side that came down, and there they would be, playing inside the truck, like a moving pageant wagon! It even had its own generator. People came and drew graffiti on it, as folk art. In interviews many years later, Justin made some funny allusions to "....the *real* action in the back of the trailer" so *young, creative and musicians*... all the gossip you heard really was true.

Justin has said they played with bands like It's a Beautiful Day, Chicago Transit Authority, and Poco (who came from Buffalo Springfield) in the early years (radio interview, April 19, 1996.) Justin also bought one of his favorite guitars at this time, off some "traveling gypsies" he met in California, for $500. It's a 1955 Martin D-28, and he says he's written many of his best songs on that particular guitar. For the guitar fanatics amongst us, he uses Guild 350 strings on it. It's the classical sound of "Nothing Changes" on the *Strange Times* album. It also appears identical to the Martin that Elvis owned.

According to Justin, they played before 20,000 along with The Airplane in Elysian Park in Los Angeles, but it must be only one of many California gigs during this time. The Elysian Park love-ins became a bit notorious in the late '60s; a vigorous search of the Internet will turn up some pretty raunchy hits, *bon appetite*; they tended to be spring break "Easter vacation" bacchanals, with the emphasis on "fertility rites." No wonder my parents kept me locked up during those years!

The Elysian Park gig in November 1969 (a beautiful day and a wonderful show, according to witnesses), was done to benefit children, and frankly might have been too cold for any serious love-in action, as people keep their clothing on, in late November in California. Justin said in a HOF interview, 21 June 2002, that this is where Dr. Tim Leary first met them, and invited them to his ranch.

Elysian Park rock n' roll love-ins became a regular occurrence over spring break in the Los Angeles area, from 1967 onward, and all young people from the area who could do it, did it. California bands like the Doors played this venue regularly. John Lodge undoubtedly was reflecting the love-ins with his song on *Natural Avenue:*

Children of rock n' roll, Raised on rock n' roll. We played Elysian Park, Until the night was dark

Amusingly enough, Ray had written about "the astral plane" in "Legend of a Mind," which was supposed to be a gaily painted biplane, barnstorming about the Bay with the Good Doctor at the stick. But Leary had a home in Southern California too. So, since they had written him such a nice song, the Moody Blues were invited to "worship at the feet of the guru" (and Harvard professor of psychology) Dr. Tim Leary. Justin, Ray and Mike stayed a few days at Leary's ranch off Laguna Canyon Road, not far from the best beach and boardwalk in the area. (*I know, I haunted Laguna during those years, too! Great tide pools!*)

During a radio interview on KROC New York (November 13, 1995) Justin would speak favorably of Dr. Leary, calling him a "larger than life gentleman" and John claimed Leary played tambourine on stage with them for a few shows.

I know some Moody Blues fans will take offense to the inclusion of drugs in this biography. It is a fact, that in many later interviews, various band members can be quoted as saying "Recording on LSD was absolute rubbish." So not for music; but socially, I think only by being honest can I be fair to the memory of Dr. Leary, who was an integral part of the times, and to the thought in the Core Seven albums. Dr. Leary was a psychological researcher whom many respect as a colleague, and as a leading voice in changing American culture of the time.

The song "Legend of a Mind" was to become a huge hit with the drug society in America, and forever branded the Moodies as "stoners."

According to the Moodies, the song refers to *The Book of the Dead.* Said book holds various spells about the Afterlife, spells which are supposed to hide your "naughty deeds in life" when you present your heart to Osiris for judgment! As well, it refers to academic research which was being done with the effects of LSD; one passage from a researcher on acid that I remember (from reading this long, long ago) was "I thought I was dead.....I was outside, looking in at life."

Ray says he meant the song "Legend of a Mind" as "…ribbing the piss outta [Leary]." It was a tongue-in-cheek look at the entire "guru" thing. Apparently Leary got the joke, and was not adverse to letting the guys crash at his place. Ray was also, by his own admission "hung over" and planting daffodils when he wrote Leary's theme song. It was not all insanity: there were actually some intelligent, serious researchers in the '60s, trying to figure out what the effects of LSD meant for mankind. They just got a little side-tracked.

All the California bands knew each other, and obviously offered bunk space to one another. Leary's home became a stopping spot for all manner of troubadours and hippies. I think it was Sean Phillips (Mama's and Papa's) who said he woke up one night and found the Moody Blues asleep all over his chairs and couches in the front room.

According to Justin, they didn't have LSD pressed upon them when they stayed with Leary, and the Moodies didn't try it until later. But Justin also said he was "tabbed" at a party for his first experience, which is not funny. For those too young to know the slang, being "tabbed" is when some fool drops a blotter square of LSD into your drink......*melts in your brain, not in your hand, tee hee.*

The Moodies did not have unique experiences.... EVERY one in California was on the edges of this stuff in the late '60s and early '70s. It was everywhere.

In another interview (found on *youtube.com*), Justin claims that he, Ray, Mike and Graeme all dropped acid (LSD) together the first time they did it, sometime in early 1967 or late 1966. They were friends with the Beatles, the Stonies, and went to the Maharishi for enlightenment. Take your pick as to where they found acid first. All stories are direct quotes from Justin interviews, also from Graeme interviews.

Mike Pinder claimed (*Goldmine*) to have been dabbling in LSD in 1966, probably due to the Beatles connection. The Moodies certainly made the connection with the Huxley book and *The Doors of Perception* prior to touring America, as per their lyrics "House of Four Doors." I find it remarkably bold and brave of Justin to discuss their drug experiences in interviews, with such banality. (That's Justin for you.)

Certainly, in the minds of most people here in the 21st Century, psychoactive drugs should not be considered criminal when used in moderation, "moderation" being the key concept. Dr. Leary testified (unsuccessfully) before Congress in 1963, urging that "all psychoactive drugs and plants be kept out of the criminal justice system." There was limited DEA back then, and *cannabis* was certainly nothing new in American border states. Possibly Leary's lack of success with Congressional hearings is what turned him into such a rebel. You can't say he didn't try to do it right.

  The Orange County fuzz (county sheriff) raided Dr. Leary's ranch more than a few times, eventually getting him for "contributing to the delinquency of a minor." (I think someone got run over by a car, the story was all over the Orange County newspapers.) Dr. Leary had returned to Harvard and was trying to clean up his act when *The Electric Kool Aid Acid Test* was written; but he apparently "backslid" by the time Mike Pinder wrote "When You're a Free Man" in 1972. Leary's outlaw existence continued until *Rolling Stone* picked up his saga in the mid '70s.***

  Being stoned all the time is fun, but has serious side effects too. It would make a good movie scene: I've always had this fantasy about the Moody Blues, along with all the other hippies, hanging out on a nice Southern California day at Leary's place, "high on a mountainside" overlooking Laguna Beach, lounging in lawn chairs or skinny dipping.... When all the sudden the whistles start blowing.....and through the weeds and sagebrush go all sorts of long hairs, wildly leaping and running ("O shit we're gonna be deported!" wails Ray) ....like something out of the Fabulous Furry Freak Brothers. I mean, it was really like that sometimes; Elysian Park was for sure raided by the police during one of the love-ins. The only thing you can do about memories like that, is look back and laugh.

  This story is real, and I think, from 1966, or early '67 (?). My eyewitness was dealing with her teenage son (a minor) being arraigned the same day (he had been caught with ONE joint in his van, along with his cousin.) She said they were standing in the Orange County Courthouse in Santa Ana, when flashbulbs went off, crowds gathered, and through the midst of all this came a horrible clanking and stomping. Dr. Leary and his cohorts were brought through, chanting, in leg chains. They were stomping in unison, making the chains rattle in time. My eyewitness was not kind in her description of the "hippie wenches" surrounding the Good Doctor; to paraphrase, they looked like something out of an R. Crumb cartoon (see the cover of Cheap Thrills); and were "grubby as hell with dirty old hair hanging down."

The Doctor didn't look too tidy either apparently, and the citizenry of Orange County drew back in alarm when they saw him. "He looked like something from Mars, from another planet" my witness claimed. "He reared back, grinned lopsidedly, and shot everyone the Peace Sign. He had long stringy hair, and looked like he hadn't had a bath in about a week."

Said eye-witness actually wound up in the same courtroom with Leary and Friends, before the same judge, with her son and his dope charge. The hippies got a little noisy a few times (leg irons and all) and when the judge yelled at them, "Hey you, quiet down over there" they more or less respectfully complied, mumbling.

The event apparently had a very lasting impression on my witness's son, who to the best of my knowledge (he's a close associate of mine) never touched weed again. Neither did his cousin.

In the '60s, the Moodies played with Ravi Shankar, John McLaughlin, and the Indojazz Fusions, which I think were bigger in the U.K. than they ever were in America. According to *The Hindu* on line (Nov 8, 2017) Mumbai singer Nandu Bhende did a cover of "Nights in White Satin" in his 70's bands Velvette Fogg and Atomic Forest. India unto this day still has a dedicated Moodies following.

Sometime during the recording of their second album *In Search of the Lost Chord*, in that eternal search for enlightenment; the Moodies attended seminars by the Maharishi Yoganda, who was getting attention from the Beatles crowd. John Lodge didn't get into it, being Christian sort of guy, and perfectly secure in his own beliefs, but the other four Moodies gave it a try. A LOT of rock stars around the world poured money into the Maharishi's coffers. I don't see it as any different from other counselors and "self-help" seminars that are offered every day in every city; they just dressed a little bit funny.

Justin claims he and Graeme once shared their personal mantras with one another, something you were never supposed to do, as your personal mantra is your "power" phrase for making magic in the world. Anyway, it turned out that Graeme's phrase was exactly the same as

Justin's, with a slight shift due to accents. Justin finished the interview saying, "I almost choked!"

Some people were and are excited by the Maharishi and his philosophies. I always thought he looked like he needed a bath. Whatever turns you on, I guess. Knowing the Moodies, they were pretty thrilled by the Kundalini stuff, so I'll leave it at that. We all find magic in our own ways. Apparently, studying chakras can be beneficial to one's singing abilities, it helps with good breathing.

Justin said in an interview that he dropped out of the whole thing about the time the Maharishi wanted him to donate a week's worth of wages to the cause.****

Rolling Stone Magazine managed to wear out the subject of Donovan over the course of its first three issues and began to cast about looking for new Flower Power bands to review. Justin hung out a bit with Donovan during the late '60s, I assume during the Maharishi period; he says he learned a lot about finger picking from Donovan, and what type of strings to use. *Rolling Stone* finally found the Moody Blues Dec 7, 1968 and did a pretentious little review of *Days of Future Passed*, and the new album, *In Search of the Lost Chord*. It's plain from the *Rolling Stone* review, the writer knows little about melody, but at least the Moody Blues got mentioned.

The "Lost Chord" album reached #8 in the U.K. charts, August 1968. The title of their second album was cribbed (by Mike Pinder) from Jimmy Durante, who in turn, cribbed it from a church hymn "The Lost Chord" by Arthur Sullivan, of "Gilbert and Sullivan." Arthur Sullivan was ALSO from Swindon, see Appendix C.

The chances of anything coming from Mars... The Moody Blues have always had a "spacey" following of fans who did more than their share of hallucinogens and are firmly convinced that the Moodies are prophets from another time and space; these are the people who approach the band "seeking enlightenment." Some of this comes from the times; everyone was a "seeker" in the '60s. Graeme would always say, "We just asked the questions, and everyone thought we had the answers, when we were just as much in the dark as everyone else!" But just the same, as a psychologist (or a Zen master) might say about Moody lyrics, *just because you wrote it doesn't mean you know everything about it!*

Many ideas from Justin's early poetry seem to come from the most famous fantasy book of the '60s (on both sides of the Water) *Lord of the Rings*.

The trees are drawing me near, I've got to find out why (Legolas and Gimli on the edges of the Fangorn forest) or *Just what is happening to me, I lie awake with the sound of the Sea calling to me.....*(Legolas hearing the gulls on the shore for the first time, during the War of the Ring). And down the road a little, did Justin write "The Voice" from reading C.S. Lewis's *Perelandra*???

Here's a direct quote of Justin's, from the *Question of Balance* songbook;: "Tuesday Afternoon: on a beautiful day, trees like Tolkien's Ents who take hours just saying hello." So Justin and the other Moodies were influenced in their writing by what the entire generation was reading and sharing as a collective fantasy.*****

I skipped over Justin talking about the writing of "Tuesday Afternoon" didn't I? According to the composer, he had in mind the writing of the new show they had decided to do, about "the day of one guy." He can be paraphrased as saying, he rolled a big fat joint, and went out under a tree on a BEAUTIFUL blue day with fluffy clouds, in the park in his home town (Lydiard Park, Swindon), and with his guitar, enjoyed the day, and wrote the song. He also claims he had a dog named Tuesday, and of course, dogs love trees. In fact, Justin always said that his dog went bonkers when the song was played, because "Toooos-day!" was how they called her. Just listen to the music someday, you can't help but hear the Ents walking at the end of the song, perhaps lifting their roots a bit quicker to avoid the sniffing of Tuesday the dog!

If Justin wrote "Tuesday Afternoon" in a park in Swindon near his parents' home, perhaps we can also assume it was written early 1967, when they came back to England from France. Quirky side note: believe me, sorting out Tuesday the dog is important to the fans! Ray had Tuesday's littermate; according to Storyteller's, Justin and Ray went together to get his dog, and Justin took a littermate on a semi-whim. Now THAT is friendship!

And since Ray's dog was reported as a Chihuahua in one fanzine (Richard Green, "Doing a Moody"), does that mean Tuesday was a Chihuahua too? Apparently not. Justin claimed Tuesday (the girl pup he took home) was a Yorkie (Cruise 2014 Storyteller's). Those who are fanatical about dogs and Moodies, can reach their own conclusions. Long-hair Chihuahuas aren't all that dissimilar from Yorkies. Justin also claimed he named his dog after Tuesday Weld, a popular performer of the time.

The Moodies frequently mention another popular author of the '60s, Arthur C. Clarke; along with producer Stanley Kubrick, he co-wrote *2001: A Space Odyssey*. The album *To Our Children's Children's Children* was influenced heavily by the first manned landing on the moon that same year. What you don't remember unless you were there, is that everyone was reading everything by Arthur C. Clarke they could get their hands on. Two Clarke books, *The City and The Stars/Against the Fall of Night* are actually the same book, one the rewritten version. Anyway, these books have a character in them, a rather charming space critter by the name of Vanamonde, who is so like the song "Watching and Waiting" it must be the inspiration of the song. "Watching and Waiting" is a tribute to the ultimate spirit of Mankind, and a "generation lost in space." It sometimes seemed we all might be lost sooner than we expected, either in reality, or in the inner space of our own minds. "Watching and Waiting" is also the closing line to Clarke's short story "The Sentinel" from whence came the story line of *2001: A Space Odyssey*.

Meanwhile--On line people will sometimes come out with interesting tidbits. Most from this time period say that Mike and Ray tended to be the "leaders" when it came to talking to the audience. Later, Mike would say that the others were usually tuning their gear (guitars often need a tuning touch up or amp adjustments after an active song) and since the mellotron needed no reset, he often introduced the upcoming song. Mike sang a lot too, in the early days.

Other early witnesses say that Mike was one of the primary "set up" guys, out before the show making sure the wiring all matched up. In the early days, like up until 1969, they didn't have roadies to help set up, and Mike did a lot of pre-show tech.

During later "Storyteller" shows, many details came out involving technology of live shows (a span of forty-five years); Justin, John and Graeme all seem very pleased that technology finally caught up to their music. In the early days, the mellotron especially would be variable in volume as they cranked it through amplifiers, due to electrical current differences in different countries (voltage/frequency.) Mike was (and is) a master electrician, he must have had all sorts of ways to rectify the house power. I bet they burned up some equipment too, *ouch*!

Another thing that bugged them was whether an acoustic instrument could be played on stage with the same veracity of tone, and this too was solved over the course of forty-five years of playing live. Justin has mentioned going from Vox amplifiers in the beginning, to Bose equipment in the later years. (Bose is very fine equipment indeed!) Justin's early sound involved a Marshall fuzz box going through a Vox amplifier, but that didn't always work too well on stage, it was more of a studio sound.

In 1970, John says (*Wild West Magazine*, 2000) Jay Silverheels presented the band with the platinum record of the album *On the Threshold of a Dream*. John and Ray of course are well known for their love of Cowboy and Indian stories. When Decca asked them who they wanted to present the Gold Record to them, they asked for "Tonto" from the *Lone Ranger* series. Apparently boomer English kids were raised with *The Lone Ranger* on the telly, much as American kids were. Jay Silverheels was happy to help out, and Justin proudly displays his photo of the moment in his music room; Ray has a similar photo on his website.

John made an interesting revelation in an article he wrote about Jay Silverheels, that Jay actually wrote poetry himself, and it was pretty good stuff. The Moodies meant to write some music to go with it, but somehow never got around to it.

Like a snowball it kept on rolling. The Moody Blues toured with Cream on their farewell tour and opened for Canned Heat too. (Ginger Baker, drummer for Cream, would later be involved with Graeme's solo albums.) *To Our Children's Children's Children* was one of the first western rock n' roll albums to go to Red China, and was taken there by our table tennis champion, Trevor Taylor. No, the Moodies didn't tour Red China as mentioned in *Higher and Higher* #3, though I think the trip was in the works, it was cancelled due to red tape. But they got their albums played behind the Bamboo Curtain, one of the first western bands to do so!

On the negative side, Justin talks about unscrupulous sheriffs in small towns walking on stage, and taking their money-box for "fees." Ray talks about fans handing them bags of weed or throwing it on stage, and him having to stand for hours, flushing the boo down the loo. I'm sure the band liked weed like the rest of us, but in those days, it was a good way to get deported if you were not a U.S. citizen, and were caught holding. Remember, these were the times when talented genius poet, Jim Morrison, was in jail in Dade County, Florida, on lewdness charges, just for waving his shirt tails on stage. Young people were rioting in the streets, and the cops were SCARED. Times were so nasty, that a nark could toss a bag of weed on stage, then have the cops tapping on your dressing room door after the show.

Since the Moodies were friends with the "notorious criminal" Timothy Leary, the fuzz were itching to bust the Moodies too, we must assume! In fact, the Moodies tell one story about a club owner who hosed them out of four days' wages by calling the cops on them. What a creep!

Luckily no one was holding when the fuzz showed up, or they swallowed quickly. As I've said before, the Moody Blues are very smart men. They never got caught!

Only dead fish go with the flow -- Sarah Palin

Make yourselves sheep & the wolves will eat you -- Benjamin Franklin

Who's running this show, anyway?--I have to add some bits about management here. Tony Clarke only handled the recording end; cash flow from touring was another matter. Sometime in the fall of 1967, in "a club up north" they met a guy named Derek McCormick. He became their bankroller and manager (money handler) about the time they recorded *Days of Future Passed* and were turning into rapidly rising stars.

According to Mike Pinder, Derek came backstage after a gig at the Cavendish Club in Newcastle. Smitten by the music, McCormick offered his services as money manager and "angel," professing to have never been anything but a Sinatra fan up to that point. A businessman in the field of ducts and venting, McCormick knew the art of accounting. To pump up their promotion a bit, in interviews they referred to Derek as "a millionaire." He was not. He found the money to keep the road show rolling in late 1967. Perhaps the "grave-digger" look the band was sporting, with dark-eyed glares and solemn songs, made people think they were starving to death. Maybe they were. They probably snapped at the deal like hungry fish.

Leaving their other managers in a cloud of dust, McCormick financially herded the band through the year of 1968 and on into 1969 as they began to record their third album; with occasional help from Colin Berlin, who handled bookings. Derek was along for their summer of '68 European tour and did Monte Carlo with them.

The promo package for *In Search of the Lost Chord* very plainly shows McCormick as management, and Berlin as their agent. The money began to come in from album sales and touring. The group was friendly with their manager, and things seemed pleasant (good times were had) even unto Derek being the keeper of much photo documentation of the band's social life off stage.

It began to fall apart in the fall '68 tour to America, which McCormick was also along for. The tour was emotionally grueling for the band; it got off to a bad start too, they had to cancel one show at the beginning when the gear plane went back due to engine problems. Justin was chastised for ordering room service while flat on his back with the flu. One can't fault him for wanting to eat peacefully in his room, chicken soup we must presume. Justin does tend to stick out in a crowd, and probably had hoards of girls chasing him even then, making eating in public a stressful situation.

And the band was also lectured for making long distance phone calls to their sweethearts and wives back home (*Record Mirror*, 1972.) Marie Hayward said of this time she was eternally grateful to Lionel Bart when he let her use his phone to call Justin, in the remote wilds of America.

The fall tour wasn't pretty, Ray referred to California of the time as "crazy." He was so shell-shocked by the experience that he asked his girl Jill to marry him, "…before his brain melted." Being treated like small children didn't sit too well with the Moodies; remember what Tony Clarke said about them "devouring producers" back when they started *Days of Future Passed*? And from McCormick's perspective, he probably saw "prima donna" behavior.

The years 1967 thru 1969 were "the best of times, the worst of times" for rock n' roll. American culture was in the throes of a thinly veiled social revolution. In December 1968, a pretty well stoned, rising rock artist named Jim Morrison (allegedly) dropped his drawers on a poorly promoted, poorly constructed stage in Florida, promptly setting off a riot. Tim Leary became Public Enemy #1 to what we called "The Establishment" in those days. The

Establishment was anyone who thought long hair on men was just this side of Satanic.

I won't even mention events in Los Angeles, August 1969, but I lived there then, and mass hysteria is an understatement. The year of 1969 was referred to in the Doors' biography (*No One Here Gets Out Alive*) as "the Year of Paranoia." John Lennon and Morrison were being tracked by the FBI, and Lennon got held at the Canadian border, thus missing Woodstock. The good news is, while societal molds were being broken in the Land of the Free, management molds were also being broken, for the better.

Between their fall 1968 visit to America, and spring of 1969, the Moodies made contact with Jerry Weintraub and Tom Huelett (WEG), then handling Jimi Hendrix; WEG was eventually to handle Elvis, John Denver, Sinatra, and so many others. (If you didn't catch it, all the Moodies are fans of Hendrix.) The Moodies have good sense, both Graeme and John have at various times in interviews discussed how they were getting into the financial end of things. They wanted to be in charge of their own money, without the middle man. Weintraub and associates offered alternatives to the classical "band manager" scenario. The new approach gave control back to the artists.

The fall 1968 tour must have left lasting scars, because the Moodies went home, and stayed in the U.K. and in Europe until Halloween, 1969. They cancelled a couple of gigs in August 1969; there are several stories there. The band claims they flipped a coin that August and went to France for the Communist Rally/rock festival. A gig is a gig. They stayed close to home, watched the moon landing, and wrote songs for their new "space" album, *To Our Children's Children's Children*. And they made changes.

McCormick wasn't too thrilled when the Moodies told him his services were no longer needed in mid-1969. According to Adele (McCormick's daughter) Graeme was fairly good friends with Derek (and didn't get involved in the lawsuit, other than to back up his band.) Justin (ever the diplomatic Libra) was nice enough to apologize when things cooled off. But it got very, very ugly.

Mike and Ray were suspicious survivors of the first band incarnation (they still claim that Seltaeb ripped them off) and didn't want their new success to go the way of their earlier try. Secunda apparently didn't do a good job, not to mention the (sadly) over-dosed Epstein. They wanted management they could rely on. Though they advertised McCormick and his duct systems during their shows, they said he was "not right for them" and slid away after being associated for eighteen months.

McCormick sued them for breach of contract, and to get his investment back! He had taken out loans to bankroll the band and buy their equipment, not to mention their transportation; there is of course a financial end to the business, you have to pay the bills! On the band side, Justin said of those times, "There I was in front of huge audiences, and barely enough money to pay my own costs." The lawsuit dragged on for years, and eventually they settled out of court in 1973. And lawyers again earned enough to pay their country club fees.

It was the band's first brush with the inevitable legal situations. I say "inevitable" for a reason: where there is serious cash flow, there also are deep pockets thinkers, who think a lawsuit is the way to tap that cash flow. Or as Mike Pinder would put it, "All that energy attracts more energy, and some of it is negative."

Graeme was to say in later interviews, that since 1973, he couldn't think of a time when the band was NOT in litigation of some kind. Remember, in civil law, you can "sue anyone for anything," and the money that the Moody Blues began to make by 1969 was and still is very attractive to the "hungry," ever-armed with confused perceptions and/or nuisance suits. Or "for real" beefs.

You have to give McCormick credit for helping the band get going in the early years, just as Secunda and Epstein helped the first band incarnation and got them their early breaks. It's an ugly business, keeping your books straight in show business; and there are a lot of coke-snorting accountants out there (I've partied with them.)

But as with all things, the Moodies ARE fast learners, and saw moves they could make to better their chances of success. The move had been made. Weintraub and Huelett now were their "not" managers, handling the cash flow. Bill Graham promoted them in the early days Stateside, and I would presume Colin Berlin mostly handled bookings in Europe.

Pete Jackson was added along the way, as roadie and security manager 'cause he's a very big dude; then Jackson became their tour manager after the rough tour in 1968. In 1972 or so, they picked up Mike Keyes as tour manager (I think this is the same as a Stage Manager, for those who do regular theater.) Mike Keyes ran their road shows for a long time, even unto the '90s. I believe Keyes first hooked up with them as a roadie, he lives in England today. The act started to grow into a real serious stage show as the cash flow improved.

Tony Clarke was along for the first tour in the States, but for later ones, stayed home. After a few years of touring, Tony finally found the time to come to the States again with the Moodies. Driving between venues, they told Tony, "Watch this." Looking out the window, he saw they were being escorted by an armada of cars!!! They became very popular indeed! The band also left behind their families and steady girls.

Those people I have talked to, who remember the Moodies in the Bay Area during this time, describe them as "a little ragged" but also as "always putting on a very good light show." The Moody Blues have always called themselves "a working band" concentrating on their live performance. There is something to be said creatively for the live, raw sound and the unpredictability of working in front of a real audience. Songs change, often for the better, with the feedback from the audience.

So on and on it rolled, touring, then recording at home, then touring some more, sometimes at colleges, sometimes at sports arenas. One day they showed up at a venue (on the same bill with Van Morrison), and asked who was topping the bill. "Well, you are, it's a Moody Blues crowd," replied the promoter. And they were. Justin said he and his manager Pete Jackson slunk out of the room, avoiding the outraged Van Morrison. Suddenly, they were the headliners, and well on their way to a cozy spot in rock n' roll history.

* I had to research this. In April 1968, Czechoslovakia began to "liberalize" and break away from the Soviet Union. THAT is "Prague Spring" which was a spring of liberal thinking. August 21, 1968, Soviet tanks rolled into the country (troops came too) to reinstate Communism and generally terrorize the populace. The rest is political, but the important point is the whole world was horrified at the time by the tank invasion, and Justin claims the band was there to do a gig when the tanks rolled in. Probably the western bands began booking in April when they tried to open up; "decadent" rock n' roll wasn't exactly welcome behind the Iron Curtain. See Radio Free Europe. There does exist a black and white film clip of the Moodies playing in a street in Prague which only surfaced in 2007 on *youtube.com*. It was done just before the tanks rolled in and has been hidden all these years. It's great, the girls are wearing bouffant hairdos, pale pink lipstick, and the Moodies are really having a good time. References say the Moodies were "the last English band to play in Czechoslovakia" before the Iron Curtain fell again.

**Spring 2013 (Moody Blues Cruise) Graeme talked about the "first time they met the Beatles" Gerry Levene and his band (Graeme drumming) on the same bill, Graeme's band went on first and "There we were dressed in orange and pink. Then the Beatles came on after us [dressed in Gene Vincent style leather, etc] if you think we didn't feel silly!" So yea, everyone agrees the Beatles changed and set the trends.

***I could probably write a book on Leary, but others have beat me to it. Thus I apologize for my vague recollections, some of my information might or might not be confirmed by research, but this is a book about the Moodies, not Leary. I and people I know remember it thus; I would not testify to it. After he finally got out of the pokey, Leary went on to live a quiet life until the '90s when he started making random news splashes. (For example, getting arrested for smoking a cigarette in an airport. Ever the rebel!) Leary would later say of his research, "LSD is a way of stepping outside of one's self." This is called meta-communication in Psychology, and it works well in couple counseling, as well as substance abuse counseling. *Psychoactive drugs should be used by those educated to use …it's natural* *and traditionally used by shamans (who are trained to use it)* (Jacquie Withrrite, "The Curious Psychic," *The Morning News Tribune*, 1992). Leary lived long enough to have a lot of fun with the Internet and developed a wonderful interactive website *(www.leary.com* of course) before "Madame Cancer" took over his body. Doing research for this book, I ran across newsgroup postings alleged to be from Dr. Leary, and they say things like "Never trust no one who uses 'quantum' and 'psychology' together," very funny stuff, some of it (March 25, 1994). There is even a possibility that Leary coined the term "websurfing" (*Higher and Higher*, May 1994). Leary toyed with the thought of drinking hemlock live on line, once he was diagnosed as terminal; he viewed death as the "last great journey." There is alleged to be a movie out where, after his death, Leary's body is decapitated to the tune of "Legend of a Mind" in preparation for cryogenic freezing of his brain. I have to confess that's one movie I've missed. A wonderful man, Leary, and like the intellectual Libra that he was, truly dedicated to the art of pushing back boundaries!

**** *Four Beatles, Three Beach Boys, Mia Farrow and me*--Donovan in Concert, talking about his first day with the Yogi. I ran into an old hippy who was into Transcendental Meditation, or TM. He enjoyed discussing Moody music, he alleged that the phrase "Are you sitting comfortably?" is the line the guru gives to the student as you begin meditation. It's also the beginning of an old radio "story time" show in the UK, so this has some cross-over, as the Maharishi got his start in the U.K. Said old hippy also had an interesting explanation of "Tuesday Afternoon," saying that it was "The third day of verification." That is, when you start and commit to the TM process, the first day (Saturday) is totally spent one-on-one teacher to student. The next three days are when "the group comes back together as a whole." Those gentle voices I hear is also supposed to be from TM, and the "sigh" it's all explained with is the word "ohm" some sort of kundalini breathing thing. Of course, we expert Moody fans know that Tuesday the dog, and Tolkien's Ents are the more likely inspiration to "Tuesday Afternoon." There is no telling how late-night conversations went at the Bag o' Nails, the TM stuff was probably being bounced about in the U.K.rock scene quite a bit! The Moodies never have said what year they were doing TM, I would guess it was when they were also working the Bag o' Nails in mid-1967, and were socializing with so many other pop stars, including the Beatles. Justin also said he never got to meet the Yogi himself, because he wasn't making much money at the time. He was passed off to a lesser instructor; the Yogi only saw the Big Bucks folks. *Time is Money*.

*****No surprise, J.R.R. Tolkien also came from Brum, as did the Moody Blues. Apparently, it is a place that is conducive to wanting to escape reality.

VIII) Across the Threshold: 1969-1970

Why is the opening of a doorway called a "threshold"? The wealthy had slate floors which in the winter they would get slippery when wet. So they spread thresh on the floor to help keep their footing. As the winter wore on they kept adding more thresh until when you opened the door it would all start slipping outside. A piece of wood was placed at the entry way, later named a "thresh hold" -- found on line

Money reveals character -- Tom Clancy

We were doing a show. Graeme's drums were up on podium, with a black curtain around the back. The podium was very small, Graeme was just able to squeeze on there. We got to a certain point in the sound where Graeme raised his arms, you know for the big hit at the end. But it never came because he lost his balance, and did a back flip through the black curtains. Fortunately he wasn't hurt too bad, and we all got to have a good laugh, including Graeme. -- Mike Pinder, *Moodymania* #17

Marriage was slow to fall into place for the band members but came eventually, as they felt more secure in their income. It's a common, normal life experience everyone feels, to want children and a family in their twenties; and the Moodies are quite normal people in this.

Ray Thomas married Gillian Jary in June 1969. Gillian was apparently a fisher-wife, and a good match for mad angler Ray. On their honeymoon in Cornwall, they got into a contest over who caught the biggest shark, according to the *New Music Express* (NME) interview in early 1970, done by Ray; it's a very funny, wonderful interview. Ray also allegedly had a Chihuahua to go with that sombrero mentioned earlier, if the NME article is to be believed. By 1970, in the interview "Three Fifths of the Moody Blues" Ray sketches a quick outline of collective family status, and says something to the effect of "We need more boys," he and Graeme both had little girls at the time.

Graeme Edge married Carol Mayers, article dated Jan 11, 1969. Graeme talked freely about his own personal life in a Howard Stern radio interview dated June 2, 1988. I'll interject this as historical information, if needed as we go along (same for the others) but suffice to say that Graeme's three wives appear to have been just as lively as he is in their personal affairs.

John Lodge married (and is still married to) Kirsten in 1968. Kirsten has family in Denmark, as per the Official Fan Club (OFC) newsletter of Christmas 1972. There is a picture of Kirsten and John in *Higher and Higher* #11/12, which is actually a poor picture. I've met Kirsten, and she's a very pretty woman, especially when she smiles. From my short ride in an elevator with her once in Tahoe, she appears to be a very intelligent, and elegant lady, and furthermore was being very good to her mum-in-law who was with her. (John has his mum's chin.)

Justin Hayward married (and is still married to) Marie Guirron on Dec 19, 1970. I've heard a fan club myth that Marie is "French" and have never been able to find reliable documentation to back this up; her accent certainly sounds English. According to other apocrypha, she is from near Liverpool. Marie and Justin share a love for horses, and I'll discuss this more as we go along too. In 1968, Justin bought a home in Kingston-on-the-Thames, which had been converted from an old coach house in the '50s; the building dates back to being a hunting lodge for Henry VIII. Justin said that they didn't have much when he and Marie moved in, and just lived in one room. Lionel Bart bought them some mod inflatable furniture. The Haywards eventually bought real furniture, and lived there until late 1997, when they sold it, and moved permanently to the Ligurian Coast.

Mike Pinder married Donna Arkoff, a "California girl" in November, 1970. There aren't too many notes about their personal life, which I'm sure is how both of them like it, but it's common knowledge their marriage broke up shortly after the band's separation in the '70s.

The Moodies did a lot of recording in Mike's "very large" garage when they couldn't get studio time; they all lived near each other around Cobham, England during the '60s. There was talk at one time of them actually buying an entire town for the band, and all their roadies and management to live in!!!

I didn't talk about the sixth member of the band, did I?? Tony Clarke grew up in Coventry near Brum, born August 21, 1941. Like Mike and Ray, he is old enough to remember bad things about WWII as a small child and says he can remember waves upon waves of bombers going over his home. Coventry of course, was bombed pretty heavily by the Germans during the War, and it apparently left lasting impressions on him.

Somewhere along the line he worked on the first Harrier jet engines! (WOW) Tony first got into music whilst in Art College, had moderate success in song writing, eventually wound up working for Decca. Some of the '60s groups Tony worked with were Pinkerton's Assorted Colours, and The Equals ("Baby Come Back") which are total unknowns to this author. Often Tony's job was to handle "high maintenance" acts. In early 1967 he was assigned to the Moody Blues.

It's common knowledge that his first marriage split up around 1978, probably as a result of the same thing that split him up from the Moody Blues: plain old over-work. That's further down the line. He had a very good biography on his website, there is another on Wikipedia that's also well written.

As this phase of the Moody Blues was involved with commitment, it seems only reasonable that this would take place in their personal and professional lives simultaneously. By 1969, the Moody Blues had more money coming in than they knew what to do with, especially with the release of their third album *On the Threshold of a Dream*.

In all fairness to McCormick, he probably wasn't ripping them off. But he wasn't handling the money as efficiently as Weintraub could, and the band was unmistakably hitched to a rising star. According to Michael Lang, producer for Woodstock, in August 1969, the Moodies told him they were in the middle of an album (*To Our Children's Children's Children*) and "It wasn't going well" so they couldn't come to the festival. That's why they're on the poster, but weren't at Woodstock.

It matches up with what was going on with Moody management at the time, leaving McCormick and going with WEG. Their tour in the fall of 1968 was pretty frustrating, and other things were happening too. Lennon couldn't get into the country, Leary (public enemy #1) was either skipping bail or being put in jail. And then, the horrible LaBianca-Tate murders happened. Riots over the draft for Viet Nam were still breaking out, plainly America was NUTS. They stayed home until the management issues were resolved and rationality returned. They focused on cleaning their own house, and created a spin-out company from Decca, Threshold Records; *To Our Children's Children's Children* was issued on the Threshold label. In the meantime, they toured Europe a bit (see *Blue Timeline*) and recorded in between shows.

WEG (Weintraub Entertainment Group) began to assist the band in management. I've turned up documents that say Gerry Hoff of Decca was their manager as of 1971, but at some point, they "self-managed," with a little help from those who were changing the business face of rock n' roll. Weintraub helped many bands get away from the "rip off" attitude that was (and still can be) common in music management. The modern singing group N'Sync complained about the same problem the Moody Blues had in 1970.

There you are, top of the bill, yet you barely have the money to pay the rent...where is all the money going? (July 28, 2000, *the NBC Today Show*.)

The new paradigm gave the band control of their investments, WEG acted more as investment counselors. As I understand it, the accountants in these "self-management" firms report directly to whatever celebrity they are assigned.

The celebrity is offered control of his/their own funds, given advice by accountants, and the company does the investments for a fee, allowing the artist to do what he/she does best, which is create!

Partner and advisor to WEG and Moodies, Tom Huelett would say later in testimony (*Moodies vs Moraz* 1992) "I don't manage the band. I help them to make decisions. They manage themselves." Tom Huelett was from Seattle, and had gotten into the business as road manager for Jimi Hendrix (he and Weintraub co-founded Concerts West in 1967.) Huelett eventually advised Wings, Led Zeppelin, John Denver, CCR, Elvis, Sinatra, Zappa, Neil Diamond, and the Beach Boys. He would advise the Moody Blues until his death with cancer in 1993. More can be found out about Tom Huelett in *Higher and Higher*, winter 1990, as well as in John Denver's autobiography and Jerry Weintraub's bio.

Concerts West folded in 1983, and Weintraub went into movie making, while Huelett continued advising musicians with Huelett and Associates. Anything the Moodies did up to the founding of Threshold Music was under the control of Decca; in May of 1992, the Moody Blues sued Decca/Polygram for control of their first three albums, and I have no idea if they were successful in their quest. I hope they were, and you will probably agree with me after reading the chapter on *Long Distance Voyager*. After twenty-five years, control of copyrights becomes pretty nebulous.

The Moody Blues considered themselves, as artists, more than capable of delivering a complete package, including the cover sleeve to their albums. Decca and they did NOT see eye to eye over this, and the argument escalated over the sleeve production of *On the Threshold of a Dream*.

Decca griped about the cost, and here the Moodies were bringing in more money with chart toppers than they could count! Money seems such a trivial thing in retrospect, when one leafs through the gorgeous lyric booklet that accompanied *On the Threshold of a Dream*, with the flowery writing and attractive art. But "money is numbers," and when Decca threatened to short them on covers, it was difficult to make it a top seller indeed.

Anyway, deciding the record company was seriously misguided, the Moodies founded their own company and christened it Threshold Records. Probably at the same time, in a legal maneuver to protect their interests, the Moodies declared a stock option, and split the interest six ways, between the five band members, and Tony Clarke, who was considered "the sixth Moody." What paperwork exists on this is unknown, but according to the band members over the years, it was always a gentleman's agreement, that they all had equal shares in their enterprise, and no one was going to hose the others for monetary gain. This simple yet effective management concept was to save their skins when the lawyers got ahold of the band in the early '80s and again in the early '90s.

The artwork was all part of the Moody package, and during this time, the Moodies started using Decca staff artist Phil Travers for their album covers. Most of his original album paintings hang on the walls at Threshold, but at least one, the cover to *A Question of Balance*, hangs on Justin's Hayward's wall in his home. More can be read about Phil Travers in *Higher and Higher* #7/8.

Threshold Records was conceived as a place to get all the records you never were able to find at your neighborhood record store. They had eleven record stores at one time, in Manchester, Soho, Birmingham, and Bristol to name a few. Eventually they shut down most of these, but for many years, Threshold had a record store connected to their offices, though you had to call ahead to make sure they were in!

The record shop in Cobham, Surrey was run by Phil Pavling, and of course carried all Moody Blues CDs currently available, as well as many other artists. Late note: as of Feb 28, 2011, Threshold Records closed shop. It has closed and re-opened at least one time prior that I know of.

THS-1, the first album of Threshold's catalog, was *To Our Children's Children's Children*. (The title had a bit to do with the fact that Tony had just had children at the time.) The cost in the States was some 50 cents more than the regular album. *(I know, because I bought it hot off the press at age fourteen and griped about having to cough up 50 extra pennies from my little coin jar.)* Possibly for this reason it was not a top seller at the time, but for the serious fans, it was a minor thing to pay a little extra. The cover was lean, creative, and it has probably the most cohesive story line from the Core Seven years; reflecting upon mankind's first steps into outer space, and where the entire thing was taking us. More can be read about this album, along with reviews and fan thoughts, in *Higher and Higher* #26/27.

Tony Clarke was heavily into astronomy at this time (owned a Newtonian Cassegrain Telescope) and built his own observatory dome on the top of his house....and drove the other band members a little nuts babbling about stars. In fact, the Four Tops came to one of the Moody star parties (June 10, 1972 *Record Mirror*), Tony was able to get the planet Jupiter into focus, and everyone was deeply impressed. Graeme and Tony were so into space-science that they were invited to see Apollo 15 launch. Mike's instrumental piece "Beyond" came from a concept that each planet had "a voice" (as a traveler might pass by and hear) and indeed astronomers will tell you that Jupiter DOES have a radio voice.

To Our Children's Children's Children (TOCCC) was supposed to come out at the same time as the first Moonwalk in July 1969, but it was a month or two late. That was ok, the point was made.

"Watching and Waiting" was released as the first single on the Threshold label, October of 1969. They said the song sent chills up their backs when they recorded it: unfortunately it failed to thrill consumers, and in Justin's words "sold about nine copies, which were all bought by me Mum." But it's a good song, and has one of the best recordings ever done of Justin's voice, in many opinions.

In the late '90s, Justin did a series of solo shows, including a live performance of "Watching and Waiting." Those particular performances showcased the song as very bluesy and eerie as originally conceived; somehow this does not come over on the album. The song also appears to have the exact same peculiar chord sequence as "Ventura Highway," a hit by the band America; "Watching and Waiting" predates "Ventura Highway" if I'm not mistaken. It also has a similar chord sequence to "Bookends" by Paul Simon. Odd how musicians borrow from each other, probably unconsciously.

Justin's father passed away in 1969, and some lyrical content in Justin's songs on *To Our Children's Children's Children* appears to reflect his thoughts at that time. There's another peculiar thing on the inside of this album; look carefully on the right side, there's a spooky black dog glimmering in the darkness. I once read a children's mystery novel wherein the Black Dog is "a death omen." Oddly, there's another black dog on the cover of *From Mighty Oaks*. There's LOTS of symbolism about the Moodies' personal lives and themes they wanted to get across, on all the album covers, if you look for it.

In addition to stress on the home front, Justin began to collect a following of fans who thought his songs were all literal; or who began to interpret them in odd ways, each as subjective as the person hearing it. Analysing lyrics was a big deal in the early '70s; this continues even unto the 21st century. At least one song, "Never Comes the Day," Justin explained in a radio interview, as being "…like painting a pretty picture; the light may be on, but no one is home." In later concerts during the '90s, Justin got on stage, and said of writing of that song "…and "I got lucky that night!" referring to some past romantic interlude. Sooooo ….. only Justin knows for sure!

The Moodies all started looking for investments to sink their money into. Most of them indulged their tastes in collecting musical instruments, and baubles for their ladies; but John, aspiring car designer, invested some of his money into cars. When asked what he thought about one critic (who was probably beating that "pretentious" word to death again), John is alleged to have quipped "I'll run over him in my Rolls Royce." There is a great article on John's car collection in *Higher and Higher* #11/12, pg 20. Among John's eventual acquisitions in rolling stock would include a 1972 Morgan, a Bentley, numerous Rolls Royces, and a Lincoln Continental, which he took on a long drive. "I wanted to drive Route 66 across America. So I did, taking in the Grand Canyon, Tombstone, Graceland, the Grand Old Oprey." Then the Lodge family (family road trip) piled all their luggage in the car, had it winched onto the RMS *Queen Elizabeth II* and shipped it home to England! Now THAT'S a dad who knows how to take the family on vacation!

 Graeme and Mike took their loot and indulged in their love for electronics. A serious student of rock n' roll should always bear in mind that the Moodies are and were a working band, with a backdrop of eternally evolving, cutting-edge music technology. Mike was to use the Moog for the first time in "Melancholy Man." to good effect. Justin and Mike both bought mini-Moogs in America, around 1970 on one of their tours (according to Mike.)

 Graeme developed and showcased some of the first synthesized drums, only to find they were too delicate to transport on tours. There was a fan chat with Gordon Marshall in the summer of 2009; he discussed this, and apparently drums are ALL electronic now, the details are complex, and Graeme was there at the beginning of it all, experimenting. The drums had something like 5,000 transistors, which was at least a step up from valves/tubes, but it was still pretty shaky.

 In his December 1972 interview with *Circus,* Graeme talks at length about electronic drums and babbles about upcoming silicon wafer chips. Apparently the drum electronics were so sensitive, the drums were thrown off by stray EMF; they whacked out to the tune of any magnetic fields around the transistors and made the drums play "better than me" as Graeme grumbled. They would "play themselves, every time the lights change from red to blue." The answer is shielding. The Mind Boggles.

Like the Beatles and their company Apple, Threshold soon grew to be a monster. The Moody Blues are intelligent men, but no financial wizards; with the sort of money they had coming in, it was inevitable that everyone would want a piece of the pie. One effective way to deal with the cash flow was to divert it back into something they felt strongly about; the promotion of musical talent. Perhaps it was a result of the horrible things they had endured in their five-year climb to musical fame.

Whatever the reasons, they started an artist's workshop associated with Threshold, and tried a hand at their own record producing. This turned out to be a great way to work with other artists in the recording industry.

Among the names and bands to be associated with the Moodies would be Medusa; their album *Trapeze*, produced by John Lodge, is THS-8, released Sept 1977. Medusa toured with the Moodies for three years during their association, apparently in the very early '70s.

Also signed with Threshold: Sally Pickard, Timon (produced by Justin Hayward), Sue Vickers, Asgard (with Rod Harrison, formerly of Bulldog Breed), Providence (produced by Tony Clarke), and Nicky James (*Thunderthroat*). Toward the end, the then "infant band" Kiss tried to sign with them. The Moodies even claimed to have early demos of Kiss in their possession; that must be interesting (*The Moody Blues Story* with Anne Nightingale, 1979.) Rumors are that Kiss actually used to play "Go Now" on stage! Go figure, in large glowing red letters!

Justin also claims they almost signed Genesis! The Four Tops also were associated with Threshold Records in a more general way, flying to London to record five or six tracks in the Wessex Studios, in 1970. I think the Four Tops' writers, Holland, Dozier and Holland had left Motown, and the Four Tops were high and dry for material. I've actually run across articles that say the Moody Blues were influenced by "R&B music like the Four Tops," heheh it went both ways!

Tony Clarke produced the Four Tops at the request of Motown Records. The Moodies jammed on some backing tracks, at least on the cover of Mike's "A Simple Game." Justin's and Mike's voices are also on the "ooooos" in the song mix, they sang back up. Justin said in radio interviews, that he also wrote some tracks for the Four Tops under the *nom de plume* of Gurron, a misspelling of his wife's maiden name. Justin and Tony Clarke wrote "You Stole My Love," the B-side to "Simple Game."

The Four Tops also covered Moodies song "So Deep Within You." A lot of these songs were never released in the U.S. but only in the U.K. The "Gurron" songs are now included in the Four Tops box set *Fourever*, and also can be found on *youtube*.

Certainly the Four Tops song "Reach Out" appears to have a chord sequence that is peculiar to some of Justin's compositions, a "C to Bb" chord shift, "Reach Out" was written by Brian and Eddie Holland in 1967. One is tempted to draw a connection to Dave Holland, who was the original drummer for Medusa, see above about Threshold bands.

Medusa eventually split due to one of the guys getting really big and going on to Deep Purple. Dave Holland played drums on Justin's *Songwriter* album, and later became the drummer for Judas Priest. One is also tempted to assume that Justin first met Dennis Lambert around this time, the producer and writer for the Four Tops in 1972. Lambert would later co-write the beautiful "Less Is More" with Justin on his *View from the Hill* CD (1996).

The Moody Blues were also alleged to have sung back up (less Graeme) on Billy Davis's single "I Can Remember"/ "Nobody's Home To Go Home To." (*Goldmine*) Graeme and Justin both worked with Lionel Bart about this time, who wrote for the insert to *On the Threshold of a Dream*. So the Moody Blues were really mixing it up in 1970.*

Justin, perfectionist that he is, voiced dissatisfaction with their Threshold artist's workshop; he was to later comment "You had to go down and take the instruments out of their hands, and do it properly." Probably the Moodies were not ready for their new role as mentors. Be this at it may, exposure to new artists also gave the Moodies the opportunity to work professionally with different and fresh talent. The Moodies are playing anonymously on the backing tracks of several Threshold albums (Justin backs up Timon with a guitar on many of his songs).

It's difficult to avoid thinking some Moodies worked on the beautiful album, *Ever Sense the Dawn*, produced by Tony Clarke, with the Portland, Oregon band, Providence. I had a rare opportunity to communicate some years ago with Bob Barriatua and Andy Guzie, the original guitarists of Providence. They still live in Portland: Bob is now a medical doctor, (yes, they call him Dr. Bob). Andy is still very much into his guitar work. Their story about becoming associated with Threshold in 1972 was, "We were just wild and crazy kids, and sent this tape backstage with a note when the Moodies played in town. A few weeks later we got a call from Threshold." It was that simple.

The Moodies, like their mentors from Decca, also recognized talent when they heard it, and were quick to bring the orchestral string sound of Providence into their fold. *Ever Sense the Dawn* was recorded in 1972 at Sunset Sound in Los Angeles, and mixed by Tony Clarke in the U.K. *Ever Sense the Dawn* sound-bytes are available on *youtube* as of this writing.

At some point, the Rolling Stones and David Bowie also tried to throw their financial lot in with Threshold, only to be deflected by the rapidly over-whelmed Moodies. "Don't follow us, we're lost too," is their general commentary about this time period "Let us come with YOU" they said to the Stonies. In an article from April 1990 (*Q Magazine*) Justin comments, "I can't even remember having an office in Soho Square.....bloody hell!" John recalled hiring a huge restaurant for a company Christmas party, and then didn't know anyone there.

Eventually they abandoned their "own record company" about the time they formed for *Octave*, because as Justin put it "The entire thing became NOT about making music, but about talking to people's lawyers." That would be enough to make anyone pack it in.

Saved By the Music --While deflecting the lawyers of their promising new protégés, the Moodies were still able to turn out some pretty good music. The last three albums of the Core Seven are *Every Good Boy Deserves Favor* (from the mnemonic for the lines in the treble staff, EGBDF), *A Question of Balance*, and *Seventh Sojourn*.

The Moodies settled into a lifestyle, recording in studios, sometimes doing their best work at 3 am, so they were up all hours of the night. Moody Blues music sounds the best very late at night, Tony Clarke would say. In fact, Tony claimed in a 2008 interview that they pioneered recording in the dark because it added to the "flow and feel." The lighting had to be just right. As English boys living far to the North, good mood lighting would be important. The effects of winter lighting on our moods is just now being understood and has definite effects on the creative process.

They hung out in their cubicles, working on model airplanes and reading; or they played football, or whipped off a game of darts. Ray is alleged to be VERY good at this time-honored British sport. There's even one very funny story about a large backboard that Graeme played drums behind, that eventually had to be replaced, due to it being chewed up by Ray's knife throwing practice (no kidding.) One can only wonder if Graeme played drums there while Ray did this. The mind boggles.

When things got boring, they dropped in on their friends, the Move, who recorded at Decca in a neighboring (smaller, the Moodies got the good one) studio. Remember them from back at Brooks Brothers in Brum, when both bands shuffled and regrouped under the kindly patronage of

Tony Secunda? The bands remained good mates all during this time. Recording studios must be the ultimate place to party, depending on the producer of course, with friends dropping by to visit at all hours.

Tony claimed the band was always arriving late to work, and of course he had to yell at them a little, but then he said he got more effort out of them if he kept them supplied in cigarettes! Ray was locked in the microphone cupboard a few times by Tony until he came up with a song. Tony alluded to Ray actually being held captive in there, and allowed only biscuits (cookies), tea and cigarettes, until he came out with a song. *(I can see this scene in a movie too: the rest of the band pouncing on Ray and stuffing him into the closet. Musicians play rough!)* Tony said in his interview, "Strange thing, I think he grew to like it!"

Then Tony locked Graeme in The Cupboard. This is prior to isolation tank research, though Dr. Lilly might have been dabbling in it, even in the '60s. Graeme, a professed agnostic, eventually came out staggering, poem in hand, astonished that he could have written anything so spiritual as "The Balance." It was a very moving experience for him. Various tribes of Native Americans have used isolation rooms as a part of their religious customs for centuries; the Moodies stumbled upon it accidentally.

There was a lot of waiting around for Tony to get to their part on the new album. On a clear night, Tony might set up his telescope, and everyone would crowd around, looking at stars. Their cubicles were described as "very '60s" so one must imagine beads, draped Indian bedspreads, lava lamps and bells, along with the inevitable burning incense.

According to Graeme, they usually started recording their albums with one of Justin's songs, "out of superstition." One witness would later mention the entire studio (Decca Three) they had set up as an indoor soccer field where they played a rackety game in the day and warmed up. Then as darkness fell, they turned into mystical musical priests, complete with weird lights and wafting incense.

When reporters asked if they could come along to the recording sessions, they were told very firmly by Tony Clarke, "No." It was probably the smartest thing Tony ever did for the band. Imagine trying to be creative and having to watch your language and behavior around a reporter, who is liable to write down everything or anything you do! [*This actually happened to the Doors, somehow a reporter crashed one of their studio cessions; Jim Morrison expressed his displeasure by lighting a match, and slowly lowering toward the fly of his leather pants. The reporter ended the article with "I did not stay to see the end of the recording." Invade the space of a working band at your own mental risk.*]

In various interviews, the Moody Blues mention opening their meetings with a few Chuck Berry impromptus before starting business. There is even rumored to be a live bootleg of this time period where they are warming up, playing "Oh Susanna!"

They also mention a coffee table that they all used to sit around, presumably at Mike's house first, then later in their own offices, or at the studio. Like the Round Table of England's ancient knights, the coffee table was where they "laid down their armor," brainstormed their strategy, and refined the concept for whatever album project they were going to take on next. Drawing pictures, tapping on the table, passing tidbits about...who knows what happened, but each album is said to have started there, with some theme as the core concept. John drew pictures of the Moodies with Dr. Livingston, on safari in the jungles. While John was being creative with pen and ink, Graeme was finding what he wanted to do with the album by whacking metal plates with a crickett bat. It was an "anything goes" process, throughout any album.

Probably the coolest bit of brainstorming that jumped directly to the album from "goofing around" has to be "In the Beginning" with Justin, Mike and Graeme just horsing around in the control room....and coming out with a very interesting dialog. If you gotta consult your counselor to get this, be my guest, but Justin is the Ego, the third voice is the Id, and Mike is the Superego. *Take that, Dr. Freud!* Someone on Facebook posted that the "third voice" in this was John Lennon!!! Good heavens! Graeme says it was him, it does sound a bit "Lennonish," so your guess is as good as anyone's; the band is not always strictly truthful. Maybe it's Varnals, he sounds a LOT like Graeme.

At the Durham storyteller show (Spring 2012) Graeme told a story about putting all their wristwatches up to the microphone during "Of course you are my bright little star," with the microphone turned up full; they had to post signs, lock doors and so forth, so no stray noises would blow out the amps.

Even unto 1991 with the release of a co-written song by Justin and Ray, Justin would say in interviews, speaking about their creative process "It was nice, just a guitar and flute." So the creative process has a lot of different aspects on the path to any Moody album. Anything goes.

Sometimes that idea core shifted, but not so with *To Our Children's Children's Children*; it had a very obvious and coherent theme. *Where is mankind now, in 1969, on the threshold of space exploration? Let's make a time capsule of this, right now, where we are.* The album was overlaid with weird sound effects and electronic music; several stories in making this album bear repeating. Like, the opening "crash" sound is a piano being dropped off the roof. For real.

When they wanted the actual soundtrack for "white noise" of a rocket launch (John claimed they sent away to NASA for it), to be heard on the first track "Higher and Higher," it was totally UNsatisfactory. They eventually took the simple sound of a match being struck and slowed that way way down; then you have good rocket noise. That's what the "white noise" is on the opening of the album. Tony later would say, "It was a statement, to use atomic power for peaceful purposes, it was supposed to be a nuclear blast." Nope. Just a different perspective on a lighted match.

At the same time, Mike began to recite the opening poem "Higher and Higher" and says he actually held his nose for the first few verses, and then spoke the rest of the words in a clear voice. And you thought it was all electronic gimmickry…..nope, just Micky the Moonboy talking through his tonsils!

John talked about tape being stretched clear across the room, and him holding huge loops with pencils and fingers, for some odd effect. If you held out the tape, then let it snap back, you get a *WHOO-oooooooooo* sort of sound, that you hear on the beginning of "The Voyage," and other places too. Yep, very creative stuff going on at Threshold Records in 1969.

Things like this made the album a technical marvel for its time, but was it good entertainment? Those who saw this tour, and the opening "Higher and Higher" performed live, talk about a total blackout; THEN came the crashing of cymbals, and overpowering bass, and slowly as the lights came up, the band started wailing discordantly.... and went into the concert. It must have been wonderful, and it's a shame no live concert videos have survived that we know of.

In 2003, following the crash of the shuttle *Columbia* and with the Iraq war looming, the Moodies put this song back into their stage show. Words can't describe it, but Graeme Edge at age 60, doing the funky chicken to Gordon's drum solo, and the lights *pok-pok-pok*-ing all over the stage, set a new fabulous level in rock performance.

In 1973, the Moodies played in concert the entire first side of *To Our Children Children's Children,* and were awarded the "golden ticket" at Madison Square Garden, which was to say (in their words) they had sold the most tickets to any event to date, in that venue.

A report from on line about the show on Nov 2, 1973 at LSU went something like this: *"Higher and Higher" led off the concert....everyone left the stage, and for a while there was only Mike with a spotlight on him* [and] *the mellotron. Then Ray was there, spotlight on him……..a huge auditorium and just the two of them playing to utter silence by the audience……*

Not everything went wonderfully though. Justin says he can distinctly remember a show when they were starting this very dramatic lead in. The smoke billowed up, and Mike yelled "Stop!!!!" having a major malfunction with the mellotron. Justin says he put down his guitar, and ambled off stage, followed by the others. As the smoke cleared and the house lights came up, the confused audience was treated to the inspirational vision of Mike head-first in the monster mellotron.

Tony Clarke says he remembers other times, when the tapes of the mellotron spewed out all over the tarmac at O'Hare Airport, as it was unloaded from a plane (they didn't pack it before loading it.) Plainly the mellotron was a high maintenance pet. During the recording of *Every Good Boy Deserves Favor,* Tony and Mike stripped all the old funky sticky tapes out, and put new ones in.

There is another interview where John tells the story about "Procession" in concert; on the word "Desolation" they cut all the lights in the house, so the audience could experience the desolation. However, instead of quiet, they heard people falling down stairs, dropping popcorn and sodas, because of the sudden darkness. Obviously the creative Muse let them down on that one!

The band was dissatisfied still. Live performance is a funny thing: not only music, but dancing and acting too. If you rehearse TOO much, it might be stale and stilted. While, if you do it quick and keep it fresh, it works and has a more authentic ring to it (but the chances of making a mistake go up too!) The songs of *To Our Children's Children's Children* were too complex to reproduce well on stage, and they decided they needed to follow the KISS principle (that is, *Keep It Simple, Stupid.*)

When they next sat down at the coffee table, this was the theme that came up over and over again: SIMPLIFY. They booked the time in the studio, and literally wrote the songs as they recorded them, trusting to immediacy, and concentrating on a raw, fresh sound, which would translate better to live performance. Spontaneity rather than simplicity became the true process; for example, they threw together "Question" at the last minute to record. They just DID it, with time ticking on the studio clock. The gods smiled, and it happened.

Justin said he literally was writing "Question" the night before they recorded, in his flat in Barnes, London; his voice on the track sounds like he's been up all night. It's in moments like this that true genius comes forth; he had two songs in open C tuning he was messing with, couldn't finish; then he and Tony got the idea to put them together. They juxtaposed nicely, one slow, one fast.

Graeme said something about soiling his bloomers (he was more graphic than that) doing "Question" for the first time, as he had nothing planned. That's the raw impromptu Graeme you are hearing on the album: the version of "Question" on the album is the first run through. The two songs that make up "Question" illustrated the most puzzling "balance" in anyone's life, Love and War (conflict.) The song went on to be a hit, and a major theme for the Viet Nam protests that were raging in the streets of America in those years.

For the record: open tuning (just one of several "open tunings") in "C" is a C-G-C-G-C-E tuning, going from the bass string to the top treble string. Justin recommends a very heavy string on the bottom for "Question," he has broken them in live performance, not a pretty sight. Justin claims that Richie Havens taught him how to use open tuning; the only other '60s artist I know of that likes open tuning is Joni Mitchell. Justin has mentioned Jimmie Spheeris as doing it too, no one seems to know where it came from! I personally learned from a friend, sitting in my bedroom in the very early '70s. All you have to do is bar any fret, and you have a new chord.

The rest of *A Question of Balance* is not to be sneezed at, despite the overwhelming positive reception of Justin's first track. The entire album reflects what was going on then, nature and Mother Earth, war, social issues, personal issues, love, beauty around us. Somehow, it all hangs together in a coherent whole.

One of the best tracks is written by Graeme; he took the entire band down a different path with "Don't You Feel Small?" with a reggae beat and flutes. It undoubtedly prompted at least one reviewer to write, "The rhythm was such that you half expected the Aztecs to come leaping from behind the stage at any minute." (*New Music Review*, Sept 5, 1970).

Question of Balance is cleaner technically, fewer generations, fewer overdubs, less "hiss" (*Higher and Higher* #33). QOB was recorded Jan-Mar, then they toured (March 13-June 1) in the U.S. and picked up the recording again in Jun. They sound as if they are under the gun at this time, from the studios. Tony Clarke said that on the end of "Minstrel's Song" the whole editing thing fell apart at the end, but most listeners thought that was part of the song! Doesn't it sound neat?

Fan: *How can a mouse play a daffodil?*
Ray: *A mouse must practice!* -- on line chat, Sept 1994

Ray had a cute story about "Nice to Be Here," the original words were about a critter who "played a guitar with only one string." It was *supposed* to be a banjo, but in Ray's words, "Justin didn't have a banjo, so I changed the word to guitar. Then he cheated and played two strings!!!" If you've ever watched Justin picking up close and live, this makes more sense. Justin only uses two fingers to pick with, and usually, yes, only plays one string at a time! Justin refers to this way of picking as the "claw style." It looks very tense too, Justin must have very strong hands indeed.

Moody Blue touring is difficult to ferret out for the year 1970, but they were headliners by this time. June 28, 1970, they were part of the infamous "Bath" concert in the U.K. (200,000 people). "Blues and Progressive Rock" was the title. It included many wonderful bands from that same time period, It's A Beautiful Day, Steppenwolf, Pink Floyd,

Donovan, Canned Heat, the Mothers Of Invention, Santana, Led Zeppelin, Hot Tuna, Country Joe (*sans* Fish), Jefferson Airplane (who got rained on and had to stop early), the Byrds (who solved the rain problem by going acoustic), and Dr. John, the Night Tripper (complete with all his *gris gris*).

The *gris gris* rained out the Moodies and they never did play Bath which "...narked them somewhat as they'd paid £500 for a helicopter to get to the site." Why does this sound a bit staged? Five good-sized Moodies, two guitars, one mellotron, several amps, speakers and drums, all in one helicopter? *Hmmm*. A Chinook maybe.

The concert was filmed on 35mm film, but this has so far failed to surface as a complete document. (*MOJO Magazine*; Issue 52 - March 1998). Again, the electronics were causing problems on the road, so maybe the *gris gris* was subtly steering the Moodies toward a simpler show, in spite of themselves.

According to articles of the time, Mike Pinder required throat surgery in 1970. He was hospitalized in Los Angeles, while the rest of the band returned to England without him. The October 14-22 tour of Italy was canceled. It was the first known incident of serious illness the band would collectively face over their years together. Having said that, remember they are normal people and have medical issues crop up, like the rest of us.

Even worse, a bit earlier in Philadelphia (September 27, 1970) Ray was in the lead going on stage, and in the blackness backstage, fell through a trap door!** They fished Ray out with a strained back and 2 broken toes; like a trouper, he played the show, and only let them cut the boot off his thrashed foot after curtain. OUCH! Both incidents impacted touring, but they did eventually tour, both the U.K. and America, supporting *A Question of Balance,* which hit #1 in the U.K. during August of 1970.

The Moodies were able to reproduce songs simply and effectively on stage. One "live" song that exists in bootlegs and on the Moodies *Isle of Wight: Threshold of a Dream*, is "The Tortoise and the Hare" which changed radically from the recorded to live version. It presented live much different, much more a "ripping rocker." Like "English Sunset" would in 1999, the song mutated and improved on tour, achieving a life of its own in live performance. The same was true of "Never Comes the Day," listen carefully to the live version on *Caught Live Plus Five* and compare it to the version *on Threshold of a Dream*.

Plainly, the Moody Blues' main strength was (and is) on the live stage, in front of an audience. *Every Good Boy Deserves Favour* is more or less a continuation of the same themes in *Question of Balance*. That is not to diminish the album. While QOB had some of the first experimental laser photography on the inner sleeve of the cover; in EGBDF, Graeme used the cutting-edge technology of electronic drums in "Procession."

The technical innovation continued, though it was restrained to "fine frills" use on the album. For example, it's recording trickery on "Dawning is the Day," the string trilling is NOT a mandolin, but some fun in the studio with stuttering guitar noise. Later in May 1977, *International Musician and Recording World,* Justin changed his mind and said they used a mandolin here: both stories are from valid documents.

And of course, Mike Pinder was constantly refining the sound of electronic keyboards, eventually using the Moog synthesizer as his instrument for the first time on EGBDF. The Moodies were true artists, and rock n' roll scientists; remember those engineering degrees many of them hold??? They were promoting new and innovative technology through the medium of music.

"Dawning is the Day" was used without permission by the U.S. Air Force for recruitment ads on American TV when it first came out. Justin and the other Moodies were not too happy about it (as there was a very ugly war going on at the time) and put a halt to it. In later years, Justin has actually had very nice things to say about the U.S. Armed Forces. Justin was raised right, his parents I'm sure instilled some history into him. The Moody Blues played some gigs at the U.S. Naval Academy and MUD Island (Marines) in the '90s. "Wildest Dreams" showed up in a Blue Angels video in the '90s, which was widely accepted as wonderful by many.

We had a beautiful day when the island gave way to the children of rock and roll -- John Lodge

You can't buy what you give us tonight, God Bless you. -- Ray, at the 1970 Isle of Wight Festival

Desolation Row --Sometime during the early '70s, promoters got the subtle hint that young people wanted to go to big four-day rock concerts, camp out, and to listen to all their favorite rock stars, all in one place. They got the hint after Woodstock (August 1969) broke all attendance records, and young people traveled literally from all over the world to be at the happening.

With this in mind, promoters in England did three years of Isle of Wight festivals. According to Justin (*Record Collector*, spring 2003) there were Isle of Wight concerts in 1968, 1969 (August 30, 1969, Woodside Bay, near Ryde); and 1970; and the Moody Blues played the last two. The first, though poorly documented, is by most accounts something Dylan was involved in; Bob Dylan DID promote the 1969 festival. (Dylan was pop god at the time.)

In the video *Legend of a Band*, John Lodge rather dramatically returns to the scene of the festival via helicopter. His recollection is of the Moody Blues going on stage right at sunset, and opening with his "Minstrel's Song," quite lovely in the video. Which "Isle of Wight" he refers to is unknown; I suspect the 1969 festival, as they played "Sunset" (at sunset) in the 1970 DVD. Remember too that the Moodies played in France during the same weekend they had been offered a gig at Woodstock (August 1969), so they were very busy boys!

The 1970 Isle of Wight festival is VERY well documented thanks to the mercenary long-sightedness of the Farr brothers, the Falk brothers (promoters) and Murray Learner. The video *Message to Love* is an absolute delight; no one is dancing naked in the mud (like at Woodstock.) BUT the cameraman catches people backstage, sitting on the loo, comedians in drag, stalkers heckling Joni Mitchell, Joni practically crying in frustration, TINY TIM (who was no goofball when it came to his dosh), John Sebastian urging everyone to share their weed, Donovan (who invited some hobbits on stage), the Doors, Jimi Hendrix looking like a psychedelic butterfly (not long before he overdosed), Jethro Tull.....and the Moody Blues doing "Nights in White Satin."

It isn't always a beautiful scene, in fact Justin Hayward has occasionally referred to the Isle of Wight festival as having a dark edge to it. The entire set has been released commercially from four bands at this festival now, The Who, Jimi Hendrix, the Doors and the Moody Blues. The whole video is one of the best cross sections I have ever seen of what was going on with young people at that time and is masterful in its production.

The Moody Blues' recollections of that concert are amusing and telling. They dedicated the song "Have You Heard" to Ricky Farr, but it probably went over his head; he looked stoned too. John says he really enjoyed Jimi Hendrix and waited for the last day to see that performance (read on, the story will change.) According to others, Graeme had his share of their money in a black grouch bag, and gave it to their driver to watch, which the driver did very faithfully, sitting on it. Then, after Graeme retrieved his loot, he lived up to the stereotype of all drummers, and proceeded to lose it! And, nicest of all, the Moody Blues were called back for four encores.

Rolling Stone sent reporters too, and the entire thing can be read in *Rolling Stone* October 1, 1970. In an article entitled "Behind the Scenes at the Isle of Wight," RS tried to make the Moodies look like whiners. Maybe they were; many others were whining along with them. There was a lot of money coming in, the cops were fugly, and so were their guard dogs. Graeme mentioned in one Storyteller session, that he saw a stoned dude freaking out badly over the dogs and struggling with the police. He finished the story during Cruise 2014. The police dog actually helped the freaking hippy to get himself together. A good story (score one for the Alsatians.)

In the video, the promoters are made to look more than a bit greedy, playing with a literal mountain of bills! Equalarian waifs and anarchists ("Desolation Row") pounded on the Wall, trying to break it down and come in for free. The good, bad and the ugly are all there, an enduring portrait of "the Real Sixties."

All the Moodies elaborated even further about conditions backstage, on the 2014 Cruise, during Storyteller shows. For one thing, there was NO food if you didn't pack it in yourself (Arlo Guthrie said the same about Woodstock in his 2014 tour), they mentioned a lack of refreshments several times.

Justin also clarified things in *Record Collector* (spring '03) and said the band Free was not getting their money (neither were the Moodies) so Free went in to see the promoters and got a *bit* aggressive. The Moodies tried the same act and *Rolling Stone* put their own spin on it. During the Storyteller Cruise 2014, the same tale went thus: wondering when (or if) they were going on, that last Sunday of the festival, Justin said he ambled into the management office. He found members of the band Free, hanging one of the promoters by his heels!! And they were going through his pockets for their pay!!! ("They got it all" Justin commented glumly.)

Backing hastily out, Justin went back to palaver with his band mates. The fence came down about that point, and Ray commented sarcastically "Well, they'll use this as an excuse to not pay US." See above about "suspicious survivors of rip offs." Ray and Mike (after a couple of belts) decided to pull the same routine Free had (they are not small men) and set off for the office. Justin followed up with "A drink glass sailed out the door and just missed my head, shattered on the wall!"

The Moodies almost pulled out, it got so ugly; the roadies were fighting, and many bands were in complete disarray (*www.zoinksonline.com*, 3-20-2014) Gear and performers couldn't get to the venue due to the hoards of hippies surrounding the place. Despite back stage carnage, the Moodies stuck around, and went on to be part of it. John said simply "It was utter chaos." The Moodies finally (according to John) just announced "We'll go on at 9 pm" which was more or less sunset.

During that cruise (2014) Storyteller, they threw out the figures of 150,000 people at the 1969 Isle of Wight Festival, and over 600,000 the next year for the same festival. Justin says he was in shock at the mass of people, and he looks pretty grim a few times in the video. But Ray acts like he is on Cloud Nine. The video is not to be missed, and if you can track down the *New Music Express* article of Sept 5, 1970, it has an even better (and friendlier) write-up than *Rolling Stone*.

After they finished their show the Moodies wisely decided to make their get-away during the Hendrix set; he was the big-name attraction, and the crowds were rapt watching at him. The Moodies all piled into their van to make the last ferry. In the distance they heard the very last Hendrix concert as poor Jimi and his techs struggled with the amps.

The outcome of all this, was that the large festival shows (Woodstock, Monterey Jazz Festival etc.) demonstrated there was a massive audience for this sort of thing. Management groups started developing into professional systems they are today, efficient organizations that see to the comfort of artists backstage and run tours with the smooth efficiency of a machine.

The Moody Blues performance for the Isle of Wight was released commercially as both a DVD and a CD, with slightly different play lists; apparently not all the video footage was worth including. John said they had the sound cranked up so loud to reach the audience, that he looked over at Ray's pant legs and saw them blowing against his legs from the sound output. (*It took our trouser links off* as John put it.) Justin variously has said "It was a bad day," "I had a few drinks and may have kicked over a few chairs" (!) and "I was just astounded." The band rose to the occasion, and the video came out pretty good. On the CD I think my favorite is "Minstrel's Song" because all those male voices blend so nicely.

I'm talking about the fan phenomenon around the Moody Blues in another chapter; suffice to say it was very weird and scary from about this time on, for the band. The stalker bugging Joni Mitchell in *Message to Love* is a perfect example. Remember too that the Moodies were young men who were experimenting with psychoactive drugs, as was the rest of the generation. It was not only a time of the big band gatherings and love-ins, but also the time of the Moodies playing before that massive Communist rally in France in 1969. The natives were restless, especially in America where the young people were rioting in the streets over the war. Overall, it was enough to make you paranoid!

The weirdness of a few erected a wall between the band and their fans, which was not what the Moodies had wanted in the slightest. About this time, they started calling themselves "The Cobham Mafia." They took to hiring huge bodyguards, and being secretive about their movements, in an effort to find more privacy, as well as to protect their creative efforts from prying fans. They also pulled up in huge black limos to their offices in Cobham, carrying oversized "violin cases" no doubt to the amusement of their neighbors in the Old Bear Pub.

They were in good company. Many bands of the '60s were humanistic but were forced by overwhelming fan adoration to isolate themselves; then the fans would scream that their band was being "elitist." The band that suffered the most was the Beatles, and the pressure eventually broke them up, prompting John Lennon to speak in scathing terms about how his name was not "John Beatle."

But all these performers were only human, and in their isolation, they were forced to socialize ONLY with each other.*** As Graeme put it, the people who did manage to break through the wall of isolation were frequently not nice people at all. The good news was it meant more jobs for security guards, but it was not a fun way to live, for any of the rock stars.

So saying, with the pressures of the lifestyle catching up with them, the Moody Blues went into the endgame of their early years.

*It may have been later, but sometime around here, Justin met a talented musician and producer by the name of Lionel Bart, who wrote *Oliver!* and the scores for the early James Bond movies. In fact, on some bootlegs of Moody concerts in the '80s, Justin can be heard jamming to the James Bond theme during "I'm Just a Singer," which is how Justin Hayward says "tribute." Lionel Bart was well-known for the lush parties at his estate (in the tradition of a good James Bond flick, of course); and apparently during the early years of the band, Justin and Marie (both young and attractive) were always welcome additions to his guest list. Marie Hayward speaks highly of Bart, saying he was kind enough to loan her his telephone to call Justin while he was on tour in America, as she couldn't afford it herself at the time. Justin recalls being impressed by the gold commode seat and mirrored bathrooms at Bart's home. Bart is one of those unsung, talented people who really helped out the Moody effort in the early days. Bart and Justin recorded demos, a musical version of *Gulliver* (aka a *Gulliver's Travels* musical: Nicky Hopkins and Maddy Bell are also part of this) as of this writing, these tracks are available on an album entitled *The Genius of Lionel Bart*; they are VERY good too. Justin was in a special about Lionel Bart in the early '90s, too. Bart passed away in 1999, his estate forwarded the *Gulliver* tapes to Justin, and they are now out on the CD. Larry Gelbart who did *M*A*S*H*, is alleged to have written a screenplay to go with the *Gulliver* tapes, and they were thinking of doing it in 1980, but it apparently never happened. Then. From John Lodge off his blogsite (I trimmed a little), 2009: *Lionel Bart was a great friend of the Moody Blues, we spent many happy times together. He wrote some fabulous rock n' roll songs for English rockers. The first song I became aware of was "Rock with the Caveman" sung by Tommy Steele and the Steelemen. ....Lionel also wrote Butterfingers, another Tommy Steel No 1. Lionel wrote most of his songs on a Danemann baby grand piano. I was with him at his home in London one day and he said to me "John this is the greatest piano for songwriting"...I went out and bought one, which I still have and I wrote "Isn't Life Strange" on it, thank you Lionel. All this is leading to Lionel writing one of the greatest modern musicals, Oliver. Last night I went to Drury Lane Theatre in London to see the musical with Russ Abbot playing the part of Fagin. Russ is a long time friend of mine......Russ is Fagin all this week, if you get a chance do not miss it!*

**Allegedly, Ray also broke a favorite black flute (Sheila) in that trap door incident, and a fan provided him with another for the show. I've seen people accidentally drop through trap doors on stage, and it's one of the worst, scariest things that can happen to a performer. When the stage is painted black, and the lighting is dim (as it has to be backstage) it is absolutely impossible to see holes in the floor; Ray just happened to be in front that fateful day. The Moodies ARE pros though, and pros put safety first. In Portland in the '90s I saw Justin hesitate during the Dino Walk, and carefully place his feet (a bit like a cautious cat!) near the very black edge of the stage right before Intermission. During the break, a stage hand scuttled out with white tape and marked the edge! Justin gets action when he wants it.

***Toward the end of this book, there is mention of a Christmas show the Moodies did in Lake Tahoe, during the '90s. I was lucky to be at that one, and I'm one of those people who tends to look where I'm not supposed to look [being married to a magician does that to you.] The Moodies and Santa lit up the Christmas tree, and then the fireworks went off. While everyone was *OOoohhing* at the fireworks, I watched down in the shadows behind the platform, where the Moodies were whisked away between security guards. Ray (who was having a great time in his Santa hat up on the stage) had a paralysed, almost depressed (disgusted?) expression on his face. After thirty years of being treated like that by control freak guards, it must get very weird to be cut off from humanity. Which brings to mind another "Ray" story. At some point during the early years, Ray said they bought some tickets from a scalper. and went out in front of the theatre and passed them out for free. No one even recognized them as band members. Ray is that kind of guy..... doesn't take the "fortune and fame" thing too seriously.

IX) Land of Make Believe: 1971-February 4, 1974

When the world gets a bit ragged, people turn back to romanticism for an escape -- John Lodge

It was like driving around in a big wad of bubble gum -- Kurt Vonnegut

As success made them mega-stars, their world got smaller. And the technology got weirder.

Seventh Sojourn was released in November of '72, but the first single from the album, that John Lodge had written, "Isn't Life Strange?" had snuck into the American top 30 some five months earlier. -- Redbeard

With their hectic lifestyle, scheduling studio time got too complex, so the Moodies began recording in Mike's garage in Beckthorns. The ceiling of the garage was high, the heat was unbearable (they recorded at night), but that was where the better recording gear was, now that Mike could buy The Best. John and Justin completed the vocals on "Isn't Life Strange" about 2 am in the morning, mixing it on the spot. The next morning the band boarded the plane for New York, with the master. The following week it was out as a single, to go with their tour. As John put it, *That's how things happened then......it's quite amazing* [today], *because we're talking about high-tech CD now, and the actual record was made in a garage. Original garage band, we were.* (from an interview with Redbeard.)

Sometime in 1971, that unique "new sound" that had gotten them the big push into the spotlight, began to turn into a monster. The conflict between good music, and the Pindertronics-Edgetronics special-effects-concept continually reared its ugly head. According to technician Tony Clarkson, the fall 1971 tour was a wreck technically. Everyone allegedly chickened out on running the monster mixing board, even unto Tony Clarke and Pete Jackson.

From his interview (*Higher and Higher* #30), Clarkson got the job by default.

After the tour (which was a technical mess), the band "cleaned house" and Clarkson was no longer on the crew, along with a lot of others. Around the same time (very early 1972), they picked up Mike "Micky" Keyes, who was to eventually become their head technician and road manager. Keyes was their road manager even unto the '90s, and next only to God when it came to behind-the-scenes work. For what it's worth, Mike Keyes looks and sounds like a twin to the Diva's road manager in a movie *The Fifth Element*. Maybe he did a cameo. Wavy Gravy did. I digress.

I had a former roadie tell me a very funny story about this era: apparently he was touring with the back-up band for the Moodies (Dr. West and the Medicine Show?) He was staggering around on the stage pre-show, trying to get set up, and had the bad fortune of falling into the drum kit. He reported that he was treated to a "Cockney tongue lashing" of magnificent proportions from Graeme! After some of the interviews of the time about electronic drums, and leaking EMF making the drums play on their own, one can only shudder to think of the chaos.

At least one accident happened this tour, in '71 or '72, in Phoenix, the truck with the gear wrecked, luckily the drivers and sound techs were ok. The only piece of gear they had for the show was the mellotron (which was rushed to the show on time) and of course, Justin's 335, which he rarely lets out of his sight and was hand-carrying. John, Justin and Mike said in various interviews, they would have extra mellotrons shipped to venues AHEAD of the tour, in case one of them died or coughed up its tape-guts in an unexpected manner.

It was either a variation of the same story, or the same thing happened in Chicago during their tour with Canned Heat, but their gear truck wiped out and they lost all their stuff. Canned Heat drove on through their day off, and set up so the Moodies could play their gig. One of the nice events in the history of rock n' roll. (Brooklands interview, April 27, 2009)

From *New Musical Express* dated September 25, 1971: the fall tour in the U.K. featured an electronic drum kit, which was rapidly scrapped when it became too unruly to play on stage. Sometime in early November, John got sick with flu, and they had to cancel about five shows. So the stress indeed got to them in various ways, both physically and electronically. They had something going for them though, even if the electronics gave them a hard time. The *Court of the Crimson King*, pretty much a cloned Moody Blues album, was selling big time in the early '70s. Imitation is the sincerest form of flattery they say. The market for the music style was there: could they keep up with the demand?

A Fish Tale..... Then you had some of the cast and crew that led an entirely separate life, free and unencumbered by space age technology. Taking the Wayback Machine to the '90s, I found myself cruising the streets of Seattle with some Moody friends, and they started talking about this four-star hotel called "The Edgewater." Yeah the Beatles had stayed there, and had publicity pictures taken with them hanging out the window, fishing! I wonder if the Moodies ever did that? Seattle is a weird town, the birthplace of not only Jimi Hendrix, Tom Huelett, and Bill Gates, but also of organized labor. Puget Sound is also the home to a primitive (and not too bright) shark with six gills.

Never underestimate a story from Seattle. Anything can happen. You often discount stray thoughts and rumors, and then you find out "Truth is stranger than fiction." YES the Moody Blues did stay at the Edgewater during their visits to Seattle.* The Moody Blues had been to Seattle in the fall of 1968 (backed up by the early Led Zeppelin.) "Fishing out the windows" was a standard thing with visiting rock bands, there was actually a tackle shop in the lobby, or near the hotel.

According to Tony Clarkson (*Higher and Higher* #30), friend and fishing crony of Ray Thomas, he and the other Moody crew-members had arrived early (this is in

1971); and finding some slack time, rounded up fishing poles and hung hooks out the windows at the Edgewater. No dice. They weren't biting.

Never fear, the expert eventually arrived, had done his homework, and Ray (Lord and Master of all fish) revealed that the lurking monsters of Puget Sound could only be lured by the prospect of salmon-belly bait. The belly bait was found, and in short order, Ray managed to land a genuine whopper. In a year 2000 interview, Ray made a very cute comment about just "kissing 'em and putting them back" when it comes to angling. I suspect he thought better of his philosophy that fateful day at the Edgewater. He hauled in a four-foot sand shark, which proceeded to thrash around his room, wrecking furniture and stinking up the carpet.

Either from his natural compassion, not having a baseball bat handy, or deciding prudence was the better part of valor, Ray and the roadies grappled the shark by the tail and heaved it bodily out the window. And you know Ray blew it a kiss as it swam away, picking the hook out of its teeth. No doubt the shark couldn't believe its good fortune and went back to lurking under the kitchen windows of that premier hotel, waiting for goodies to fall.

When they told the desk staff the story, they were met with peals of laughter. Ray, Tony and crew, not being very pleased by the lack of faith on the part of their hosts, proceeded to fill up the bathtub with a large assortment of small sharks and cod. We presume Ray showered with fish fins between his toes! We all get our thrills in different ways. Then they checked out and never said a word to the staff. (FYI John told the same story at the Cruise IV/Storyteller II, with embellishments.)

The Moodies were lucky: they all got along fine (sorta) in their fame-generated isolation; they dealt with the pressure with humor and referred to the repeating conversations by index number. But many popular "superstar" bands of the late '60s and early '70s did not fare so well. Even with the even-tempered and intelligent

Moodies, it was bound to catch up with them. Touring stress was beyond belief, considering some of the wrinkles that arose. It may have been this tour when their van broke down a mile from the airport in a blinding blizzard, and the only way to catch their plane was to run down the freeway, guitars and bags in hand. It all seems glamorous until you have to do something like that....

Graeme in some interviews, said he was mildly annoyed with the idolizing that was part of their fan following. In response, he wanted to change the format of the band and was all in favor of issuing an album cover along the lines of "Phi Zappa Krappa" (a very funny poster from the time period, which, if you have never seen it, would probably not be appropriate for our present tale. I don't wish to shock any children. Google it.) But the collective band thought better of their public image and continued to promote a "gentleman band" front.

As has been said elsewhere, the Moodies may have had indiscretions like every normal human has in a normal life; but they maintained a clean-cut public image, and no one has been able to dig up much dirt on them. That may be why they have not ever been overly splashed in the spotlight. The private lives they live are much too clean and rational for the tastes of salacious reporters.

Like it or not, about this time the Moodies began to get treated like "cash cows" by promoters, which would wear on anyone with brains. Most creative people would rather be recognized for what's in their hearts and minds, or for their accomplishments, not for being a Boy Toy Doll. However, just the same, the promoters started making the Moodies into sex symbols. Pictures of Ray and Justin, wearing fur coats, began to pop up in promotional photos and fanzines. Ray has a huge moustache, wild hair, and looks like a mad Viking.

This trend continues even unto the 21st Century. Photos of the Moody Blues are hot sellers on Ebay, while tour t-shirts and collectables languish without bids. Even unto the '90s, frantic fans would wrestle security guards for telescopic cameras and film, in the front rows of every Moody Blues show. Even with all the beautiful music produced and orchestrated by this very talented band, even with their intelligent thoughts about the world, and their interesting history, it seems the only way some fans can relate is through a "pretty boy" sex objectification. It makes about as much sense and is about as productive as a Miss America pageant.

Having said that, Graeme and Justin have both, at various times in their interviews, said they enjoyed being "sexy and attractive" very much during this time, and really had fun with the birds!

Never underestimate a story from Seattle. (I said that already didn't I?) According to myth, sometime in 1972, an all-night DJ in Seattle ran across the re-released "Nights in White Satin" single. He had this problem: every night around midnight, Mother Nature murmured to him, so he took a magazine and retired to the "library," leaving the tape to roll. As it turned out, "Nights" was nice and long, with a juicy dramatic poem tacked on the end of it, and just fit his break slot. Other documentation will say he was signing off with "Nights," no doubt "sleepless in Seattle." (Yes we have White Nights in Seattle.)

Anyway, he started giving "Nights" a lot of air-time. The whole thing snowballed again, and suddenly the Moodies had a chart-topping single in America, and a chart-topping album *Days of Future Passed*, five years after its first release. Later that year, *Seventh Sojourn* would join it in the Top Ten. The concept behind *Seventh Sojourn* was to have been, like *Pilgrim's Progress* or the *Canterbury Tales*, a tale about people sitting around a campfire telling stories to one another. Never mind that the pictures of the campfire were really on *To Our Children's Children's Children*, or that the driftwood on the cover wouldn't manifest poetically until Justin's song on *Octave*, four years later. It was where they were at that moment: in between.

"New Horizons" and "Land of Make Believe" are obviously a reflection of Justin's joy in having his daughter in 1972, and in making his house a *home*. Mike's "Lost in a Lost World," the most raw and gutsy song on the album, reflects the discouragement of six young men who really thought they were going to make a difference, and who thought they had failed. John's "I'm Just a Singer in a Rock and Roll Band" is a forlorn attempt to ground the growing madness around the band, and bring everyone back to reality.

Their music was a reflection of society at that time too. The Viet Nam War was getting worse and worse. The album opens with the words "I woke up today I was crying." That pretty well summed up their feelings, and the feelings of many young people. There were pictures of scorched Earth on TV. There were photos of little children with napalm burns, we saw it all in prime time, on the evening news, with our suppers. Our best and brightest young men were forced to fight (and die) in a war that no one wanted. The Moodies were in a position to do something about it (or so they thought) but here they were in the lap of luxury as rock stars, watching young people riot in the streets of America. It all felt WRONG. "I'm Just A Singer in a Rock and Roll Band" was how John expressed his confusion and concern.

The other half of the equation was that the Moodies were turning out to be like the Beatles, people chased them down the streets and security kept them isolated from the rest of humanity. Graeme had his brush with Beatle-hunting maenads back in the "Go Now" days (so did Mike), Graeme (as the survivor of a neck choking incident with groupies) was all in favor of the low-profile approach. He and Mike especially became wary and convinced the rest of the band to go easy on spreading their faces across too many fan magazines. Weintraub confirmed this in his autobiography, he marketed the Moodies as "Everyone's second favorite band," which kept them flying under the radar without stopping the cash flow. That was just fine with the Moodies.

Mike Pinder says that the year 1972 was a happy time for him (*Goldmine*). I think the band must have been considering Southern California in the early '70s, for recording (as per *Ever Sense the Dawn* which Tony Clarke produced, recorded in L.A. then mixed in U.K.) Both Mike's wife Donna and Ray's wife Gill had family there. No coincidence that Southern California is where Mike would settle to live when the band split up in 1974; Mike started building a studio in Malibu during 1971.

People react to the same situations from different perspectives. The whole band sounded like they were really strung out, and maybe trying to do too much with too little time. The Moodies start to show the strain in photos: their eyes take on the appearance of deer caught in the headlights of a car, or they clutch guitars, looking a bit insecure.

Seventh Sojourn was certified as Gold before it was even released, on advanced sales. (If that doesn't impress you, nothing will!) The Moody Blues were awarded "Vocal Group of the Year" by *Playboy Magazine,* 1972 (I'd call that "arriving"!)

Even so, it sounds like a lot of hot air was being blown around and memories were strained. For example, various reports about their pipe organ (upon which John wrote "Isn't Life Strange") were that either it was "there already in the studio" (as per Mike) or was carried in (and rebuilt) from a nearby church. John tells a lovely story about the writing of "Isn't Life Strange," that it "wrote itself." He claims literally to have heard their pipe organ playing it (with no one at the keyboards), and so he walked in to write the song. It's one of John's favorite stories, and easily found in many interviews. Then in later interviews he claimed he wrote that song on a piano! (See earlier footnotes on Lionel Bart.)

"Isn't Life Strange" was released as a single before the main album. Much of the album was recorded in Mike Pinder's garage, rather than the expensive studio they had at their beck and call. The Moog was used on "Melancholy Man." Mike said he had been trying for a "French sound" for the song, and apparently got it, as that song was very popular in France. As well as the relatively new Moog, Mike used a Chamberlain synthesizer (an upgraded version of the mellotron), on *Seventh Sojourn*.

Behind the scenes, they flatly were having trouble getting something on tape that they were satisfied with. It just would not come together, the cause being technical as well as emotional. The gear in Decca One was not up to their standards, and they had better equipment in the garage.

The album, like the year it was born, seems scattered to the four winds, and lacks a central theme. John had a serious case of pneumonia during this time and was hospitalized. They toured and toured. They recorded stuff and didn't like it. It all "sounded alike" or was "stale." Graeme claimed their lifestyle and work got to him when he had hippies come up and prostrate themselves in front of him, asking for his blessing. (Yes this really happened.) There stood Graeme "with a drink in one hand and a fag in the other" and this hippy had been on macrobiotics for a year, preparing himself to be blessed by his heroes. *Blblblbl.*

Despite their weary souls, the books looked pretty good. Things were going so well financially, that they started setting up a world tour and had plans to go to India, where oddly, some 300,000 albums had been sold in one small village! They looked closer at the stats and found that village only had 500 people in it. It turned out that someone was buying the albums, then shipping them by mule, over the Kyber Pass into the USSR (which the US had a trade embargo with at the time.) I don't think the Moodies ever DID get to India. (Interview with Edge, *Morning Call* 7-31-14)

Early 1973 was taken up with legal matters; Justin had a new daughter, too! Then they finally got back together, did a world tour, and tried recording again. Graeme says in interviews of late 1972, they dumped and demagged enough music for a double album. In fact, they told the press they were going to issue a double album in 1973, after *Seventh Sojourn*, and they dumped that too. Justin would say later "we had 'arrived,' and we were unhappy." I guess they were, to be so disillusioned.

Out take: *I once had the pleasure of getting acquainted with a major league rookie baseball player who was first with the Cleveland Indians, then went to another major league team. He's good hitter, and awesome in his physical abilities. But, people are human, and they are going to have "off" days. For a young athlete, no matter how gifted, to hit a homer EVERY time he gets up to the plate, is........ well they don't all change their clothes in telephone booths, after all! No surprise, his wife has a degree in psychology. The stress and pressure on young men in their twenties, suddenly shoved into the limelight is incredible, not just to achieve, but to MAINTAIN that level. And when my rookie friend was traded, he got only ONE HOUR notice to pack his bags. Talk about feeling like a pawn in a very nasty game!*

Graeme Edge would later say "Music is a dirty, dirty business" in one of his radio interviews, and he's sadly correct. It's the same for *any* high-profile celebrity in our society, when fans demand so much from our heroes and public figures. So, bear that in mind whenever someone you like, who is a "star" or a public figure, "transgresses" in some way. We truly are only human, all of us. The need to out-do your last spectacular deed can be a heady spiral to stress indeed.

One wonders if it was really bad, or if the Moodies were just deeply unhappy with the way things were. One major problem was obsolete gear. As of August 1973, they had a new studio in the works (Decca One), which would eventually become the state-of-the-art recording studio in England. They wanted to go home and use their new studio, not tour forever.

Out take: <u>Seventh Sojourn</u> *is very dear to me now but was not at the time, oddly. In 1972, the Moody Blues were "all the rage" finally; for me it was senior year and the ending of my childhood. My high school friends and I had been getting together for four years now, comparing our collection of Moody albums; each of us had two or so albums, but between us, we had them all; we loved to get together and play them. I distinctly remember my friend John McCarron looking up when some casual acquaintance of ours had gushed about "Nights in White Satin" which was currently reaching #2 status. With a snarl and a lift of the lip, John muttered "Where have THEY been for the last four years?"*

Really. It was kids like us, and our big brothers and sisters, bringing the Moody albums back from Viet Nam, and from college, that got the songs out to the rest of the people, who got that Underground band the "popular" recognition they deserved. The senior poem for my Class of 1972 (in Southern California) was Graeme's "The Dream." My brother, who had brought home <u>Days of Future Passed</u> in 1968, bought me <u>Seventh Sojourn</u> for Christmas of 1972. It was brand new. I listened to the tracks, loved "For My Lady" but somehow failed to get into it, because it doesn't really hang together well........and I put the album away among the others while I settled into my early college years. The Moodies were too popular. They were no longer "cool," when the entire world knew who they were. We all had other things to do. The Moody Blues were going the same way the Beatles had gone, the commercials were now going to ram them down our throats with ads for perfume and cars.

In 1972, Richard Nixon, terrified he was going to lose the election, finally wound down the hideous war in Viet Nam that killed so many fine young American men in my generation, or left them maimed in mind, body or soul. It took Nixon over four years to make good on that campaign promise that won him the first election, and only the threat of political defeat got him off his butt. (That and giving 18 year-olds the right to vote.)

With the Fall of Saigon, America lost our only armed conflict in our 200 year history. The veterans came home, confused, shell-shocked, and terrified to wear their uniforms in public. I know American sailors who were actually spit on for wearing their uniforms in bus stations. They didn't want to go to war either, but they joined the Navy voluntarily to keep their hides out of the Draft and rice paddies. Those who had not gone to war were shell-shocked in their own way.

If the interviews James Morrison gave are to be believed; one of his favorite quotes is that *more young people died in the streets of America due to drug overdose, than died in the trenches of Viet Nam.* Jim was intelligent; his sources are unknown. But it brings up a good point. By 1972, rock stars Jim Morrison, Janis Joplin, and Jimi Hendrix (among so many others) also had passed over to the Other Side, in very creative ways, with the excessive use of sex, drugs, and rock n' roll. The Beatles break-up (and documentary *Let It Be* showing the entire process) in May 1970, must have affected the Moodies. They knew the Beatles. It could happen to even the most talented bunch of guys, if you pushed matters too far.

In the early '70s, England wasn't "swinging like a pendulum" anymore, at all....in fact, the whole bunch of us, on both sides of The Water, seemed to be doing a lot of dangling. Like warriors returning home, the entire generation decided to take up ploughshares; the "war" (whatever war they happened to be fighting) was over. Everyone moved to the country and started making babies and growing things.......

There's something really weird about the cover art for *Seventh Sojourn*, which was painted for the album in early 1972. The scene is of piles of driftwood, laying about on a very deserted beach; it's dead, and looks like a moonscape. But if you look closely on the inside of the album, there is a little sprout of tiny leaves trying to grow and renew itself on one of the logs. That's how it was in the early '70s. It wasn't just the Moody Blues, it was our entire generation that felt the same way.

San Francisco in the middle '60s was a very special time and place to be a part of. .... we were riding the crest of a high and beautiful wave. ... Now less than five years later you can go up on a steep hill in Las Vegas and look west and with the right kind of eyes, you can almost see the high-water mark, that place where the water finally broke and rolled back. --Hunter Thompson

John Lodge always says, the turning point for him came when they were flying around on their world tour in 1973/1974. They played that year in Japan (Tokyo, Osaka for two nights, and Nagoya), Hawaii, Europe and America.

The band was in their own 747 jumbo jet, dubbed "Starship One," with the name painted down the side of the plane. John realized there was an organist playing somewhere, and here were all these bedrooms with palatial furnishings. And just the band there, up in front, talking with the crew; no wild parties; by now the Moody Blues really were family men, and didn't have wild ongoing orgies with their entourage.

And John said he got up and wandered around the plane, and it was a big flying NOTHING (his words). They had arrived at the height of luxury, and it was not all that exciting; they had isolation with nothing but each other for company. That was John's turning point. Their world tour terminated in California (February 4, 1974); and shortly thereafter, they decided to let the entire thing rest for a while. *Rolling Stone Magazine* did not announce the split until October 10, 1974, eight years after the adventure began.

To show how confused they were, Graeme remembers the tour as ending in Los Angeles, yet others remember it as ending at the Cow Palace in San Francisco, on Feb 4th. One article of the times claims John actually ended their last concert with the words "I'm just a singer in a Rock and Roll band." It's a wonderfully dramatic and fitting closure, if it's true. With seven albums on their resume, "after seven days they rested."

In an interview, Graeme Edge remembered the split as him walking down a street in Los Angeles and wondering if he would ever play the drums again. For some reason, that vision is more poignant than John's story of the break up….it seems so forlorn. Graeme is the Aries "clown in the show" but this was one show he didn't know how to laugh with.**

Mike and Ray have never had public reactions to the split, but you have to assume that, being Capricorns, they both greeted the decision with visions of long fishing trips with sons, dancing in their heads. Seldom mentioned, they lost the windshield on their plane on the way to Japan in 1974, had to make an emergency layover in Alaska, and were stuck in an unheated terminal for a few hours. (They all bought fur coats!!) (Justin Q&A March 17, 2011) Different things get to people differently; Justin tells the tale with typical banality, but it might have had some thinking too much about their collective karma.

In his autobiography (*When I Stop Talking You'll Know I'm Dead)*, Jerry Weintraub claims the Moodies broke up due to one of them thinking he could do better on his own without the group. It's not uncommon with many bands. If that really WAS the reason, it's band business and they aren't talking. Read on.

Justin recalls the breakup as happening in Decca's studio canteen in Tollington Park (*Record Collector*, 2003.) Justin said he and Tony Clarke were doing some tracks; they recorded a song eventually called "Island" around this time, for the "new album" that never happened. Remember, for "luck" they always started recording with a Justin song. Anyway, Tony and Justin came down to the canteen, where the rest of the band had been holding a meeting while Justin sang, and they told him they wanted to "put things on hold." According to Justin (Q&A Mar 17, 2011), Mike acted like he didn't want to work with Tony anymore, and Mike was moving to California.***

Justin always says of that moment "At the time I thought we were crazy, as we had just achieved everything we hoped for, but looking back, it was the best thing we ever did." Justin would also say in later interviews, that he really took himself far too seriously back in those early days......

* Justin mentioned in an interview that Tom Huelett, their good friend and quasi-manager lived in Seattle, and the band used to visit him, go to baseball games, and hydrofoil races too!

** In fairness to Graeme, it's entirely possible that they DID break up in Los Angeles, as the band has often done business there; for all any of us know, that's where it really did end, rather than right after the last show in San Francisco. Perhaps it is most accurate to say, the break up happened in different places for different people. Obviously they weren't talking to each other very well, were they?

*** Mike has said in later years that he was under incredible stress with the way the band was going when they broke up, and it's a fact that Mike and Tony began working together again toward the end of Tony's life.

X) Middle 8: Further from the shore: 1974-1977

There is a timeless feeling in a recording studio-no time passes at all while working. -- Jim Cockey (interview, *Higher and Higher* #7/8)

We're much more an introverted band, talking about things that happen personally to us. Those things are universal, that's why Shakespeare is still a great playwright, everyone can still relate to him -- the actual basic human condition has not changed....we split up when we ran out of ideas --Graeme Edge, *The Source* (audio interview 1984)

The Moodies were gifted a spot in a "Top Ten Progressive Rock" show that aired in the U.K. (March 3, 2001). The premise of the entire special was that the top blew off music in 1967, and "Prog Rock" was the result. Sadly, this special lumped Hawk Wind in with Jethro Tull and the Moodies. Music-wise, the '70s got pretty weird, many bands spent the next ten years wearing bat suits, or things even stranger. They tried to re-invent a Bohemian movement by doing ANYTHING on stage (the more gross, the better.) I would hesitate to call this "progressive." Just my opinion. Everyone has one.

People enjoy "weird" but this is not new; sometime in the early 1900s, the Marx Brothers made a living out of chasing cockroaches across the stage and betting on them, to point out just one example of The Weird. Pop music got just *nasty* in the '70s, and it is no wonder the Moodies took some time off. You can't sell Nice Hippy Music when surrounded by Satanic verse.

All was not happy in Moody Land in 1973. Another fan sent me this article over the Internet, he didn't know the source, and neither do I (he suggested *Audio* or *Stereo Review*.) However, I'm going to transcribe a quote from it anyway, as it says a lot: "The Moodies were getting ripped apart," John said. "We were only 'passengers' on this express train, where we had been the drivers. The last tour took five lawyers, ten accountants, fourteen road managers, and twenty thousand other personnel, all of them arranging *our* lives to earn *their* livings." In another interview with Michael Jackson (L.A. talk show host), John sums up their breakup as, "We were suffocating." And in *Moodymania* #3, we find a quote, "We had become too big and we were trapped in the MOODIES and we were living our lives in rooms and out of boxes."

So, despite what Justin said about being crazy at the time, maybe there was something right about their decision to take a short hiatus. They sold their jet airliner *Starship One* to Led Zeppelin and took it easy. They backed off from the HUGE touring, but they also had to keep managing their lives. The band was still based out of their offices in Cobham, Surrey, and they saw each other on a very regular basis, dropping in to their various offices and desks, doing the business that a band must do day to day, to remain a viable commercial entity.

It was also a good thing to take a break for personal reasons: at least one (maybe more) Moody Blue took the time to have work done on teeth. (The jokes in *Austin Powers* are too true!) We Americans don't always appreciate this, but English families in the '50s didn't have the cash for braces, and crooked teeth can do bad things to a young man's ego. If nothing else, getting nice teeth was worth all the long hours touring for the good pay it brought.

At various times in interviews, over the years, all of the Moody Blues have professed more than a passing interest in gardening; Justin had palm trees in his garden in Cornwall, due to a quirk in the Gulf Stream. Graeme spent much of his off time in "knee waders" bug-hunting in the Wetlands, waving a net and capturing newts. (No kidding, in fact he wanders off golf courses to do this sometimes.) Ray enjoyed playing his flute by his own fishpond. They ALL had small children, and a little more "at home" life was going to make for happier families.

So, in 1974, they STOPPED and paid more attention to personal matters. December 21, 1972, the article

"In Search of the Moody Blues" in *Rolling Stone Magazine* also said a good deal. Mike Pinder, even then, was pulling away from band activities. Sure, he was one of the guys when the rubber met the road, in the studio recording. But it was plain from the article, done at the real height of the success of the early days, that Mike was resisting the direction of the energy in the band.

Mike's quest for his spirituality would be a serious factor later in band history. In his FoMP newsletters, Mike says that in 1971 he was building his OWN studio at the Indigo Ranch in Southern California. The songbook *A Question of Balance,* distributed in 1970 by MCA Music, has the foreshadowing of things to come in the future decade for the Moodies, only (of course) things didn't turn out quite that way. The articles of the time reflect the same; the Moodies wanted to break it down a bit and had different ideas on what makes "good music."

As of 1970, the score was: Mike and Graeme were going to do a more electronic album together; one interview goes so far as to dub Graeme's electronic drums "Edgetronics." Ray wanted to do a song that would cause bowel movements in the Albert Hall. (Leave it to the Capricorn to crack the scatological jokes.) Justin makes romantic, cryptic comments. Justin and Ray were discussing doing an acoustic album together "with just a flute and a guitar" we must assume. Justin and Tony probably kicked in together on *Ever Sense the Dawn*. At one point, Graeme was talking about making an album with Ray Thomas, to be called *Tops and Tails* but (bummer) it never came about (*Music Week*, Sept 6, 1975).

And who eventually made the "most Moody-like" album together, but John and Justin (and Tony) on *Blue Jays*. Ray sang back-up on Graeme's *Kick off Your Muddy Boots*. Ray and Justin both performed on Nicky James' *Thunderthroat;* Ray plays bass flute on "Maggie" and Justin plays quite a bit of guitar on "Bottle of Cheap Red Wine." (*Thunderthroat,* THS-19) Even though Graeme and Justin had been roomies, and chased birds together; even though Ray and

Mike went to the fleshpots of cabaret Germany together; and even though it all started at age 14 with Ray and John meeting on a bus...there was no ganging up of two against the others. They all had different personalities, yet stayed one group of friends and mates, and even extended that to their old Brummie friends.

At the Crossroads--According to *The Source* (a radio interview done in 1984), after the early '70s split up, Mike stayed in Los Angeles where his wife's family lived. Justin went to work recording with him, and they waited for the rest of the band. Eventually Tony Clarke showed up, and Mike seemed ambivalent about the whole thing.

So Justin and Tony packed up and went back to England, not only to home, but to check out their new space-age studio, which was almost finished. Graeme said the studio had an oval shape to it for the acoustics, and others said it looked like the bridge of the starship *Enterprise*. Justin would later talk about "going through countless remodels" speaking of horse farms, studios, and homes, so I would say he was around for the building of their West Hampstead studio. Remember, Justin started out working in a building supply store; he seems to be a bit of a closet architect.

In later years, according to interviews, Justin was the one who would walk around the Royal Albert Hall (for example) and along with the sound crew, test the place for acoustics. This is an obscure side-light to architecture, the acoustics of buildings. Certain shapes encourage certain sound waves is the simplest explanation. Justin is a musician who understands this. Be impressed.

Their new studio was finally finished and opened on July 17, 1974. Tom Tompkins would later say of the New Improved Decca One Starship Studio that "We could fly this baby to Mars!" They actually called the control room "The Bridge." The Moodies claim they got some of their recording gear from NASA in Houston; why NASA needed recording equipment I don't know, Westlake Audio is mentioned as the manufacturer. One visitor dubbed the huge tape machine from NASA "Big Bertha." The studio had state-of-the-art technology; cameras were put in every corner, so they could monitor all movements from the control room, like Big Brother.

For the record, the first song to be recorded in the remodeled West Hampstead studios, is "Remember Me, My Friend" for *Blue Jays*. It wasn't just about John and Justin: it was about the entire band. Justin said later that the song was "so good" that they just kept on playing, for like nine minutes. Tony Clarke talked about coming into the studio at 4 am to work with Justin and John on the *Blue Jays* album, as Graeme was working on his "Muddy Boots" album at the same time. The weird hours began to get to Tony about this time, and in later interviews, he says of this time, he was "physically exhausted" and unable to do more than one album at a time.

We Like To Do It--Graeme Edge, as forlorn as his parting thoughts that February day in Los Angeles must have been, didn't waste any time finding out if he was to play drums again. He didn't wait for the official announcement that was to come in *Rolling Stone* later that year, he was the first to release his own solo single "We Like To Do It." A honky-tonk special, it's one of the cheeriest songs done by any of the Moody Blues in any of their combined repertory and was gladly welcomed by the Moody fans of the time.

Kick Off Your Muddy Boots was supposed to be a fun album, more loose and open than work with the Moody Blues. Unfortunately it was not a huge success; it seemed that no matter how good the song, it needed that magical "Moody Blue" label to be stuck on it, or it didn't sell. "We Like To Do It" was the first released commercially from the new studio. Graeme must have been breathing down the Jays' neck to get that one out!

Free of touring and the demands of recording by Group-think, Graeme turned to private pursuits (as did the rest of the band.) He has a huge love of flying and sailing, and didn't hesitate to indulge himself, with all the free time he had on his hands. Sometime during the '70s, in between his two solo albums (to little or no notice from the musical world, despite them being rather good); he did a solo trip around the world in his boat, the 75-foot *Delia*. It had to do with being a "tax exile," he had to be out of the U.K. for a year. He parked the *Delia* in the Mediterranean for a while, off the island of Corfu, then went around the world; which way was not made clear. He said of that time later "I thought I was God," finishing the statement with a hysterical cackle.

According to the promo package for *Paradise Ballroom,* Graeme's sailing claims are a bit more modest, he hung around the Greek isles for a while, absorbing Greek music. (If you ever visit Greece, you'll feel like you've fallen into a *Zorba the Greek* soundtrack, great music, very fun.) After that, Graeme sailed the *Delia* over to the Caribbean, arriving in the Bahamas at Christmas of 1975; and of course, he absorbed all the reggae he could while there.

In April 1976, he sailed back to the U.K. to start recording *Paradise Ballroom*. In later interviews, he said, "I ran out of money and had to go back to work!"

Graeme got into hang-gliding with an Eagle II ultralight, and eventually had to give it up around 1986 as "the insurance companies caught up with me." Plainly Graeme is the sort of guy who loves to feel the wind in his hair. As well, all his globe-trotting exposed him to various drumming styles, a definite enhancement to his art. Drumming is perhaps the most universal music of all cultures.

Sometime in the '72-'74 time frame, Graeme met Sue, (who was to become Mrs. Edge #2) working as an office manager, and was smitten. Sue's sister was married to one of the Gurvitz brothers, and they all got together for an album. Graeme did his two solo albums from 1974 to 1977, with the Gurvitz's. The Gurvitz's have their own following in the music world, and I've actually found *Kick off Your Muddy Boots* filed under "Gurvitz" in used record stores. And the store owners then say "Who is Graeme Edge?" No kidding.

Graeme later, in his "Nightbird" interviews, alluded to having been more involved in the writing of many of the songs on their albums than he wanted to admit. Ginger Baker, former drummer for Cream, also worked with Graeme and the Gurvitz brothers on the albums. Baker has worked with the Gurvitz's on their albums too, without Graeme; all are associated with groups like The Baker-Gurvitz Army, The Sex Pistols, and The Gun. So again, various Moodies were benefiting from getting exposure to other artists and ideas.

Later, the issue of "some of the band lives in Los Angeles" would be a sticking point in Moody album production. The point being, that when you are making an album, you really need to be on-hand, and can't be jetting half the way around the world on a spur of the moment. Adrian Gurvitz lived in Graeme's Surrey home during the making of their solo albums, and they happily used the Decca One Studio.

Carol (Mrs. Edge #1) had left Graeme not more than a year after they were married, and moved in with Terence Stamp, the accomplished actor who played General Zod in *Superman*. (And he acted in other movies of course, at least one of the "Star Wars" movies. Terence Stamp was in India from the late '60s until the late '70s, so I'll leave that up to you to figure out. In April 2018 Justin did say during an interview that all their girlfriends also did TM, and Stamp went to India to the Maharishi's ashram. I *think*.) The last I read, Carol wasn't living with Stamp any more either, and she continues to make random splashes in U.K. social circles.

Graeme's second serious lady was named Sue, and he makes a very funny comment in one of the fan club magazines about why they were not married, even though I think she had already had Graeme's son. Matthew was born just as they started to record *Octave*. You'll have to say it to yourself but think about how it sounds: Sue Edge. Oh dear, *cringe!* Be that as it may, I think Sue and Graeme finally married, and lived in relative sanity a few years at least.

During Howard Stern's interview where Graeme chatted about it all, he certainly didn't seem to bear any wives ill will, nor was he secretive about any of it.

Graeme was not the only one to have a boat. Ray also had a yacht named *Mfawnwy* (Gaelic for "beloved"). John Lodge was allegedly into speed-boat racing for a bit, and had a boat called the *See Saw Blue*. (One of the Moodies let slip they used to hang out at Tom Huelett's home in Seattle, and there is a lot of hydrofoil racing here. *Never underestimate a story from Seattle!)* John too had a yacht at one time (Brooklands, April 27, 2009.)

Graeme was serious about his sailing, his ships over the years have been the *Delia* in the '70s (75 foot), the *Sojourn* (32 foot) and the *Cutter Edge* in 1985 (52 foot). The nice thing about shipboard living is that you can up anchor and go where the action is. Graeme was anchored in Boston for a long time in the '80s, and then anchored his *Cutter Edge* in Florida, where the good golfing is. I think he sold the *Cutter Edge* in the '90s, as he wasn't using it. AND by the mid '70s, all the Moodies had pool table rooms in their homes (they call it snooker in England) so plainly, as English gentlemen, they had "arrived."

Meanwhile Back in Pinderland--I do favor unexpected chord changes -- Mike Pinder (07-15-04 in chat on *moodytalk.com*) After the Moodies went their separate ways, Mike Pinder lost no time setting up housekeeping in California. Mike had the garage studio in Surrey which the whole band used, but the English economy took a dive, so he changed his focus to California, and shipped his equipment there. At the time, a lot of rock n' roll artists from England were "under the gun" from a ravenous tax situation in England, and were doing a lot of things, like moving elsewhere, to avert this. Justin has talked about this in interviews; at the time, 83% of their income was being taken for taxes in the U.K.

The laws were something like Mike could not be more than sixty days per year in the U.K. without violating tax directives. Mike Pinder claimed in *Moodymania* (1994 interview) that U.S. state department had messed up his paperwork pretty badly, and lost his green card, or he was working on his citizenship (two stories.) He was afraid to leave the States during the recording of *Octave*, lest he not be able to come home to California again.

I clipped this directly off Mike Pinder's website, fall of 2002 *Having moved to California in 1974, I returned to England for a visit in summer 1975. I was trying to get the band to do an album, but the response was so weak I returned to California with my two new MK5 Mellotrons and began work on my solo album <u>The Promise</u>.*

Oddly "weak response" is almost exactly what John, Justin and Tony all said about Mike! Perhaps it was only all a matter of good intentions, but very bad timing. Mike of course, got re-interested AFTER the *Blue Jays* was a hit, reviewed by *Rolling Stone*; and Weintraub had played their album at Carnegie Hall (as we shall soon read.) As John and Justin were committed to a *Blue Jays* tour by the summer of 1975 (and Graeme was out to sea somewhere), there is no mystery about the *weak response*.

Pinder built his own home studio at his Indigo Ranch in the hills above Malibu. The site had been owned by various Hollywood celebs over the years but was originally built as a refuge for John Barrymore (a place for him to dry out!!) At least one interesting story surfaced about Mike in the early '70s; he was summoned by Yoko and John to play the mellotron on the *Imagine* album. When Mike arrived at the studio, he found the mellotron he was assigned to in an advanced state of disrepair, and not fit for being much of anything but a large paper weight. Not wishing to miss the scene, Mike grabbed up a tambourine and played rhythm on "Don't Want to Be a Soldier, Mama."

Mike's wife Donna had family in California, Los Angeles, so it DID made sense; in any case, Mike wanted to be close to his son, and it was a family decision for him. In the *Orange County Register*, dated October 16, 1994, Mike discusses how his marriage was "breaking up" at this time, around 1975. He would eventually produce *The Promise*, which was commercially non-robust, but the cover is very lush and pretty, and has nice graphics.

The general gist of the album is heavily spiritual. Graeme has said of this time (in his *Modern Drummer* interview), that Mike was "A Hopi one week, and the next week a Sun worshipper." After Mike turned down the *Octave* tour, and he and Taralee were married (not sure which came first), they moved to Hawaii for a few years; sons Mike Jr. and Matt were both born in Hawaii. Other rumors persist of Mike raising finches or opening an electronics store.

Mike did an *Innerview* radio spot with Jim Ladd mid-1976, and many, many things came out which explained where Mike and the band had gone in the two years of their split up. The fame overwhelmed them, and Mike said he was one of these people who runs on a slower clock and was NEVER on time for things. He also said he couldn't deal with inner cities, and had to be "out in Nature, in a calm place" to write, or to even exist for that matter. It was not an uncommon thought for the '70s. He took his time off from the band, going from hysteria to confusion to "finding a new norm for inner peace."

He talked about lying in a box, watching the stars wheel over him at night, and about taking "the journey out and in." It's a radio spot that is filled with wisdom, and very much should be on the "list" for the discerning Moody Blues collector. Mike talked about people who had auras who "attract energy." all sorts of energy, some of it not nice at all. And how things got twisted around "closer to the center" of any high energy situation, such as what the band went through at their height of fame. (*After being in their fan club for over twenty years now, I can wholeheartedly agree with Mike on this point.*) This all was to be a factor in the reunion album in 1978, which "came just the same."

Then something happened that surely shook Mike's deep spiritual faith in the ideals of the '60s. Remember that PhD. of psychology that the Moodies used to hang out with? The one with the West Point diploma, who served with honor in World War II? They finally captured him and locked him up for ten years, because he had two roaches in his car; and I'm not talking about small crawling critters! Later, Leary would say he was locked up for "poor use of the First Amendment."

When *Rolling Stone Magazine* came out August 28, 1975, Mike must have choked on his corn flakes. You will recall the plaintive song about Dr. Leary back in 1972? "When You're a Free Man" is very deliberately dedicated to the guru of LSD, who was at that time on the run from Johnny Law. Little did Mike realize when he wrote the words "How are the children and Rosemary," that Tim Leary, in the throes of a flaming case of midlife crisis, was (according to *Rolling Stone*) dandling a hippy vixen the likes of which even Mata Hari would blush to contemplate.

There is no way I could top the stories of the master gonzo writers of *Rolling Stone*. Go to the library, get the article and read it yourself. It's probably the most ludicrous tale of head-tripping from a doctor of Psychology that has ever been spun on this Earth. The cloak-and-dagger jail breaks are not to be topped in the wildest adventure novel; someone should make a movie!

The Moodies, upon reading the article from a usually "pro-head" magazine like *Rolling Stone*, must have decided it was time to distance themselves from the drug culture, and thus the serious, *very* serious swing to more family-oriented themes in their solo albums. The video to "Question" that came out in the late '80s, shows the Moody Blues on a projector in an FBI investigation room. It's probably not too far from the truth, considering the two rather harmless songs they wrote for the Good Doctor; and *gasp* considering that Communist rally they played some peaceful songs at in 1969. Certainly we have found in later years that the FBI was tracking John Lennon in the '60s, and that's a fact. I'm just glad I've never had to go through customs in the entourage of the Moody Blues!

I'm a goin' fishin'--Ray ran for the English countryside. It still is not public knowledge where his home is, but I think it's in and around the Cobham area (seven acres in Surrey); he also has a home in the wilds of South Wales, and his own fishing pond by which he was (and probably still is) accustomed to play his flute. Those fans who have seen pictures of his home describe it as "very like a country gentleman's place." *Moodymania* #31 has some interesting notes about Ray's home life, itemizing his dogs, talking about him stocking his pond with carp, and "fishing with blokes from a local angling club.... *When you get up at five in the morning, and you are messing about in the mud with the lads, it's so divorced from the music business that it straightens your head out.*

Ray is very down to earth and loves to cook. In the '70s he concentrated on his family life, and (like Ian Anderson) tried his hand at endangered salmon hatching and farming. His two solo albums done between 1974 and 1977 are *From Mighty Oaks* and *Hopes Wishes and Dreams*. Both covers have beautiful artwork by Phil Travers, and several of the songs are about his family, notably "Adam and I." Nicky James (Ray's old pal from Brum) and his band are integral to both the albums.

According to documents, Ray hired a 39-piece orchestra for his albums. He was even considering touring with this full orchestra; however, the microphones, mixers and amps then were not sophisticated enough in 1976. By 1992, the concept became a reality, the Moodies were able to finally do this with the Red Rocks orchestral tour. Emerson, Lake and Palmer also tried touring with orchestra in late 1970's and didn't have much success either. They had to wait for the technology to catch up.

Ray was obviously a man with vision, and (having time on his hands) worked with a man named Hoff to remix the earlier Moody Blues albums in the new studio, thus more clearly preserving what Derek Varnals had originally done. Derek is credited on both *From Mighty Oaks* and *Hopes, Wishes and Dreams*. These cleaned-up later album versions were eventually remastered into the CD's currently on the market. They were working with the very earliest Quad technology (*Billboard*, 8-30-75). For years, Ray's solo albums were totally out of print, unless you could find them in used record stores. In September 2010, they were released as boxed remastered CD sets.

Graeme's CDs go in and out of print. (Buy 'em fast when you see 'em!) However, various spies have informed me that all the songs off their four albums are readily available from on-line sources, as MP3s. Mike's and Ray's solos are available on their websites, *www.raythomas.me* and *www.mikepinder.com*.

Don' chu Walk Thru My Words--In the '70s, Justin spent his new-found time off from the Moody Blues hanging around with other musicians. He guests on *Flash Fearless Versus The Zorg Women Parts 5 & 6*, recorded at the Chrysalis Studio in London between October and December of 1974. Justin performed guitar on two tracks, "Country Cooking" with vocalist Jim Dandy of Black Oak Arkansas; Justin plays guitar. On "Space Pirates," he performs with vocalist Alice Cooper, and Justin plays acoustic guitar.

Justin also found recording action not very far from home, with Lol Crème, Kevin Godley, and Eric Stewart. These future 10cc members (formerly of Hot Legs, which toured with the Moody Blues in 1971) were caretakers of Strawberry Studios in (Stockport) Dorking, not far from Birmingham. In Justin's "Caroline" interview, February 2001, he reveals that he was actually a stockholder in the Strawberry Studios at the time. There is a very funny radio production *The 10cc Story: Well Above Average* which Justin narrated, and in which he tells the graphically anatomical origin of the name 10cc. I omit this bit of music history in case any small children are reading. Despite his margarine-melting smile, Justin can get pretty raunchy.

It's probable that during this time, Justin and a LOT of British rock stars were in the habit of taking vacations in the Caribbean on Barbados. One verse in the 10cc song "Dreadlock Holiday" is about Justin being abandoned to the dubious humor of some locals, in a boat far far from shore. One can imagine Justin, tall, skinny and blonde (and with a very red lobster sun burn), being heckled by these huge, healthy, and very dark Rastafarians, who were plotting to peel his gold bracelet off him. And his meek explanation and plea, "It was a present from me Mum."

They said, you have a blue guitar
You do not play things as they are
The man replied, things as they are
Are changed upon the blue guitar
--Wallace Stevens

Once their suntans were finished, in the spring of 1973, 10cc and Justin spent time lolling about their English studio, doing what musicians do for fun, writing songs, and recording demos. The result was the beautiful "Blue Guitar" written by Justin, originally called "New Day." (Actually it might have been recorded in 1972, but who's checking?) They were messing around with a guitar device called the "Gizmo," a thing with six whirling plastic rollers that touched down on the strings of the guitar, and gave a spacey, odd sound by buzzing the strings. They first used the Gizmo on "Blue Guitar" as an experiment (at Strawberry Studios). It was used as well on *Long Distance Voyager*, and on 10cc albums (*Consequences*)

Justin claims he literally forgot the "Blue Guitar" demo tape was there, when he started recording with John Lodge for a new album. When *Blue Jays* became a huge hit, Eric and Lol rang Justin up and reminded him. The "Blue Guitar" single was doctored a bit by Tony Clarke, some Lodge bass added, and it was released under the "Blue Jays" name. It too, was well received, going to the Top Ten in the UK (*Higher and Higher* #31). Unfortunately the Gizmo didn't catch on in the recording world, but there is a very interesting adaptation of "gizmo" technology in the huge guitar sculpture at the Experience Music Project in Seattle, WA. *Never underestimate a story from Seattle.*

In *Saturdag* (April 14, 1977), Justin says that he and 10cc recorded MORE songs, which were sitting on the shelf, but due to his contractual situation, was unable to release them; the only way they could release "Blue Guitar" was under the *Blue Jays* label, thus it stands today. Justin indeed almost joined 10cc. How different rock history would have been.

The Man With the Blue Guitar is a poem-book written sometime during the '30s by Wallace Stevens; it is reprinted in *Eternity Road* #3, and is easily found on the Internet. Stevens said of his poem cycle, "The blue guitar in his poem is a symbol of the imagination, a reference to the individuality of the poet."

I was fortunate enough to see the (I think) first live performance in twenty years of "Blue Guitar" at the Portland Brew Pub in the '90s. And I've seen it live more than few times after that, at various shows Justin did solo in the '90s. It's a very complex song, and well worth watching Justin's fret hand for, if you know anything about guitars. "Blue Guitar" was to become so popular, that Gibson Guitars in Nashville actually made two Blue Gibson 335s, giving one to Justin, and selling the other to a private collector (*Higher and Higher* #6.)

In the late '90s, rather excitingly, B.B. King gave the Pope (of all people) a Blue 335 Gibson ("Lucille's Sister" as B.B. put it, on CNN); so in the meantime between 1975, and the late '90s, Gibson issued a few more Blue Guitars. I think I even saw one of the Rolling Stones playing a blue 335 during the *Bridges to Babylon* tour, and a band called the Editors from Brum also used one on the Jimmy Kimmel Show in 2007. They Are Around.

Did I just say there were more Blue Gibson 335's made? Here's another clue. *I was at the EMP once with the daughter of a "Texas Playboy" session musician (on same trip we spotted the Gizmo); and she was having a good laugh at the museum. "My Dad has several of these guitars that are 'under glass' at home in the closet!"* So you never know what people are going to find in the closet.

I clipped this off line June, 2005: *Justin said that Gibson made only two blue 335 guitars after "Blue Guitar" was released in the U.S. with the picture of the blue 335 on the 45 picture* sleeve. Justin said the other blue 335 was given to a contest winner in a contest run by Gibson. One of the two blue guitars appeared on ebay within the last [few] years..... One guitar was given by Gibson to Justin in recognition of "Blue Guitar," and its twin was SUPPOSED to be given to a contest winner.... that never happened. The radio station manager never did what he was supposed to do with it, instead he took it home and put it in a closet where it sat for years. Only after he retired from radio did he pull it out and sell it. I guess he saw it as a little retirement bonus! The guy who had it, listed it with a starting bid of ... 2 or 3 thousand to start.* [A classical cherry red Gibson 335 costs around $3,500 if not more.] The really INTERESTING things were the photos. That poor guitar that spent its life unloved and unplayed had turned GREEN. There was definitely a green cast to it. ... I understand that Justin still has his Blue Guitar. I wonder if that one has developed a green cast?*

One indeed wonders. In November of 2017, Justin mentioned that he sometimes used spare parts off the blue 335 in his possession to repair his other Gibsons.

Blue Jay Way--About *Blue Jays*. Without a doubt, John and Justin made the largest splash during their "solo years." As related earlier (in 1974), Justin began to mess around in the new studio, still hoping Mike would show up and work on an acoustic album. Tony was amenable to a new album, but he and Justin could not get any other Moodies to join them!

Then John got interested. Having produced the lush *Ever Sense the Dawn*, and having developed a taste for classical string sounds, John, Justin and Tony proceeded to contact what they could find of Providence's Idaho string section (Jim Cockey, Tim and Tom Tompkins). Then they rounded up a drummer and piano player (Mel Galley from Medusa, a band produced by John.) Justin rang up Peter Knight to help out with the lush orchestrations on "I Dreamed Last Night." (I have notes saying Justin played drums on this song! In a chat with Gordon Marshall, July 5, 2009 Gordon refers to Justin as "a tasty drummer" who occasionally sits down to the kit and whips off some acceptable rhythms.)

And they proceeded to record. Some of the songs on *Blue Jays* are a bit experimental in melody, and confusing to the ear on first listen. But over all, it's a euphonious package, well worth having in ones Moody collection. *Blue Jays* was the first full album produced in the new studio; it had advanced technology which translated later into a very nice CD. Older albums, such as *To Our Children's Children's Children,* really suffered from the CD re-master treatment.*

Jim Cockey interviewed for *Higher and Higher* (#7/8) and tells much of what went on at this time. After their two weeks of recording *Ever Sense the Dawn* in Los Angeles in 1972, Providence toured the West Coast a bit, and split up in Portland. Some returned to Idaho, and two settled permanently in Portland. *Ever Sense the Dawn* was the first Threshold album on 16 track, and *Blue Jays* was on 24 tracks.

"Remember Me," the first track, was recorded in 1974 without the Tompkins brothers and Cockey, but the other songs of *Blue Jays* have two or all of the three string musicians on them; they were in and out of the studio at irregular intervals. Providence did their own string arrangements, left largely to their own devices by Clarke and the Jays.

Cockey's interview is well worth reading for Moody information. My favorite part is where Jim talks about the paper airplane contest they had, and he proclaimed Justin the paper airplane master of the studio. The Decca studios were a great social center; over in a smaller Decca studio, the Moody Blues' old Brum mates, the Move had changed into ELO (Electric Light Orchestra) and were doing their own recording.

One song on *Blue Jays,* "My Brother" is sometimes acclaimed by reviewers to have been "a song about Mike Pinder." In no article or interview have I found Justin saying this is whom the song is about. Does he have to? It could just as easily be about Justin's real brother who was in the Navy, or Graeme who might have been sailing around the world at the time; or any other number of people Justin might call "brother." The point is, there is no reason to interpret the songs without the input of the writer.

I'm on top of the world. I haven't slept for four nights I'm so excited. It's been a hell of a year, a hell of a gamble. Justin, Record Mirror and Disc, Nov 22, 1975.

On March 10, 1975, *Blue Jays* premiered "non-live" in a strange show at Carnegie Hall, perpetrated by their publicist Jerry Weintraub. They just set up a record player on stage and played the vinyl. That's all. There were no performers on stage. John and Justin said it was pretty weird, but Weintraub was insistent that they not even consider going on stage live! There was applause after every track. Radio station WNEW had something like 35,000 requests for tickets to the show, and only 10,000 to go around! It was reviewed in *Rolling Stone*, dated April 24, 1975. The playing was so well attended, that Jerry Weintraub even considered piping it into the streets outside; but the New York police wouldn't let them, for fear of causing major traffic problems.**

In his autobiography, Weintraub describes the aftermath of this audacious performance, it has to be read to be believed, the press conference afterward was close to riot conditions. In fact I thought Weintraub's explanations were sheer genius. As per Justin's and John's reports, they were more than willing to go out and perform live. Chalk it up to a fabulous publicity stunt, which worked quite well, the album sold in respectable numbers.

Then in late 1975, *Blue Jays* toured 21 dates in Scotland and England, with their "string quartet plus." Though they got off to a "timid" start (as per one review of their performance at London's Odeon); they eventually picked up the energy and toured with resounding success and standing-room-only crowds. Justin's daughter Doremi says she remembers being in the limo and Justin's fans cheering for him outside; apparently it was pretty impressive for her as a child.

For the record, the *Blue Jays* tour line-up was Saved by the Music, Remember Me, The Story in Your Eyes, This Morning, You, You and Me, My Brother, Isn't Life Strange. The first part of the show was done with a mellotron and/or synthesizer, and the full instrument line up. They then reset the stage, and just Justin and John came out for an acoustic set. The feeble bootleg I have of this show (very faded with age) sounds remarkably like later orchestra shows in the '90s. The next songs were Who Are You Now? New Horizons, Emily's Song, and I Dreamed Last Night. Then the rest of the "Blue Jays band" came out, and they finished up with Nights in White Satin, I'm Just a Singer in a Rock and Roll Band, Blue Guitar, When You Wake Up.

They were so successful, that Tony, John and Justin were afraid if they continued, the Jays might replace the Moody Blues, and they didn't really want that to happen. So after the *Blue Jays* tour, John and Justin struck out on their own to produce separate albums, in both instances, with the able assistance of Tony Clarke.

Justin got it together first and found a little bit of heaven in a remote part of England. He and his growing family (wife Marie, daughter Doremi, horse-pal Toggs and a dog named Peggy Sue) settled down in a tiny Cornish community right where the deep turquoise Gulf Stream runs smack into the English seacoast, where the temperature is usually about 10 degrees higher than the rest of the country. They could grow palm trees in their garden, and there are all sorts of flowers, the area is noted for their floral festivals in the spring. Migratory birds of all varieties flocked to their small hamlet. There's a salmon stream that runs into an estuary, crossing a spacious, uncrowded beach where you could ride horses during low tide. Gorgeous views of the ocean are everywhere, from high cliffs and walking paths.

The Haywards also maintained their home in Kingston-on-Thames near Cobham, but in sunny Cornwall they were riding horses, hatching rare breed ponies, and raising their little girl who was now three. I think Justin's mum Gwenda retired to Cornwall too.

About this time, Justin's horse buddy Toggs becomes an integral part of fan attention. Every hero has a wonder horse, Justin's horse was Toggs; Justin described Toggs as a "clapped out old race horse." Justin was really attached to his horse! He would refer to Toggs as "a perfect gentleman" in one interview.*** Justin has said in interviews that he "likes riding as it allows you to see into other people's gardens." There is a very nice article on Justin's riding abilities in *Higher and Higher* #9.

Justin really did almost retire during these years. In his website blog, Jan 2002 he says, "Sometimes I'm almost tempted to chuck everything, and just disappear into Cornwall's beauty and mystery (I have to tell you that there was a time in the Seventies, when I was close to doing just that.)" In *Saturdag* (April 14, 1977) he mentions with some pride about being hired by the London Symphony Orchestra to do a guitar solo of "Nights," and talks about working as a session musician. But thankfully for lovers of rock music, Justin continued with the Moody Blues.

Not surprisingly, Justin's solo album *Songwriter* has the voices of children (Doremi, and Tony Clarke's little girls in "Raised on Love"); even Marie Hayward and Tony's wife Lynn sing on various tracks. Tony also sang back-up. Considering the Hayward's lifestyle at the time, it's surprising there are no whinny's of horses on it!

The album is very nicely put together, and the songs and lyrics are pure Hayward (that is to say, wonderful); but at the same time, Justin's voice sounds a little thin without the chorus of deep masculine voices backing him. Justin talked about touring with *Songwriter* music, with Mel Galley (Piano), Dave Holland (drums), and Aj Weber (vocals), but that tour never got off the ground.

Tudor Lodge--John, ever the family man (first priority), apparently didn't lock himself right into the music room, so he took a little longer to put a nice album together. His home was dubbed "Tudor Lodge," and as with the other Moodies, was not far from their offices in Cobham. He bought his home in 1968, but talks very rarely about his private life, which is understandable. John eventually was to have a second home in Spain, which he also talks little about; I think his Spanish home might have been near Andorra, as the Lodges loved to ski.

John and Tony put together *Natural Avenue*, two of the more notable songs on it being "Summer Breeze" and "Street Café." John even did a video of this, with street violinists (Nicky James on the violin) and pink balloons. It's a very neat video, and well worth watching on the fan club cassette readily available from Threshold Records (or like everything else, on *youtube*). Important to note: "Street Café" wasn't on the original *Natural Avenue* vinyl, but was tacked onto the CD. It was produced by Pip Williams, who would eventually be the producer for their next two albums: *Long Distance Voyager* and *The Present*. A look behind the making of *Natural Avenue* can be found in *Higher and Higher* #32.

John says that before he recorded *Natural Avenue* (and after the *Blue Jays* tour), he once again took to the road, this time in a Winnebago with his wife and kids. Some articles say he toured for eighteen months across Europe, playing in small bars on occasion, but mostly just seeing the countryside. He wrote as he traveled (he may have done all this before and during the album recording too, taking his compositions to the road.) There are also articles and interviews in which he says he traveled across America in the Winnebago (in 1977 on Hwy 66); this is not shocking, as there is a lot to see in North America. John by his own frequent admission loves to travel with his wife and is a bit of a shutter-bug.

"Threw It All Away" was released as a single during this time period. According to John (Brooklands, April 27, 2009) he wrote this originally for Elvis! Elvis was handled by WEG, as were the Moodies. Elvis tragically died on August 16, 1977, so you can fit all that into the timeline.

All of the solo albums are to be found (with some persistence) in used vinyl record stores, and even sometimes from Threshold, or from the artists themselves; John was selling them on-line at one time. *Songwriter, Natural Avenue* and *Blue Jays* are still available in CD form, the others are VERY hard to find as CDs. *Kick off Your Muddy Boots* is wonderful on CD, well worth buying if you can ever find it. *Trapeze* by Medusa on CD used to be easy to get from Threshold Records, and there is even an illegal CD from Japan, of *Ever Sense the Dawn* on the loose. All of the solo albums have something of worth on them, and it's a great part of the Moody Blues to explore if you never have heard of some of them.

From an article on the Moody Blues in *Melody Maker* dated July 30, 1977, the direct quote is "All members are residents of America except for Justin." I missed when and where Ray moved to the U.S. so perhaps *Melody Maker* was stretching it just a bit. I think a more accurate report would be that Ray, Mike and Graeme were married to American gals, and could claim residence in America. John's and Justin's wives are both European, but John's family may have actually had a home in the Bay Area at the time (again, an obscure reference.)

John's and Justin's albums both were released in early 1977. In Justin's interview in *Satudag* April 14, 1977 he seems to be setting his course on a solo career. He talks about finally getting his *Songwriter* album out, which had been done "since September," and he was very frustrated about it being held back. And he talked about touring with his own band around England in May, but this never happened. Justin did an interview with *Sounds* "Going Broke the Blue Jay Way," and the handwritten date is 12*8*77; I suspect it's actually from Dec 1976.

At any rate, Justin is, as of that interview, suing Threshold Records to release his album! And everywhere he turns, lawyers and accountants are pouncing on him. And they all want money. It appears to be the same with several of the Moodies, from his interview.

Even though they are all turning out some nice work on their solo albums, the label "Moody Blues" is going to net them more money in the popular market, than going it alone. So it seemed a forgone conclusion that the Moody

Blues were indeed destined to make music again together. The only problem was, to get all six of them into the same room at the same time. That winter in 1977, they went to Southern California, and began to record *Octave*.

*I can't recall the interview, but Justin has been (thankfully!) rather "perfectionistic" about the remix of their albums for CDs, saying he has actually sent them back to "be done properly" (paraphrase). Some early rock vinyl albums have NOT weathered the digital shift to CD well at all, notably Led Zeppelin albums; they have a sorta "dead" feel to them (has to do with cutting off part of the "highs and lows" long technical explanations). Core Seven Moody Blues CDs are the best sound that can be pulled out of the old master tapes, and they sound pretty good comparatively. As of 2007, technology took another leap and the Super Audio CDs (SACD) were released, taking the enhancements even further.

**Tom Huelett, the Moody Blues manager through the '90s, and Weintraub were still buddies, and in the '80s they worked on *Karate Kid II*, in which Moody Blues music is used. (Super good movie!)

*** "Toggs" or "Toggle" I think is a generic horse name, possibly like how Americans refer to a cow as "Old Bessie"; Hugh Lofting used the name for a horse in his Dr. Doolittle stories too. Either that, or Justin really likes Dr. Doolittle! Toggs had a "real" registered name, but Justin never used it.

XI) A Higher Octave: Slide Zone 1978-1980

"I was involved with very little of the <u>Octave</u> fiasco. It was not a very mellow time." -- Mike Pinder, 07-15-04 on chat, www.moodytalk.com

"...there is a type of constructive tension that is necessary for growth..."
-- Dr. Martin Luther King, Jr.

In late 1977, Tony Clarke managed to herd the entire band to Southern California, where they had time booked to record their eighth album at the Record Plant in Los Angeles (Malibu to be specific). Tony said of this time, that he spent a lot of time "doing Henry Kissinger," calling and visiting, and trying to get everyone to paddle their separate canoes in the same direction. He had to line up the recording space once it was decided to go to California, and then arrange for places to live.

They were only in the studio for three months out of the six months it took to record the album, so imagine three months taken up by all the interruptions. Some of it was perfectly understandable family stuff. Things were just fine once they got everyone in the studio, and the music rolled right into the can. Tony pronounced that it was good, even "challenging" to change the pace, and to become involved with different people and different places. It was better for the "creative soul."

Even though the Moody Blues were truly back together, and wanted to make music together, everyone was still trying to go different directions, like driftwood in a whirlpool, either shoved here and there by the will of uncontrollable tides, or by the earth dropping out from under them. The word "octave", in a musical sense, implies going to the "next level." Maybe they did, but while getting the Moody Blues going the first time was like having a newborn baby, getting them going the second time was like giving birth to a full grown human being. Life has that habit, of getting more complex as we go along.

Octave was apparently the first album the group did without first playing and breaking in their songs in front of a live audience. Every band member would say later that the entire process of making *Octave* was the recording session from hell. The first signs of trouble had been when Mike Pinder refused to come back to England to record, despite the "super studio" they had built in West London. Mike's home was an Eden on Earth (you can see the Pacific Ocean from the Indigo Ranch), and he also wanted to be near his son; I think he was starting to go through divorce. People can do nasty things during custody battles, and there is no father alive who could blame Mike for his actions, if this was the case. It's a measure of how highly the Moodies all thought of Mike, that they sacrificed their home comforts in England to come to California where HE was and record their reunion album.

It wasn't just Mike's stay-puttedness either. Tony Clarke really thought it might be good for them to get out of their "rut" in England and be exposed to new influences. Justin would say in later interviews about this "We were like fish out of water," going to L.A. to record. BUT given the money and tax situation in England that year, it was more favorable then for band business to come to California and do it.

The Record Plant was found to be in a terrible state of disrepair, holes in speakers, and wrecked equipment. Mike said of the recording period that "The vibe was weird and negative," and people weren't really communicating well with one another. Certainly Mike is one of those dudes who runs on his own time and shows up late; that had to be annoying to the others. Oddly, Mike has a saying about "Order to Chaos" (Rudder, 1-13-08), so perhaps the others were just more accepting of chaos than Mike. Maybe it was just a lot of Alpha Male ego all around.

Perhaps a "strange vibe" is no surprise considering all the lawsuits that several of them had been going through just prior. We must assume that whatever legal battles everyone was doing (Justin wasn't the only one); they were indeed resolved, but perhaps not forgotten. According to Mike, John was totally obsessed with money. No wonder! Graeme managed to terminally piss Tony off during this time period. Graeme's son had just been born, so I bet he wasn't real pleased about being away from home.

So things started out with a very rocky beginning. They knew it, too. The first day everyone showed up at the studio to record, they just sat around playing Buddy Holly songs all day.

Apparently, Kirsten Lodge uprooted the family and moved to California to be with John; here I have a scrawled note found on-line "John DID live 18 months in the States." Documents of this time say the Lodges had a home in the Bay Area. Ray's wife Gill had or has family in Los Angeles, so they had no trouble with the move. And while Graeme had the *Delia* to live on (if he wanted to take her through the Canal), his lady Sue stayed home in Monaco, with the new born son Matthew.

Marie Hayward declined to come to California to be with her husband during the recording of this album. She had a daughter who was just entering school, and she also had horses to feed at their ranch in Cornwall. Justin recalls being on tour or away from home, and when his daughter got on the phone, and said with her little girl voice "When are you coming home, Daddy?" it was enough to set him off more than a little. The OFC newsletter of this time documents Justin making at least two trips back to England during the recording of *Octave*; according to Mike, Justin "bailed for Christmas." It had to have been disruptive to the rest of the band for their guitar lead to be taking off like that, but at the same time, Justin was perfectly capable of song writing on the road.

Indeed perhaps the tension of "back and forth" is a great creative motivator. "Driftwood," arguably the finest love ballad ever penned by Justin, was written in Cornwall during this time, and recorded for this album. In an interview in June 2002, Justin talks more about the writing of "Driftwood" and alluded to Tony Clarke's home turmoil as being part of his inspiration, rather than a spat with Mrs. Hayward. Tony Clarke spent his energy getting the band together, at the expense of his own domestic bliss, going through divorce during the making of *Octave*.

In the later interviews, the Moodies would say "Both our keyboardist and producer quit half-way through the album." Justin literally had to talk Tony down off a cliff once, according to Graeme's '80s interview in *Modern Drummer,* March 1987. Incidentally, this article is one of the finest interviews done by the collective Moody Blues regarding their musical style and philosophy, and if you can find a copy of it, it's a "must" for any Moody fan. It shows up for sale on Amazon.com sometimes. Say what you will, I say "good for Justin" if he was the one who got Tony off the cliff. It could happen to anyone.

In Tony's defense: in later *Higher and Higher* interviews, he would emphatically state that he did NOT "bail" on the Moodies during *Octave*. It was he who spent the long hours after the recording was over, mixing tracks and putting the thing together, while the rest wandered off on Winnebago trips, sailed away, went home to weed the daffodils, or ran home to distressed families. I would say the proof of this is that the album is a very fine package, and certainly as good as other Moody albums. Clarke also said in his interview, and Mike says the same; Mike was not very involved with the album, and that John and Justin played a lot of the keyboards on it.

Justin has said that when it came to mixing the album, Tony got so distraught listening to "Driftwood" (still trying to deal with his divorce) that Justin had to mix the song himself. (*Lost 45's*, aired 4-19-09)

Where their heads were, is very plain from the opening sounds on the album. It sounds like chirping crickets, then four car doors slam…..and then you suddenly realize….it might not be crickets chirping at all. Maybe it's really UFO noises. And later in the album, the five note "greetings/ handshake" sequence from *Close Encounters of the Third Kind* is heard. Odd isn't it, that a "handshake" is also a computer term, and that it has a musical analog. Reaching out is what it's all about.

Graeme has said they usually have a "superstition" to start off with one of Justin's songs. This time, they departed from tradition, because a song that John had written was so perfect for the entire theme of the album: "Slidezone."

In a chat room on July 15, 2004, Mike Pinder alluded to "the Ancient One" or the "Citizen Ghost" that lived at his Indigo Ranch in Carbon Canyon, near Malibu/Santa Monica. This was a pretty rustic area in the '70s; in fact, the whole area was well infested with hippies in those days, as I recall, communes and such. He said something about a local nature spirit, "we are not alone." He may have been right, the Indigo Ranch was an ancient site of the Chumash people, and some ornery spirits seemed to be hanging around. Mike says the "Ancient One" didn't care for Heavy Metal but does like Rock.

After the Moodies abandoned the burnt-up Record Plant, they took a limo every day from Malibu (where they were living) and drove out to the Indigo Ranch, sliding all the way on muddy dirt roads. "Around the bend" has more than one meaning perhaps, in John's song, because some very weird vibes jumped on board with the Moodies. If you listen to the words to "Slidezone" you'll find a tiny bit of *Pilgrim's Progress* in it, too. A very neat song once you pick up on where it came from.

Mother Nature even seemed to be in dissonance with them. The Record Plant was the victim of poor inspections, too: first the roof fell in. Then it not only caught fire (they managed to save 2 or 3 of the masters), but what was left of it slid down the hill in one of those mudslides that Malibu can be notorious for. A side note: according to Ray Coleman, Steven Stills was actually in the Record Plant when it caught fire, doing some hot licks*, ha ha*....

Somehow, the ever-active John Lodge managed to break an arm in the middle of it all, and of course, couldn't play a note. John Lodge says in their DVD interview that

"Everything that could go wrong DID go wrong." Justin got caught in one of the rain downpours (while driving) in the California winter, and (with Tony in the car) managed to get in a wreck. It makes one wonder; the whole *Octave* production really did seem haunted by poltergeists.

All these complications might explain something unusual that Ray and Justin finally did. They said when it came time to record "Had to Fall," the two of them just went into a vacant studio next to the one they were working in. And they did all the parts themselves, the (open tuned) guitar, the drums, keyboards, harmonica and all; they mixed it themselves. Talk about the KISS principle!!! (Justin blog, Sept 2008)

Stories of the Indigo Ranch would tell about long hikes, early mornings, with flashlights, on muddy trails in the winter rain. They had to hike over California chaparral, in order to reach a studio that was separated from the main house. Recording at Mike's homestead sounds like it was a pretty primitive affair, one not willingly repeated.

The magic in such places will "take back their own" I suppose, because the follow up is that Carbon Canyon (Justin says "Coral Canyon" in one interview, anyone have a SoCal map on them?) caught fire a few years after this, and Mike lost some of his ranch, and a mellotron in the flame. He moved north to the Sacramento area in the early '80s.

Mike has talked a lot about the reasons for his leaving the band emotionally at this time, saying that he had a really wonderful life in Carbon Canyon, and was totally into the peace and quiet of his lifestyle. He talked about how he got into his own time rhythm and what a shock it was to deal with all the inevitable ego around recording a new album. Above all, he talked about how much he was into being a father, and not into the rock star lifestyle anymore. He wanted to bring order to his chaos.

In their 2006 DVD biography, EVERYONE interviewed about the *Octave* recording period seemed terribly saddened by the memories, and reluctant to talk about it. The photos on the *Octave* cover say it all. Mike

Pinder is obviously looking somewhere else, while the rest of the Moodies make eye contact with the camera. No one has ever said if this was intentional or not in the planning of the album cover. According to later interviews, Mike was apparently "matted" into the shot, and is not in the same room with the Moodies for that cover photo. Everyone is shown going through the metaphorical door, "into the light" and coming out just fine on the other side. And they did.

All the songs on *Octave* are up to the usual standard of the Moody Blues. The album was eagerly greeted by Moody fans, hungry for new material and continuing magic.

The promotion behind *Octave* was staggering. Sir Edward Lewis was at the time still head of Decca records. Lewis held a huge "garden party" on his estate, inviting press, and the Moodies (*sans* Pinder and Moraz apparently, but PLUS Tony Clarke) and all their families. The band is treated like royalty, and good cheer is in evidence everywhere in the rather lengthy, newsreel-like video that is shot of the event. The Moody Blues are photographed time and again, holding up platinum albums and cheering like soccer champions gloating over a win. At that time, they were estimated to have sold 26 million LPs world-wide. Possibly for the first time, their ladies are videoed, at least Marie and Kirsten are very apparent. Kirsten has a glass of wine and seems very elegant and composed. Marie is laughing and lighting up a fag. I think the "other blonde" must be Sue, Graeme's lady.

The tour for *Octave* had a slightly different line-up music wise, than the early '70s (obviously). At least a few of the songs in the new line-up were "Twilight Time," "The Balance," "I'm Your Man," and "Legend of a Mind." They appeared on T.V. shows and on tour, rising out of the center of a pyramid, complete with flash pots and wild lighting effects. It must have been a wonderful tour.

Tony Clarke at this time fades away from all things Moody, and moves on, to other pursuits and occupations. In his words, he was "run ragged" by *Octave*, it was very hard to come up with new ideas. *Blue Jays* was very experimental, as was *Songwriter*, but things were not fresh with the Moody Blues; what was fun in 1967 was just tedious by 1978.

After wrapping up *Octave*, Clarke went on to produce other artists. One group he became involved with is the ethereal Irish super-group, Clannad, related to '90s top-seller Enya. Clarke also did the sound effects for *Supergirl* the movie, which wasn't exactly a blockbuster, but is a worthy movie. In 1986, he worked on a double album for Rick Wakeman. Tony had his own label, TC Records; and lived aboard his yacht the *Tao Princess* with a new lady, a new recording studio on his boat, and appeared to be a very happy man. More can be read about Tony in his interview, in *Higher and Higher* #5. He also posted occasionally on Mike Pinder's website and newsgroup. A good Google might even turn up his own website on-line, and his Wiki.

Graeme says that in 1977, Mike Pinder got as far as having a pen in his hand, when it came time for the band to sign papers that would put them on the road again, with the *Octave* tour. And he couldn't do it. (Mike said this was dramatic embellishment in a 1995 interview, but basically true, he just didn't have a pen in his hand…) Going on the road, being away from family, it was just too much for Mike. In his words, he had just found the girl of his dreams (Taralee), and when he looked at his new family, thought about what the tours of the early years had done to his home life. He just could not do it. So the Moody Blues were left high and dry for their *Octave* tour, without a keyboardist. Something had to be done, and they went out, looking for backup. That replacement would turn out to be Patrick Moraz.

The direct quote from the *Octave* tour program; "Patrick is the touring replacement for Michael Pinder, who is on leave of absence." Draw what conclusions you will from that.

One more note should be added. During what were to be Mike's final years as a Moody Blue; even though he didn't want to tour to support *Octave*, he was still officially part of the band. 1980 was the year John Lennon was shot by a stalker in New York City. It seriously rattled the pop music world; every high-profile rock star immediately thought, "It could have been me." They ALL had weird fans. John Lennon had been a friend to some of the Moodies, mentor to others, and it had an effect. The event was probably taken very seriously by those who declined to stay with the Moody Blues during the '80s.

Certainly the event cast a shadow on the album *Long Distance Voyager,* then in production. According to Pip Williams, the day Lennon was shot, they all came in and just sat in silence, until Justin finally said, "Let's all go home." So, bear in mind that the next phase of the Moody Blues is colored by this event; John Lennon, standard bearer of English rockers, was suddenly and tragically removed from the scene, much as Buddy Holly had been in 1959. Pop music took a radical swing away from its melody-laced roots (the Beatles) and veered toward a love affair with technology, and electronic embellishments. It became DISCO.

We're not closing the door on Mike, but by his refusal to tour, he has walked out through it -- New Music Express, September 30, 1978

Patrick Moraz came first from the band Refugee and then Yes. He was (and is) a noted keyboardist (he does runs and scales especially well), and he was looking for a job. small dab of his history: Patrick is Swiss-born (raised French I think), and the son of diplomats. He joined Yes as a replacement for Rick Wakeman, who had left the band. When Patrick accepted the job with the Moodies, he had "been replaced" by a returning Rick Wakeman, in 1976. Patrick wasn't real happy about being replaced in Yes, and had drowned his sorrows in Rio, Brazil for two years, where he avidly studied a form of shamanism called Macumba. A good interview with Patrick Moraz can be found in *Higher and Higher* #5.

Still looking for a gig, he found it in France. He was playing the Montreux Jazz Festival in 1978 and was hanging out with the likes of Chick Chorea. It was there that Graeme Edge found him, invited him to meet the Moodies, and suggested hopefully that he might fill in their large gaping keyboard hole for the upcoming *Octave* tour.

They auditioned Patrick in their Starship Studio. Everyone was suitably impressed, they were a good fit, and Patrick was a great technical resource. Moraz knew all the songs. He was eager, high energy and dressed flamboyantly. He got married to the girl he met the same day he met the Moodies and was a regular "Steady Eddie" just like the rest of them. He was "with" the innovative, new electronic MIDI sound that was sweeping modern music in the early '80s. He was in. The Moodies signed him for a touring contract, in the amount known only to those involved, and everyone was happy.

Reviews of the times talk about a "Sixties revival." This was the first of many "Sixties revivals" which were to happen every other year all through the '80s and '90s. The Moodies toured in 1978 for *Octave*, first in Europe, and then in America. The tours were marvelous, Patrick was a phenomenal addition to the touring band.

Then it was time to record. According to *Melody Maker* (May 26, 1979) Patrick was held back contractually from recording with the Moodies, so somehow that was gone around, since Mike didn't show any signs of putting in an appearance. Patrick eventually arrived at the Decca One studio, with an impressive array of keyboards, synthesizers (17 total), and (count 'em) three MacIntosh computers, all used to produce "his sound." *

Even though Patrick's fairy-tale with the Moodies had an unhappy ending, his addition to the band at the time was a real boost to their sound, as evidenced by his lush arrangements in the *The Polydor Years* boxset. It just goes to show, that even the most talented performing artist might be on the heights one moment, and then make a sudden decline to the depths. I wonder where that musical genius went to, that was captured in those live recordings.

Graeme was later to talk in interviews about making his electronic drum set send signals to Patrick's keyboard. In a 2009 chat, Gordon Marshall said this technology was a reality, so Graeme was in on the ground floor with this sort of thing. Graeme had in mind a musical cascade effect, wherein one certain drum rhythm would set off a melody sequence on the MIDI. MIDI and synthesizer music was, and still is, such a changing, rapidly evolving field, and all the Moodies were in on the cutting edge of this technology, field testing the latest in every tour. It must have been very exciting to do technical work for them during this period. It too, might have been just a little overwhelming. I wonder what everyone would have thought, had they realized then that all of Patrick's gear would be replaced by one suitcase-sized keyboard by the end of the decade. More can be read about this in *Higher and Higher* #10.

Looking back, the late '70s and '80s were really a cultural wasteland, even with the technical advances happening. Some nice movies came out, but the only two that really come to mind, and which altered the landscape of society as we know it are *Saturday Night Fever* and *Top Gun*. A lot of the pop bands (like the Village People) did a fast fade after just a few years. However, other stars of the '80s (the Muppets and Robin Williams) stayed on to become true legends, so "being silly" is perhaps what lasted best from that time period.

People were making money and living life in the fast lane, all going somewhere (did we know where?) in a hell of a hurry. In retrospect, there's a hard edge, and a cold, glittery feeling to the entire era, even if it masquerades under the annoying sound of goofy "whoop whooPs." Pop culture beat to death the catch-all phrase and plastic-edged "disco," and then the phrase "New Wave" (from Nueva York). Baby boomers were still competing in the work place, and the younger generation was growing up to challenge them. We were all working hard and grasping for money. Somehow, in the bustle and fast action, some of the softness and joy of living, that is humanity at its best (and so indicative of '60s and '70s music), was lost and forgotten.

While *Octave* had turned out to be a farewell gesture to the magical '60s and '70s, as well as closure (in the pop arena) for the marvelous musical talents of Mike Pinder, there was still something left. "The Voice" truly opened the "nueva" era for the Moody Blues. Justin would say, looking back on it, "There was an energy, a new vitality to it that was wonderful." But listen to the lyrics. There is still the uncertainty and the seeking for answers that was there in Moody Blues music in the '60s. The same questions were being asked, the band was just taking another approach to match the times.

The Moody Blues didn't waste time moping about over the lost '70s. While the others have hobbies, like traveling with family (John), flying and sailing (Graeme), fishing and thrashing about in the snow (Ray); Justin's hobby is making music! In 1978, having finished the *Octave* tour, Justin found himself approached by many artists in the recording industry. One was associated with old friends from 10cc; Justin sang a track for the lush fantasy album *Eye of Wendor*. Involved with this album would be Eric Stewart of 10cc, and David Rohl, who had done the infrared photography on the inside of *A Question of Balance*.

Eye of Wendor was a take-off on a rock opera, loosely based on a Tolkien-esque mini-novel. Whether this was even intended to be more than a record and small novelette is unknown, but as far as I know, it was never a play or video. The illustrations look like Bakshi's *Wizards*; the map looks like Middle Earth, and the music sound track certainly sounds like a precursor to music of a later fantasy movie, *Conan the Barbarian* [Basil Poledouris.]

The chances of anything coming from Mars--In this same time period, through a contact with David Essex (a friend of Justin's); came Jeff Wayne's *The War of the Worlds* album, based on the classical H.G. Wells novel by the same name. Students of science fiction know that the original novel is set in England. The outstanding movie by the same name, shot in America during the late '50s, is much different than the original novel; Spielberg did even more twists in his American version, produced in 2005.

Wayne intended to go back to the English roots with song and animation (yes there are animated clips of this series still in circulation among Moody Blues fans.) Wayne was experimenting with new techniques called Rotoscope, in which animation was used over live actors. (Rotoscope would eventually be used to good effect in 1978 by Ralph Bakshi for an animated version of *Lord of the Rings*.)

In William Shatner's book, *Memoirs*, he mentions a revival of the series *Star Trek* being considered along with a T.V. series of *The War of the Worlds* in the late 1970s, for a new sci-fi channel. That new channel never got into production during that time period. We might assume (should we?) that Shatner's recollections, and Jeff Wayne's (early) ill-fated production, are one in the same.

A T.V. special of this version of *The War of the Worlds* was allegedly done in August of 1980. Whatever the details of the project, a wonderful job was done on the album, the original vinyl contains a gorgeous graphic magazine. The sound track features not only actor Richard Burton, reading from the novel (Burton was doing *Equus* at the same time), but also includes incredibly dynamic music with Justin Hayward singing on two tracks, "The Eve of the War," and "Forever Autumn." AND in the Collector's Edition of *The War of the Worlds*, there lurks a copy of "Thunderchild" with John Lodge playing bass on it!

There was a tour of a multi-media stage show based on the album, in April, 2006 in the U.K, June 2009, Dec 2010 in the U.K. AND September 2007 in Australia. Richard Burton was turned into a large digital Talking Head, and yes Justin Hayward sang live in the shows. The show was a massive hit in the UK, but sadly never made it across the Pond to America. *UUUllaaahhh!!!*

"Forever Autumn" has, putting it mildly, a checkered history. Wayne refused to give up his wonderful song, and after selling it in 1972 to Tyco for a Lego commercial, Wayne revived it in 1978 for his T.V. project. "Forever Autumn" released as a single, with Justin's singing, was to go into the Top 10 singles chart in America. Again, Hayward was tops in the fame game. Justin was to say later that Jeff had the studio all set up and the orchestration all set perfectly for his voice, and right in his range; it was one of the easiest songs he ever recorded. Justin's solo career REALLY kicked off that day when Jeff rang him up to do "Forever Autumn." See *Higher and Higher* #3, and *www.thewaroftheworlds.com*.

When it became a hit, "Forever Autumn" was featured on *American Bandstand* (America) and *Top of the Pops* (U.K.), bringing Justin a whole new wave of fans as the song shot up the charts. When Justin settled and lit after *Octave* touring (1978/1979), he found he had lots of job offers, all from the "Forever Autumn" backwash.

In February 1980, Sir Edward Lewis died, and the handwriting was on the wall. It had to have been a shock, Lewis was a real father figure for them, and Decca was going to go through some sort of corporate restructuring (like it or not.) That same February, Justin got a call from Mike Pinder, who wanted to get together and work as a band again. On Feb 19, 1980 they started production in Decca One, for the next Moody album. The first producer didn't work out, and they dumped much of what was done in the March/April time frame.

By July of 1980 when Mike finally arrived in London, the rest of band had scattered to the four winds (possibly with an aftertaste named "Octave" on their tongues.) Justin was moving on, and busily promoting a new "solo" album. I DID find a reference to Justin "recording a song" right before an interview, the article (*Liverpool Gas?* By Peter Trollope) is dated July 2, 1980 (look on *Moodybluesattitude*, Time Capsules for 1980.) This would have been between June 20 and July 1 by the timeline. So the band was all "in studio" recording at the end of June, 1980 (unless Justin was telling a little white lie, you really can't tell.) Justin did so much in this time period, he could have been recording with someone else too.

Jeff and Justin had so much success with "Forever Autumn," that they went on to make the album *Night Flight,* released June 13, 1980. (It is unknown if this was a tip of the hat to Antoine de Saint-Exupery, who wrote a biographical aviation novel by the same name, during WWII.)

Justin, ever with a good song up his sleeve, used this opportunity to record four of his own tracks, and sang on Jeff's songs as well. They would go on to be undistinguished in Moody fame, but are still perfectly good songs. Dave Holland (from the band Medusa) worked on "Crazy Lovers." The only criticism that has ever been leveled at the album is to say, "It's too disco," and it does indeed have elements of the disco beat. But it's inoffensive, and rather a good album for easy listening, light and airy. Indeed, the disco beat is such that one is mildly reminded of Motown and the Four Tops.

There's always been a joke in the fan club, and possibly with the band, that when Justin starts making a good go of it solo, the others can't stand to be left out. And they suddenly get it together to whip out another album. There's probably some truth to it. Suddenly, the Moody Blues decided they needed to all do another album together. And so they did.

*This was pretty flamboyant in itself, I only saw MY first Apple I PC in 1978; it ran off cassette tapes! The first floppy disc came out commercially in the fall of 1978. While I took this information right from a newspaper interview, I'm sure a more accurate view would be that Patrick started buying the latest Apple technology for music as soon as it reached the market. A new model came out every year. If this techno-geek stuff thrills you, go find a movie called *The Pirates of Silicon Valley*. Apple is now the standard in music production, and the Moody Blues were one of the bands who pioneered it.

XII) Veteran Cosmic Rockin' 1980-1982

I admire "Boogie Bass" and it developed from listening to the "Left Hand" of boogie piano from the South -- John Lodge, *Official Fan Newsletter,* June 1992

Simply put, major business changes happened for the Moody Blues during this time period. Sir Edward Lewis had a tough time through the '70s, and slowly sold Decca to Polydor/Polygram; his subsequent death was the end of an era. The Moody Blues officially became Polydor property in 1983 with the release of *The Present. Octave, Long Distance Voyager,* and *The Present* were all under the Decca umbrella, though other labels are slapped on top of that; Threshold music was no longer in the vinyl producing business. I'm not sure how all this affected the band accounting-wise, but poor sales on *The Present* probably had something to do with poor promotion and a new company.

There's a MAJOR amount of information on *Long Distance Voyager* in *Higher and Higher* #31, with extensive tech notes. It was the only full, true Moody Blue album done in Threshold's Studio One (formerly Decca One). Mark Murley, and the entire *Higher and Higher* staff, have done a masterful job of interviewing and recording the history of this marvelous album, the album that really gave the Moody Blues back their full level of status in the world of music.

Enter Pip Williams. John Lodge had made his acquaintance when he produced "Street Café," a song that was issued as a single (Oct 1980), independent of *Natural Avenue.* "Street Café" was intended to be the beginning of John's second solo album. It's a nice song, featuring Nicky James on the violin (and with a very cute video), but alas it disappeared charts-wise.

So Pip and John abandoned the second Lodge solo album, gathered up their material, and set their focus on another Moody album. This was fine with Justin, who had even MORE songs (he's always writing.) Whither goest John goes his mate Ray. So at least three of them, and an acceptable producer found themselves by Dec 9, 1980, sitting in Decca One (when word of John Lennon's murder came down.)

Pip's history is a bit vague (which is probably how he likes it) but here is one thing of importance; Pip Williams is a fly fisherman and ties his own flies! There's a lot of fishing and football in the history of the Moody Blues, isn't there? Pip's interviews in *Higher and Higher* are really great; one theme sticks out for me. He talked about the Moodies as having "a Magic that happened when they played together." His thoughts are very similar to those of Yoko Ono, when she was speaking of the Beatles. The same thing happened with the Doors, and with so many other gifted musical groups. A magical interaction happened and produced "that sound" that even the band members marveled at when they put on the headphones and listened to a play-back.

With the overpowering electronic pop-disco music market in place, they incorporated some of that into their approach. Wild horses couldn't have dragged the Moody Blues back to California for a repeat of their traumatic *Octave* experience, so they got to work in England. *Long Distance Voyager* is the only album the Moodies were to record in the studio they had built in West Hampstead, London. *Blue Jays* was not done with the entire group, and *Octave* was, of course, recorded elsewhere.

When they returned to the studio in early 1981, it was a certainty that Decca was going to disappear from under them, along with the beautiful starship studio (Decca/Threshold One.) So it was a matter of "get off the pot or sh**" as we say in America. Patrick Moraz was there, Mike wasn't, so Patrick was suddenly the new keyboard player. Why Mike remained uninvolved after July 1980 is not publicly known. (Tony Clarke at least was straight up about it, and said he was "run ragged" by *Octave.)* In later interviews, Justin was asked a question "Who gets their music played on albums?" Justin's answer? "Those who show up for rehearsals!" Ever hear the story about *The Little*

Red Hen? We may never know who hung up the phone first between the Moodies and Mike, but it happened. No one likes a busy signal.

They turned out the album for final play-back on April 13, 1981. Decca closed its doors the same day. From reading articles, there appeared to be a lot of "hang around the studio" people, who would drop in, perhaps party a bit, and cause distractions from the main purpose of recording. "When there was a record in production, it was a flag to show up" to paraphrase Pip. So, apparently every British musician was fully aware they were recording. It wasn't a secret.

Justin tells a hilarious story about inviting friends from a local soccer team to the studio for the playback of "The Voice," he said they had a great time, dancing around the studio. Can you imagine a bunch of huge, pro-ball players cavorting to the Moody Blues? (Lost 45's, 4-19-10)

Pip, Patrick and one of the engineers at least went elsewhere during the production and did other work, so that took time out of production as well. "Life happens" tended to be the byword to the lengthy production schedule. Weird wrinkles arose. Even though Patrick had arrived with enough gear and Macs to fill half a studio, he didn't have an electric piano; they had to go rent one for "Meanwhile," and I'm glad they did. It's a neat tinkly sound. As well, Patrick didn't have the foggiest notion of who Fats Domino was when Justin mentioned the style for a piece they were recording. (Patrick is classically trained.) I wonder what Patrick thought of John's boogie-woogie bass style!

There was not supposed to be a heavy concept to the album, it was just the band getting together to make good music. Even so, once the promotion started, John talked about the album in heady terms, such as, "It's the ninth album, there are nine planets, there are nine tracks, and the *Voyager* spacecraft is just leaving the solar system."

Justin said he found the 18th century picture for the cover (*Higher and Higher* #31) in a photography studio, and decided that somehow, everything they were saying on the album was said in that picture. If you can find a theme to the album cover, I guess that's the theme to the album, too. John Lodge claimed to have found the print to *Long Distance Voyager* in his grandma's attic (*Moodymania* #9), and it hangs framed on John's wall at home as of last word. Or darn, maybe he found it in an antique store? One of these days, maybe John and Justin will confess to who REALLY found the darn picture! In a Storyteller show in 2011, Justin asserted, "It's a well-known picture." Ok, it was *storytelling*, and the picture's title has yet to surface!!! Check out *Appendix D: The Art of the Moodies* for more information on this cover. There is more here than meets the eye!

They sometimes found the message was getting lost in the technical details. It was not always fun dealing with the electronics, high technology sometimes squeezed all the juice out of the creative process. But with the coming of computer technology, synthesizer sound was an unavoidable certainty, as well as a little disco flavor. They had cover art from the 18th century, a lovely English afternoon with people listening to a traveling musician. Inside they have an album full of space-age wizardry.

"22,000 Days" took the longest to record of any Moody song up to that date. From the way it sounds, even though the poetry is Graeme's, it was apparently conceived and engineered by committee. No wonder it took so long to find their way, with all the different directions they were trying to travel!

Do you want marzipan or icing on that cake?-- a Moody comment about recording

"Veteran Cosmic Rocker" is a departure from the norm, with "the sound of an Arabian kootch dance." Ray always claimed the song was influenced by *Lawrence of Arabia*, and by *King Kong*, perhaps one should read a bit of tongue-in-cheek to that. The careful listener will also hear a decided bit of "Night on Bald Mountain." Justin laid a little bit of sitar music on top of "Veteran Cosmic Rocker" to put "icing on the cake," and it stands today as one of the better rocker songs in their line-up. It was played live in tour and was well received.

Justin talked about the incredible energy on "The Voice," which was the first thing the band recorded together with Patrick. For "In My World," B.J. Cole used a pedal steel guitar, something a little different from a regular electric guitar; it does sound a bit Western, doesn't it? Dave Symonds, the DJ who first sponsored their return to the U.K. in 1967 and contributing writer to *Threshold of a Dream;* did the recitation of "Painted Smile." Pip said he has this imagery about "After You Came," of teams of slaves rowing Roman galleys. So there are a lot of different facets to the album, and a lot of fingers in the creative pie.

From interviews with Gordon Marshall in the '90s, it appears that the Moody Blues are mildly socialistic over their musical instruments, with the exception of Justin, who would probably bite your arm off if you touched his 335 without permission. In a Moody Blues recording studio, everyone is very generous in sharing gear with others as the need might be. "No ego" is the byword, any band member can pick up any instrument and add to the soundtrack. John and Mike Pinder were both on cellos for "The Balance," and Mike often played rhythm guitar behind Justin as he was picking.

In bad times, that door swung the other way, with good reason after the "burn" the band got when Decca broke up (as we shall soon see.) When the Moodies and Moraz got into conflict in 1991, the Moodies locked up Patrick's studio full of keyboards and Macs, leaving the poor man in serious withdrawal. Justin's bond to his 335 has been mentioned. But once, in concert, when Ray had a problem with his flute, he literally chucked said flute over his shoulder and called his roadie for a new one, which appeared *post haste*. So in the Moody world, ownership of musical instruments can be a bit nebulous, and differ from artist to artist.

During the year in *Long Distance Voyager* production, little men had been mysteriously appearing and putting inventory stickers on their microphones and equipment, in preparation for selling the Stuff due to Decca bankruptcy. Decca vanished a piece at a time. Their orchestral equipment was all sold out from under them, and they had to finish recording the orchestral parts at CTS in Wembly.

The final crowning blow was when they went to look for their Steinway grand piano, and found it missing in action. A search of the area turned it up for sale in a local music store; the vultures had literally wheeled the thing away in the middle of the night. The piano had been a gift to the band from Sir Edward Lewis and was not property of Decca; this was taking socialism just a bit far! Happily, in a later video interview, the piano turned up in Justin's front room in Kingston, so he was able to reclaim it somehow.

Today, Decca's old studios are used as a storage room for the National Opera's scenery. The accounts were so cannibalized, for a while it was risky to say who owned the Moody Blues' publishing rights; it seemed to change every six months (Universal as of 2007.) The playback party on April 13, 1981 was more than a little emotional, as it was also the end of Decca, and of their magical studio.

Voyagers--In 1979, according to *Higher and Higher* #41, a seven and one-half hour composite video of the *Voyager* space probe, with various space scenes; was all set to the music from *To Our Children's Children's Children*. It was presented at a $1000/plate dinner for the benefit of the National Space Institute in Las Vegas. John Denver, himself a pilot, was one of the chairmen of the NSI. Denver also had corporate ties through Weintraub and Huelett to the Moodies.

The group who produced this video (also loosely associated with JPL) did such a nice job, they were asked to cook up the lighting and set designs for the *Long Distance Voyager* tour; this included the plastic *Voyager* spaceship and the inflatable planets that "floated" overhead. The entire thing was intended as a prototype for a hoped-for larger

Earth Space Expo. Jim Dilettoso and Alan Ames also came up with the lighting effects and served as consultants on all Moody Blues tours up through the "Red Rocks" tours. It's really neat reading in *Higher and Higher* #41.*

With Pip Williams producing, *Long Distance Voyager* was released May 15, 1981, and went all the way to #1. They toured successfully from opening May 26 (in Germany) to closing, Dec 6 (Florida); they generated countless rave reviews in the music magazines. "The Voice" and "Gemini Dream" both won ASCAP awards. *Long Distance Voyager* also spawned many single hits, and established the Moody Blues as electronic wizards, well able to keep up with the rest of the popular music world.

John would later say the *Long Distance Voyager* tour was like something out of *This is Spinal Tap*. The blow-up balloon planets developed leaks, deflated as the night wore on, and by the end of a show would be "pear shaped" with fat bottoms. Saturn started out in the entourage, and as the tour wore on, the inflatable rings fell off; and suddenly they had Jupiter hanging over their heads. There's a story that the rings actually fell on Graeme during a show; one can only imagine Graeme thrashing around, trying to play drums while the slowly deflating rings settled about him. The sets generated a good deal of mirth among the band and crew, prompting Justin to say of the *faux* planets, to one reviewer, "I don't know how they got there. They just follow us around." Even the program from this tour has a little astrogation star chart showing all their venues as stars, and some guy in a space suit is standing with the band in the group photo. (Maybe the band was radioactive.)

The Moodies say at this time that a younger audience began to come to the band; there is the feeling of nostalgia about the LDV tour, but also a freshness brought about by the electronic keyboards of Moraz. The fact is, the rest of us were getting older, and kids always like good rock n' roll. But in addition to the young party hounds, they were joined by the older dedicated fan group who truly loved the music and would show up even if the album was not in the pop charts. The Moody Blues appeal, even still, to a very wide spectrum of age; it's a point that the marketing companies for a while, failed to realize. "Gemini Dream" was very pop for the time, and it spent some time in the top of the charts.

It's interesting to note that the early '80s are when the fan club really began to take shape and become part of the developing rock history surrounding the Moody Blues. People passed around bootlegs of Moody performances and interviews, just from contacting, networking and "sharing with friends." The best-informed fanzine in the Moody fan base, *Higher and Higher*, edited by Mark Murley and Randy Salas, issued its first publication in the spring of 1984. In twenty-two years they published fifty issues, averaging three per year, full of interviews, and news clips of the Moodies, as well as interviews of people associated with the Moodies. They offered information about where to find more information. Indeed, *Higher and Higher* #6 offers a fine bibliography of video bootlegs for the beginning collector.

Taken as a whole, the *Higher and Higher* database is incredible source material on the band and is highly recommended. Other fan-based "newsletters" would surface in the next 16 years, but none with the comprehensive scope and professional approach Mark and Randy were able to achieve.

By now, there are so many Moody Blues video and audio boots, they are impossible to catalog, even for the most dedicated collector. And there is a legal aspect to this tape documentation too; many collectors are mum about exactly what they have, and about sharing it with others. Then you have people blatantly selling bootlegs on Ebay, so many that the FBI would have to generate an entire department just to track Moody bootlegs, not to mention all the other classic rock groups from the '60s. The most recent news on bootlegs is that *youtube.com* seems to have an unlimited, unregulated supply of Moody videos, legit, illegitimate, fabricated, bogus; copyrights have apparently flown out the window on this matter. Ain't the Internet *wunnderful?*

Melancholy Man--Long Distance Voyager was released May 15, 1981. The same day, *Pinder v. Decca Records Co. Ltd. and Another* was filed. The album went on to sell wildly (went to #1) and the touring band toured (to rave reviews) up until Dec 6, 1981. So I have no idea when the actual court dates were: sometime 1982 I presume, as there is no touring that year. This leads me to believe Mike blocked the band from using the name Moody Blues for 1982, once their touring contract was fulfilled.

This is a direct quote in *US Magazine* (September 1, 1981), a year and a half after *Long Distance Voyager* started production, and WELL into an American tour: *All efforts to keep in touch with Pinder have mysteriously dead-ended.* I just report it, I didn't write it. According to Graeme in his *Modern Drummer* interview, they only communicated with Mike through his lawyer after 1978, regarding royalty checks.

Once the *Long Distance Voyager* promo tour dates started appearing (spring 1981), THAT got Mike's attention in a hurry. The exact timeline is thus uncertain, but in the Steve Goss interview of Feb 8, 1997, Justin states that Tony Clarke and Mike Pinder put an injunction on the release of *Long Distance Voyager.*

In *Moody Blues vs. Moraz* (1992, televised on *Court T.V.)* Patrick's lawyer brought up a point during the trial (what brought it on I don't know, as Mike wasn't anywhere near the courtroom, but remember Patrick's lawyer was also Pinder's lawyer at the time); that Mike had been deeply shocked in 1981 to find a whole album had been recorded and produced, without him even knowing about it.

Mike likes money like everyone else, he sued the Moody Blues for breach of contract, and also for the right to control the name "Moody Blues." This does make sense, as he was a founding member of the band. But, several interviews (before and since) have pointed out that Ray Thomas and Denny Laine also took part in the naming of "The Moody Blues," so Mike was not exclusive in this. Tony

Clarke was also part of the suit, as he had left the band, but was considered "a member" and also had rights to the name "Moody Blues." As gentlemen in business, the agreement had been that the six partners, Hayward, Lodge, Thomas, Pinder, Edge, and Clarke, all had equal shares in "the Moody Blues." Their company Threshold, which was now no longer producing records, was their property, equally.

On May 1, 1977, a Decca service contract had been signed by all six (Tony, Mike, Justin, Ray, John and Graeme) saying that the Moody Blues were the six of them, essentially making them a band, and functional property of Decca. Part of the eventual settlement (1982) was for the four remaining band members to buy out the shares of Clarke and Pinder, leaving Thomas, Edge, Hayward and Lodge each with 25% of the stock. Money changed hands. Paperwork was generated. Decca was restructured at a higher level.

According to Diane Palermo, who posted this on *Lost Chords* (a Moody Blues newsgroup), she saw the trial, and "Justin had to sing in court to prove who was the 'voice of the Moody Blues.'" We must presume that the judge (and/or jury?) decided Justin sounded more like the Moody Blues than Mike Pinder did.

During the trial the judge pointed out that the touring band had been out promoting their catalog (touring for three years), while Mike was resting at home, therefore some of his complaint was out of line (my paraphrase.) In turn, both Tony and Mike said that contractually, without THEIR input, *Long Distance Voyager* was not a "Moody Blues" album. It got a little ugly. This suit was somewhat "normal" in that often the closing of a large corporation generates many lawsuits, as various participants cover their bases. Sure, feelings were hurt, there were emotions, but some of it was "self-inflicted wounds" too. Those who kept it professional came out unscathed. Some of the problems were surely male ego, and a lot of it can be chalked up to plain ol' DENIAL.

Ultimately it all boiled down to just sorting out the royalties. Mike sure didn't want to tour any more. Tony didn't want to produce the Moodies anymore. I would assume Mike, and Tony's estate still get royalties off the albums they worked on, the "Core Seven" plus *Octave*; all of them still in commercial production.

In hindsight and in my humble opinion, it's a good thing that they DID charge ahead with *Long Distance Voyager*, without waiting for Mike to make another appearance. They ALL (past, present and future band members) might have gone down with the sinking Decca ship. The album was a #1 hit. All ships rose with the tide. Mike wound up with enough money to buy a nice piece of property in Northern California, in the Sacramento area; the deed is dated April 1984. Tony bought a boat and turned it into a floating production studio. Mike eventually wound up with enough boys in his family to have his own band! (Google them under "Pinder Brothers." They are on twitter, facebooks etc.)

Mark Murley and friends found Mike Pinder in 1985 (if not before), and there is a very informative interview with him in *Higher and Higher* #5. Otherwise, like Tony Clarke, even though *Higher and Higher* gave him lots of coverage every issue, Pinder begins to fade from the serious Moody Blues musical mainstream at this time. Many people have tried to "make it happen" when it comes to a "reunion" between the remaining Moodies, and Mike Pinder. From what I have read, it does not seem a likely issue to spend time struggling with**.

In 2009, Tony Clarke, Ray Thomas and Mike Pinder all got together for Ray's second wedding and had a "reunion" or fifty percent thereof you could say. Later that year, Tony Clarke passed away with emphysema.

*The *Long Distance Voyager* tour was calculated to please and astound. Comparing what I read about this in *Higher and Higher*, and from my own sources, the tour of *Long Distance Voyager*, had its conceptual beginnings in the mid-'70s. Sometime circa 1975, a theatre artist by the name of Megan Terry, loosely associated with the Mark Taper Forum in Los Angeles, had conceived of a notion of "multi-media entertainment." I'm not even sure she was the one to originate the concept: extravaganzas such as she envisioned actually go very far back to the designs of grandiose and radical stage designer Craig, in the 1920s. The concept was to have a "Space Pirate" chase, that ran in live action across a stage, continued in a filmed overhead projection, ran through three different screens around the room, showed up as blips on the radar scope, and if she could get away with it, would have projected hologram images into your lap. It was pretty radical for the time, early virtual reality! I'm not sure anyone to date has been able to do the complete concept, some 4-D shows at Disneyland come close. Certainly Batt's *The Hunting of a Snark* had elements of this, so did *Outside Blake's Window*, a ballet/opera done by Tandy Beal in San Francisco during the '90s. Multimedia is very familiar now. Cirque de Soilel does it, but it's really hard to take on the road, as the designers for the Moody Blues would attempt. In 2006-2007, Jeff Wayne has taken the concept of "projecting holograms" combining live action and singing and applied them to *The War of the Worlds*. And it's getting very good reviews too. Hot on Jeff's heels, Tony Clarke was talking about (in 2007) a show about the Pioneer Spacecraft, called *ARC*, and it too sounded very multimedia. Theatre and entertainment just keep on evolving! In the 2009 Moody tour, technology caught up with concept. The backdrop of the Moodies' set had first projections of star galaxies, and then live movies of the band projected and "mixed" (that is special effects) done live during the show. And they even turned the camera on the audience a few times. We live in an age of miracles, don't we? The cameras were very small and not visible to the audience.

** Mike and Tara's first son was born in Hawaii in 1980, which may have quite a bit to do with Mike just not being able to make it for the production of *Long Distance Voyager*. He had moved to another life and had other priorities.

XIII) No Time Like the Present: 1983-1986

People behind the scenes are really what has made the Moody Blues happen as a band. Before the 1980s they apparently wallowed in a legal and financial mess, but there was so much money coming in, no one noticed it. As per a 1970 *New Music Express* interview, John was trying his best to handle it, but obviously he would rather play music than hustle money, and it was just too much for him. Justin said in an interview he even wound up suing himself once!

Wyn Mather came "on board" in the early '80s as accountant and office manager for the Moody Blues, at Threshold Records in Cobham. She also probably helped protect them financially from things like the collapse of Decca. Wyn seemed like a very cool lady, and the only videos we have of her are from the *Moodies vs. Moraz* trial, December 1992. She passed away right around New Year 2000, having guided the administration of the Moodies for almost twenty years. A lot of fan club secretaries came and went over these years, but Wyn was always around.

Another backstage person worthy of note is a Sasquatch-sized roadie with the handle of "Mother" (John Bennett) who was signed on as Ray's personal flute technician. He also doubled (for obvious reasons) as security, and (from other little hints) was the keeper of the hootch as well.

Two other people who helped out backstage at various levels during the 90s and into the new century, are Mark Hoague and "KC." I think the world of KC (her nick name) she often liaisons with fans for things like backstage tours and VIP events. I first saw KC waving costumes in cleaner bags around outside the stage door of the Schnitzer in Portland, cussing a blue streak and trying to find the backstage entrance!!! That was maybe 1992? She a tough lady and seems the type to hold a Black Belt. ALL these folks are very professional and it's a very refreshing thing to see in a rock and roll band. Things Stay Organized.

The early 1980s were not good times for the band, according to interviews with Justin, though in other interviews he refers to the late '80s as "good years." Besides losing their guardian angel, Sir Edward Lewis, and having to deal with lawyers and piano thieves, they had human tragedy beset them. Sue Coulson, their beloved fan club secretary, was a personable young woman. But she was also gravely ill and wasted away before everyone's eyes with leukemia. To this day, the Moody Blues put leukemia charities and donations at the top of their list when they do non-profit performances. Justin's older brother Richard, also passed away around this time, in 1984, of a heart attack. After that shock, Justin says he started taking better care of himself.

Ray's first marriage broke up around this time, too. In a remarkable show of class, Patrick Moraz deflected some information about this during *Moodies vs. Moraz* 1992, when his legal counsel brought up the story. I don't think the details would be appropriate to repeat, but as has been said before, the Moody Blues are all very human people, everyone makes mistakes, and when marriages break up, usually there are two people to blame, not just one. Graeme says he wrote the song "Going Nowhere" as his second marriage (to Sue) was breaking up, in 1983; and "I'll Be Level with You" as his first marriage (to Carol) was breaking up, for the record. Plainly things were not perfect in their personal lives.

Justin was apparently doing fine in his personal life, and later would say that he found the '80s to be among his happiest times for his home life. He bought Toggs (his main squeeze horse buddy) in 1973. Then in 1980, he bought a stud farm, the Soley Farm in the Wiltshire/Berkshire area, with forty horses (this in addition to his menagerie in Cornwall.) [In 2015, I visited the west country in England, and found the general Soley Farm area is close to "The Old Hayward Farm" so I wonder if this was not right where Justin's grandparents lived. It's a lovely area, and the back roads there reminded me of Hobbiton.] The accommodations included living quarters for five humans, forty-eight horses, and assorted guest cottages: see *Higher and Higher* #21/22. The Haywards had many hours of enjoyment, doing whatever it is horse fanatics do when they are communing with their equines, and avoiding the rest of us yahoos.

From the articles, Justin seems to be a bit of a closet architect and planner, as he spent a good deal of time building the 400 acre, run-down farm into a notable stud ranch, "making it into all the things horses like" as Justin put it. It sold in 1987 at considerably more than he had paid for it. Justin buying and selling the farm coincided with his daughter "getting interested" in horses, and then at the age of 17, probably "getting disinterested" in horses. I think he lost Toggs around 1990 too, so that had to have put him off horses a bit; he really liked Toggs. Wow, what a nice dad Justin is! Some daddies buy plastic horses for their little girls: Justin bought the whole farm!!!

John and Justin took over most of the song writing duties of the Moodies about this time. Considering what the others were going through in their personal lives, this is no shock. The facts are that Justin and John had wives who stuck with them no matter what. That has to be something that lends itself to a stable, calm lifestyle that, in turn, lends itself to good writing.

It seems a shame the others didn't contribute. One of the best cycles of songs on any album certainly has to be "The Veteran Cosmic Rocker" song and poem on *Long Distance Voyager*, penned by a very talented Ray Thomas. This is not to overlook songs like "Legend of a Mind," "My Little Lovely" (*Strange Times*), and "Nice to Be Here" on *Every Good Boy Deserves Favor*. Ray not writing, and Graeme's poems missing from albums in the '80s are a serious loss.

So in the mid '80s they seemed to lose direction; the album done in 1983, *The Present* (also produced by Pip Williams) did not make very much money at all, and fell into pop obscurity with a pitiful plop. They may have even lost money on it; go figure, because it's as good, if not better, than their other albums. Perhaps the world was too tangled in the throes of Reaganomics, and too busy stripping S&Ls to pay attention to a few romantic rockers. [*In fact, we Americans almost went to war with the Soviet Union over KAL 007 being shot down, in August of 1983.*] The world was just not going the same direction as the Moody Blues. This would be Pip's last album with the band, and like Tony Clarke, he too cited "exhaustion" as a factor in his dropping out as their producer.

The Moodies themselves weren't even sure what they were doing. Justin wrote "Running Water" on a small Casio keyboard he had bought for daughter Doremi, and even played it in concert with the same Casio. And it sounded great; Justin says he wrote the song just sitting in his front room one day, it was one of those songs that just "pops out." Then as a contrast you had Patrick with three Macs, and seventeen monster keyboards, frankly getting no better musical effect. No one came right out and said it, but "sometimes less is more." *

Looking at low sales on *The Present*, the Moodies decided to offer Patrick Moraz a stock option. It was a good deal, I think they offered him 19% of the stock in Threshold, in lieu of some of the contract pay he was to get from working on *The Present* and in lieu of some of his tour money. It was their way of saying, *join the group, take part in our faith about our future success*. Like all stock options, it was a way of having security in the company.

Patrick weighed the money he would get for his contracted pay, and the money he would get for being a stock partner in Threshold. And he decided he gleaned more money via contract. So he signed a document saying he had refused the stock option, sometime around the year 1983. At the time, it made no difference, other than he got a bigger immediate pay check; but that simple sweep of the pen would later make a huge difference to the entire band.** It's hard to believe Patrick allegedly has a marketing degree, and failed to take advantage of the stock option, in retrospect.

The Moody Blues again toured, to support their new album. During this tour, Ray got a pretty rude review about his stage performance, for the Wembly Show. This show may be the video which Graeme referred to as "a great rip-off" in an early *Moodymania* interview. Heaping insult upon the injury of his recent divorce, it's a wonder that Ray didn't pack it in after that. In fact, the entire 1983/1984 tour got some pretty snide reviews, apparently press people lost their sense of taste during this time period. The Moody Blues were showing their age, and the world of popular music can be very cruel at times.

The good news is that the cutting remarks had an effect, and a couple of the band members stopped drinking and eating like they had been, and adopted health programs, to excellent effect, as they still looked pretty good seventeen years later in 2000. None had dropped with heart attacks, overdoses or strokes, that we know of. Probably around this time, as exercise, John, Graeme, and Justin's wife Marie took up golf, at the Coombe Hill country club, near Cobham. They were eventually joined by Graeme's drum technician, Alan Terry. John claims to have always been a tennis player and fit into the country club set well but refers to his chosen sport of golf as "Zen."

Justin apparently found golf a bit slow and took up working out in gyms. The Haywards were both avid equestrians in the early '80s and didn't get into their other exercise programs until the late '80s when they sold their stud ranch. Justin took up weight lifting when avid "buff master" Gordon Marshall joined the band in 1991. In all cases, "exercise is good" and they all took their physical well-being very seriously. Note: we must assume Ray, a dedicated fisherman, got his exercise wrestling whoppers into his boat!

Money must have been tight, and in 1984, when the company released a compilation album, *Voices in the Sky*, the Moodies toured to support it. As well as making their dosh (enough to cover expenses), they netted over $100,000 for NSPOC, a benefit for abused children.

The fan club starts to really take on interesting aspects by this time; *Long Distance Voyager* brought more fans to the band beyond what had been around in the early Core

Seven days. In 1984, the Moodies held one of their Christmas parties, which would eventually become a regular matter for them, inviting some of the fans to meet and greet the band. A LOT of people would be running in and out of the home offices in the next decade, from reports. An intern named "Christine," who worked for the Moodies in the early '80s (apparently helping out as Sue wasted away) says she got the opportunity to ride along once on the tour bus from Los Angeles to Las Vegas during these years. I asked her the obvious question; "Well was there anything juicy going on? Did you have to defend your honor?" "No" was her matter of fact reply, "They are really truly gentlemen! John has a wedding ring about this big," here she held her fingers out in simulation of a very fat band. "They are very clean behind the scenes!" She also baby-sat John's kids on occasion.***

It's consistent with reviews of the times. The reporters meet the Moody Blues gathering in the hotel lobby before they can board their bus and depart. They can't find Ray. He finally comes in, not reeling in the arms of babes, but holding up a string of fish he had gotten up early to catch.

Graeme, ever active, started sitting in with a little group called Loud, Confident and Wrong, as per his interview in *Modern Drummer*. Mike Gallaher was on keyboards, and Robin Lumley also played in the group. Robin is a bit of a wildman (no shock being a friend of Graeme's; he has some interesting friends!) Anyway, Robin wrote a very funny story for the OFC newsletter in the '90s, dubbing Graeme's lady of the time "Commander Amander" and his son Matthew "Medge." Graeme is likewise known occasionally as "Gredge."

She, Shoes and Wolves --Justin (as always) continued to write poetry and songs and managed to maintain a fairly consistent solo career. In 1985, he penned the closing love ballad "Eternal Love" for the movie *She* (apparently based on a female "Valkyrie" comic-book warrioress. It's a fairly amusing movie.) "Eternal Love" was written twice, from

Justin's interviews. He wrote it the first time and took it to the director; the director said "it's nice but not what I want; write it again." Justin described the first version as being "more punchy" than the final version.

He rewrote it, and the final song on the movie is the result. Apparently that's the only existing track of the song, and it's impossible to hear some of the lyrics over the chomping of horses. Rick Wakeman, eternally fated to be peripherally linked to the Moody Blues (or maybe it's the other way around), did the rest of the score for the movie. The words to "Eternal Love" can be found in *Higher and Higher* #21/22, as well as more about the song and movie.

Justin also penned a short song for children, entitled "Shoe People" in 1986. It's a very neat little ditty with the flavor of a skiffle band (or English Music Hall) and easy words. By Justin's account, he wrote it for a friend (James Driscoll) who did the animation of the popular children's cartoon *Shoe People*. In the States, this show has syndicated on *Eureeka's Castle* over the years, and (according to my son, who was an avid viewer) the entire theme did not always play with it. I went out searching for it on the webs, found it (Justin wasn't credited); and the MP3 download said "Warning, this will get stuck in your head!" Alas, it is now considered one of the "lost cartoons" of the '80s.

Swinging to the other end of the spectrum, around the same time, Justin penned a lovely, dark song "Something Dangerous" for *The Howling IV*. It's a terrible movie, not even very good horror, and even worse acting; I was cheering the wolves on by the end. The song alone is worth checking the video out from the local rental store; as Mark Murley put it, Justin's song is "a rose in a landfill." The song is a clear copy on the movie credits, and definitely a departure from the usually positive, humorous music of the Moody Blues.

Beach Boys Summer--The "solo years" in which John and Justin cut such a wide swath with their *Blue Jays* album, were not lost upon the music world. In 1986, the Blue Jays were invited to participate in 4th of July festivities, along with the Beach Boys, and Ringo Starr (among others) at the Washington Memorial in Washington, D.C. The Secretary of the Interior actually tried to block the Beach Boys from playing at the Washington Monument that 4th of July, citing that they were "not indicative of true American music." President Reagan (and Nancy!) stepped in and cleared the way for the California band to play after all! It's a great video, everyone in the audience is rocking out in shorts and halter tops.

An amusing story from Justin about this concert, surfaced in *Juke* January 31, 1987. Mike Love was trying to explain to Ringo a rhythm he was supposed to pick up for "Help Me Rhonda." Ringo replied, with a totally straight face, that he had never bought a Beach Boys song, and didn't have the slightest idea what Mike was talking about. A shaken Love regrouped and asked Ringo if he could do "Back in the U.S.S.R." Ringo, obviously having a good time (no doubt John and Justin sitting in the back of the dressing room, also keeping typically British straight poker faces) replied that Paul had done drums on that Beatles tune. (Dang Brits, what were they doing playing on our Independence Day anyway???)

British humor aside, the video to the 4th of July, 1986 Great Beach Boys Musical Meeting is wonderful, and very worth watching if you can lay your hands on it.

Obviously the Moody Blues and Beach Boys are fond of each other's music, not surprising, as both groups are so heavily influenced by Buddy Holly. The Beach Boys blanketed the radio in the Los Angeles Basin in 1968 when the Moodies first toured here, so it's no shock they like them. Brian Wilson was able to travel to the U.K. during the '80s and did some live music in England after one of the Moody shows at Wembley Arena.

John was in contact with Bias Boshell during this period (1986). Bias initially came on board The Good Ship Moody Blue to work on John's second solo album, which never happened. So Bias eventually became the second back-up keyboardist during the '80s. Bias has an impressive resume, and when John met him, Bias had been touring with Barclay James Harvest (April/May 1987). Barclay James Harvest also worked on the *Eye of Wendor* album. More can be read about Bias in *Higher and Higher* #6. Bias would go on to be a fun addition to the show, wearing some really wacky things on stage: purple frock coats, and a red t-shirt with Sylvester the Cat come to mind. He actually appeared in a Santa suit during curtain call of one Christmas concert at Caesar's Tahoe, in the late '90s, getting wild laughter from audience and the rest of the band alike. Bias dropped out of the touring band in May, 2001. In 2009, Ray and Bias were said to be working on more music for release.

Going to the Mountain--Justin was able to do his own solo album from 1980-1985, with a distinctly different flavor (almost steel guitar, or Western) entitled *Moving Mountains*. Released in 1985 on a very obscure label that went out of business shortly after issuing the album (Anchor Records), the CD (or vinyl if you can find it used) is well worth buying and owning. It differs from a normal Moody album by having a neat steely twang to the guitar tenor.

With Jeff Wayne, Justin co-wrote the dynamic (and yes, punchy) "Silverbird." They not only released it as a single, they cut a rather abstract video to go with it, filmed near Lizard at Land's End in Cornwall. In June 2014 (Q&A on his website), Justin talked about the production of this video, saying the director had a "pal" who filmed the scenes, flying in an ultra-light. Quite advanced work for the time. Although interesting, the video is not quite up to the standards of what was to become a burgeoning market on the new MTV stations. But it is cutting edge, and interesting to note that Justin was getting his foot in the door early on with the video market. According to notes from a September 2007 interview in Australia, Justin wrote the lyrics, and Jeff Wayne wrote the melody to "Silverbird."

When he was recording the Clifford T. Ward song "The Best is Yet to Come," Justin said it was him just standing in the middle of the orchestra, and singing, mixing it all together on the same tracks. Clifford T. Ward was another Brummie, quite popular with U.K. music lovers; I had never heard of him here in America, until this album.

Other artists worked on *Moving Mountains* as well: Eric Stewart from 10cc, plays keyboard on "Goodbye." And Martin Wyatt, whom Justin had known from his solo years before the Moody Blues, was the album's producer. It was something Justin took his time with and worked on with friends over a five-year period. It shows: it's a very good album. *Martin Wyatt incidentally is very cool: he was along as Justin's personal manager during the Justin Border's tour in the late '90s; I heckled Martin a bit from the crowd, and got a pretty good response from him. He's ok in my book. [Sorry, Martin, for the heckling.]* More about Martin Wyatt can be read in *Higher and Higher* #10.

This was to be Peter Knight's last album; he passed away shortly after the release of *Moving Mountains*, and the album is dedicated to him. Peter of course, was the one who composed and did the orchestral scores for *Days of Future Passed,* and he worked on *Blue Jays* too. He also worked on the theme for *The Bounder*, a UK/PBS series in the '80s. He did the music for Jim Henson's *Dark Crystal!* His wonderful orchestral work on *Moving Mountains* "tied it all together," and really made the album what it is: an outstanding cohesive collaboration of many talents. There is a very good biography of Peter Knight to be found in *Higher and Higher* #9.

Again, perhaps spurred by Justin's acceptable solo attempt on *Moving Mountains*, the Moody Blues rallied to follow Justin in recording another album, this time entitled *The Other Side of Life*.

* A basic tenant of the Bauhaus art movement, early 1900s

**Moodies vs. Moraz*, December 1992, Los Angeles, CA (Court T.V.)

*** She has told other interesting stories about stone circles in the garden outside Threshold, to "tap cosmic energies." The band was apparently experimenting with feng shui principles in their garden in the early 1980s! One of my readers piped up upon reading this, saying "It's not feng shui, it's one of those alleged primitive things Atlantian hippies love!" I haven't seen it, but the garden was landscaped pretty weird at Threshold. An "English Garden" thang apparently. And yes John Lodge is into antediluvian stuff (look up the Wiki, I dare you), maybe other band members too. Atlantis is said to have had nine stone circles. Anyone have a photo?

XIV) On the Sea: 1987-1990

Justin Hayward is the most gracious dinosaur around -- Dennis Hunt, the *Los Angeles Times,* 1986.

"Doctor in Distress" -- *we always knew he wore a dress* -- Moodies on line chat, 1994

"Doctor in Distress" (single - 1985)/ *Justin Hayward and John Lodge participated in this charity single for Cancer Relief which also was part of the effort to stave off cancellation of the TV show "Dr. Who."* -- off a newsgroup

[clipped on-line] Date: Sun, 6 Feb 2005 *I was reading the booklet, from my newly purchased CD of Bowie's early album, "Space Oddity." I noticed that the bass guitar is credited to "John Lodge, Tony Visconti and Herbie Flowers." Looking at the original vinyl album I still have the credits are, "Hank, Tony Visconti and Herbie Flowers."* [Herbie Flowers also played later with Justin and Gordon Marshall in *The War of the Worlds* stage show.]

Well, the Moodies weren't poor. But they weren't ready to quit working and retire yet, either. There was no denying that their last studio album had flopped, and they were minus a producer with Pip gone, so out they went hunting for a new one. Enter Tony Visconti. They say that John and Justin first talked with him in his kitchen. This sounds like an Italian, doesn't it? More business deals have probably been struck in Italian kitchens than have been struck on golf courses, which is saying something.

In the mid to late '80s, technology was doing another subtle shift. Patrick was synched in as part of the "sound" and the old electronics/acoustic debate again reared its ugly head. In *Higher and Higher* #5, Justin is talking about valves/tubes in amps; and the beginnings of solid-state technology in guitar amps, which were apparently a bit slow to accept transistors. A big debate between the "warm" sound/feel of analog versus digital becomes a serious consideration for the band around this time. Justin preferred the warmer sound of analog, and "valve" technology. In 2002, my sources told me musicians were again going back to tube technology, for a warmer sound in stage amplifiers. Where will it all end?

    Into this stepped Tony Visconti. He arrived with his own impressive history; he was an American who moved to Brum in the '60s, met Denny with his Electric String Band, then produced ELO and David Bowie (the Goblin King *hisself!*) among others. Apparently the change-over to Visconti was welcome by all, as Tony "cracked the whip" and set down limits on what was going to happen. It was more disciplined and orderly. No more hootch in the recording studio, for one thing, and regular hours for another. The Moodies who interviewed during this time liked it that way, which makes one wonder what had been going on before, that Tony had to change! It also makes one wonder why some Moodies chose to not be around for the recording of *Sur la Mer*.

    During their settling in period, Tony had worked on Justin's solo *Moving Mountains*, producing the ballad, "One Again." It sounds little like *Star Cops* doesn't it? Tony also would use Justin's talents in the popular U.K. *Star Cops* TV series, with his romantic ballad "It Won't Be Easy" as the title track. By adding a simple line, "reach across the stars" suddenly cops, lovers, romantics and space operas become part of the same theme. *Star Cops* is very worth watching, especially for the avid Moody Blues fan, as several of Justin's solo songs are done instrumentally over the action. For example, "Nostradamus" as a dark, chilly guitar solo, is heard over a lunar rover scene, a wonderful effect.

    Justin commented in interviews, that he learned a lot from working on the show; and he makes some very intelligent observations about how the music should NOT be heard on film track. That's something the show director has to deal with, where to bring the focus, to the music or the visuals. Lots more about Tony Visconti can be read in

Higher and Higher #7/8; he also has a very nice website, *www.tonyvisconti.com*. He has an impressive resume!

Other little things have come out in the years that Tony has interacted with Moody fans on line: he claims to have photos of the band at a nudist colony, wearing "nothing but daisies." (April 24, 1995 on line chats) I don't know if this is cause for thrill or for laughter. Imagine comparing "how many daisies it takes" to cover your favorite Moody! Tony is a real character and has done a lot in documenting the goings-on of the Moody Blues, in a positive yet honest way, and is a great favorite with fans whenever he shows up for a Moody show.

Visconti also did a very enjoyable interview with *Higher and Higher,* which can be read in issue #25. And Justin was best man at Tony's wedding to May Pang, so obviously their relationship went a bit deeper than just recording.

What I really like about Tony: he is honest (unto blunt) about the music business and tries to tell it like it is. For example, we have a certain contingency in the Moody fan club that goes on and on about mellotrons, like they are fantastic machines. Visconti in no uncertain terms has said they are piles of junk, and very hard to handle. Mike Pinder has been the only Pop musician gifted enough to really wield the mellotron properly, in my humble opinion. In today's electronic age, it is ridiculous to deal with antiquated machinery; speaking as a former electrician myself, and knowing what I know about mellotrons, I have to agree with Tony. Adding the mellotron back in the '60s was better than hauling around an upright Baby Grand when the Moodies got their start, but today you can get the sound of a concert piano, or a mellotron, out of a suitcase-sized keyboard that you can carry under one arm.

Justin claims Tony saw to it that every sound from their mellotrons was sampled before (as Justin put it) they turned to dust; so allegedly all their electronic sound is STILL mellotron based. (*Goldmine*, Aug 13, 2010)

They say that in your '40s, everyone goes through a thing called "a midlife crisis." The Moody Blues, being normal people, undoubtedly found themselves suddenly "mid-life," and wearing the daisies to prove it! While Ray and Graeme coped by struggling with divorces and tried to fill in the gaps by wenching a bit, Justin wrote a song about it.

Without belaboring Justin's inspirations for writing the hit song "Your Wildest Dreams" released in 1987 on *The Other Side of Life* album, it seems a simple enough concept. He wondered whatever happened to the first love in his life and wondered where she might be. For his inspiration he turned to a quasi-Irish melody, tucked in a rock beat. And (no doubt inspired by the swooping music soundtrack to *Top Gun*,* released the same year the album was written) added lush, ethereal filler and dynamic rhythms with synthesizers. In his *Higher and Higher* interview, Tony Visconti says he played the lovely introduction to the song on synthesizer; probably Patrick was away in Los Angeles at the time, working on one of his numerous movie scores.

I Want My MTV--Next came the video, and for this newly open MTV market, the Moodies tossed something together that was genius in its simplicity. They envisioned several scenarios for the "meeting of lost loves" twenty years later, the funniest of which was for the girl to run into Graeme's arms, not to Justin! She had been looking BEHIND Justin all those years, from the front rows!

But the famous, award-winning video is now as it stands. The lead singer's (*that other Justin* as Justin calls him) old girlfriend, facing her own mid-life crisis, goes to look for her lost love, and they are pulled apart by different worlds. In a way, it's very poignant about the isolation of the rock world, showing a tragedy of true love torn apart by (as Justin would put it) "the road that I must choose."

The Moody Blues struck a mythological baby boomer chord that even they didn't realize was there; everyone went bonkers over the "Wildest Dreams" video! EVERYONE was having a mid-life crisis, wondering about lost loves. And of course, the hit video, which played over and over on MTV, brought more and more fans to the fan club, every one of them smitten by Justin's blonde surfer hair and good looks. The other band members are really in the background, as it's supposed to be a story about a lead singer.

Another neat thing about the video is the '60s costumes, the Neru jackets and so forth. When Justin got a look at what they were supposed to wear in the video, he went home and dug the REAL stuff out of his closet. So, what they have on in the video is real clothing from the clothes-horse himself, Justin. And the nice thing was, it all still fit. The video "In Your Wildest Dreams" went on to be *Billboard Magazine's* Video of the Year for 1989.

In 1987, home video cameras were just becoming a thing you could buy in the stores and play with, if you had the money to do it. I was still in the Navy in 1987, and of course, took my video camera overseas with me. I did a (non-profit) video scrapbook of my squadron's (VP-46) adventures overseas and used "Your Wildest Dreams" as the background music to some pirated aviation clips from Top Gun *(my old squadron, VF-126, was in many of the frames in* Top Gun*). My amateur home video made some travels: imagine my surprise when in August of 1994, the Blue Angels would actually do a commercial video with "Your Wildest Dreams" laid over footage of one of their aerial ballets! Dang and I didn't even get credit for the idea! But it just goes to show, that good ideas are what Moody Blues music is all about.*

In later years, Navy Commander and chief astronaut "Hoot" Gibson would present the Moody Blues with a plaque containing a tape of Moody Blues music that had traveled numerous times in orbit with him on the space shuttle. Aviation and Moody Blues make a good combination! It also proves that sailors have excellent taste in music.

I think the real unspoken effect of the Moodies' MTV video was, to point up that the band was looking BACK at the audience. "You and Me" (*Seventh Sojourn*) and "Blue World" (*The Present*) are plainly songs written in reflection of the audiences that shared the music with the band. Now suddenly, a mythical "love interest" develops between the band and the audience, taking the relationship to another level.

  I guess it would be fair at this point to correct what I said earlier about "wenching." Around 1988, Graeme started keeping company with Amanda, who was a resident of Florida. As per the *Herald Tribune* (Sept 2002), Graeme started hanging around Southern Florida (Manatee County) at this time. Amanda met Graeme when she was a make-up artist; she might be the one working on Graeme's hair in the video *Legend of a Band*; and he mentions her in his Howard Stern interviews. He's a bit naughty too, I would have whacked him for talking like that on public radio, if I were Amanda! Golfing is also great in Florida, no doubt another allure.

  So in 1988, Graeme started sailing his yacht, the *Cutter Edge*, into Floridian ports, for lengthy stays. For all the wild stories that have followed Graeme in his touring legends, I suspect he is more "down home" than we know, as he hung onto Amanda for almost twenty years!

  The video of "The Other Side of Life" is a definite flip side to the usually clean-cut image that the Moodies try to put forth about themselves. Having a new producer might have made a bit of a difference, too: Tony Visconti, talented and personable, had them recording in the Soho district, which is dark and mysterious: a very old part of London, full of interesting characters. For their first meeting, the whole band met Tony at an Asian restaurant, and sure enough, that same restaurant pops up in the video.

  Graeme was later to say he was bored out of his skull during the shooting of this video, so it must have taken a bit of time. It was all worth it. Justin claims the video was written by a nineteen-year-old! In a very dark sort of way, it's a wonderful and rather funny video, but it's also very creepy and scary, people tearing off masks, and playing with human limbs in a very dark burlesque of occultish cults. It's leather, punk rock and grunge, it's German cabaret. It's the sleazy bowels of the city. And it's also a very cool song, no matter what you want to say. Patrick's usual frenetic scale-running is tied down and kept calm by a steady cool beat, and the balance is perfect.

"The Spirit" is one of the last tracks Graeme is involved in for a LONG time, and he co-wrote with Patrick on this. I've always thought the melody sounded more like Graeme; it doesn't have enough scale runs for it to be Patrick's work. Patrick was doing his own albums and movie sound-tracks about this time (1986, *The Stepfather*), and had a lot to keep himself busy. Later in the hearing *Moodies vs Moraz* (1992), he was to complain that he was being ignored for input on the albums.

Plainly the entire group wasn't sure if they should go with the electronic sound or with the ballad format. This album really shows that conflict, while still hanging together somehow, only by the grace of Visconti's talents as a producer. In *Higher and Higher* #11/12, Patrick is a bit critical of "political decisions" on who writes songs for the album. In retrospect, the two guitar players have pretty strong personalities, and may not even have known how much they were dominating the entire band direction. In fact, to them it probably looked like the others just weren't interested. One indeed wonders who showed up for rehearsals, and who stayed at home in front of the telly, sipping brews.

"Talkin' Talkin'" must have been a very weird song to put together. It's heavily synthesized, electronically laced in a straightjacket! And it has an annoying tone whooping up and down, only rescued by a wonderful ripping guitar riff about halfway through, done by Visconti; he called it a Chuck Berry riff. The song had a curious history; apparently it kept getting sent to Ray Thomas by mistake (something about a dingbat assistant.) Ray was still in retreat at his Welsh "Walden Pond" and, being a low-tech sort of guy (and liking it that way), only had an answering machine to play the tape on. He kept getting "Talkin' Talkin'" on his answering machine. Somehow it sounds very funny, this *whooooPPPEE whooooPPEEE* song playing on an answering machine. I bet Ray thought he was having flashbacks. (This was prior to him meeting his second wife Lee, Ray was a bachelor for a long time.)

It doesn't get any better after that. John's "Rock and Roll Over You" might be "punchy" and to Justin's liking, but frankly is too disco for a good Moodies song. Thankfully, it's followed up by one of the simplest, and most effective ballads ever written by Justin, "I Just Don't Care." Songwriters are funny: they don't always write about personal experience, they could be watching and eavesdropping on a couple at the next table in a restaurant and get the idea for a song; you get that feeling about "I Just Don't Care." Whatever the inspiration, Justin gives full throttle to his Libran tendencies to "be in love with Love" and it's a wonderful ballad, one of his best.

The stage performance of "Running Out of Love" was shot for a video and is frankly pretty good for the times. It was included on the "purple box" video from the fan club. And as if to make up for the disco song on the first side, John did a wonderful ballad, "It May Be a Fire" on the flip side.

The body language of the band photo on the back of *The Other Side of Life* is interesting in the same way the cover to *Octave* is. Patrick is standing apart, in fact he might even been seen as "pulling away" from the rest of the band. And Justin is reaching out, trying to include him. The front looks like something that escaped from the *Superman* movies, with their heads floating about in loose frames; and in the foreground, lab equipment. One can only imagine what heady substances they might have been distilling in those mad scientist bottles. (Or maybe Graeme was having General Zod nightmares!) It's a dark album cover, perhaps trying to balance out the very light and elfin art of the prior album cover, the album that had flopped. What the heck WAS going to sell the music, anyway?

The Other Side of Life tour t-shirts were quite clever, and several Moody Blues can be seen wearing them in video interviews of this time. The tees had the word "Life" printed on one side, and "Other" printed on the other side.

Some of my friends were around for *The Other Side of Life* tour and have odd stories to tell about it. One story involves Patrick; my friend had somehow gotten backstage, was fishing for Patrick's signature, and Moraz turns to him and says, "Do you know what the other side of life really is?" Then Patrick scrawled a four-letter euphemism for excrement on the page. I don't know if you should consider the source for that story or not, but it certainly was out of the norm for the Moodies. It WAS quite Gallic though. Patrick IS very French. *Merde* indeed.

Graeme says something in *Higher and Higher* during the winter of 1990, that the band is "skittish" of too much video exposure, and shy of the press. It could be with good reason: apparently Justin (still a good-looking blonde with surfer hair, at 46) began to have people walk up to him on the streets and say "Hey aren't you the guy in that video?" ("Wildest Dreams") Up until that point, the Moody Blues were fairly safe, and didn't have troubles walking around in public. Being famous is fun, but when it impacts your personal time, you have to find a good balance, and the Moody Blues were hard pressed to maintain their distance from what was becoming an increasingly intrusive fan base.

This is the time that, while touring, they started doing what would eventually become a part of EVERY stage show, the Dinosaur Walk. Justin is alleged to have dubbed it such. In fact, the term "Dinosaur Rock" started about now, with young reviewers griping about the Old Guys (like the Rolling Stones, and Bee Gees, and Beach Boys) sticking around, dubbing them fossils and so forth.

So the Dinosaur Walk became a permanent fixture in Moody Blues concerts. I've always thought three or four rockers all walking downstage to the right during "Story in Your Eyes" more resembles a dinosaur in a Mummenschantz show. Certainly it's an interesting effect if you happen to have a seat right under them (against the stage) as they walk up; it's a bit like laying underneath a locomotive as it runs over you. For those who have missed it, it's a lot like a ZZ Top "strut," and may indeed be where they got it from.**

    The show *Miami Vice* was hugely popular during this time, and it turns out that the star of the show was a major Moody Blues fan. The Moodies were supposed to guest star on the show, but most of their shots wound up on the cutting room floor. They had to reschedule the shooting a couple of times, as word leaked out, and the fans showed up, *en masse*. The episode was "Better Living Through Chemistry," and it still plays in syndication. Don't blink, you might miss the Moody cameo.

    Touring takes on new aspects around this time. During the tour, John and Justin flew to Miami to film the *Miami Vice* episode (several times), and then in September 1986, Justin collapsed on stage. Those I have talked to who were there, said they took him off feet first, and the rest carried on like troupers. The story is to be found in *VH1's Rock Encyclopedia,* but I DID find errors in that tome, so I would not swear to this event in a court of law. The tour certainly ended there in Costa Mesa, and then resumed in November. No one has ever said what happened, and I won't speculate; they were all working very hard, and it catches up with one.

    Justin wouldn't be the first, nor the last Moody to collapse on stage. I almost saw Graeme go down once myself; he only saved himself by clutching his cymbals and grinning real big. The poor guy had a cold bug at the time, we heard; Tahoe has a pretty high altitude and is not conducive to good health for those under stress! Ray went toes up on stage once too, and I lost that reference. Gordon DID collapse on stage at the Tropicana in Atlantic City, spring 1996 (and likewise went off feet first!) and he's a very healthy specimen! *(Moodymania* #22). So it can happen to anybody.***

    Interesting note, in 1986 The Fixx toured with the Moodies as an opening act. The Fixx went on to gain their own faithful following among the Punk Rock generation, showing that Tom Huelett knew how to pick bands; he also "managed" The Fixx. In the early '90s the Moodies toured with another Huelett band, Cinderella, and I was sad to see they didn't go very far. They played good music and had great costumes.

Moody Birds (The BUVs)--I never could figure out if it was insulting to call the Back Up Vocalists "BUVs" or not, but certainly for a few years, on the female-dominated Moody newsgroups, BUVs became synonymous with "bimbos." Terribly unkind and catty, thus I spend a good deal of time in this chapter setting the record straight, for the ladies. Those gals griping about the BUVs online probably can't sing a lick, either.

Over the years, while middle-aged women like to go to concerts and watch the Moody Blues, of course, their long-suffering husbands like to "look" too. So, I think it was a good move on the part of the band to add the girls for a little more spice to the show. And of course, the feminine voices would add texture to the vocal mix in concert. However, it's possible there was some "overkill" here. The evidence is plain in bootleg videos of this time. Wendy is wearing little more than a corset, and is doing a rather interesting kootch dance, sandwiched between Justin and Patrick at one point. (Montreal, 1986). *Yike!*

The Moodies have gone through twelve female backups since they started using them in 1986. The best list made so far is something like this:

>Bekka Bramlett and Jeri Wood early 1986 (?) also the same time they added a second keyboard, it was Bias' very first tour with the Moodies. Bekka Bramlett is the daughter of "Delaney and Bonnie." Some nice person online had this to say about her and Jeri Wood: *When they did the 'aaahhh's on "Your Wildest Dreams," it just sounded so friggen perfect. None of the other backup singers have EVER gotten that sound.* Bekka Bramlett had a short-lived stint in Fleetwood Mac. [That was a good tour too, they did with Crosby, Stills and Nash in the mid-'90s, she replaced Stevie Nicks!]
>Wendy McKenzie & Janis Liebhart July 1986-July 1987

>Shaun Murphy & Naomi Starr July 1988-Sept 1990
>Sue Shattock & June Boyce Aug 1991-fall 1992
>Sue Shattock & Tracy Graham Jun 1993-2000. They kept Tracy around (solo, and she could handle it well by herself) until spring 2001, when she and Bias both left at the same time. I think Tracy was the only one of the back-up gals to cut her own album up to that point. Later, Julie Ragins and Norda Mullen BOTH cut albums, and I find Norda's work head and shoulders above the crowd!!! (recommended) Her voice is beautiful, calm and mellow.
>Bernie Barlow, keyboards, guitar and vocals, summer 2001 to 2006
>Norda Mullen: flautist, guitar and vocals: spring 2003. She worked with Justin's solo band mid '90s, and then was added to the Moody Blues when Ray dropped out. She's still with the band as of this writing, and also tours with John's solo band.
>Julie Ragins: vocals, keyboards, guitar, sax: first appeared summer of 2007, when Bernie dropped out to have a baby. Spring 2009 was with Julie, summer of 2009 with Bernie again, then Julie toured in 2010. Bernie and Julie both have their own websites, which are linked, so apparently they are friends. Julie wears interesting, cool skirts, and Norda wears gypsy skirts; they are very visually fun to watch. Norda does ballet kicks once in a while, too! In heels!!! Julie tours with Justin in his solo shows beginning in 2013.

1986 was the first year they added two back-up singers, Bekka and Jeri didn't make it through the year, so a couple of California girls named Janis Liebhart and Wendy McKenzie joined. The usual rumors you might expect from two ladies on tour with a bunch of very male men, followed them. Most of this can probably go in one ear and out the other. They seemed like nice gals and got a good write-up in *Higher and Higher* #6. In later shows, after Wendy's kootch dancing of 1986, the girls cleaned it up a bit, and stuck to bumps and grinds on the back platform. Wearing corsets on stage wasn't so shocking for the times, if you ever saw a

Madonna performance in those years, it was quite mainstream for rock music.

Naomi Starr and Shaun Murphy replaced Janis and Wendy in 1988, and were, in the words of one reviewer "more restrained." No word on what happened to Wendy and Janis, but where ever you are ladies, it sounds like you made a lot of men happy out there during your time with the Moodies.

This is clipped and edited off line: *Shawn Murphy is currently the lead vocalist for Little Feat, a position she's held since 1993. She called her time with the Moodies a wonderful experience.*

Tracy Graham had to be my personal favorite back-up singer. There are bootlegs with the vocals of her, Justin and Ray mixed on "I Know You're Out There Somewhere" that literally send shivers up my spine. Tracy is an Aquarius and showed it; I spotted her running around Tahoe one time in green high-topped tennis shoes, which clashed horrible-wonderful with her flaming red henna'ed hair. Tracy has a fine, rich, sultry alto voice, one of the best I've ever heard, and one could only wish her the best in her career, making good music.

Bernie Barlow was added to the lineup, as of 2001; she not only is a pretty lady on stage but plays the keyboards quite well. (She also played barefoot at times, which was fun. She would come on stage, kick off her high-heeled mules, and get to work!!) Bernie has her own extensive history, knows a lot of musicians in the Los Angeles area, and you can read more at *www.berniebarlow.com*. Bernie has a fine mellow alto voice, beautiful resonance.

Norda joined when Ray dropped out. She's an excellent flautist, and a pleasure to hear in concert.

As Long as the Moon Can Shine--Back to our history lesson, I got a bit ahead, didn't I? Clipped off line: *The second half was The Hunting of a Snark which had been released earlier on CD with Art Garfunkel as the Butcher; but he was unavailable so Justin stepped into the part - there had been numerous TV interviews during rehearsals and Justin featured heavily. The whole event was phenomenal but most memorable was Roger Daltrey standing at the front of the Albert Hall stage, putting down his microphone and singing a line which reverberated throughout the auditorium without electronic aid. Of course, Justin's performance was also outstanding, as were the rest of the performers.*

All in all a tremendous evening which raised a large amount of cash for a deserving cause - and a chance to rub shoulders with the star studded audience.

1987 was an interesting year for Moody Blues touring. They traveled to the Land of Oz (Australia), and toured there for almost two months. They did stopovers in Tahiti and Tasmania, though no one seems to know if they played shows there. They also were alleged to have toured Japan, Canada, and possibly Europe and Israel during the early months of 1987, essentially doing a world tour. Most references say the Moody Blues have never toured Israel due to security issues.

By April they were back in the U.K. and Justin was doing "Snark." One of the most interesting threads to follow through the Moody Blues history is the periodic desire, expressed by usually Justin, sometimes Graeme, to do a musical on stage, or to be in the movies. Justin was breaking into the world of movie soundtracks; now he tried his hand at stage musical performing. Justin and Mike Batt (the composer) were already friends; when Art Garfunkel was unable to do the part, Justin was tapped to replace him.

Batt took the children's poem, *The Hunting of a Snark* by Lewis Carroll, and turned it into a very likeable musical production. It's an abstract theater piece, with staging a bit odd to the modern eye, but actually bearing a good deal of resemblance to Stuart England and the Court Masques of 1601-1630. Justin is the quasi-romantic Butcher, and a wonderful cast was assembled; among them Julian Lennon as the ill-fated Baker, he who meets the Boojum.

As far as I know, though he has staged it elsewhere, and it exists as a CD, Mike Batt's "Snark" of April 1, 1987 is the only video of Carroll's famous not-so-nonsensical play in existence. Some factoids about *The Hunting of a Snark*: it took place on April Fool's Day, a date more noted in England, an honorable and very serious holiday to the sometimes very serious English people. This show was a Royal Command Performance at the Royal Albert Hall, attended by Lady Sarah Ferguson. There was a rumor that Princess Di was supposed to do it; she couldn't make it, and Fergie stepped in. It was done as a benefit for The Royal National Institute for the Blind.

The major theme of the musical is the touching and lovely "Children of the Sky" penned by Mike Batt and performed by the all-star rock cast. If you've never read Lewis Carroll, I might point out to you that *The Hunting of a Snark* is about "looking for something." Justin will say in the next few years, that his hit songs "You're Wildest Dreams" and "I Know You're Out There Somewhere" are both inspired by "the eternal quest for something."

Royal designers David and Elizabeth Emanuel did the costumes. Batt directed the ninety-piece London Symphony Orchestra. The fine dance performances of "the other Butcher and Beaver" (Justin can't dance) were by members of the Royal Academy of Ballet. The cast of "Snark" was a hodgepodge of musical aristocracy from all over the rock and art world: Julian Lennon, Justin Hayward, Billy Connolly, Roger Daltrey, Captain Sensible, John Hurt (the Narrator), Deniece Williams, Midge Ure. Rock and orchestration successfully intertwined in several ripping good solos by Ure.

The orchestra was dressed in black-white striped traditional British Naval Uniforms. Mike Batt himself wore the uniform of an admiral, with the medals pinned on his back! He both conducted and sang. The actors and dancers ran about on various risers and platforms, and it is impossible to understand the set design from the video. But it never fails to delight the eye.

Probably my favorite Snark song is sung by Captain Sensible: he is the Billiard Marker, and a total ruffian. His solo is rollicking, funny; he delivers it with appropriate goofiness and an impromptu dance. "It's only a game so put up a real good fight, I'm going to be slithering in tonight." I think Lewis Carroll would have liked this; he was always writing about "slithy toves" and such; one can only wonder what a meek Victorian math professor REALLY did on his off nights!

Billy Connolly does the Bellman with a lot of humor, and his solo is very baroque; one can only be deeply impressed with the different styles in which Batt so easily composed for different moments.

Julian Lennon is, with a good deal of genius, cast as the Baker, the spaced-out member of the crew who is destined to finally find the Snark and meet the Boojum. His solo is one of those touching moments in rock history that brings back sad memories, as he looks and sounds like his father standing on stage, singing. *Vanish away like midnight smoke.......and never be seen again.* The melody is haunting, ghost-like, touching. His father met his own Boojum (in the guise of an insane fan) and has vanished away from life; it remains one of those great tragedies that can never be forgotten. Julian handles the role better than many rockers would; he is humorous and witty throughout, and once when he and Justin Hayward bow to one another, you can see this look pass between them that speaks chapters.

Casting the Butcher and the Beaver as star-crossed lovers is another stroke of genius on Batt's part. Justin Hayward, ever the romantic figure, is of course, the Butcher, and has grown long mutton chops for the occasion. He is cast with Deniece Williams as the Beaver, a lovely lady who handles the role well. The Beaver's costume is all frills, puffs and lace, because the Beaver was forever making lace in the poem. The music appears to be in a key higher than Justin's usual range; hearing him deal with that, and stretch his vocal talents is one of the enjoyable features of the video; he does it very well. Art Garfunkel, the original "Butcher" can sing quite high indeed. It is a tribute to Batt's talents as a vocal coach; Justin's higher vocal range also shows up on the subsequent album, *Classic Blue.*

The staging of Justin's solo is a high point of the show, and it brings wave-like applause from the otherwise silent (respectful) crowd of the Royal Albert Hall, while he is singing "As Long As The Moon Can Shine." Juxtaposed in front is a second "Butcher and Beaver" (Robert North and Janice Smith) identically costumed like the singers, dancing an authentic French-bistro adagio. Smith is a gifted ballerina and handles VERY well her limited dance space. The trust and intimacy between the two dancers is awesome, backed by Justin's voice and Batt's music and poetry, it makes for one of the finest stage events I have ever seen.

Mike Batt is still around. One of his songs was done on the Moody Blues album *December;* more of his stuff can be found on his website, *www. mikebatt.com*. My favorite is Ergo the Slug, very cute for kids. He Twitters too *(abandon hope all ye who enter there.)* You can even buy the CD of "Snark" on his website. In 2009, this production finally came out on DVD, vastly better than those grainy bootlegs, and less hassle than tracking it down online. But you'll have to order it from the U.K. if you're American, and it's in PAL. Justin's "As Long As the Moon Can Shine" turns up on *youtube.com*.

Extra Tours--Justin's solo career takes another interesting veer during the late '80s: he begins to find singing ladies to work with, with some beautiful results. Talented Japanese singing star Nana Mouskouri did a lovely version of "Nights in White Satin" and Justin did the guitar solo in the bridge part of the song, a nice rendition. She also did "Morning Angel" which was written by Tony Visconti, and vocally backed by Justin. "Morning Angel" is really worth tracking down, it has a Japanese flavor to the melody and beautiful harmonies.

In 1985, Justin's friend Eric Stewart (of 10cc) was contacted by Agnetha Faltskog (ABBA) who wanted to record for her album *Eyes of a Woman* something by "the guy who wrote 'Nights in White Satin.'" So Eric got them together, and Justin presented Agnetha with a song Tracey Ullmann had rejected. They slowed it down a bit: by reports, several of Justin's songs have benefited from a slower tempo. Thus was "The Angels Cry" recorded, and Justin provided lead guitar and backing vocals for it as well.

In 1989 Justin would become involved on an album by Annie Haslam (her first apparently) again doing his song "The Angels Cry" as a duet, Justin mostly backing. The neat thing is that also on the Haslam album is Peter Bliss (NOT Paul's brother, but they've worked together), and Mike Oldfield songs (Mike Oldfield did *Tubular Bells*, the theme to *The Exorcist*). And no shock, in 1989, Justin does an "Extra Tour" in Germany with Sally Oldfield, Mike's sister, and the two sing some awesome duets, including "Let It Begin."
****

le Mer--The Moodies were originally scheduled to return to the studio and start *Sur la Mer* by May 4th but didn't get back there until October. Another tour fit into the summer months, and they toured America through July and June, 1987. *Sur la Mer* rolled right off their guitars and into the can; indeed some would say that *Sur la Mer* was just a continuation of the recording they had done with *The Other Side of Life*.

Sur la Mer was released by June of 1988, and a tour followed it up. Production of *Sur la Mer* and *The Other Side of Life* sounds very business-like, as befits a senior rock band. *Sur la Mer* is probably one of the best albums to find on vinyl for the avid Moody Blues collector, as all the Moodies (as well as Tony Visconti) have photos of themselves as children on it. It's a really nice concept and works well as a fold-out album; the CD version has little dinky postage stamp photos that are no fun at all!

One interesting note that came out in Visconti interviews was that when John was working with him, Justin would frequently excuse himself. John and Justin both being intelligent and very creative, have definite ideas about how things should be done, and it must lend itself to creative disagreements at times; it can't help but happen. A few years before Tony joined them, all of the Moodies (especially John and Justin) began to save studio time by doing work in their own home studios. They then brought the tapes into the

BIG studio, where other effects and performances could be layered on top. The hit song this time turned out to be "I Know You're Out There Somewhere" and the video was done to this as a sequel to the first video, "Your Wildest Dreams," trying to capitalize on the storybook quality of the running saga.

The band began to pick up a significant Japanese fan base, and in an interview published in Japan, Justin explained his inspiration for the song series. He had bumped into one of his original band mates from Swindon, a good friend who had dated Justin's best girl's best friend, as young people do, they run in groups and date friends of friends. Justin's friend was still married, quite happily to his original lady; and Justin began to wonder what had happened to HIS girlfriend, when he was just a lad of 16. And how his life might have turned out quite differently. Haven't we all had these moments in later life?

One song, "Breaking Point" was supposed to be for a movie theme, but the directors hassled the Jays about changing it, and to quote John "We decided it was too good for them and kept it for our own album." Good call: it's one of the best songs on the album, just the way it is. The movie *Breaking Point* DOES however, use "Nights in White Satin" over a love scene, which was something the Moodies couldn't do anything about. Justin doesn't own the publishing rights.

"No More Lies" turned into a very charming animated video that was well received by the MTV stations, and "Vintage Wine" plays frequently on classic rock stations. All in all, *Sur la Mer* is a nice album with a good balance of rock n' roll and ballads. BUT there is no music from Ray or Graeme. According to Visconti, Ray didn't even show up for the making of the album.

Guy Allison filled in on the *Sur la Mer* tour for Bias Boshell, who might have been touring with Barclay James Harvest at the time. Among old standards, the Moodies were still performing "Veteran Cosmic Rocker" on stage.

The opening acts would be Glass Tiger, and later in the year, the Fixx.

After riding the heady wave with the success of "Your Wildest Dreams" and "I Know You're Out There Somewhere," it looks like the Moody Blues took a lot of time in 1989 to rest and get their stuff together. See above about Justin's solo work!

Somewhere in the Eighties, Justin started singing and recording songs in Spanish, attempting to crack the huge Latin America market with his ballads. He did a nice job on a Spanish version of "I Know You're Out There Somewhere" with the single "Al Fin Voy Encontrarte" (*como, quando...*) He started singing the song half in Spanish and half in English in concert, at least up until 1990. He also did "Nights In White Satin," in Spanish, re-entitled "Noches de Seda," translates as "Nights of Satin." Good luck finding it, and Justin even denies its existence! The pronunciation isn't quite as nice on this one, and apparently neither song impressed many South of the Border. But they are nice experiments, and if you speak Spanish, a lot of fun to try and translate. (Justin is much better in French, from later interviews.)

During this time, Justin also did a really nice recording called "Tregardock" on an album *Poetry in Motion*. Mike Read (the producer) hosted *Top of the Pops* in the U.K. for a period and knew just about everyone in the business. Justin is in very heady company on this album, the music is by Mike Read, and the talent includes (among others) Donovan, David Essex, and Annie Haslam. Frankly Justin's track is one of my least favorites on here, which will give you some idea of the superior quality of the artists involved! It's an outstanding album; get it if you find it.

All of the lyrics are the poetry of Cornish poet, Sir John Betjeman, well known in the U.K. and barely known Stateside. He is funny, witty, wise, and it's gorgeous, wonderful stuff. The music is a fine match for the words, and I was very happy to find out about Betjeman through this CD. Release was held up in litigation with Sir Betjeman's estate until 1991. In an August, 2007 radio interview, Justin said that HIS father was good friends with Betjeman, and he (Justin) had met Mike Read at Radio One. So when *Poetry in Motion* came up, he was more than glad to record "Tregardock" as his part of the album.

In 1989, the Moody Blues settled into Caesar's Lake Tahoe and the Tropicana in Atlantic City, for a total of 16 shows between those venues, essentially following (again) Tom Jones into the world of lounge acts. This would start their long and favorable relationship with the casino world, bringing many Moody fans together in "Moody-fest" weekends at resort hotels. The bad thing about the casino shows is the band rarely brings their good stage lighting, like they do elsewhere, but it's still fun to take a vacation (especially during ski season at Tahoe) and see the Moodies. Lots of people plan their entire vacations for the year around these shows. The good thing about going to these shows is, you can party with all your Moody friends, from all over the country.

Later in the year 1989, Justin and Mike Batt, his mentor from *The Hunting of a Snark,* got together and talked about doing an orchestral album with "all their favorite songs." Justin talked about this album during a Storyteller show (Toronto) in 2011, saying that he and Mike had just been talking about the project, and they were surprised when someone (unnamed person) put up the money to record it with the London Philharmonic! *Classic Blue* was recorded on Abby Road (EMI?) Two of the tracks on this *Classic Blue* album are penned by Batt, and at least one, a love ballad, "Railway Hotel," is apparently not available anywhere else. I think it's the best song on the album.

The opinion of many is, the original artists did the songs fine to begin with, and they didn't need the *redeux*. Having said ALL that, it's an enjoyable album, a good experiment, and very worth adding to one's collection. Batt is apparently an excellent voice coach; and under his tutelage, Justin's voice reaches into a very wide range of vocal performance, about three octaves, which is really good for any vocalist.

This presaged the "Red Rocks" show. The door to orchestral Moody Blues music was being kicked open in no uncertain terms, and the next decade would see them reinventing their sound again with a live orchestral format. Like any good idea whose time has come, it was bound to make money once it got rolling.

Where there is money, there are lawyers, trying to keep up their country club dues by doing what they do best: advocating adversarial legal situations…..

*Kenny Loggins added a sound track note to *Top Gun* on the DVD, that is when he auditioned in Los Angeles to compose/perform music for *Top Gun* (1985) there was quite a cattle call; he was not the only musician there. "Wildest Dreams" lends itself so well to aviation footage, one is tempted to assume there was a Moody somewhere in that cattle call. Of course, Kenny Loggins is a friend of Justin's too. *Who knows….*

** John and Justin also presented musical awards to ZZ Top during the late '80s; obviously they are fans of other rockers!. For those wondering about the song "Everybody Walk the Dinosaur" by Queen Latifah, do a Google on the song title (it's in *Ice Age III* FYI). Came from a hip hop song c. 1987.

***Gordon was very sweet to explain his collapse in the OFC newsletter, summer of 1996 (flu I believe.) Apparently he collapsed into the arms of Alan Terry, the drum technician, who lugged him off stage. Ray is alleged to have turned at this point, and commented in his dry British accent "Well, he's out" and they kept on playing. Some of the songs were cut though, as the drums were just too complex. Alan Terry and Gordon were met by an ambulance and concerned family offstage. In Gordon's words "The hospital staff was impressed that I showed up with my own heart specialist," who happened to be a friend of his family, watching the show!

**** "Let It Begin" was on *youtube.com* last I looked, and it's a good video, too. Mike and Sally Oldfield actually recorded an album together prior to *Tubular Bells*, and it's alleged to be worth looking for.

XV) Keys of the Kingdom: 1990-September 1991

...when it is evening, ye say, It will be fair weather, for the sky is red. And in the morning: It will be foul weather today, for the sky is red and lowering. Oh ye hypocrites! ye can discern the face of the sky: but can ye not discern the signs of the times? A wicked and adulterous generation seeketh after a sign, and therefore shall no sign be given unto it.......oh ye of little faith....upon this rock I will build my church: and the gates of hell shall not prevail against it. And I will give unto thee the keys of the kingdom of heaven: ....and whatsoever thou shalt loose on earth shall be loosed in heaven. Matthew Chap 16, King James translation *The Bible.*

I was thinking about how people seem to read The Bible *a whole lot more as they get older; then it dawned on me . . they're cramming for their final exam.* -- George Carlin

  Sometimes when reading the history of the Moodies, you get the feeling all they do is record and tour. But they managed to fit in a real life around it. Justin found time to sing at Jimmy Tarbuck's wedding, sometime around 1990. In between recording four songs for *Keys of the Kingdom*, in the fall of 1990; John and Justin sang "Across the Universe" for Yoko Ono's concert, to celebrate John Lennon's birthday in Oct, 1990. Sadly, Yoko cut the Jays out of the *Tribute to John Lennon* American release, and Moody fans had to get their friends in the U.K. to send them copies.
  In the fall of 1990 while the Moodies toured, Doremi Hayward (now 18) came to America and toured with her daddy. For a young British woman doing a major in American studies, this must have been like heaven.
  The 1990 tour had started off well enough. They opened July 21 at Husky Stadium in Seattle at the Goodwill Games, and the Moody Blues got a better round of applause than President Bush did, playing to an International television audience. They played a song that Justin said was about "reaching out" "I Know You're Out There Somewhere."

By the time I saw them at the Concord Pavilion, fall 1990, they had been on the road a month and a half, and it must have been tiring. This is where it gets difficult for the writer to be objective, without letting my UN-objective feelings come into it. Although I've listened to the Moody Blues since 1968, my first concert seeing them live was September 2, 1990, at the Concord Pavilion, Northern California. The play list was shorter this year. I recall the duet between the keyboards (Patrick) and Ray on the flute, during "Legend of a Mind," was much shorter than for other shows in later years, after Patrick was gone. Ray also started doing less and less in shows during the next few years. This was a sore point with many of his fans.

This was to be Patrick Moraz's last tour with the Moody Blues. From my recollections of the night I saw them, he was very active on stage, in sharp contrast to the other rather calm, sedate, professional band members. John was wearing a very flamboyant denim jacket, with long, long fringe, and was having a great time showing it off, but he was also very collected. Ray looked a little paranoid. Justin glared a good deal, looked like he was going to bite someone's head off at any minute, and had not bothered to cut his hair since the tour started July 21 (and it grows fast!)* Patrick jumped around like a raccoon on hot coals, making imperious gestures. He flamboyantly directed and coordinated with Bias, who was dutifully playing his keyboards on the other side of the stage. At the end of the show, Patrick threw his towel near me into the audience. I don't pick up other people's used towels, but I saw someone else snatch it up. In retrospect, how prophetic.

I remember that fall 1990 being the time period in which Kuwait was invaded and ravaged by her unfriendly neighbors to the North, Iraq. Patrick Moraz is Swiss-French; the French are a nationality notorious for being outspoken on international politics, and usually against the British-American alliance, just out of pure orneriness. I think anyone who cares about World Peace was upset that fall.

No matter what the Moodies might say in public, that they are non-political, one can only imagine what might have been going on behind the scenes during this tour. It seems plain from the Los Angeles interview with Justin, just a day or two before the show I saw, that everything might not be well in Moody Land. Justin mentions "conflict" as a creative force and gets a little testy with the two horny gonzo DJs (Mark and Brian) who are interviewing him.

This is the year shock jock Howard Stern started doing interviews with the Moodies. They were first on his radio show, one with Justin, one with Graeme, one with both Justin and John; then Stern did a TV spot with all the Moodies. Howard even brought out Go-Go girls for their TV gig, a scene which is best left to the imagination. Try *youtube.com*. A lot of interesting things come out in these shows, and Howard is up to his usual shocking habits, which the Moodies weathered rather well, especially Justin (I think he likes to banter.) Graeme is the only one that really does the "kiss and tell" thing, and I saw nothing wrong with just being truthful. I think Howard was a little shocked himself; Graeme was quite forthcoming about his private life, unto banality; he turned the tables rather neatly. They're really good interviews: Howard obviously likes the Moody Blues and has a lot of respect for them, or he would have "dug in" more.

Q: *What would you say is the cause for Moody Blues' continuing popularity and admiration?*
A (JH): *I wish I knew, but I suppose it's because we didn't follow the normal rules and just went our own way, and I always like that in music. Most important of all though is the contribution of our fans --- they, and only they (no record company or promo outfit) are why we are here!* ---Justin interview, *moodybluestoday.com*, c. 2008

1990 continued a cycle of reflection on their past lives and trying to make some sense of it all, not only in their lyrics, but by, of and for the fan base. This had really started when Mark Murley and Randy Salas began doing history spots with *Higher and Higher* in the early '80s. People who, before, had just liked the music, now wanted to know the people behind the music, and the Moodies were more than happy to oblige. So they hired a new fan club secretary in the spring of 1990 (I think the previous secretary stopped working for them due to having a baby!)

The new secretary, Ivy Stewart attempted to integrate with the existing fan club and organized a Christmas party. Little did Ivy know, she was grabbing the proverbial tiger by the tail. The heavily female weighted, baby boomer fan base, was collectively entering the menopause. *(~~~~AGHA~~~~~)*. Need I elaborate? (I can say that, I was one of them!) Fan things got pretty crazy for a few years.

The 1990 Christmas party was a pretty weird one from some of the reports that came back. Char Kemp, who reviewed the party for *Higher and Higher* would say diplomatically "some fans over-reacted." The exact stories don't bear repeating, but the phrase "very weird head trips" comes to mind for me.

Justin was apparently mobbed by enthusiastic women. Ray didn't bother to show up….and was missed by some of his friends who DID come. Patrick was sighted eating a vegetarian plate. Poor Graeme was ignored and slid out the door early. Justin eventually escaped and did a fake "flash" on the crowd with his raincoat before bolting into the dark, cackling wildly. Once Justin and his dubious humor had gone, John led the crowd in a group dance around the Christmas tree. All in all, it was a complex social event, and it would be six years before Ivy would organize another Christmas party for the fans.

As per the Dec 12, 1990 "Rock over London" interview with Justin; Tony Visconti was still working with the band, and would be, up through February 1991. Chris Neal (who also produced Mike and the Mechanics) is mentioned as a co-producer. As of the Christmas party Dec 1990, Patrick had been in Switzerland (and just made it for the party), working on a score for film *Eye of the Snake*. He went to Los Angeles for other projects right after the party, so he apparently wasn't around much for set-up work on this Moody album, being made in the U.K.

If you ask me, things just flatly fell apart on *Keys to the Kingdom*. A certain amount of metaphor can be read into the title, in retrospect. In 1978, the cover of *Octave* showed the entire band going through a open door; then the album started with the sound of doors closing on a car. A transition, a passageway to another world, was sensed perhaps; at least, they found the key this time. The question was, which door exactly did it go to?

There is an obscure reference during this time, to Graeme being run over by a golf cart and breaking an arm (he should know better than to fall asleep on the Green, eh?) Perhaps that small event affected things more than we know. *Keys of the Kingdom* is riddled with synthesized drums, for the worse frankly, as much of the album sounds mechanical and very *ooompahish*. Graeme fled in the face of this technical take-over, going out for a long, long cruise on his yacht, far far from shore. Gordon Marshall was brought on board at this time, to help out. When Graeme recovered, they went to a "two drummer" approach, and it worked out GREAT.

The 1990 tour ended sometime in September, the band went into the studio to work on *Keys of the Kingdom*. It sounds like it was done piece-meal, in home studios, here and there as people got around to it. If the *Octave* album was the session from Hell, this one must have been several levels lower in the circles of Hades, because they couldn't get Graeme to show up, barely got Patrick there for a couple of songs, and went through three producers, one of whom was Tony Visconti.

Mike Pinder has said over the years, that his real contributions to the Moody albums have been to "fix up" and add bits to the songs when others were stuck on them. Boy, did they need Mike on the *Keys of the Kingdom*! Did I actually say that? Oddly Tony said something similar to the band during an interview around this time, mentioning a "reunion with Mike." In Tony's words "This was met with the same reaction a ham sandwich might have at a bar mitzvah."

From polite commentary by Graeme in an interview with Dana Grubb, it seems that Visconti was attempting to take the band in a direction they were not comfortable with, which had to do with them parting ways. Tony definitely had other ideas than the Moodies. Visconti did the vast majority of producing on this album, but was only with them half the time, during 1989-1990. Visconti's six songs were apparently recorded and mixed by the summer of 1990, before the tour. I'll leave it up to the reader to track down Visconti's biography explaining this time, but the band had some real turmoil going on. After the tour was over, they attempted to finish. It didn't gel very well, at all. Visconti wasn't asked to return, and they found other producers.

I think the recording company also was breathing down their necks for a new album, so time was a factor. All sorts of weird things happened: Patrick was summoned from Los Angeles, then when he found time to come to the U.K. was left wandering around waiting for his parts to come up. So he got tired and left. Others were not happy with the production either; one Moody commented in interview, "Some geezer even put in a brass section after we left!"

At first, Ray just was not to be found for "Keys." Tom Huelett sent Visconti to dig Ray out of his house, where he was found sitting in his happy position, on the couch with a remote control in his hand. As it turned out, Ray had a very nice song, called "Celtic Sonnet," which he had considered for the new album; it was taken from an old Celtic blessing, but set to music. The original "Celtic Prayer" aka "Celtic Sonnet" is reprinted in *Moodymania* #18. Donovan Leitch also did a nice, but vastly different version of the "Celtic Prayer" on *Sutras* in 1996.

Tony tells a wonderful story about going to Ray's home and hearing it for the first time; Ray sang it *a cappella,* with the orange rays of the setting Sun coming in the window. Somehow that image failed to come over on the album, but it was nice to see Ray contribute something so pretty to the album after being missing in action for several years.

Ray is heard singing back-up and whistling on "Is This Heaven?". Tony claims to be "the nut" screaming "I love this world!" on "Is this Heaven?" (down a drainpipe I think.) Once Tony had found Ray, Justin and Ray made the time to sit down together "with just a flute and a guitar," and pen "Never Blame the Rainbows," which Visconti produced; not too bad a song.

"Highway" (released as a single) comes from William Blake's writings. "No one else can see things like I do," is a Blake quote, and the song also borrows lines from *Songs of Innocence*.** "Highway" was left off the CD, because the band thought it was too "oompahish." It's a great song though, laced with bag-pipes, and would eventually be heartily welcomed by fans who felt keenly the lack of real exciting material on the main album. Curious note: had "Highway" been put on the CD, that would have had thirteen tracks, and this is the 13th studio album, not counting *The Magnificent Moodies*, with the Mach I band. I won't say the Moody Blues are superstitious, but sometimes I wonder.

There is also a mix-up in the tracks and outer label on the first printing. "Say What You Mean" (a weird *gobbldygoop* song anyway) comes over as two tracks digitally but is listed as one track on the label. This mistake threw off the track numbering and was to really screw up one Christmas 1991 interview (WNEW) with the Moodies, where the usually even-tempered Justin shows one of his rare flashes of public anger. The poor sound engineer keeps hitting the requested track, but repeatedly gets the jarring Hendrix-esque opening guitar chords to "Once is Enough" rather than the placid "Celtic Sonnet." Justin, by his own admission in other interviews, says he rarely listens to the finished product after it's released.

Keys of the Kingdom is (in my humble opinion) full of half thought-out songs, that would have been really nice had they taken some more time with them. It darts in different directions with no predictability, like a frightened school of fish. I think "Hope and Pray" upsets me the most, as it's a VERY nice tune, with good lyrics, but it's seriously marred by the synthesized drums, and yes, is too "punchy." It should have been the *bluuuuess...*

There is an overall feel that they had to rush to get the tracks out. I won't make up your mind for you; get the album and listen to it yourself. It's not my favorite album. Having said that, I think Lodge's ballads are really nice on here, much better than those he did on *Sur la Mer*.

Curiously, on the cassette tape version of "Keys," they left off another wonderful, and "different" song, "Once is Enough," but put it on the CD. Plainly someone could not be objective on this album, in deciding what is and what isn't a "good sound." Graeme was not to mince words and called *Keys of the Kingdom* "a load of bollocks."

What happened after those first tracks were done, is anyone's guess. Tony isn't nasty about not finishing "Keys," but he did say diplomatically "They like to shuffle the deck" about his departure. Patrick was let go two months after Tony, in March 1991. Tony did dig Ray out of his house, so that was good work as a producer. Graeme had gone sailing and was impossible for Tony to catch. Some Moody fans have hung out with Tony Visconti over the years: he was married to May Pang, herself a very good friend of John Lennon's. Tony and May have two kids between them, and May Pang occasionally shows up at shows (even unto 2017), usually backstage with Marie Hayward and high-end cameras.

Tony seems a very kind, intelligent guy, and it's a tribute to his talents as a good producer that he was even able to pull Ray and Patrick both into the recording process for "Keys." Mostly, the lack of spontaneity and the lack of keyboards began to get to them. John and Justin were showing up with bits and pieces of stuff they had done at home in their own music rooms, but there needed to be other band members "on hand" for filling in the backgrounds to these songs. If Justin or John got the idea for a keyboard piece in a certain spot, or Ray would suddenly appear with something everyone thought really needed a piano line for it, it was just too complex to call up the guy living in California and get him there. And the guy in California was apparently busy with other projects and couldn't come when the slot fit with other people.

During *Moodies vs Moraz*, Patrick complained about the "sitting around, waiting for your part to come up" while in the U.K. Patrick being as hyper as he was, probably WAS bored. His home was in Los Angeles too (I think his wife is Californian, she certainly sounds like a Northern Californian in the hearing tapes); it was a long way for him to come. He had other fish to fry, one of which was the *Star Peace* show, which was supposed to include Yoko Ono and other cohorts of hers.

By March of 1991, Patrick had been interviewed by *Keyboard* magazine, the interview came out later in May. Lots about Patrick's ill-fated *Star Peace* plans, and the birthday celebration of Switzerland, can be read in the *Keyboard* magazine May, 1991. The designs are interesting, a bit like the Olympics opening/closing ceremonies; but the war in Iraq hung up finances somehow. Even once that was resolved, no one would finance the thing.

In that *Keyboard* interview, Patrick was not complimentary to the rest of the Moodies, essentially saying he thought they were "stale," and that he really had better things to do than hang around with them. I think even with such a blatant public chop as that, the Moody Blues might still have asked Patrick to play with them, had he not become like Mike Pinder, and just plain hard to get ahold of and unavailable.

According to the testimony in *Moodies vs. Moraz;* when *Keys of the Kingdom* had promotional spots, and a small European promo tour come up in early 1991, the missing Graeme was found, but the missing Patrick was not. They did their TV spots in Europe without a keyboardist, and frankly, they looked and sounded pretty good. But they were plainly upset by it, the matter of the unavailable keyboardist comes out over and over again in the hearing. I think some spots in Europe the year earlier are also without Patrick, one of them being a lovely video with candles; so the lack of

Patrick's reliability in making little promo gigs must have been a long term matter. One look at Patrick's work and dates in the same time period on his website, *www.patrickmoraz.com* will show just how busy he really was from 1980-1990. The Moody Blues were a low priority for him. They needed a reliable keyboard player.

When Scott Muni interviewed Justin in June of 1991, Justin says "Patrick is no longer with the band," that Patrick had another career in Los Angeles. Not to speak ill of Patrick (who is gifted in his own way), but looking at his work schedule, and reading over some of his comments during this time, you wonder if he ever took time to slow down and listen to crickets or take a deep breath of fresh air. One can almost see John and Justin listening *patiently* to Patrick talking *excitedly* about how he thinks the songs should go, and then doing it *exactly* the way they wanted to do it anyway. Deep breaths of fresh air are what the Moody Blues is supposed to be about.

Patrick seemed on a wild roller coaster by 1991. A lot of his fans (he was interactive with quite a few Moody fans during his time with them) worried about him during the trial, and one can only hope he is doing better as of this writing. I do think it was a bit unfair of him to call the Moody Blues "greedy" though, just because they found two keyboardists who not only believed in the Moody Blues, but who were willing to be there when he wasn't. (*Akron Beacon Journal,* Sept 29, 1991)

The Moodies for sure toured a few paying venues in Europe in the spring of 1991, in England, Holland, Belgium, and Switzerland. Justin wrote one letter for the fan club newsletter during spring of 1991, from a bus somewhere in Germany. According to his letter, they were not getting much of a turn out, in Germany anyway.

Stress can manifest in scary ways. In July of 1991 (John's birthday), David Lee Travis "DLT" on BBC radio, did an interview with the band about their upcoming album release. Paul Bliss makes his radio début as a Moody Blues keyboardist. Justin and DLT discussed biscuits (cookies), beans, and underwear; it's a really funny interview. But they also talked about John, who was supposed to come along with Justin; John was hospitalized "with the flu" as Justin called it. Justin's well wishes for his band mate are a bit naughty, but very heart felt; you have to listen carefully.

In an article c. August 2000, *Charisma Magazine*, John discusses his illness at this time; apparently he was laid low with some sort of paralysis of his arms. It makes sense, he plays the guitar and golfs too, both stressful on the upper torso. He goes on to discuss a prayer meeting that apparently pulled him out of it, and the profound impact it had on his family. This was a very tough time for the Moodies, and emotions often manifest as physical illness. Poor John is on an interview with CNN Aug 2, 1991 (after they had to cancel some dates early in the tour, Justin allegedly had a sore throat), and John looks ragged, obviously still recovering from illness.

A media blitz was launched to support the American tour of the new album, and Justin's pretty daughter, Doremi, then in modeling school, began to pop up in articles and promo bits. It worked too; reading about Doremi and her daddy during 1991 was a lot more interesting than the stories about Moody Teddy Bears in *Moodymania*. Eventually Doremi got out of modeling, and went to college, where she was an American Studies major.

The other Moodies had children who were growing up too; Matthew Edge studied Physics if I'm not mistaken. Adam Thomas, Kristian Lodge, and his sister Emily would eventually start doing liaison work with the fan club, to good effect; Adam looks just like his father. Kristian went on to study film-making at UCLA and turned up at more than a few Moody shows with his camera in hand. Doremi did a year of extension at UCLA, too. Smart kids! You don't get into UCLA unless you have good sense.

Touring is always lucrative, and the parties can be fun.*** While various band members have opted not to be heavily involved in making albums (which yes, can be a source of creative ego conflict, and a lot of hard grueling work at times); everyone seems to like the idea of touring. When Patrick found out he was not going to be invited to tour in spring 1991, he wasn't real happy! September 21, 1991 he served the Moody Blues with legal papers at the Whiskey A Go-Go in Los Angeles, for breach of contract; and for kicking him out of a band when he was supposed to be a "lifetime member."

In my opinion, the Moody Blues reached a low emotionally in the year 1991. Justin's throat was reported as raspy, among other negative comments in reviews (he quit smoking shortly afterward.) They had a thirteenth studio CD that didn't hang together coherently, it had been cobbled together by three different producers, and probably did the worst statistically of all their albums. They also failed to pick up their previous year's sponsor, Budweiser. At the Concord Pavilion in 1991, their sponsor was a hair treatment (VO-5 or Vitalis). No kidding. The arena was only about 1/3 full, if that. They wore coordinating shirts of pink, purple and mauve, to match the new album cover, but they all looked ill at ease on the stage. They had new back-up singers, June Boyce, and Sue Shattock. And, they had a second drummer, a muscular, young fellow named Gordon Marshall and (in addition to Bias Boshell) a new keyboardist, Paul Bliss. Boy they really HAD shuffled the deck!

In addition to a slump in sponsors, the fan club was taking some very strange, and rather childlike turns. I joined the fan club in September of 1991, and I kid you not, the only fan merchandise that was advertised at the time was Moody Blue Teddy Bears. It was pretty disappointing; I was hoping they at least sold key chains or something. Nope. Thankfully this trend changed in the next ten years, but 1991 was pretty pitiful for fan merchandise.

Another way to look at Patrick's departure from the Moody Blues, and the change in personnel: there was another technology shift going on. *Keys of the Kingdom* is heavily laced with technology (almost to the point of tackiness) and has no central theme. They WERE stale. It was time to go back to the melodic roots they had come from. That would turn out to be live orchestral tours, which even in 1991 must have been in the planning stages.

To make up the missing keyboardist, they found Paul Bliss, who had a very solid resume; our first introduction to Paul was summer, 1991. Gordon showed up first with snare drums, performing "God Save the Queen" to open the new American football (gridiron) season in the U.K. When Paul and Gordon auditioned for the Moodies, Gordon claimed Justin referred to the coming 1991 tour as "Bookem and Riskitt." Their talent showed through, and the dynamic duo of Paul and Gordon became part of the Moody Blues.

Bliss and Marshall both arrived as side men with impressive resumes. Paul has composed and recorded as a keyboardist (he plays the guitar too) with numerous other stars, among them Celine Dion. He's the composer of the beautiful theme to a show called *Star Fleet* in the U.K. (kid's show.) Gordon, in addition to being one of the most sexy, athletic, attractive drummers I've ever seen in my life (truly a joy to watch in performance); Gordon is educated in orchestral techniques & functions. He was to serve as the vital link to a new enterprise in the planning stages: the orchestral tour. Gordon is a very competent reader of music, not just a drum basher!

An INCREDIBLE chemistry between Graeme and Gordon soon manifested itself on tour; Gordon knew how to party as hearty as Graeme, who was already a legend in his own time for his tour shenanigans. AND wife Susan Marshall seemed a very nice gal, and real trouper; a good cook too, by Gordon's report. Paul integrated well with Bias Boshell, whom the Moodies were happy to invite in lieu of the departed Moraz. Bias has a good interview in *Higher and Higher* #17; there is a lot in this interview on how they split up the electronic piano sounds.

Gordon and Paul both work together a good deal, and eventually formed their own band outside the Moodies. I've peeked into rehearsals before Moody shows, and seen them in there noodling together; they have worked on each other's solo albums. They both continued to do odd work, and gigs in between Moody Blue shows, as did some of their steadier roadies during the '90s (Rene Martinez comes to mind, he has toured as head guitar honcho for several big-name Rock bands, not just the Moodies.) Gordon Marshall has an interview in *Higher and Higher* #37, and of course, has released his own book *Postcards from a Rock and Roll Tour*, recounting adventures with the band. He has done some commercial jingles in the U.K. and earns a steady living as a musician. He's also a martial arts enthusiast, and at various shows, has doubled as security (never mind the details). He loves weight lifting, and apparently got Justin into "buffing out" when he joined the tour.

Did I say that Gordon is educated in music and orchestral method? Did I say how much he was going to be an integral bridge to the orchestra? What? You didn't know the Moody Blues had NEVER played live with a full orchestra???? Nope! BUT some big ugly metaphorical dragons stood between our heroes, the Moody Blues, and a true orchestral tour.

*We fans have heard rumors that Marie Hayward has been sighted, dragging her resisting husband Justin to the barber shop at various stops in the tour.

**They aren't the first '60s rockers to do it. Jim Morrison did it for the Doors in "End of the Night" as well, snitching lyrics blatantly from the same poem *Songs of Innocence*. I've seen Madonna recite William Blake on the telly, too.

***During their first orchestral tour, I happened to attend a show at the Concord Pavilion. At Intermission, we walked up to the pit, and looked down into it.......and smelled the distinct odour of pizza wafting up from the dressing area beneath. Security assured me the Moodies had bought pizza for the entire orchestra!

XVI) The Dissonant Bar: March 1991-April 1994

Proceed until apprehended-traffic sign in Mexico

SNAKES-label on the side of a Moody Blue stage box

But first we have to turn to something of vital importance, that everyone has been holding their breath about. *Ta dahhhhhh!* (Drum roll please.) Mike Pinder came out of hiding!!!! As he would later put it, he finished raising his kids, and turned back to his original love of music. Oddly, this coincided with the advent of the Internet, which was rapidly becoming a major component of the Moody Blues fan base. And of course, Mike had/has been on the cutting edge of the musical electronics and computer world for years, as had Graeme. In fact, some of Mike's "coming out" process had to do with being a spokesman for Atari. Atari, of course, has been as seminal in the world of recording as Amiga/Commodore.

Little did we all know! In 1986, Pinder had signed with Wizard Records in California; he was eventually to instigate his own "Wizdom Road" series under the name of One Step Records. This would include semi-mystical folk tales and children's readings, all set to his esoteric-cosmic electro-musical backgrounds. Although Pinder had been on excellent terms with the staff of *Higher and Higher* since 1985, he was also to eschew what he would later call "fan adulation" apparently having had plenty of this in the '60s.

The good news was that he would eventually go on to give some really good interviews in the '90s, especially about the history of the band, and his musical roots. He also did a series of free tours and readings for Borders Books in the middle and late '90s.

Wherever Mike was in 1991, he sure got a copy of the Moody Blues fan club newsletter. As soon as I joined the OFC in September 1991, and had my name put on their pen-pal list, I got his snail mail ad, selling old Moody posters. They were priced between $350 and $400, "some have water stains" so said the flyer (perhaps they had been stored in a very dark wet place.) They were to be signed by Mike himself. It is indicative of the high prices that vintage rock posters were now commanding, not just old Moody Blues posters, but anything from the '60s and '70s.

One should also keep in mind that in the early '90s Mike Pinder and Patrick Moraz both retained the same legal counsel.

In the fall of 1992, the Moody Blues landed in Las Vegas, worn out and taking the proverbial well-earned rest from their lengthy planning of the Red Rocks concerts of Sept 9-10. This was after a five-month tour across the United States. They did legal depositions in Vegas, and Patrick was spotted in the light booth, so all sorts of rumors spread about *that* through the fan club.

Things indeed were happening on the legal front, but frankly the Moody Blues all seemed to be having a wonderful time. Graeme was frequently seen in the company of a lovely, bubbly young woman whose name turned out to be Amanda. She was to become a favorite and worthy liaison with the fans, and eventually she and Graeme married. They were to live in Florida, near a golf course, in a house no doubt full of aquariums and computers. (Graeme over the years has developed a love of aquariums, and breeding newts).

I joined the fan club in 1991 and was able to observe the fans from a worm's eye view. I'll address this in another chapter, that's enough to say (for now) about fans and casino antics. In some ways, it's more interesting to go to the shows and casinos and watch the fan shenanigans, than it is to watch the concerts. It was the ultimate reality show!

Back to the music, which is the most important part of what the Moody Blues do. The first orchestral show of the Moody Blues was filmed at the last minute by Public Broadcasting System. The concert was conducted by Larry Baird, then leader of the Colorado Symphony Orchestra. Larry was very impressive to watch conducting live, I was lucky enough to see the orchestral show several times.

Baird's resume includes arranging and conducting the Los Angeles Pops, Les Brown and his Band of Renown, and he worked with Count Basie, The Who, Gladys Knight and the Pips, Bob Hope, Leon Russell, and Procol Harum.

In 1992, technology finally allowed for the effective mixing of live rock plus orchestra. In these live rock/classical shows, each and every classical instrument, from the harp to the cello, has a little microphone clipped on, and is mixed via computer.

I said at the beginning I was not going to count beans, so I have no idea what the gross monetary gain was for the first orchestral show at Red Rocks. What everyone waving legal papers around in the next few years (hoping for a cut of the pie) failed to understand, was that with a show that size, there are union stage hands and musicians to pay. This does not include electric bills that resemble the national debt and feeding/housing/insuring stage hands and performers for the tour.

So to talk about a "gross" take is one of the most ludicrous matters ever to cross the tongue of anyone in regard to the orchestral tours. It made money. The bills were paid. The Colorado Symphony was put on the map, which was wonderful for their civic pride. The same would be true across the country in the next decade. The Moody Blues would team up with orchestras in cities everywhere and give the anaemic classical music world a major shot in the arm, to the delight of music lovers everywhere.

It also put the Moodies back on American TV in March of 1993, when the taped orchestral show aired on PBS. You guessed it: the Moody fan base again swelled to astronomical proportions. The Moody Blues all still looked pretty foxy and a lot of lonely Boomer women in their menopause suddenly decided the Moody Blues were the band they wanted to go see over and over again.

The good news about December of 1992, was that the Moodies were able to do a Christmas song for a children's benefit CD entitled *The Gift of Christmas*, singing "What Child is This?" It's a wonderful rendition of the old

English Christmas carol to the melody of "Greensleeves," they sound like Gregorian monks! Several of the Moodies are Christian, they probably had good reason to pray that year, as we'll soon see. A lovely Christmas carol should be what this time is remembered for, rather than other ugly situations.

He's Swiss, we're English. What's it got to do with California? -- The Moody Blues, concerning *Moodies vs. Moraz*, 1992

Say What You Mean--Christmas Season of 1992, the Moody Blues were supposed to do a tour in Australia. They attempted to settle out of court with Patrick Moraz the night before the civil hearing began, so they could do the tour! But he refused the settlement. The Moodies had to cancel their Oz tour and were forced to sit through two weeks of courtroom banter, as to whether Patrick was unfairly kicked out of the band. Patrick more than had his say in court, fully and at length, for several days. The emotional appeal of the prosecution was casebook, detailed and impressive. However, even though Patrick's lawyer did his best as Patrick's advocate, I'm not sure Moraz hired the right *type* of counselor.

There are about eleven tedious hours of *Court TV* video on this hearing in circulation among the Moodies fan base, and it eventually turned up on *youtube*. It's a fascinating to watch, and very educational about legal matters, as well as providing a few peeps into the psyche of the Moodies. *Court TV* might even sell it to you if you contact them.

The band and their families actually changed seats once, so as to be off the camera as they sat in the audience; their body language was really interesting! Several Los Angeles fans found out about the case, and went down to watch, sitting in the courtroom. Some of the ruder fans wanted to flip pennies at Patrick as he came out of the courthouse (*how L.A.*) but luckily cooler heads prevailed.

The Moody Blues' counsel was a paternal sort of fellow, their accountant a nervous, yet competent young man, Wyn Mather (their office manager) got on the stand and seemed very charming. Tom Huelett was very professional and honest. The Moodies for the most part are themselves, a little more testy than normal; no shock, as they are "hostile witnesses."

The entire Moody team is very professional and intelligent overall, unless you want to count the one alleged instance of a band member verbally baiting a lawyer outside in the hall. We all have our coping devices. Counsel for the prosecution "got back" at them in his closing statements about a "Byzantine Brotherhood," which probably went right over the jury's collective head but made Kirsten Lodge squirm visibly. It was a scurrilous, cheap shot, and of course untrue, but reflective of the thought processes of the speaker

I do directly quote the commentators for the *Court TV* broadcast when I say that Patrick's lawyer was described as "showboating."

A lot of fans have said they didn't want to see the hearing due to the adversarial nature of it. Strictly my personal opinions: I thought Justin and Graeme were a little more annoyed than normal; Justin is usually so pleasant, but he comes over like a pirate in the hearing, when he isn't cat-napping in the audience. And I really thought Patrick over-reacted. He wasn't starving or out of work. In fact, the problem had been getting him to find time for the MOODIES in between his other gigs in Los Angeles. Business was good for Patrick Moraz, from the sound of things. I would refer the reader back to that *Keyboard* interview of May, 1991. Or better yet, read his website for his work (projects) of that time.

The upshot of the hearing was that the judge took away the decision from the jury as to whether Moraz was "kicked out" of the band. The Moody defense counsel produced the paperwork from 1983, in which Patrick signed away his stock option in lieu of a bigger paycheck via contract. Legally, and by his own choice, Moraz was never any more than a sideman under temporary contract, the same as all the back-up singers, as well as Marshall, Bliss, and Boshell (etc). This is a clear legal precedent; the stock option "band membership" was defined back in 1981 when Pinder filed suit (if not before that), and the same has held true in other similar cases with other bands. So, Patrick signed away his "lifetime member of the band" option in 1983.

The rest of the hearing had to do with monetary award for back royalties and such; the jury was so confused by the disparity between the accountants that they just split the difference.

Another thing came out in the hearing: apparently the Moodies locked up Patrick's keyboards at some point. I wonder who owns the instruments and the music software, Threshold or the artists? And when Patrick left, and they finally let him have all his Macs back, the MIDI software for the upcoming 1991 tour vanished. So Bias and Paul had to reconstruct everything from scratch. Being men of great talent, they did just fine.

Everyone lost on the hearing, except the lawyers. Patrick would have netted more money had he settled out of court the night before they started. The Moodies would have made money, touring Australia, and saved legal bills. Australian fans would have been very happy for their Christmas holidays. So, like the old saying goes: *the next time you think talk is cheap, try hiring a lawyer.* [an aside: I have two close friends and a first cousin who are lawyers, and I get most of my lawyer jokes from them.] More can be read about this hearing in *Moodymania* #10. Mark Murley, editor for *Higher and Higher*, was actually called in to give depositions, and wouldn't touch the case journalistically with a 10-foot pole!!!

A lot of dirt flew around behind the scenes during this hearing process. Around the time Patrick was at Vegas for those depositions, really REALLY salacious rumors circulated about groupies and which band members they were sharing hotel rooms with. It took over 20 years to sort out the rumors (they circulated a few times, like a virus mutating each time it leaped from fan to fan) but in each case, the rumors traced back to Patrick's "friends" in the fan base, and he had quite a few. We knew for sure that Patrick and his lawyer obtained taped radio interviews from his time with the band, and they were used as "evidence" proving he was considered a full band member. He got those tapes from fans. So, rumors about "affairs?" Yea. Music IS a "dirty dirty business," to quote Graeme.

Taking the Way Back Machine to 1990, and reading *Higher and Higher,* winter of 1990, we find a curious note in the "news tips" section. Seems information had surfaced about Mike Pinder selling off a Gold Record award in Van Nuys. Nothing more is heard of this, but it's perhaps an indicator of what was to come.

January 11, 1994: Mike Pinder, using the *same* legal representation Patrick had hired, filed against the Moody Blues, alluding to owed back pay. The (public domain) document, available from the Los Angeles county recorder, sounds like the sarcastic sign you see posted in someone's office cubicle; "Everyone around here gets plenty of exercise jumping to conclusions and flying off the handle."

However, the professional view should be, that "same lawyer" was simply advocating for his client, who was totally "in the dark." Mike claimed to have lost all his documentation from his earlier court proceedings with the Moody Blues in 1981/1982, when he had agreed to part company with the band. And no one at Threshold would send him copies, probably because they would have had to dig back 13 years! There were audits and deals throughout the '80s, with Decca/Polygram shifting to the new CD technology. It concerned Mike's shared royalties on the first eight albums (nine if you count *The Magnificent Moodies*), of which no one had apparently (so he said) bothered to send him copies of; neither Decca/Polygram nor Threshold.

In April 1993, (right after the PBS *A Night at Red Rocks* special got Mike's attention) the Moody Blues had agreed to talk to Mike if his "advisors" (the band was really miffed at this lawyer obviously) were not present; apparently

Pinder declined. Remember, the same legal counsel had just wrapped up *Moodies vs. Moraz* in January 1993 and had all the band's audit information throughout the '80s.

It sounds like Decca/Polygram didn't bother to do the paperwork they should have through the '80s, and Threshold didn't know they were supposed to. Of course, it's anyone's guess who owned Decca by 1993; that's why doing audits over seven years back are a joke, and lawyers usually lean on emotional appeal in such cases. It worked: I was pretty angry by the time I got done reading the lawsuit.

Having said that, I suspect the Moody Blues were more complete with their records than we might expect, as the lawsuit was dropped quickly. It just boiled down to a good audit.** Actually, every person with royalty rights to a Moody album should get copies of the documents when a record deal happens to "their" work; that could include not only Pinder, but Moraz, Dave Holland, Tony Clarke, Bob Barriatua, and so forth. The list is endless, just read the album credits. Tom Huelett had passed away in the middle of this, not making things easier, as he had been a driving force to the organizational details.

Two things bother me about *Moodies vs. Pinder*, 1994, and this is a "just the facts" sort of thing. One is that Mike issued a letter to various fan clubs, in which he says,"Have you never quarreled with dear friends?" and, "This action is not a personal attack upon the remaining members of my band." In the court document that Mike Pinder signed, on pg. 7, line 8, it sure looks like a personal attack to me, on Hayward and Lodge! As well, pg. 11, line 5 states very clearly, "The Moody Blues should be liquidated." If that is not an attack on "remaining band members" I'd like to know what is!

Secondly, I don't claim expertise in legal matters. However, in the world of *psychological* counseling, at least in California, for a counselor to commingle two clients in this manner, as this lawyer did with Pinder and Moraz, it's a serious breach of professional ethics. Perhaps it's ok to do in the legal world. He most assuredly had access to the Moody

Blues financial records for the *Moraz vs. Moody Blues* hearing in 1992 and was able to find out confidential matters between them and Mike Pinder, which should have been a separate matter.

Whatever the details to this Pinder/Moodies case, the cyberspace Moody Blues fan-base *exploded!* Eventually the Moodies and Pinder settled out of court in April 1994. It only took 4 months to resolve; the details are unknown to the average Moody fan, which is as it should be. I would assume Tony Clarke was included in the settlement, as he has equal rights the same as whatever Mike had coming to him: 1/6th of whatever profit was realized by the band as a group on the Core Seven albums (plus *Octave*), as well as subsequent royalties.

Mike Pinder issued several statements during early 1994 to his cyber fan base, which was growing by leaps and bounds, the Friends of Mike Pinder, or FoMPers. These releases showed the power of the Internet to take the place of official news outlets. Mike and the rest of the band had so many memories together, it's difficult to think that they could ever totally hate each other. They were happily able to talk it out; John and Justin even got some photo opportunities in with Mike at a Tahoe show, after the dust settled: see *Higher and Higher* #25.

Mike started his own cottage industry in the midst of this, issuing his new albums right after everyone's finances were straightened out, and the rest is covered in Chapter Seventeen.

Forever to Be Alone--One final bit to this chapter. In late 1992, when the inevitable bootleg of the Red Rocks orchestral concerts circulated among the fans, there came a little surprise. This was some months before the professionally mixed CD was released, which was wonderful and much better than the bootleg obviously. There was a little tidbit tacked on it. In fact, I almost wrecked my car when I heard it on my tape deck (and Paula didn't send it to me, it was a third party.) A "lost" recording by Justin, dubbed by *Higher and Higher* "Forever to Be Alone" was on the end of the Red Rocks concert tape. The story to this can be read in *Higher and Higher* #18/19 (pg 33) and #21/22 (pg 70).

The most upsetting thing we were to learn about this was, Justin said that the demo had been *stolen* from Threshold offices in Cobham, and he didn't even know it was missing until a fan had sent him a recording, asking him about it. This brings up the question, what else "vanished" from Threshold in the early '90s?

This particular demo was apparently recorded in the late '60s. Justin doesn't say why it was not released, but my guess would be it was too much like another piece, "Songwriter." There are undoubtedly other Moody demos like this that we don't know about, among them "Peeping and Hiding" by Ray Thomas, a lost bluesy piece. But some were redone and became other songs; therefore the original demos were held back, and possibly forgotten.

At any rate, the story that I got from Paula Woods (a truly philanthropic lady who was kind enough to return the stolen demo to Justin) was that the "Forever To Be Alone" demo came from a dealer in the U.K; it was then sold to an American dealer. That's from whom Paula got it, before the fan club heard it had been stolen, for a three-figure sum, which I don't feel like repeating; but which makes me squirm a good deal. I was lucky enough to see it before it was returned to Justin when he did his Dallas Borders signing show: it was black and plain, the size of a 45 rpm vinyl. It had only the words "The Moody Blues" on the yellowing label, hand-scribed words, and didn't have any tracks on the back, just slick black plastic! One chip on the edge, small enough to not be a problem, thankfully.*

People who have never seen it have repeatedly claimed it was "metal acetate." It looked like a klunky chipped vinyl record to me; if it was metal, it was black all the way through. And I'm not an expert on recording tech, just telling it like I saw it.

Paula waited until she had the opportunity to personally hand it to Justin, as too many fans had the experience of sending things to the offices at Threshold, and never hearing a peep back about it. Everyone had agreed, when we found out it was stolen, that the right thing to do was to return it to Justin.

Justin was so rattled, that he signed TWO items for Paula, instead of just one!

The story I got from Paula was when the American dealer got his hands on the demo, he recorded it and passed the tape to two of his trusted Moody fan contacts in America saying "What the heck is this? Did you ever hear of it before?" At least one of those two people recorded it and sent it to THEIR trusted friends. The last I saw, this lovely unreleased song was available as a "put together" unofficial video on *youtube.com*. The song was not widely in circulation as a bootleg prior to 1991. You can draw your own conclusions as to whom pinched it from Threshold (some **greedy** person), but no one has 'fessed up to the original peccadillo as of yet.

Once the legal niceties were out of the way, it was "full steam ahead" for the Moody Blues and their Red Rocks tour, which was to take the music world by storm.

*Curious foot note. Paula let me in on her plans, so as far as I know, I'm the only person with photos of this particular happening. I actually took a picture of the demo itself "for the record," but the Force was apparently with Justin. That photo DIDN'T COME OUT. Man.........*go figure*. So my recollections are totally from memory. It was a great signing anyway, Justin sounded great, he got his record back, and I got to meet a lot of neat Moody friends I'd never seen before. An amusing side note: some of the fans (the ones who go bonkers over photos and stand around with cameras glued to their eyes) actually whined to the management of Borders Books that "No one told us Justin was going to get his record back!" *hehehe* No one knew but me, Paula and a few friends. Poor Larry at Borders, all dressed in a fishing vest and ready to bolt out the door after the show was over, beset by whining fans! It's amusing to see living theater go off script like that.

** A good example of what happens when an event is seen from different perspectives. I did run across a tidbit from Mike, in which he said he had only sued the Moody Blues ONCE. I presume he means the early '80s courtroom episode, which blocked touring and *Long Distant Voyager* release? Not to dispute an intelligent dude like Mike, but I have a copy of the (second) lawsuit from the early '90s (write the County of Los Angeles, maybe you can get a copy too, it should be public domain); it sure looks like a lawsuit to me! However, Mike did not take the rest of the band to court! Also flashing back to the chapter on *Long Distance Voyager*, the Moody Blues were not specifically mentioned in the 1981 lawsuit title, but the effect was the same. I shall leave it up to the reader to make the final judgment and parse appropriately. I'm just REALLY glad they all got over it and are talking again, more or less. And are all still putting out good music!

XVII) Red Rocks, Moody Blues: Fall 1992-March 2000

There are never enough violas! -- Larry Baird, 1992

Just crank up the amps and let 'er rip....(one of the Moodies to Larry Baird)

Before the creation of Man, the Great Spirit (whose tracks are yet to be seen on the stones...... in the form of a large bird) used to slay buffalo and eat them on the ledge of the Red Rocks... and their blood running onto the rocks made them red. - Lakota legend as recounted by Catlin and pinched from a book by Ken Davis

    The Moody Blues have modestly claimed in interviews that they started playing "rock with orchestras" more or less by accident.
    Some accident.
    1992 was not the first time the Moodies played at Red Rocks, nor were they the first to combine rock with orchestra. There was plenty of popular music set to lush orchestrations in the early '60s; Nat King Cole comes to mind; there were others. George Martin was merrily mixing Beatles music with orchestras during the same years; "Sergeant Pepper" was released only three months before *Days of Future Passed*. The Sixties was an era of daring and creativity; it only took people willing to experiment to fulfill the concept.
    The Moody Blues were willing in those early years, and had every instrument ever made laying around their studio in 1968 to prove it! Maybe it all started as a "tour" idea, on that 1972 night in Portland, when a bunch of crazy kids sent their rock n' roll *cum* string quartet tape backstage, and were recruited for *Ever Since the Dawn* and *Blue Jays*. Justin carried on the trend, not only in working with Peter Knight on *Moving Mountains* in 1985, but with *Classic Blue* in 1989, with help from Mike Batt (an extraordinary

experimentalist in his own right, and a very funny guy on Twitter.)

    John and Justin continued to test the waters with orchestral versions of "Question" and "Isn't Life Strange" on a Moody Blues compilation album in 1990. When *Keys of the Kingdom* came out in 1991, the Moodies cut a demo of "Bless the Wings" with full orchestration. It indeed got backers interested in the Red Rocks project.

    September 1992. Everything changes after this. John has said in interviews that he lay awake at 3 am night before that first show, wondering if it would work.

We're fortunate, because three of us can sing, and use our voices to give an orchestral feel to our harmonies...and then we add the flute. -- John Lodge, *The Star-Gazette* (Nov 11, 2000)

    Much debate comes up in interviews with the Moodies, and with Larry Baird, who scored (re-scored) the music. WHY does Moody Blue music lend itself so well to orchestration? The Moody Blues write melodies with more than three chords, that's why. Three chords more or less is what distinguishes folk music: three basic chord songs are easy to learn, making it "folk." The Moodies had written complex melodies for a long time, without trying (same with the Beatles.) Slapping an orchestra on top of rock n' roll is just gimmicky, unless there is a well-developed melody there to begin with.

    The other good thing about the orchestral tours: it forced the band to look at their song writing roots. Discounting the dinky mikes on all the instruments, it nudged them away from the electronic trickery. By 1994, Graeme was backing away from his former love of electronics; from *The Journal* (Rapid City, SD) Edge found the advancing technology hardest to accept. "I don't enjoy it as much now," he says of recording, "You hardly ever play at the same time." It eliminates learning by error. The things you miss are the glorious mistakes that don't happen now."

And this man had the courage to play drums with a full orchestra behind him!

For the record, the first live Moody Blues orchestral concert is Sept 9, 1992, with the eighty-eight piece Colorado Symphony Orchestra. It happened at the Red Rocks Amphitheater, conducted by Larry Baird. Those eighty-eight pieces in the next eight (or so) years would vary from forty up to ninety pieces, depending on the city they played in; it was rarely the same orchestra two nights in a row!

Emerson, Lake and Palmer had tried to tour with a whole orchestra in the late '70s and had not done so well. Ray Thomas had also considered it with his *Hopes Wishes and Dreams* album. *Blue Jays* did it on a very reduced scale in 1975, touring with a trim ensemble of two guitars, a string quartet and a Mellotron (and they sounded pretty good). Larry would configure for his orchestras "Eighteen violins, eight woodwinds, four violas, cellos, basses and horns, three trumpets, trombones, and percussion, one tuba, synthesizer, harp and timpanist." (*Houston Chronicle*, May 30, 1993)

Barry Fey promoted Red Rocks, and showed up for the event dressed in a tux jacket, and shorts. Obviously a man with style! When Barry was interviewed Sept 1, 1992 he was already getting nibbles for other shows from other orchestras across the country. The first orchestral "Moody Blues at Red Rocks" sold out in two hours, and it's a Very Big Place.

A couple of DJs from Philadelphia rang up Graeme in Palm Beach in 1996 and quizzed the drummer about how they managed to pull it off. "Sometimes by the skin of our teeth...our conductor Larry Baird discovered we don't have the right kind of discipline! We do dinging and banging and bumping....a rocking good blast from an amp, and in the violin section one of the strings would break!" Even better, the DJs asked him about the poem he recited so seriously every night on stage. "I actually do forget them [the lines]. Just before I went on one night, one of the road crew said in my ear 'Breathe sheep, and gather the wool' and it came out on stage.....by then it was too late!"

The Moody Blues did a "normal" tour in early 1992, with the band Chicago. It went like any rock n' roll tour, with a new combination of keyboardists, new back-up singers (Sue Shattock and June Boyce), and new drummer (Gordon Marshall.) Tom Huelett had them slotted to tour to Kuala Lumpur in Ceylon, prompting Justin to ask "Do they know who we are in Kuala Lumpur?" At that, Tom is alleged to have returned "They might not know the Moody Blues, but they sure as hell know what 'Nights in White Satin' is!" Don't let Justin's innocence fool you: one of his favorite authors at the time was Nigel Barley, noted anthropological author who wrote some incredible books about Indochina. Justin and the rest of the band were itching to tour that area.

Sadly, I don't think they ever got there, due to the lawsuit that overtook them at the end of 1992. That wasn't the only tour mix-up that year: their last show at the Sunrise Theatre in Florida (July 29, 1992) got cancelled due to the wrong dates being on their work visas, and they had to leave the country with the last summer show undone.

In later eons, we may even see 1992 as a watershed year socially and technologically. Two interesting things happened with Red Rocks 1) technology caught up with the long-frustrated desire to blend live orchestra and rock music. Although various bands attempted to tour with live orchestras in the 1970s, it was not until the '90s that each instrument would be individually wired with a tiny microphone, and then mixed with the aid of computer technology. And 2) Moody Blues fans were able to network via computer bulletin boards, and "tribalize" via the computer. These Internet fans from all over the world, showed up at Red Rocks in September, all waving blue glow sticks, during "The Other Side of Life." As far as I know, this is the first online fan group to do this sort of thing.

I joined the Moody Blues official fan club in September of 1991. By early 1992, I had run an ad in the OFC newsletter, trying to find people who had sheet music of the Moody Blues, with a mind to playing it myself on the guitar and piano. I was contacted by a "fan" who quizzed me regarding "had I ever seen any orchestral scores for Moody music?" I hadn't (I'm probably one of a minority of fans who would recognize it.) Neither had anyone else. Peter Knight had passed away in the '80s; the scores he did originally in 1967 have long since vanished or have yet to be discovered. Possibly they were scooped away into a dumpster when Decca One was cannibalized, but if I were to make a guess, I'd guess that Derek McCormick (or his heirs) might have them, as he was planning to do an orchestral tour in 1968 with the band.

Anyway, I remember discussing via snail mail, that the only thing left to do was to take the sheet music as it stood in the songbooks and start scoring the various melody lines for the different instruments, listening to the original orchestrations from <u>Days of Future Passed</u>. It's not hard for a musician who reads music, just really tedious. And I know there were various computer programs out there at the time (Deluxe Music on Amiga) that allowed cut-paste-drag of notes onto the music staff, so this might have been less difficult than we realize.

However they did it, they did it fast, and they did it well. *Higher and Higher* #18/19 has lots of great notes about the development of the Red Rocks concert. In May 1992, poor Larry Baird finally had the news broken to him that there were no original Knight scores to be found, for love nor money. Refusing to panic, Larry dove in, burned a lot of midnight oil, and did a magnificent job. It took from six to ten weeks (depending on the interview) to reconstruct faithfully what Peter Knight had originally done in two weeks. Larry also did new scores and additions.

The results were wonderful. Most notable was "New Horizons," which was for the first time orchestrated, and is ethereal on the video. You cannot imagine what a huge amount of work all this was; whatever Larry got paid, it was worth it. He even scored in the cat that accidentally knocked over the bell tree during the crescendo at the end of *Days of Future Passed* (which always causes a good deal of mirth among the band.) One song for an orchestra would run to around 200 pages, including fine details such as whether the violin was bowing "up" or "down."

The task was so complex, that Larry eventually hired two more young musicians to help proofread the scores. The very coolest part of his orchestrations is the opening chords of the Red Rocks Overture. You have to listen very carefully, but it's actually "Ride My See Saw" that opens *A Night At Red Rocks*. For so many years, this has been the finale for the Moodies, and now here it is, full circle, opening one of their greatest accomplishments.

Sadly, the entire Overture was not part of the original CD, but exists as many, many bootlegs, spread across the world in the numerous collections of Moody Blues fans. If I'm not mistaken, a Red Rocks CD released at the end of 2002 might have the entire overture included. On the Overture, Larry began with "Ride My See Saw" altered in tempo just a bit, then slipped into the harmony line to "I Know You're Out There Somewhere." and then went into "New Horizons"; the whole overture was well worth hearing without the rock concert.

For other additions, Larry used a lot of brass in "Isn't Life Strange" and "The Other Side of Life." He used a Debussy flavor in "New Horizons." used a celesta on "Emily's Song." [The celesta was first made famous in the Sugar Plum Fairy's dance in *The Nutcracker* ballet, if you are a classical music fanatic, a tinkling "music box" effect.]

All of the Moodies pulled out songs rarely performed live, but which meant the most to them, tunes such as "Emily's Song," and "For My Lady." Justin says on the video about "New Horizons," "It's a family song."

Luckily the advances in technology were such that the world was *just* into the FAX age in 1992; email was still "iffy," and you couldn't attach files like you can today. The scores were easy to send ahead (via fax) to prospective orchestras, as well as to the Moodies themselves for fine adjustments. The concert probably couldn't have happened if it hadn't been for the FAX, especially with the short amount of time they had to pull it together.

Musicians are not known for small egos, and can be faint with praise, but in the case of Baird's scores, there seems to have been nothing but good feedback from the professionals. Phrases like "fairly complex scores," "of exceptional quality," and "a few tricky spots," are but some comments on the score. Word got around in the music world that it was a good show and fun to be part of. Baird would tell the musicians, "Play the songs as you know them," hoping the musicians would pick up the crisp rhythm the Moodies originally imparted to the music.

Sometimes the magic worked: sometimes it didn't. At least one orchestra member mentioned in an interview that playing with the Moody Blues was a bit like being the original orchestras that played with Bach or Beethoven; doing the music with the original composers. Certainly it must have been nice to get quality scores that were more current than Beethoven, and just as enjoyable.

Rehearsals could be weird. The orchestra members sometimes wound up gawking at the band rather than playing the music, so eventually the band stopped showing up for rehearsals; tapes were used. There's nothing like putting "the real thing" in front of a live audience to sharpen concentration.

After the bugs got worked out in the first two years, the year 1994 has the best reviews of the orchestral show. This is the year that *Starlight Sojourn*, a bootleg CD, surfaced. Recorded (off the radio?) at the San Diego concert of September 29, 1994, it's possibly the best mix of the show to date, far surpassing (in my humble opinion) either the Red Rocks show in September 1992 (the first) or the sluggish Royal Albert Hall show, the last (May 2000).

Sometime in 1994, Justin worked with studio recordings of other songs he had written, and they were to surface in Germany under the title of *The Frankfort Rock Orchestra*. There was litigation over this: some of the tracks are really not quality, but more experimental in nature. For a while they were considered "bootleg," and then suddenly they were being sold as legitimate CDs. The songs that Justin sang with orchestral backing on this CD are "Forever

Autumn," "Running Water," "Blue World," "Blue Guitar," "Voices in the Sky," and "In My World."

While the Moody Blues were eventually able to tour the U.K. with an orchestral show, they would find that Europe was not cost effective when it came to orchestras. The European groups wanted to hire the Moodies to play with *them*, thereby keeping control of the revenue! So it just didn't work out to tour anywhere but England and America with the orchestras. In England, they apparently lost money, but it was worth it to take care of their hometown fans. And, much of the U.K. proceeds frequently go to charity, which is a good thing.

One of the neatest things the Moody Blues said (in interviews) about the concert tours, was that total strangers would walk up to them, profess to being lifelong Moody fans, and then would say, "Do you know I have never seen a live orchestra perform before?" If that doesn't give you faith in what was happening, nothing will.

One would think that combining the English and concert music would make the Moodies "stuffy." Not at all, it seems. In Bournemouth in December of 1993, when the sound system went on the fritz, the Moodies all did stand-up comedy until the problem could be fixed. And at the Royal Albert Hall (May 2000) one of their more sprightly fans did several handsprings up the aisle, in full view of the PBS cameras and band, during "Your Wildest Dreams." It got a big round of applause and lots of grins from the musicians.

Ugly rumors spread at one point, about Graeme and Gordon doing a wonderful drumstick juggling act during "You're Wildest Dreams," and accidentally hitting a valuable violin, catastrophically removing the bridge. Another time, a flying drumstick hit an amp, turning off the power switch. Graeme started appearing in a Plexiglas box; possibly their life insurance rates improved as well, as Ray and John had more than a few near misses from the juggling act. It was a good deal of fun to see Justin, usually the center of attention, being totally upstaged by the flying drumsticks: he knew it was going on but was powerless to turn around and watch. It was also a lot of fun to watch John peering down myopically at a drumstick skidding to a halt at his feet.

One reason for the "drummer box" could have been that everyone (including the orchestra) was thinking of preserving what little hearing they had left after thirty years of touring rock n' roll. Graeme would say of his plastic box "[It] had me cut off from everybody. Everybody can see into you, but I spent the entire show looking at ghosts of the band." The real reason for the box was probably keeping the sound mix clean, and to eliminate the bleed-over sound from drums to orchestral tracks.

The first official show of the Red Rocks tours happened in June 1993, at the Starplex Amphitheater in Dallas, Texas. Justin was interviewed before the show and had the most serious cases of pre-show jitters ever recorded in a Moody Blue. The poor man stuttered.

One major change happened; June Boyce dropped out of the lineup to start a family, and her replacement, Tracy Graham, was hired. Tracy soon developed her own fan club of admirers, not just for her pixie-like beauty, but for her melodious contralto voice, the likes of which has rarely been heard on a rock stage. At least one on-line dude fan would be moved to comment gallantly about Tracy, "She has moves that would stop a Sherman tank!" At least two good digital recordings of the Red Rocks tour, *Starlight Sojourn* and *Hall of Fame*, really showcase her voice in the mixing of "I Know You're Out There Somewhere." Between Ray, Justin, and Tracy, the harmonies are worthy of shivers up the spine.

The Moodies would tour for the next seven years, taking mastermind conductor Larry Baird along. Larry wrote up a really nice review of their backstage happenings in the OFC newsletter for summer, 1996 (well worth reading). He coordinated rock/orchestra arrangements with the Moodies' musical powerhouse, Gordon Marshall. According to interviews, Gordon got his cues from Larry, and then he cued the band (*Higher and Higher* #18/19.)

Sometimes they played with a local orchestra, and sometimes without. Some orchestras, like the Baton Rouge Symphony and the Spokane Symphony, were "small town," very talented, and very happy to have Big Names come to their "second fiddle" towns and play. I've become convinced, after substitute teaching music in rural area schools, that musical talent is something you find more readily in small towns, not in the big city. Musicians don't like the inner city, you might say, or at least they are more humble about their talents when they live in the country.

In larger cities, sometimes they would pick up big, formal orchestras (like Los Angeles, and the Hollywood Bowl), with mixed results. Take the familiar, strong-willed leader away from the big city orchestras, and put in a "new guy," the extremely talented Larry Baird; and it was often a matter of Larry trying to drag a reluctant orchestral elephant along to the crisp pace he wanted for the show. Compare Larry's own Denver Symphony at the pace it should be in *A Night At Red Rocks*, to the Royal Albert Hall show, seven years later. You'll get the picture. Interestingly, April 30, the night before the commercial version of the RAH, the pace was much crisper, from the bootleg. Go figure why they used the slower second night.

Some established orchestras (luckily, a minority) just couldn't be bothered with the Moodies, and they "picked up" an orchestra in whatever city they were in. Portland, Oregon was a prime example. The real orchestra was busy the nights the Moodies played the Rose Quarter in the late '90s, and several of the members of the Portland Festival orchestra turned out to be high school students, hired as a last resort.

Sometimes, the Moodies hired musicians (viola players) to come along with them; I think they gave them money and told them to get there on their own; they made their own travel arrangements. Whatever the logistics, many of the Moody Blue's orchestras-of-the-90s were "made-up" orchestras, and the entire thing must be recognized overall as a feat of genius in management.

Something cool happened when they got to Boise, Idaho. Some of the original members of Providence; remember them back in the early '70s? got to play in the orchestra. Talk about full circle!!!

Not all of the shows went off smoothly, and it was all part of the fun, to see what went different each night. The orchestras had musical scores faxed ahead to them, and tapes of the rock portion of the show, to practice with. I know of at least one case, where a local fan was able to slip some very good bootlegs of other orchestral shows to the Baton Rouge Symphony, with excellent results.

The orchestra would rehearse early the same day with Baird and tapes, then the Moodies arrived and "just did it" on stage. Sometimes the band and the orchestra would get on different tracks, and it got muddled. During the '90s, another technical leap happened, and everyone in the band started wearing earplugs that gave mixed sound back to them, so they could synchronize more efficiently with the orchestra. Justin took time to explain this in one show, which was very nice of him, and I bet it was nice for him too!! Much ground-breaking musical technology has developed during these shows, and other musicians will, and have been able to follow in their footsteps.

They sold out the Hollywood Bowl the first time they played there with the symphony. However, not all shows went off well that first tour. The talented Spokane Symphony was destined to play the Gorge for three years with the Moodies. (This would not be the first time for the Spokane Symphony with pop stars; they backed Natalie Cole in 1992.) You haven't lived until you see the Gorge amphitheater: the Columbia River Basin is as beautiful as the Grand Canyon and makes a wonderful backdrop for the stage.

Unfortunately, on bad days the gusts of wind are hurricane in proportion; the first time the Moodies played there, the wind came up, knocked down the big screen, and nearly wiped out people in the front rows. Luckily the fans who had those seats were still in their car, stuffing flasks and tape recorders into their underwear. During the next two years for the Gorge shows in May, the weather would play dodge-ball with damp musicians, and I have no idea how everyone managed to stay in tune, as moisture affects every string and drum membrane.

The Gorge may be beautiful, but the people of Seattle and Boise for the most part didn't relish driving out there; only the hardy few made it and camped over-night on the hills overlooking the canyon. One of my fondest Moody memories is of those Gorge campgrounds, bending over a very poor field recording of "Strange Times" after only the second public performance of the song, and trying to pick out the words. The wind was whipping, the light from the lantern was an eerie blue glow, and I looked up to realize two of us were Native American and one was Buddhist, lending a very spiritual air to the night's proceedings. Everyone's hair was flying in the wind, high on that mountainside. The Gorge is a great place, go out there sometime if you get a chance.

In 1996, new arrangements such as "Never Comes the Day" were added to the show and can only be heard as orchestral pieces in bootlegs. Also, "Strange Times" was apparently written with an orchestra in mind, and actually debuted in Portland, without ever having been sold commercially. I was there for that one: people sat in stunned silence after the song finished, then hesitantly broke into a welcoming applause. It was a very weird, and wonderful event.

The orchestral shows usually changed every year, during the eight years of touring, just to keep the show fresh and alive; and to keep from boring the performers too much! The Moody Blues have such a huge list of songs to chose from, it was no strain at all to find good material.

An entire book could probably be written about the orchestral tours. A tour documentary was done for New York PBS by Laura Vitez, entitled *The Other Side of Red Rocks*, very worth watching if you can find it. I was pen-pals with Laura's sister at one time, and she about drove me nuts with "not too subtle hints" for a year preceding the first Red Rocks show. According to her sister, Laura is alleged to have eight more hours of documentary, but much of it never made it to commercial video, due to not only space considerations, but copyright issues with union musicians in the orchestras.

The band loosened up a bit in the later '90s and started letting fans back-stage, in small, well-supervised numbers. Many of the backstage passes would be generated by auctions for charity through the Official Fan Club.

When they were without the orchestras, they were able to do other charity work, such as the Hungerthon '95 at the Beacon Theater in New York. Soon after that, Justin did solo work for Annie Haslam's "Lilies of the Field" concert for Bosnia. In 1996, on Bastille Day, Justin was able to do a solo show for UNICEF in his home town of Swindon, Wiltshire. Those are but a few of the benefits the combined Moody Blues did during this time.

1994 was noted for the contribution the Moody Blues made to a World Cup benefit CD, recording "This is the Moment," a song from the Broadway show *Jekyll and Hyde*. It's a great song as done by the Moodies, and very worth tracking down if you haven't heard it yet. Ice skating stars have used it in skating competition, and people play it at weddings.

During the same year, they released a boxed set *Time Traveler*, which is a "best of" album. There are some noteworthy differences in this and other compilations; *Time Traveler* initially contained CDs of the leftover songs that did not make the final cut for the live Red Rocks CD, released in 1993. And they also included "Highway" (left off *Keys of the Kingdom*) and "This is the Moment." The biographical essay has a funny slant, and the pictures included make it one of the nicest boxed sets to hit the market; it reads exactly like a book. If you can find a boxed set with all five CDs in it, you are a very lucky person indeed.

1995 saw Mike Pinder, suddenly finding the resources to do it, releasing his first album in seventeen years, *Among the Stars*. He managed to coordinate his mini-signing tour with the Moodies in Las Vegas, capitalizing on the momentum behind the fan base, to market his album.

September 27, 1994: the Moody Blues were inducted into the Hollywood Rock Walk, on Sunset Boulevard in Los Angeles. The videos and photos of the event are pretty trippy; confronted with a large pile of mud, the Moodies were all asked to contribute their handprints. While Justin peeled off his rings, Graeme was the first to smush his hand in, apparently enjoying it. Ray, not to be outdone, put his mitt in next, and lifted a lip in mock (or real) disgust. Justin, smiling with the boldness of a Zen master, calmly placed his hand in the muck, and John (who was hanging back), reassured when Justin didn't "ick out" put his hand in too. The attending fans loved it. The whole band played later that day at Tower Records in Hollywood, more or less the same acoustic set that they were to do later in South Africa for a radio interview.

By the end of their 1994 tour, the Moodies were exhausted. Not only had they released and promoted a major boxed set, and toured with the orchestra, but they had dealt with a major lawsuit and audit that year, enough to tire anyone. They relayed to a fan who crashed their end of the tour party in Texas, that they needed to take a year off.

1995 was a slow year, the Moody Blues only toured South Africa, and without an orchestra. Much of this tour was captured on a video available through the OFC, and they included some home videos of their sight-seeing. The video showed South Africa as a land of many contrasts, with a long way to go before catching up to the rest of the Western world.

Marie Hayward, John, Graeme and Allan Terry got in some golf on a South Africa course riddled with crocodiles. The crocs were in a sand trap and got a few balls for gizzard stones. Justin's wife had the bad fortune to knock her ball into said pit, and John whispered rather fiendishly "Go get it, Marie."

1995 also saw the Moody Blues touring to all the Caesar's casinos. The following year, 1996 would see a major media blitz, numerous press releases outlining their many awards and kudos, more interviews (especially in casino newspapers) and another year of orchestral touring for the Moodies. People still wanted the orchestra tour, the demand continued until 2000 when they more or less ended the orchestra cycle.

In later years, an occasional orchestral show happened (Hard Rock Park, Myrtle Beach in 2008, and Dallas 2009) but it was very much a "here and there" situation. In the '90s, in between Las Vegas and Tahoe, Justin was able to swing through Los Angeles where his daughter was working for VH1. One of the nicest TV spots ever done by the Moodies, is Justin and Doremi on Father's Day 1995. One look at Justin during this, coming out of a dressing room on Rodeo Drive dressed in yellow vinyl should convince everyone that Justin is anything but stuffy.

While his wife was busy at the golf course, Justin put his mind to serious musical pursuits in his mini-studio, based at his home in Cote d'Azur, on the Ligurian coast. Always full up with song, Justin didn't wait for the rest of the band. He veered sideways and with a little help from his friends in Italy, recorded a most wonderful, well thought-out solo album: *The View From the Hill.*

XVIII) A View from a Certain Hill: September 1991- 1999

And the spirit that breaks free from the cage is the one they cannot kill-Micky Feat

I dug out my notes, and here is the best I can do about the [Portland] Brewpub show order. I KNOW for sure that he did "It's Up to You" then "Land of Make Believe" and then "Blue Guitar" in that order. I wrote it down. It was a very very weird moment, because the friend I went with actually said "Play Blue Guitar" quietly, right as W**** and M***** were simultaneously requesting it under Justin's feet (he was on a high balcony). And we were nowhere near each other. There was some psychic vibration going around the room apparently. I don't know what he opened with, but he did (somewhere in the night) "Driftwood," "Forever Autumn," "Wildest Dreams," (I think he did that in open tuning, which was different), and he closed with "Raised on Love." He probably did something very close to the show in Seattle the next night, because I talked with Nida about it afterward and the line-up was very close. -- notes from the Portland Brewpub

    The real first solo show of Justin's is lost somewhere in the mists of time, as Justin started out prior to his Moody Blues days, doing small coffee-shop gigs in the U.K. in and around his hometown of Swindon. For that matter, his first solo shows would have been in Swindon at high school, or in Lyme Regis!

    As far as I can tell, after he joined the Moodies, and discounting a few solo appearances on the telly, Justin didn't do any solo shows until the "Swindon Be-Bop" benefit in October of 1991. This was really the first of Justin's solo shows in which he did what he darn well pleased.* In interviews he has said, the Moody Blues as an entity on stage can be a little stifling for doing ad-libs.

    This begs a moment of explanation about music history. Depression era musicians had a fairly standard format that has come down to us in the form of coffee-house entertainers. (Call them modern troubadours if you like.) Arlo Guthrie is the only big-time entertainer I can think of, still treading the boards, that does this as a primary form of performance. The format is, you sing a song, then you stop and tell a story about how it was written, or you do a comedy patter, and then you sing another song. And so forth. The stories can get quite elaborate. (I'm thinking of a masterpiece Arlo did called "The Clam from Oklahoma.")

Obviously, Arlo learned it from his dad Woody Guthrie. Those who visit Branson, MO a lot will also recognize the format, *Legends and Lyrics* in Nashville does it. Yeah and they do it at the Bluebird Cafe in Nashville too, as "songwriting in the round." They call it "taking a pull at a song." Groucho Marx did it in *An Evening with Groucho*. British music hall artists did it. Vaudevillian and burlesque "top bananas" did it. A gifted story-teller is a thing of beauty, and not something modern listeners are used to, considering most of us think television is a high form of entertainment.

When I saw Justin do his solo shows, he did a lot of coffee-house patter, and the smaller the venue, the more relaxed he became. The Santa Barbara show is the best show I've seen Justin do solo (they only squeezed in 200 patrons); he told many stories, and ad libbed a LOT.

In October 1991, after finishing up the set list for the Swindon Be-Bop show, Justin broke out into a series of oldies, including "Be Bop A Luma," "Rave on," "Twist and Shout," and other Buddy Holly songs, music from the era he grew up in, the early days of rock n' roll. Paul Bliss played with Justin at this Swindon show, done as a benefit for Justin's high school classmate. The proceeds went to the Princess Margaret hospital in Swindon, to build a new cancer ward, "The Sunshine Room." It was dedicated to his classmate's husband, who had passed away with cancer. So thankfully, Justin found time to touch base with old friends during his hectic schedule. The show was home-videoed, and Justin's friend was able to sell those as well, to further benefit the cost of the Sunshine Room. Very cool, that the sales of the video eventually doubled what they thought they would make off it, and they put in two wards instead of one.

Normally British fans would have sent the video bootleg right to their American friends, but those who know their electronics understand that England and America run on different systems. PAL (British) has to be converted to NTSC (American). About the time I got into the fan club, I connected with people who tried to loop me into a scheme for getting a "converted copy" of this video from some woman in Arkansas who was selling them at $35 a pop. The scheme was, I was supposed to get one, then copy it for all my friends who kicked in on the original price.

In the fan club, prior to the Internet and *youtube*, the issue of black market bootlegs came up over and over again; one look in the *Goldmine* ad section gave you a hint on how widespread this is. Anyway, at the time (smelling a fish) I declined to get involved, and I'm glad I did: the OFC newsletter came out, June 1992 with a rather nasty note about this operation, citing the fan who sold these "for her own profit." If I'm not mistaken, the same fan managed to push her way backstage at Tahoe to get her picture taken with Justin, claiming to be terminal with leukemia. Sad, but some fans can be really conniving in their fandom. The problem was finally solved by doing the PAL/NTSC conversion, and offering it for sale Stateside through the fan club.

Justin would later pick back up the general format he did in Swindon, playing solo his favorite songs he's written over the years. In the '90s solo shows, he ended with "Raised on Love," which sums up much of what Justin is all about. He's a family man, and if his fans haven't found that out by now, they have missed the entire point. In a sense, the Moody's finale "Ride My See Saw" says something similar: "Take this job, I have my own life when I walk off the stage."

Grand Ol' Oprey. *For every English guitar player, this is a dream. It's Mecca. You bow down and say your prayers to Nashville* -- Justin in a Nashville interview. Justin's performance at Tin

Pan South is written up in *Moodymania* #19, and also in *Higher and Higher* #26/27.

The original Grand Ol' Opry, known as the Ryman Theatre, was once a church, and still has wooden pews. It's quite a nice theatre with lots of history, and well worth the journey to see if you are a music lover. The Moodies play there whenever their tour takes them through Nashville.

Justin seems to be a very active person professionally and is well known in the international music community. In April 1995, he was invited to perform acoustically among his peers at the Ryman in Nashville, at a songwriter's event known as Tin Pan South.

A word of explanation about American "country" music. There is a bit of the lurking "hick" in Nashville, and a pressure to be "just folks." The challenge of Tin Pan South, was for the people who wrote the music to get up, with just a guitar or a piano, and do the song like you are at home playing with friends. Just sing and perform the song. One of the neater clips I saw from this same show was the couple who wrote "The Way We Were" doing the song on a piano. Neither one of them was comfortable singing (certainly not feeling up to following Barbara Streisand) but it still came over as a very nice song, with no hype.

The Nashville reviewers would say of Justin, "Without the layered arrangements familiar in his work with the Moody Blues, Hayward's songs displayed elegant folk roots." (*The Tennessean* April 18, 1995) No higher praise could come from the heart of American music!

One more thing to note: Justin took two guitars with him to the event, one of them in open tuning to play "Question." Another songwriter arrived with his music in hand, but somehow neglected to bring a guitar, and wished to borrow one. This is about like asking to borrow someone's toothbrush, to many guitarists. Justin rather fiendishly stepped forward and (never cracking a smile) offered his open-tuned 12 string to the guy. Much fumbling ensued, and the good people of Nashville never caught on to Justin's joke. Those that did, kept straight faces.

After Tin Pan South, Justin (much emboldened) did a solo benefit show for Annie Haslam. "Lilies of the Field" has an excellent review in *Moodymania* #21. It had much the same line-up as Justin's other solos.

troubadour \TROO-buh-dor\ (noun) *1: any of a class of poet-musicians flourishing especially in southern France and northern Italy during the 11th, 12th, and 13th centuries 2: a strolling minstrel; also : anyone who in music, verse, or rhetorical prose promotes some cause* ...FYI: The Troubador was also a coffee house popular in Southern California during the '60s; it's still there, and worth a Google to check out their website's musical history section.

The concept of "romance" did not exist at all (early Greeks and Romans didn't practice romantic love, not publicly anyway) until introduced by the troubadours of the Middle Ages (Crusades era.) The troubadours were the shining knights of poetry; in fact, some were ranked as high as knights in the feudal class structure. It was troubadours who made romance a high art, writing poems and singing about chivalrous love, creating the mystique of refined damsels, and glorifying the gallant knight on his charger. "Troubadour" was a fitting name for such creative artists; it derives from an old Provencal word meaning "to compose." Lest we forget, Justin Hayward lives in the south of France, on the Ligurian Coast.

You fit my hand like a new guitar -- John Lodge.

The process of song writing is one that mystifies not only listeners, but often the songwriter as well. For example, Willie Nelson made a nebulous statement regarding his music; "The tunes are just out there, you only have to pick one out of the air." (*The Big Six-Oh*) Justin calls driving "Zen" and says he does a lot of song writing while driving.

As well, every time a Moody Blue (especially Justin), gets a new instrument, they go out and write new songs.

Justin had this happen with a toy keyboard (Casio) he had bought for his daughter in the 1980s. Some friends were visiting him in his home, and he just started goofing around with the keyboard that was laying around in the front room. The result was the lovely ballad "Running Water." When Justin was having his home remodeled in Kingston, he struck up a conversation with the carpenter, and wound up borrowing a Juno keyboard which the carpenter wanted out of his house ("His wife was nagging him about it.") Justin wound up writing "Say it With Love" on that Juno. "Nights in White Satin" was written on a twelve-string guitar borrowed from Lonnie Donegan, which Justin had been fixing. The song sometimes comes from the instrument.

    A change in locale seems to be inspirational to Mr. Hayward as well. Justin had more or less moved to the Italian Riviera as of 1987; he didn't move there permanently until 1997, still having a home in Kingston, U.K. during the '90s. Going back and forth wasn't a problem at first, but eventually he sold his home in England, and moved to the Ligurian coast permanently. He picked up a new guitar in Italy, having not brought all his favorite guitars down from England yet. In his words "The songs just poured out" with the new feel of the guitar and the new surroundings. The result was many of the lovely songs on *The View from the Hill*.

    With his relocation in the 1990s, Justin found himself hanging out with other musicians who also lived on the Riviera, two of whom were Mickey Feat and Phil Palmer. In Justin's words, they started doing parties and informal gigs at nightclubs around the community, and a stage act, a "synergy" started to gel. Paul Bliss and Justin also had plenty of contact during their Moody Blues tours, so they both had some ideas of what they wanted to do on albums. They all heard about a place, the Mulinetti Studios, family-owned and operated by the Parodi's, near Genoa; and THEN *hey presto*, found themselves doing an album there.

    When Phil Palmer took over the producing duties for Justin, it was apparently the perfect partnership. Phil Palmer's uncles are Ray and Dave Davies of the Kinks, a band the Moodies toured with in the early years. Chris Neil also worked on *The View From The* Hill (he worked on *Keys of the Kingdom* too) but he is not mentioned on the album credits. Phil Palmer worked for the Italian division of Sony at one time. He also toured and recorded with Pete Townsend and Eric Clapton; Phil knew Paul Bliss, and is associated with Dire Straits. Phil Palmer had apparently been a member of the Bliss Band. I think as well, Justin might have guest-sung on a Bliss album, so we are talking about a group of musicians who all know each other rather well. On "Troubadour," Palmer is the person playing that great country western "dueling guitars" with Justin at the end of the track.

So the troubadours took themselves to the Mulinetti Studios in Genoa, Italy, a fairly short drive from Justin's home in Liguria. The studio was an old 19th century house that has been converted into a state-of-the-art recording studio and is run like a resort for bands and entourages. The family who ran the place cooked home-made meals and made the place comfortable and homey. It even has a website. (Alberto Parodi, either owner or co-owner of the Mulinetti Studios, had won the Italian lottery, so he was able to set up a studio in style! After *View from the Hill* was released, Parodi and Justin have continued to work together, re-mastering the Core Seven albums in the early 21st century.)

Phil and Justin both arrived at Mulinetti Studios with traveling guitar museums, twelve and seventeen respectively. More information on *The View from the Hill* can be found in *Higher and Higher* #32. The album was smooth, on time, in budget, it had a smaller recording group. Phil is a very organized person, clear-headed, and there was less arguing. Justin had nothing but good comments about Palmer, saying that Phil was always ready to go when Justin showed up to record. He always had the mikes set up. A funny thing about good singing: you have to be relaxed to put out good vocal sound, and when a producer is not ready, Justin's natural Libran anxiety probably makes him seize up.

(You'd seize up too, if you belted out a song a few times and found out the microphone was not plugged in.) Phil got quick takes and got a more natural sound.

Mickey Feat was first spotted by Moody fans the same weekend the Moodies were doing their Christmas tree lighting at Caesar's in Tahoe. There he was roaming around the hotel all by himself and unrecognized (and looked to be enjoying himself too!) Mickey, Justin, Paul and Gordon all broke-in their act (in private) at Caesar's, while the rest of the Moodies went out in the cold and lit the fireworks. (It was all very top secret.)

Mickey Feat has made the rounds in the rock music world, having been a session player with Tina Turner, Dave Gilmour (of Pink Floyd, in fact he toured once with Floyd), he has played with Art Garfunkel, and Van Morrison. Feat is Parisian born, but raised in England; by his report, he was working on his "A" levels in England; and somehow veered sideways into music, found he loved it, was good at it, and he could pick up work in it. Up close Feat comes over as a bit nervous on stage, but during their show, I was so blown away by Mickey's outstanding fretwork, I almost enjoyed watching him more than Justin!

The best interview I have found about *The View from the Hill* is one with Justin in *Goldmine* May 23, 1997. One song on the album is worthy of note as to "how it was written." Justin says his inspiration for "The Way of the World" came from walking around his home town and going by what used to be the prison for the French Foreign Legion.

Justin was able to play "Children of Paradise" live and acoustic on the radio before the album was released, and the bootleg flew around the fan club like wildfire; people were kind enough to post the words on line. It had been five years since we had had new Moody Blues music, so the fan club was understandably excited. Anyway, Mickey Feat co-wrote "Children of Paradise" with Justin, and specifically wrote the song's last verse. Justin works with some pretty awesome talent.

A very cute letter came into *Moodymania*, saying that "The Way of the World" even moved gnarled bikers to tears; a fan named Gail Bennett did a cartoon of it.

At least one song on *The View from the Hill* is NOT done by the Phil Palmer & Co. but was produced by Dennis Lambert, the song "Sometimes Less is More." In the '60s, Lambert was the noted songwriter who wrote "Has Anybody Here?" (*seen my old pal Martin...* a hit song about all the assassinated political figures of the '60s.) Lambert also produced "This is the Moment," the song the Moodies did as a benefit for a World Cup soccer benefit CD; the song is originally from the Broadway musical *Dr. Jekyll and Mr. Hyde*.

Justin talked about the song "Broken Dream" (apparently a very special song for him) being done in a planetarium for the proper ambience. (Scott Muni, radio interview, Nov 26, 1996) There's a thing about navigation and stars that popped up on Justin's first website, a sextant (used for navigation by the stars) and a guitar collage with "Broken Dream" in the background. Alas that site introduction is gone, it was beautiful.

Justin and Phil Palmer would carry the "out into the stars" theme, onward into the song "Skimming Stones," which was written for an Italian movie. Curious note, later when the IMAX production of *Amazing Caves* hit the theatres, one of the opening scenes was a dizzying display of stars, with the Gregorian voices of the Moodies in the background. As I sat in the darkened IMAX theatre, I grinned to myself and thought about Justin and his "planetarium" music. That scene didn't make the cut to VHS conversion.

Palmer was certainly not remaining idle in Italy while the Moodies toured in 1997. Possibly running right over the period they worked on *The View from the Hill*, the same three (Mickey Feat, Palmer, and Justin) worked on *The Phil Palmer Project,* also known as the sound track to the Italian comedy, *Three Men and a Leg* (*Tre Uomini e Una Gamba*). The movie is a murder-mystery/comedy (if you happen to run across it at the video store, is very funny, and well worth watching, even with subtitles.) Much of the sound track is instrumental, and very lovely, very worth having in one's collection.

Two tracks feature names from *The View from the Hill:* Mickey Feat sings on "Hot Wheels" (very bluesy vocals) and Justin sings the beautiful, lush "Skimming Stones." Apparently the movie got rave reviews in Italy. Justin and Phil worked together on "Skimming Stones," the romantic ballad of the soundtrack; it has numerous non-vocal pieces, mellow "easy listening" music. One of the best is a gorgeous duet between a piano and guitar, titled "Chiara Theme." *The Phil Palmer Project* is definitely worth tracking down, if you are into some good music, it can be found on *www.amazon.co.uk.*

Moody Blues touring continued during the '90s. By 1996, we fans were expecting the solo album from Justin at any time. There is and was no jealousy from other band members, because Justin has forged ahead with a solo career independent of the Moody Blues. In fact, Justin says Ray is ALWAYS supportive of his solo efforts, which is really sweet of him. (WPCH Atlanta 2-8-97) And Graeme would say of his former roomie, "Justin is often full up with songs, and would burst if he couldn't record them!"

When the Moody Blues tour came to Nat Bailey Stadium in Vancouver, BC (May 1996), I was there with a friend, who has to be the boldest and prettiest stalker ever in the fan club (and whom shall remain nameless, because I kinda liked her). She always figured out where Justin was staying, and always arranged to "bump into him" in the gym. Being a pretty lady, she usually managed to draw out Justin into conversations. One of the more amusing backstage cracks came from one of these encounters: "Our dressing rooms are full of water," Justin asserted to my friend in a disgruntled way. Adding insult to injury, the rehearsals had to be done in the concession stand area (and a grubby one at that) due to the stage being caught in a downpour.

As Larry Baird would later write for the OFC newsletter, "Like in a fairy tale, the skies cleared up and the sun came out." It did. I was there and saw it, and the very same thing happened the next night at the Gorge. Once they left, the skies clouded up and poured buckets. (Angels doth hover over the band, in Eugene 2011, the same thing happened AGAIN. I don't know how they time those shows and slide right in between weather fronts! And it happened at Edgefield in Portland, in 2017. Buckets of rain, then it cleared up for the show, perfect timing.)

Anyway, after my friend's encounter in the gym, we got the inside scoop that Justin's solo album was done but held up for some reason. The original company that was going to back it bailed on Justin, so he wound up going to BMG Records, a company that specializes in productions by classic rockers.

There is currently real political pressure in the music industry that is opposed to people like the Moody Blues, and Joni Mitchell (as an example) who are still producing quality work; but who are not cute, young, and easy to manipulate. Let's be blunt: would you rather market a young boy band, who are still easy for an unscrupulous manager to milk? Or would you rather work with experienced, suspicious rockers who know the ropes? Ugly but true: some backers can't tell the difference between good music and bad. One can only pray that the Internet stops this sort of thinking by cutting out the middle man standing between the musical artist, and her/his consumer.

The View from the Hill would not appear commercially until October of that year, 1996; it enjoyed fair success, once it got to the market. By this time, of course, the Moody Blues and their solo albums were not exactly enjoying the cash market that N'Sync or the Backstreet Boys might have been at the time. But sales were steady and adequate.

After it came out, Justin began to do free mini-concerts in promotion of his album. These free shows were always crammed: I think that Justin was genuinely shocked that he had such a large fan base, all by himself. Kevin Johnson of the *Akron Beacon Journal* (7-16-97) would have the best newspaper review of the solo shows, calling them "stripped down versions of Moody songs" with a notable exception being "The Way of the World." Johnson would praise this as the best live song in the show, impressive with full electronic back up.

Between the Vegas and Tahoe shows (fall 1996), Justin would fly to New York for promotional spots, somehow fitting the entire schedule together. He earned his dosh by zigzagging the country to shows, some free, some in small nightclubs. They were great. Mike Pinder helped Justin's momentum (and *vice versa*) by doing his own west coast Border's shows in January of 1997, and later some east coast as well. Borders Books liked what they had and wanted more Moodies.

When doing solo shows, Justin was usually a bit nervous for his first song or two, but once he relaxed and got into it, he was funny, interacted well with the audience, and joked around (indeed, a master showman.) The Borders shows were even better, as there were no lighting effects or back up. It was just Justin up there with a battered black Guild guitar, plugging away at his songs. Anywhere from 130-450 people came, depending on the city; Justin would just arrive at some Border's and make cracks like "It looks like Graeme's living room!"

In March 1997, *Moodymania* #27 does a very good job covering the various solo shows. I was able to see Justin at Border's in February 1997, in both Phoenix and Dallas for these free shows, and really enjoyed seeing Moody music in a totally different way, in the daylight, with just one songwriter up there, with his guitar. It all seemed very wholesome.

Another show that was without parallel in Justin's solo tours, was the Portland Brewpub. It was free, and I think I was the first in line that morning. It was cold and blustery and yes I am very dedicated! I actually got into a fight with some folks who tried to move my lawn chair, and then made very good friends with them. They weren't fanatics in the fan club: they were just folks who liked the Moody Blues, and had heard about the show on the radio the day before. They turned out to be lovely people; we spent the entire rainy afternoon, in this sports bar, drinking beer, and playing Hearts. Before

Justin did his show, a very interesting young man (who frankly played the guitar as good if not better than Justin) came out and did some really wonderful old songs, terminating with "Irene Good-Night." (Sadly I think I was the only one in the room who knew the song and was singing along with him at the end: he was just as enjoyable as Justin.)

Then Justin came out, bumped his head on the low ceiling of the balcony he was standing on, and gave us a wonderful performance. We were so looped by this time he probably could have recited the phone book and we would have cheered. He also did signings afterwards, and was there several hours, just talking with a long, long line of people, one at a time. Justin has been really good about signing things for people; truly he is thoughtful to his fans.

The fans were well behaved at ALL Justin's solo shows in the 1990s; there was minimal security, Justin waived body-guards. Indeed, in Dallas he was joking with the manager of Borders (a guy named Larry, who was wearing a fishing vest and Levis) who was supposed to give him a ride; then Justin pulled a stub for the city bus out of his pocket, getting a huge laugh! It was a very friendly show in Dallas, with the exception of Justin "siccing" his manager Martin Wyatt on someone who was grinding with a huge professional video camera in the audience.** I don't blame Justin, and he was legally within his rights.

Phoenix in contrast had been very uptight, the fans crowded, the manager in a stiff tie; such a difference in the friendly state of Texas! Doremi Hayward was able to accompany her dad on the tour, and the last I saw of her, she was staggering under a huge pile of books in Dallas somewhere. The Haywards apparently enjoy bookstores in the same way other people like candy shops. At least one of the songs "Land of Make Believe" is undoubtedly inspired by her birth in 1972, and there she stood in the background as her daddy sang it, a full-grown young woman that any father would be proud of. So it was an added dimension for any Hayward fan.

Coach House--By the time the main Moody tour ended in 1997, Justin went on to his own solo tour, starting in San Diego. Then he went to the Coach House in San Juan Capistrano for the second time; he also did the Coach house the year before, in December of 1996. And then the (1997) tour went up the coast to the House of Blues on Sunset Strip. I was able to catch all the Southern California shows that year, all wonderful. Then the tour went on to the Supper Club in New York and finished up somewhere in Chicago. I have no idea if the shows made money, but they sure were enjoyable. The "Justin and Friends" band was Gordon Marshall, Paul Bliss and Mickey Feat (on bass).

They did at least three different tours through the Coach House in San Juan Capistrano during the '90s. For the first Coach House shows (Dec 1996), Justin hired a young lady by the name of Norda Mullen to play flute; one of my friends who saw the shows described her as "dressed like a gypsy." Some years later, when Ray decided to retire, Justin said he took forever to find her, but eventually tracked down Norda, and the Moodies hired her to fill in the flute parts of their show. She has become a welcome addition to the Moody Blues' shows, vocally and as a flautist. She plays guitar sometimes too!

During Justin's solo tours, I was more impressed with the performance chemistry of the "Justin Band" than that of the Moodies. Paul and Gordon carried over that "Moody Blue" bond they had made, and Justin and Mickey were obviously very close friends from some of their work on stage. Off stage at times, you could see the guys doing *Benny Hill* routines, following waitresses around; nothing serious of course, just guys horsing around. I won't mention names as all of them were married at the time, but it was very funny, and I don't think they were serious, just being "boys." (The bistro waitresses ignored them, which made it even funnier.) Afterwards we found out the Moodies actually watch *Benny Hill* and *Monty Python* on the tour bus while traveling. I guess when you get punchy traveling, even the most silly things are stress relievers.***

In 1998 Justin and Friends would do a smaller version of this solo tour, three shows for the Coach House in Santa Barbara, and then three shows later in San Juan Capistrano for the third time. These shows were filmed April 3 & 4 (1998) in Capistrano, for sale commercially. People in the front rows had on different things each night (the 3rd and the 4th), but sat in the same seats, so (via editing) people actually change clothes in the front rows!

My son (age thirteen at the time) was able to see the shows at the Coach House in San Juan Capistrano July 5, 1997, and he proclaimed "Something to Believe In" and "The Way of the World" the best. And he *really* liked them, which goes to show that the clowns choosing singles and pop songs for the radio are NOT tuned into what teens like.

The Santa Barbara shows were in the worst theater possible; it was a small warehouse once. (And when I went back in Spring 2009, it had been torn down. A miserable place!) It had just opened when Justin's road show arrived; "Berkleyesque" would be the kindest description one could give it. It had rained, and it had leaked.

BUT having said that, those three shows were probably the most enjoyable shows I've ever seen Justin do. He dropped lines, he laughed about it, it was small and intimate, he talked to the crowd, and he did the finest live rendition of "Broken Dream" on April Fool's Day that has ever been done. A look of genuine shock crossed Justin's face after the opening number at the Santa Barbara shows, the applause was so loud! The Santa Barbara shows were without a doubt the best shows I've ever seen Justin do, and of the three, April 1 was best.

The solo tours were very cool, to see how they split up the musical duties of the larger band. The third and last year they toured the solo show, Gordon showed a great deal of courage by picking up the flute and doing the ending "doodle" part on "Tuesday Afternoon." Ray apparently coached him a bit. Gordon said he had played a woodwind before, and was able to adapt.****

Paul left a simple synth line to Gordon at one point, and picked up a guitar to play rhythm to Justin's lead guitar. And probably the most impressive, Mickey Feat was able to learn all those Moody Blues songs (he already knew the Justin solo songs of course) and play them masterfully, stepping into some very large boots by doing John's part on bass.

The most tired I saw them was at the House of Blues in Los Angeles, 1997. LA is enough to burn anyone out. The wives had shown up to shop apparently, and the entire band acted a little odd on stage; nothing you could put your finger on, but after seeing them the previous two nights, you could tell. But they sounded great!

After the show, Justin (though obviously exhausted) was sweet enough to stick around and sign so many things at the stage door, for the "faithful" who had waited over an hour for him. His daughter, his chauffeur for the night, was waiting in the car and got this momentary look of concern on her face, as her dad scribbled his signature, in a punchy fog. It was nice to see that bond, proving that Justin is indeed a good family man, and just like every other father on the face of the earth, has a daughter who worries about him.

Justin found time in between touring to do other recording. In 1999, Rick Wakeman came out with a sequel album to *Journey to the Center of the Earth,* the second being entitled not surprisingly *Return to the Center of the Earth.* It's a lush orchestral rock-opera, with alternating tracks of music, and narration, featuring Patrick Stewart as The Narrator. The format is very similar to *The War of the Worlds* in 1978. Justin sings on the track "Still Waters Run Deep," composed by Wakeman. Justin spoke favorably of the recording session, saying that Rick was very open to suggestions Justin made on the song.

As predictable as day follows night, the Moody Blues rallied once more, and followed Justin to Italy, where they began work on their album for the new Millennium, eventually to be entitled *Strange Times.*

*Graeme even alluded to some of this in an elevator once, when some friends and I bumped into him. He had broken loose that night (it was his birthday, after all) and mangled the opening poem in some way, "senior citizens wish they were strung" something to that effect. It was very funny. Anyway, he was sorta mumbling to himself, "I don't even know what I said on stage!" as if he felt a little guilty for it! You got the feeling another band member was pissed about it later backstage.

**This brings to mind another really nasty incident in the Moody tour. At one Las Vegas show during the '90s, the band (and Justin in centre stage) were actually being hit with a laser beam, apparently from a video camera. It was very obvious, glancing off the cymbals and bouncing around the auditorium. Being very brave men, they did not bolt for the wings (like I would have done!) but they did send a manager out with nasty words during the break. That's just a minor chapter in the rudeness of just a few, and how the band handles it.

*** Justin also mentions touring Caesar's Las Vegas, and having dressing rooms in the "tunnels under the casino" and walking (as many times as they could get away with it, apparently) past the open dressing room door for "Cleopatra's handmaidens." So touring is indeed fun for all. (Ref: Justin's website, early 2001)

**** Year 2003, Gordon picked up a flute again, and played a duet during "Are You Sitting Comfortably?" and it was wonderful. And he played it some more with the Moodies in 2007, 2008, and 2009. Gordon is very, very talented, plays keyboards, woodwinds, and drums. During *The War of the Worlds* tours with Jeff Wayne, he has also been instrumental in setting up and coordinating the Ulla dub Ulla Strings, and Black Smoke Band.

XIX) Step Into the Light

If I don't see you through the week, I'll see you through the window! -- Brum saying as per Pinder (chat Jan 5, 2008)

Life is what happens when you're busy making other plans -- John Lennon

Follow your bliss -- Joseph Campbell

      Loads about Mike Pinder can be read in just about every *Higher and Higher* issue, they usually dedicated a couple of pages to him. During the '80s, Mike moved to the Sacramento, CA area. He now has a home in a remote area, complete with a recording studio and lush herb garden. His whole family (he has three boys total from both marriages) plays musical instruments. One of Mike Pinder's sons belonged to a band called Velvet Jones, in Northern California. Mike has done some work with California recording artists, but mostly seems to be a homebody. Indeed, when one calls One Step Records, Mike's production company, often he or his wife Taralee will answer the phone themselves!
      Mike Pinder opted out of the band in 1982 (officially), while the rest of the band went on with their career and did some very good stuff without him. There is no mistaking either, that Mike's stuff still sounds like "Moody Blues," and he's a damn fine composer, indeed. One day I hope Mike Pinder writes an autobiography, because something tells me he's had a very interesting life.
      Higher and Higher Magazine was totally up on Pinder; and in the '90s even more newsletter action from The Friends of Mike Pinder kept fans up on his doings. The enquiring reader is highly encouraged to track down those publications. (The *Higher and Higher* website is a disconnect these days, but the archives do show up on *https://www.tapatalk.com/groups/moodybluesattitude* as of this writing.)

Lest we forget, (just the facts!!!) Pinder did file suit twice against the rest of the band, and both times, he attempted to gain legal control of the name "Moody Blues." I came into the fan club at a bad point on the Pinder (and band) timeline; it's been a struggle for me to be objective about Mike. Shortly after I got into the fan club in late 1991, the Moraz hearing was going on; and then a year later the fan club was clobbered with the *Pinder vs. Moody Blues* lawsuit (which never went to trial and was resolved within four months.) By this point I had developed a serious taste for the live band, and MY perspective saw Moraz and Pinder as some sort of hustlers, intent on getting a share of the Red Rocks pie. Maybe they were just that, but MAYBE THEY HAD CAUSE. This is why we have a legal system. It's not for me to judge in the slightest.

But I sure copped an attitude about Mike after that; sorry for being human, but I'm not a robot. I couldn't begin to tell you when the Friends of Mike Pinder (the FoMPers) pulled together because I tried very hard to ignore it. The FoMPer magazine began in the '90s, to document that splinter fan group. First issue of the magazine came out in Jan 1995. I have to confess it did nothing to improve my bad attitude toward Mike; the FoMPers spread a good deal of "Mike adulation" around the cyber newsgroups, which (said cyber network) were collectively developing into a formidable on-line community. It might have had something to do with reading the *Pinder vs Moody Blues* lawsuit, which a well-meaning friend of mine sent me (and how she got it I don't know, she was a legal stenographer). That legal document will never leave my hands. It was just too disturbing, too toxic. It tain't fit for the eyes of the average Moody fan.

What Mike has put out as philosophy is a rehashing of Joseph Campbell, which is not to say it's bad, but it's just very well-known to many. Campbell in turn, was simply rehashing well-known Jungian principles, applying those principles to modern mythology like *Star Wars*. Growing up in Red Neck California, I've never been much of one to rabbit on about New Age philosophies, as it tends to repeat after a while, and is about as fulfilling as cotton candy. It was disturbing to me, to see FoMPers lap up Mike's recycled Joseph Campbell philosophies like manna from heaven.

Imagine though, if you wanted to talk to "a Moody Blue," good luck because they actively avoid their fans. (With good reason, I've hung around with many, many Moody fans, and they *Overwhelm*.) If you called up Mike's company One Step Records, however, you might stand a good chance of talking to Himself or his wife in person! All those fans who craved recognition from the Moody Blues finally found someone who could fulfill their desires to rub elbows with their rock gods.

I guess it was in the early 21st century that I began to really appreciate what Mike had done. And after seeing his sons come into their own professional legacy as musicians, that was when I began to deeply admire and respect Mike AND Taralee. He did it right after all.

Mike Pinder went on after he and the Moodies settled their suit in April 1994, to issue some really nice CDs of children's books, all narrated in his wonderful voice. The stories have backdrops of luscious instrumental music, all played by his family of boys. The albums are entitled *A Planet with One Mind,* and *A People With One Heart.* They are truly worth owning, especially if you are a teacher or a parent with small kids to keep entertained. It's even nicer if you can get the books that go with them; they are easy found in most bookstores or libraries.

Mike did a series of enjoyable tours to Border's Books. The FoMP magazines document these promo tours. I was fortunate enough to make one of Mike's Borders Bookstore signings, where he treated us all with a live reading of *John Jeremy Coulter*. It was one of the highlights of my Moody adventures over the years, and I could do nothing but hope that Mike is able to finish the three CD series "The Wizdom Road" that he has planned to release. (He was not chipper the day I met him in Tigard, OR; he seemed asleep, staring kinda vacantly. But he read *John Jeremy Coulter* quite well.)

And his CDs. I can still remember hearing one for the first time, I popped it in my trusty walkman and went for a walk. I soon found myself dancing to the lovely music behind the stories on his first children's album. What a delight! How could this man have ever left the Moody Blues, and how could he have ever sued them? They were all really on the same page, how could it have come to this?

Mike released *Off the Shelf*, his first album since *The Promise*; and then issued another CD, *Among the Stars*, in and around 1993-1994. Mike has at least one poem on that CD "Among the Stars" which is rather nice; the spoken word has been overlooked in later albums by the Moodies, a serious omission. I don't know if Pinder's CDs have done much commercially, but a lot of Moody Blues fans bought them

Mike would also promote the philosophy "Follow your Bliss," following in the steps of Campbell. Mike has always said that being a "rock star" was great, you were able to do large scale communications with people, to raise awareness about various things. For what it's worth, I think Mike truly wanted to help the fans who came to him seeking guidance, by putting out Joseph Campbell's philosophies. Having been at one time, a young seeker himself, in his older years he felt the call to put those "lessons learned" back out there for younger folks. There is a lot of *need* in the Moody fan base, this seems true in many fan clubs.

But to quote Bruce Lee it can also be a matter of *we are taught in accordance with one's ability to learn*. If even one fan felt more enlightened after listening to Mike's presentations, then it was all worth it. So (for what it's worth), here is what I have put together about Mike in his post-Moody life. And you don't have to listen to me anyway, you can always go to *www.mikepinder.com* and read up on his Pinderings yourself. They are very good, he writes well.

While still with the band Mike's interviews are quite worthy from a philosophical perspective, or on the flipside, just plain funny. (It depends on the mood of course.... He's not a robot after all!) Sometimes he talks about the Beatles days. George Harrison and Mike Pinder apparently hit it off philosophically, in those early "Maharishi" days. Mike's Pinderings can be incredible; I clipped this from his website. (I think he got it from *Tao*, don't quote me on that.) It explains much to any artist who has had the experience of creating "something from nothing." Sounds a bit like "Tomorrow Never Knows" by the Beatles too.

I don't think ideas are individual by any means. I think of it as a river of thought, a river of ideas that are there. ... Late at night when everyone is asleep is a favorite time to 'fish.' ....I like to visualize that creative ideas are being poured out of an urn, almost like Aquarius pouring out the water. Instead of water coming out, there would be musical notes and [art] .... the wind would blow them, and they would be moving ...like a river. Alongside the river would be people sitting, with pencil in hand, an empty notebook, and a guitar on their knee, which is really their fishing tackle. As these ideas come by, you try and grab one for you. .... I remember buying a George Harrison album, and hearing a song, and thinking 'That's the one that got away.' I didn't get it, but further downstream--and George used to live about three miles away--George was up that night and he hooked the bugger."

Sometimes Mike comes out with personal stories, and it sounds like his dad might have been a real adventurous dude as well. Mike's dad told stories about being in the Army (WWII), and shooting baboon's arses on the temples in India. *(I wonder if they were alive, or stone baboons? Imagine: Mr. Pinder Sr, wearing pith helmet, running through the jungle with a bunch of butt-peppered baboons chasing him.........)*

I found one early article about the band that forecast it all: Mike was spotted reading a New Age Christian book in a 1972 band interview. Musicians read a lot on tour. Can you imagine being on a tour bus with a bunch of Moody Blues, reading all that heady philosophical stuff, and discussing it? *Peripatetic* indeed!

Beyond a doubt, Mike Pinder was responsible for many of the modifications to the mellotron, which was used by various rock bands over the years. (It was used to record "I am the Walrus" too, *goob goob a joob*.) The history of the mellotron is very thoroughly written out in FoMP newsletter #11 and #12, excellent reading for the technically minded. Mike also showed up in the *Threshold of a Dream: Isle of Wight* DVD and demonstrated the internal workings of the mellotron. What a fascinating machine, and how much we have advanced since then.

The Indigo Ranch apparently hired out as a recording studio during the '80s, to various independent bands totally disassociated with the Moodies or Mike Pinder.

Write in a quiet voice -- Mike Pinder

Releases since 1978 (post-Moody Mike albums):
- *The Promise*
- *Off the Shelf*
- *Among the Stars*
- The Wizdom Road Series: *Planet with One Mind* and *A People with One Heart* (yet to come) *An Earth with One Spirit*

Off the Shelf was made up of demos saved from 1979. Mike started collecting his songs in 1980 or so, and they languished on the shelf until the early '90s. *Among the Stars* came out a bit later, with the same songs, plus a few more. *A Planet With One Mind* was a finalist for the Benjamin Franklin Award, 1996, and has a silver medal to prove it!

This is not even counting what the Pinder boys have done. All of the Pinder Brothers releases are available from *www.mikepinder.com*. This now is the on-line Mike Pinder store; the One Step Records is shut down.

Newly-wed Ray Thomas, and Mike Pinder (and Tony Clarke too!) got together at Ray's place in Wales, in the summer of 2009, to make music. *Travelling Eternity Road* (an online newsgroup) had the photos last I looked.

The Pinder Brothers--Mike's first wife was Donna, and Dan is her son. For those concerned, Donna and Taralee are on each others' Facebook, or were at one time (so they are friendly and have moved on.) Dan lived with his mom Donna and her Hollywood family, grew up knowing that business and has done quite well in movie scores.

After Mike dropped out of the Moodies and married Taralee, they moved to Hawaii for a while. Matt was born in Hawaii in 1980, and Mike Jr was born after him. All of the boys play various instruments, the Pinder Brothers have put out their own CD called *Jupiter Falls*. Dan is the eldest of the Pinder brothers, he's into anthropology and electronic recording. Dan is also an excellent bass player and photographer!

They come over like a lovely clan, and indeed seem to have adopted Tony Clarke as extended family. Mike and Tony were always talking about doing a project together, but so far nothing has appeared. I'll buy it. They all had a chat in 2007 (2008?) which was really fun. All the brothers chimed in, I think Tara was typing or lurking for Mike, and Tony Clarke also joined in. Quite a group!

The Pinder Brothers (Mike and Matt) started as a band called Spiderplant, band names changed and this falls outside the scope of this book. Dan studied music at Sonoma State. *(Woo ee that was a rocking place in the '70s, I went there! NO telling what it's like now! Very experimental music department, that's for sure!)* Dan's movie scores (I don't know if he composed or edited) were used in *The Da Vinci Code, Angels and Demons, Frost/Nixon, Made of Honor, The Simpsons Movie, Transformers, The Holiday, Flicka, The Island, End of the Spear, The Ring Two, Civilization of Maxwell Bright, Spanglish, Catwoman, 13 Going On 30, Hellboy, Pirates of the Caribbean: The Curse of the Black Pearl.*

March 30, 2009: Mike Pinder newsletter: *Mike's son Dan Pinder and his music editing team recently received an Oscar for The Dark Knight.* Double wow, eh??

The Pinder Brothers have websites, and Facebook sites; a good vigorous search on Google will turn up lots of hits on them. A review clipped off line and dated summer 2006: *I received the new CD from Mike Pinder's sons .... Mike himself, is the executive producer. Both brothers, Michael Lee and Matt look and sound quite a bit like their dad. The 10 songs on this CD were all written by Michael Lee except one that he co-wrote with Nick Cohen. They are joined by some other musicians on some of the instrumentals and vocals, including Mike Pinder himself on mellotron, synth, Chamberlain, strings and flutes and percussion and tambourine. These songs are really nice and it is obvious that Michael Lee inherited a good amount of his Dad's musical talent for writing and arranging songs.* (Betsy Kishlansky)

Add to that: I think it is Michael Lee who has the soul-melting voice, really stunning. Of course, he had all the advantages of voice lessons and musical support, but voices like that are a gift. The Pinder Brothers songs are very worth tracking down, but for the most part fall outside the scope of this book.

Spooky Stories--It's hard to tell if Mike is just telling ghost stories, or if it's for real. But he seems to relish spooky experiences. There is a school of thought that puts forth a model that "weird stuff" happens around us humans all the time, only we choose to not see it. Maybe Mike is just seeing stuff the rest of us can't or WON'T. Perhaps he sees outside the perceptual box within which the rest of us seek comfort.

Mike told some stories about his Indigo Ranch, in the FoMP newsletter #4 that really give you the willies. There were dreams and such that pointed to there being extensive secret caves and caverns underneath the ground there. This is not all that far-fetched. The hills and canyons around the Indigo Ranch DO have caves, they reach down unto North Hollywood.

Mike had several names for the spirit (ghost) who lives at Indigo, including *The Ancient One, the Old One* and the *Universal Citizen.* The spirit will turn up reflected in windows; his description is a bit like the lyrics to "Slidezone." (That should give you a new perspective on the song!)

Mike's home was partially burned out, in one of those notorious Southern California brush fires, back in the early '80s; he lost one of his pet mellotrons in the fire! The people who bought the property were burned out completely in summer, 2007. Yes the spirits will take back their own eventually. The Indigo Ranch was originally a Chumash site, and it's never wise to build in an ancient place without permission from the local spirits. Mike may have moved further north to Sacramento for just that reason.

In either FoMP #1 or #2, Mike talks about seeing UFOs as a small child (not bombers.) Whimsically there is a cartoon captioned "The True Story of Mike's Abduction by Aliens" and is on pg. 7 of FoMP #2. There is an interesting story about an exploding UFO fireball over the canyon (Indigo Ranch) in FoMP #4. I would hesitate to call this a "UFO" but would rather worry that Vandenberg (just over the hill near Point Mugu) almost dropped something on his house, he should be glad a stray bomb didn't land on them! YIKE! Or it could have been a flare from a military over-flight too. The USN uses that ocean area a lot for air operations.

Graeme told a really wild story about "being abducted by aliens" in an early *Higher and Higher*, and the story was retold in the book *Alien Rock*. Mike finally told his version of this tale, online at *Cara's Basement*: May 2009: The band (early version with Denny Laine) was coming back from a show in Manchester, "doing about 85 mph" as Mike put it. They were totally alone, 'way out in the country. They realized they were being followed by a red light which they first thought was a radio tower, but it didn't recede as they sped away. Finally they went into a forested area, and they could see a red light thru the trees. Graeme's story would start here, and he says they were suddenly "filled with unreasoned dread" and left the scene, quickly. Mike finished HIS story and said when they got back home, they were three hours late. So they "don't know what happened" and those three hours are missing. <insert *Twilight Zone* music here!>

His Happy Ever-after in the Post-Moody World--The FoMP newsletter is long a thing of the past, though it has been reposted on various sites since then, most recently at *https://www.tapatalk.com/groups/moodybluesattitude*. At the time, I sneered at the whole thing (sorry, please see the beginning of this chapter.) But I eventually came around and read through the entire set (thanks to Taran and Jill, the admin ladies of *Moody Blues Attitude*.) The newsletters were fun and informative and gave me a much better perspective on the Pinder clan.

Ever since he got his website up and running, Mike has been sending out periodic newsletters of his own (right to your own email box), keeping subscribers up to date (all totally free); they are very enjoyable. Mrs. Pinder also has a Facebook account, and she shares photos of family weddings, and their everyday lives. Taralee *rocks*, I can't say that enough!

Mike yes is a cook! His recipe for shepard's pie was in *Backstage Gourmet* by PJ Grimes, and they reprinted it in the FoMP magazine. Taralee, is indeed a Master Gardener. Their old English herb garden is a showplace they will happily take you on tours of. She used to be a real estate agent.

After the lawsuit was settled in the early '90s, the rest of the band seemed a little testy with Mike, but they eventually settled down about it. In FoMP #6, there is a lovely story about Ray and Graeme when they met up with Mike at a TNN party for a Country western star. Hard feelings are all over with.

Mike has done some workshops around California, he did a "State of the World" forum, rubbing elbows with the likes of Maya Angelou, Jane Goodall, and Mikhail Gorbachev! (Nov 1997). He read for the forum, stories from his album *A Planet with One Mind*. In Oct of 1997 or 1998 (perhaps both!) he did workshops at Esalen (wow!!)

The Pinders have a cottage industry website which may or may not be making a lot of money, but it certainly keeps Taralee and Mike busy. When the Moodies do releases that involve him (box sets), he offers them for sale on his website, and tends to sign them too!

Mike Pinder was always a vegetarian, and his family is the same. Of late, he has been griping about his bad ergonomics; in spring 2000, Mike Pinder suffered what is called "cumulative disorder syndrome," that is, too many long hours at the computer, with a bad chair, and no flicker guard on the screen. (People can actually get carpel tunnel syndrome from clicking the mouse too much, what a thought!)

Mike has also been working with a gal named Patty McAdams in Northern California, recording apparently (interview with Richard Silverstein.) There are reports of him working with Tony Clarke and Denny Laine as well, over the Internet. Other sources have told me that Mike and John Lodge swap keyboard info over the Internet. So Mike stays in touch.

In 2009, Mike was involved in a "Song Wars" project promoting young song writers, here is the link: *http://www.youtube.com/user/MikePindersSONGWARS* Some of Mike's thoughts included the factoid (heard from many other older recording stars) that the people running recording companies are running it because they love money and the stock market, and not music. *Hear hear!*

Mike has his own website (*www.mikepinder.com* of course) and the stuff on there is pretty good reading. He used to have a free forum on his website, that seems elusive as of this writing. But it's still a very nice site, many news bits, blog thoughts and Pinderings from Mike himself.

XX) Strange Times: unto the New Millennium

Can we still find enough experiences to put down into lyrics and music?—John Lodge

We're living in strange times — Marcia Clark, opening statements to the O.J. Simpson murder trial (from *Without a Doubt*)

This is the beginning of discovering Man's true legacy — Mike Pinder

We managed not to fall into the trap of over production -- John, speaking about *Strange Times*

They are searching for the perfect balance between modern technology and genuine music inspiration — Alberto Parodi (owner and operator of Mulinetti Studios)

Take the Way Back machine to the late 1960s. Remember an old song from the musical *Hair*, about the dawning of the Age of Aquarius? Odd, that at the true Millennium, so few people mentioned this astrological tidbit. According to astrologers, the vernal equinox, at the Ides of March, shifts every 2000 years to another astrological sign, due to the precession of heavenly bodies. In the year 2000, the Equinox moved the sign of Aquarius. It's the ruling sign of electricity, communication, ruler of the Information Age, and "strange things." It's an air sign, yet called the *Water Bearer*.

By the time the year 2000 rolled around, the Moody Blues had written an entire album about it, prompting at least one cynic online to quip *Strange Times? Strange times in comparison to what????* How could anything be stranger than the Age of Acid in the '60s, and Timothy Leary??? The Moodies have always been a very "normal" band, doing normal things that everyone around them is doing. But consider the strange happenings that suddenly occurred to the band in the '90s:

In 1993, Chief Astronaut "Hoot" Gibson turned up at the Hollywood Hard Rock Café. He presented the Moody Blues with a framed and mounted tape of their music that had orbited the earth numerous times with him in a space shuttle. Those who have watched *Apollo 13* know this is common practice, for astronauts to take along their favorite music, and then drive their shipmates crazy with it. According to the Fan Club newsletter spring 2000, Hoot used Moodies music to get to sleep while in orbit. For a few years, Hoot showed up at Moody events, giving and getting what we Navy people call "face time," but it's a good thing in this case. As a former Navy Airedale myself, I'm proud to call Skipper Hoot a shipmate, one with good taste! Mrs. Gibson, also an astronaut, was sweet enough to have "I Know You're Out There Somewhere" piped up to her husband as a wake-up call the last time he was in orbit.

The Moody Blues have successfully toured with an orchestral show, from San Francisco, to the shores of England, from September 1992, to May 2000. That is eight years of the same format, and logistics. Strange, in that they were able to pull it off at all!

Although they started out flying their own 747 with "empty rooms" as John put it, shortly before they broke up in early 1974; here at the turn of the new Millennium, the band has taken to flying about in their own chartered corporate jet, dubbed the *Lone Ranger*. In *Moodymania* #21 one of the pilots of the *Lone Ranger* complained that the band liked to sing Buddy Holly songs while flying along. (And we all know how Holly went, pilots are very superstitious!!) Moody rumor has it that they played bridge on board the *Lone Ranger* to pass the time.

The band toured South Africa in the summer of 1995, coinciding with a rugby playoff; all the band members are sports fanatics, much of their touring in recent years follows good golf weather. More can be read about the South Africa tour in *Higher and Higher* #28.

One of Graeme's more legendary exploits has to be the scaling of a large statue of an elephant, accompanied in this harmless schoolboy prank by several members of the Springbok Rugby team. They then all sang ribald fight songs once they got to the top. Considering Graeme was fifty-five at the time, you have to sit up and take notice.

Graeme went on to vacation in the Australia after that, and partied hearty with friends down-under. Ever a trend setter, Graeme even found time to kibitz with the "Stone Age natives" in Indonesia over the noble art of drumming, and in his words was "regarded somewhere between a semi-deity and a musical genius."

The Moodies contributed a song to a benefit CD, *Soccer Rocks the Globe,* called "This is the Moment." The song was from *Jekyll & Hyde*, which debuted at Houston's Tony Award-winning Alley Theatre, breaking box office records, and playing to sold-out houses. What could be stranger than singing a song for a soccer benefit that was originally intended for a story about a mad bipolar doctor?

The tour in 1996 is noteworthy for a strange and sad reason. Dr. Tim Leary actually died while the Moody Blues were touring, on Memorial Day. That night, Ray was kind enough to get up and say a few words before doing "Legend of a Mind." (You know, the song that starts out *Timothy Leary's dead?*) Anyway, a rough paraphrasing would be "We talked about not doing this song tonight, and we decided that Tim would really have wanted us to do it." And for the first time, they did the song, with Tim really "outside looking in." Prior to his passing, the band was able to call up the Good Doctor and sing him a few bars from the rewritten "Legend of a Mind" with the words "Timothy Leary Lives." Leary apparently burst into tears.

There is a mysterious story in the fan club, that after his death, a spectral, rotating figure of Dr. Leary sometimes appeared during "Nights in White Satin," projected into the full moon on the stage backdrop: *Moodymania* #29.

The main Moody Blues tour of 1997 was distinguished by the surprise addition of a song from their unreleased album, *Strange Times*. They opened in Portland, Oregon, and I was there that night. The second night was at the Gorge (I was there too.) At every stop, Moody fans tried to write down and post the new lyrics of "Strange Times" online, so by the end of the tour, the audience was singing along with the new song like it was old hat! There's lots of information on the making of *Strange Times* in *Higher and Higher* #41, in case you don't find me covering the subject sufficiently.

There IS no overriding theme to *Strange Times*, as with the original concept albums, other than the Moodies felt like relaxing on the beach perhaps, and they indeed did just that for most of the album. Plainly the old formula of "Justin did an album, let's do one too" worked again, but it would take some time for the entire thing to fall together. The song itself "Strange Times," was recorded first by John and Justin as a demo song, and then the Jays decided it was the beginning of a real album. The debut of a song to live in concert (for the first time since 1972) was a "back to roots" thing.

Aforementioned, I was fortunate enough to be there in Portland when the Moodies first played "Strange Times" in public, with an orchestra backing them up. As I recall, the entire audience sat in numb shock (silence) after it was over....it sounded totally different from anything we could have expected. You could hear the gears grinding in the collective audience Head, "We've just heard a new Moody Blues song." All the regular fans (and I) finally came to and jumped up, applauding loudly. Justin rapidly dove out of his guitar strap; you could tell it was a risk he was nervous about. Honestly, people weren't sure what to make of it at first. (I loved it, the strings and cellos were great!)

Trying to begin the 14th studio album, the Moodies just didn't seem to be able to get into the studio to start; some of it was delay in rounding everyone up, but real blocks might have been their tight purse strings.** While the Moodies were haggling over the price of recording at

Mulinetti, they were outbid by the Spice Girls, and lost that time they had set up in between tours, May-June 1998. Tight purse strings may also have had bearing on their canceling the last week in late 2000, touring the west coast. It's not cheap to tour.

The Moody Blues toured the casinos before Justin's 1998 solo tour and toured the country after "Justin and Friends" closed. It looks like the 1998 tour ended pretty much in July, and after that we have to presume is when *Strange Times* was recorded at the Mulinetti Studios in Italy. Main production of the album must have been completed by January of 1999, as the band reappeared in Lake Tahoe and Vegas in the spring. They then did a casino tour swing though the south, and then went into the studio to render final touches to the album, finish the packaging and so forth. By August 1999, the CD was released, commemorating the coming new Millennium.

The theme repeats over and over again: technology-and-flashy-glitz vs. something that sounds good, bare bones, on an acoustic guitar in your front living room. Melody vs. technology is the collective hang-up of the Moody mind; they went from four channel mix in 1967 (DOFP) to thirty-six track mix in 1994.

Like the rest of us, the Moody Blues were finally overwhelmed by the electronics in our dynamic pop western culture, went back to the organic sound, with minor electronic embellishments. For *Strange Times*, they set up real drum sets and went back to the real sound.

Recording in Mulinetti was a working vacation indeed! The Moody Blues could probably write their own book about the good time they had in Italy recording the album. Hearing Justin rave about a beef noodle dish that the "Mum" of the studio family made for them will tell you where the older rocker's true priorities are these days (bed and breakfast services, like a resort!) John had a real cute story he told about a "chugging" boat that used to come by their windows every morning, like clockwork, apparently waking them up. (Can't you just hear all the Moody Blues in their various rooms, "There goes that bloody tug again!" *Chug-chug-chug...)* Leave it to a bass player from Brum to notice something rhythmic and mechanical like that.

The Tuscany Red winery was only a stone's throw from the recording studios at Mulinetti. Graeme tried to record the sounds of thumping on a wine vat (a bit like the sound of a ripe watermelon) but wasn't successful. Indeed, the entire recording session sounds like a very epicurean adventure, as several musicians were mentioned as falling asleep in the studio after a particularly tasty Trofiette al Pesto*** feast. "Mama Nella" and "Auntie Graziella" are mentioned as the architects of these meals and are certainly worthy of recognition for keeping our favorite musicians well fed and happy.

Now we have to bear in mind that the Moody Blues write and continually mess around with new songs, in their own home studios. When they finally all rounded themselves up and arrived at Mulinetti, there was a fair amount of material in their sweaty hands. But the live element had to be added, so (perhaps having learned their lesson while doing *Keys of the Kingdom*) for *Strange Times*, the band worked as a collective again, rather than patch-working it together. For example, "The Swallow" was done right in the studio with VERY few overdubs and is mentioned by Justin as being probably the "purest" song they have on the album. It's just the musicians in the room, playing their instruments, with minimal electronic trickery or over-dubs. A wonderful, freeform flamenco rhythm is mixed in for the song's opening.

One of the euphonious additions to the Moody Blues at this time is a fellow named Danilo Madonia. They tried to talk him into being the producer of the CD, and he graciously refused, so the band just did the producing themselves, and Danilo helped out on the keyboard compositions. He arrived at some shows with the Moodies, filling in on keyboards occasionally. Paul and Bias both had other projects on the side, being equally busy musicians. Danilo showed up in Florida for the first *Strange Times* concert and helped set up the keyboard programming. He also filled in on keyboards when the Moodies played as the "house band" for *Regis and Kathy Lee,* on the Embarcadero of San Francisco, 1999, and on a German television spot in November 2004.

There are rumors that Ray was "pinned to the wall" and a song literally pried out of him. When they got it, it would turn out to be one of the most well-received songs on the album, "My Little Lovely." It's apparently written for his grandson, who is an utter doll; we fans were lucky enough to get to see a picture of Ray and grandson in the OFC newsletter.

One inside joke: Ray says "More tea, Vicar?" on "English Sunset." Apparently this is a very British thing to say, when an awkward moment needs to be covered up, like when someone "lets one slip" at a formal dinner. Ray says it with a mischievous gleam in his eye in concert, perhaps thinking of low oscillating bass notes at the Albert Hall.

There is a lovely introduction to "Haunted," which at first listen sounds like a Japanese water harp. It turns out to be an instrument known as the gamelan (both instruments are made out of bamboo), which was by the sound of it, used on *The Zodiac* (mentioned earlier as being seminal to music of the Doors and the Moody Blues both). It's interesting to note that the Moodies have many Japanese fans, the band is sent paper cranes and paper dolls from Japan all the time. (It's a Japanese thing.) While researching this book, an interview with Justin, written entirely in Japanese, surfaced on the Internet. From what we could figure out of the translation, Justin very much recognizes the Japanese perception of simplicity and beauty. Very cool, and a nice angle to think of for this song.

Graeme delivered an incredibly beautiful poem that said more about the "strange times" that we live in, than many have realized yet. Thank goodness the spoken word returned to Moody Blues albums. The last poem (and album) ends with a rhythm, "CQ." The first time anyone in the fan club noticed this was almost three weeks after the album's release. A Ham operator posted about it to the newsgroup *Lost Chords*; the *dot dit dot dot dot/ dot dit dot* (my best approximation) rhythm in Graeme's poem "Nothing Changes," is a signal. "CQ" means "Is Anyone Out There???" (Seek you, CQ.) The really funny thing was that people on *Lost Chords* called the guy a fool and had to argue about it for a week! CQ is indeed what Graeme intended on the track, and it's a common Ham signal (another of Graeme's multiple hobbies.) It's all about "reaching out."

The rest of the album is beyond wonderful. There is not a moment of awkwardness on the album, as there is with *Keys of the Kingdom*, the lyrics are mellow and straightforward, no gobbledy goop like "Say What You Mean." The CD cover is plush and gorgeous. It's truly a masterpiece from a master band, and well worth the wait of eight years to get.

Some of the neatest things to pick out of the lush orchestral backings are the different guitar sounds that Justin uses for *Strange Times*. He says he used his 1955 Martin D-28 on the last song/poem, and it is so well amp'ed it sounds like his James Olsen. I think he uses the James Olsen on stage for this. He also managed to get a very "steel guitar" sound, and I think he mentioned using a "Dot 335" Gibson for this, a brown sunburst Gibson that he uses sometimes during tours (identical to the one he has on the cover of *Moving Mountains*.)

The Moodies said they just did the album cover design at the last minute, as the first design was not what they wanted. It's a last-minute computer clip and paste, the seashell on the cover is that of a chambered nautilus, an ancient sea creature that can let out air at need, to drop to lower depths, or rise to higher currents in the sea. A certain symbolism can perhaps be dug out of that.

If you've ever held a large shell up to your ear, you can "hear" the magic, primal music of waves, a magical voice hidden within. Primitive societies have long held the shell a magical receptacle, a doorway to Dreamtime. Polynesian natives blow on conch shells to communicate over long distances, and to open ceremonies. Muskogee natives of Alabama used conch shells in purification rites before their stickball games, and the Hopewell Mound Builders revered the shell as well (from the number of them dug up in mounds). The Ocean is very much a Jungian symbol of the great Unconscious; the Shore is the boundary of sleep. So even if the cover was just "thrown together," there are subtle symbols there, which makes it wonderful art. For what it's worth, Justin's daughter Doremi had a pet snail in the '80s. We all pay tributes to our departed pets in different ways. Several girls on line with Moody chat groups have said the shell looks like it's pregnant, with the Earth inside.

After *Strange Times* was released, the Moodies launched a three-month tour to support their album, with only a three week lay-over at the end of September. One of the cutest interviews that most of us were eventually able to see was on the Wherehouse chat lounge, which was broadcast digitally on Justin's birthday (1999). There was definitely something very cool about Justin getting a birthday cake on a cyber channel, when you know every fan tuned in was singing "Happy Birthday" together, all over the world.

Not all the shows were with an orchestra, some of the best were without, specifically the show in Kennewick; I was able to see that one. They really rocked out with "English Sunset," rapidly becoming the tour favorite. They did "English Sunset" to promo *Strange Times* on a few television shows, breaking in the song prior to tour.

During one of the best promo shows, the laughs came not from the Moody Blues, but from Robin Williams. The day the Moodies were there, the audience of Barbara Walters' talk show *The View* was chock full of Moodies fans, and they were primed for action. Barbara and her roundtable of feminists were holding forth about "how lewd TV was today." I've roomed with Moody Blues fans. I know how they talk. Was Barbara dreaming? After this lead-in, Robin Williams came out and proceeded to tear their discussion to shreds (Barbara Walters actually cringed with laughter), then Robin mentioned a gay bar in San Francisco called The

White Swallow. True ladies and small children won't get it, thank goodness. *Disgusting.*

The Moodies fans in the front rows were by this time howling on the floor in hysterics, as one of the prettier songs on the new Moody album was "The Swallow" (*ahem* about a beautiful bird) and this whole degraded joke had already been batted around on Moody newsgroups. Robin Williams was a Moodies fan as well, and I wouldn't have put it past him to lurk on our newsgroups to get material; it was just too coincidental. He's been in OFC newsletters: I believe John and he played doubles for a benefit (he and John Lodge share a birthday.) I can't begin to imagine what went on in that Green Room prior to the show. I don't want to know.

The Moodies came out to play music after Robin made his escape, smiling quietly to themselves. It was a great show.

It's in the 21st century where technology takes another leap in Moodyland. The Moodies start doing a lot of interviews online, with DJs and computer broadcast stations who are eager for a famous band to interact with them. Sadly they have left a lot of people with older (or no) computers behind, many fell out of the information flow. None of the Internet protocols match up when you go to an online chat, it can be quite frustrating. Even more frustrating is the overload on popular Moody Blue chat sites; so many people are online posting about anything except solid information about the band, that it's a challenge to wade through. THAT has been the case online since 1990. Facebook has been a godsend to the on-line Moody community, because we can now block the people who post irrelevancies and focus on the good info. Welcome to the Age of Aquarius, you will shortly be drowning in minutia and useless trivia.

Talk about the REAL strange times; the Moodies are on the marquee in 5.1 Microsoft Flight Simulator. It's the sign at Caesar's in Las Vegas as you fly over Vegas. Then they were on (voice over) *The Simpsons*, "Viva Ned Flanders," which is even funnier if you've also seen the movie *Fear and Loathing in Las Vegas*. The Moody Blues suddenly are becoming a "staple" act at Las Vegas? Strange times, indeed!

Their personal lives continued, as normal. Justin's daughter Doremi has been spotted numerous times on tour with her dad, as has Ray's son Adam. Kristian and Emily Lodge did a lot of public relations work with the fan club in 2000, coming to various fan get-togethers. Emily sometimes comes incognito. I met her at one Las Vegas fan party in the mid '90s, and she's a very nice woman, quiet and observant that day.

Kristian was involved in a video of the back stage Moodies during their final orchestral show at the Royal Albert Hall. Other than putting in occasional appearances and traveling along to spend time with their dads, the families of the Moody Blues seem mostly grown and involved with their own lives. Ray has a charming grandson, the one he wrote "My Little Lovely" for, and Graeme has a granddaughter named "Tiger" born to his daughter Samantha; he claims two children and seven grandchildren. Mike Pinder is also a grandfather. Justin's daughter Doremi is married and has a family in Cornwall, so the Moodies are normal families, like the rest of us.

John continues to do benefit appearances, mostly revolving around tennis and golf. Much John history is on his website *www.johnlodge.com*, as well as several really good articles he has written for various western magazines. He's a pretty good writer! John has also taken up painting in recent years, and his website might turn up more info on this. I think he sells that sort of thing via auction for charity.

Justin writes for magazines less frequently (good articles when they appear); he also turns out a wonderful blog of his own adventures and recollections on *justinhayward.com*.

Justin has continued to work with other artists off and on, notably Jeff Wayne, singing "Forever Autumn" for the stage production of *The War of the Worlds*. It toured in the U.K. to coincide with the release of Spielberg's chiller movie version of *War of the Worlds*. In September of 2007 Justin and Gordon headed to Australia to reprise their roles, then played the U.K. later that year. It earned rave reviews everywhere; the special effects include "the fighting machine" with lasers shooting out into the audience, and a holographic projection of Richard Burton (who narrates the original album.) In the 2009 UK tour they added wonderful 3-D effects sprinkling paper leaves on the audience during "Forever Autumn."

*Justin was able to work in one of his "snake dances" with "Strange Times." Justin's "snake dance" has only been captured on film once, to the best of my knowledge, Tom Jones variety show, 1969; he doesn't do it often. Speaking of Justin's stage antics, I've actually seen him do Buddy Holly imitations on stage with the Moodies, too. I kid you not, he was doing backbends at the Arlene Schnitzer during the Moodies show in 1992. He usually doesn't get that wound up, so anyone who finds the Moody Blues "boring" on stage just hasn't been to enough shows, obviously.

** After one of the casino shows in Tahoe (mid '90s), one of my friends knew a limo driver, and apparently they had passed on some inside scoop about the Moodies. "They didn't tip." Talk about tight! (I think it's pretty funny.) The good news is later reports have them tipping after all.

***This is a recipe for pasta, beef, basil, garlic and olive oil. Yumm.

XXI) Winter's Tale: 2003

Hold on to warm September………..

"The Sun is shining, the grass is green, the orange and palm trees sway. There's never been such a day in Beverly Hills, LA"-- Irving Berlin, "White Christmas"

"And why should the world take notice of one more love that's failed?"--Mike Batt

Well who would have thought it? I began writing this book before the Moody Blues started their last album, *December* (a collection of Christmas songs) I actually had a chapter called "Christmas" set up before the holiday album was heard of, because there is so much Moody Christmas artwork and photos.

Not too much has come out about the production of the holiday album, but Paul Bliss did say he was on the album, as well as Danilo Madonia. It's a pretty package, with bits taken from the cover of *Long Distance Voyager* (originally an 18th century art piece.)

Christmas in England is a very special time and place, and it seems a natural. Why didn't they do this years ago? The album was released in the fall of 2003. The first two tracks are penned by the songwriter, Justin Hayward, "Don't Need a Reindeer" and "December Snow." While "Reindeer" seems like a fun-loving song Justin just "threw together," of course there is a lot of thought in it. Possibly (?) two songs were put together in the same way that "Question" was composed, so many years ago.

Of "December Snow," Justin said in a brief interview that, "We would have done this song anyway, even if we weren't doing a Christmas album." It's a beautiful love song, one of Justin's best. It stayed in the live line-up until summer of 2009, and I enjoyed it every time I saw it live.

"In the Quiet of Christmas Morning" is such a great choice of Bach! Years ago, a famous contemporary of the

Moody Blues, Ian Anderson (of Jethro Tull) used Bach's "Bourree" to excellent effect. This being the first album in which the (Mach II) Moodies did music by other composers, it's only fitting they should do something by The Best. Justin's tenor vocals over Bach make the song a true jewel.

"On This Christmas Day" I found rather generic, but some fans online seemed to think it might be about 9/11. As with other Moody songs, it's a matter of perspective. "Happy Xmas" lyrics by John Winston Lennon, caused a very amusing stir in the online Moody community, as the melody sounds remarkably like a song, "Stewball," a folk tune done by Peter, Paul and Mary back in the late '60s or early '70s. The melody goes 'way back to Irish folk music. It's a great sentiment, but oddly Justin said, "I wasn't into doing it, but I was overruled. I rather like the original by John Lennon."

"A Winter's Tale" was written by a SODs friend of Justin's, Mike Batt. This story can be found on Batt's website. He said something to the effect, "I had just broken up from a girlfriend when I wrote this. I'm now married to her." So listening to the song, and realizing that it actually had a happy ending rather adds to the music. *Winter's Tale* is also the title of a Shakespeare play.

The other songs: I would hesitate to put an interpretation on them, and the lyrics are mostly self-explanatory. "In the Bleak Midwinter" comes from a poem by Christina Rossetti "A Christmas Carol" and set to music by Holst, so the Moodies incorporated a fair amount of the traditional in their presentation.

"White Christmas" is done very up-beat, a distinct difference from the usual Bing Crosby version most are used to hearing every Christmas. *Unless you have been in the military, and overseas, you don't understand this song. I was in Diego Garcia sometime in the '80s when I first heard it in its true context. Loretta Lynn's USO tour sang "White Christmas" in 3-part harmony, and there I was on a tropical island, sitting on the floor of an aircraft hangar, remembering all those old movies....... and I burst into tears. The follow-up is CNN stuffed their cameras in my face at this point, and my family back home got the special holiday treat of seeing me weeping on the 6 o'clock news. How embarrassing!!! It's very weird, but something hits you when you are out there on foreign shores, defending our way of life as a soldier or sailor; and you understand that the sacrifices you are making, being away from your family at Christmas, are the same sacrifices your fathers made, and that your children might make too someday. And they all heard, and will hear this song, "White Christmas." It's like it's all one big USO show, and this song is the jewel of the line-up. So take my word for it, the Moody Blues' version of this as an up-beat, rock n' roll song, is wonderful beyond words! Don't even sing this song slow and mopey around a veteran, because they will get very weepy!*

One final note about Christmas. December 10, 2011, Justin and Ian Anderson did a "Christmas at Canturbury" show, and the bits and bobs of that performance turn up on *youtube.com*. Alas it was never released commercially. It was a beautiful show from what I've seen, and you'll enjoy the look up on line.

XXII) 21st Century Moodies

The years 2000-2002 showed heavy touring in eastern U.S. With less distance to travel, and higher sales, the eastern seaboard seems to be the most profitable tour area.

There was an extensive orchestral tour in the U.K. in April and May 2000, culminating in a two-show concert at the Royal Albert Hall on May Day. This was filmed and released to PBS; it's a nice show and commercially available. The OFC was able to get good tickets for many fan club members, and the entire front section of the house can be seen singing along with the band.

Sometime after 2000, the Moodies were able to tour Buddy Holly's hometown in Texas, and visit Holly's grave, which was an important matter for Justin and John both. John talked about the visit in his interview, Brooklands April 27, 2009. According to John, he felt he should leave something to honor his hero and put a plectrum (guitar pick) on the grave. They elaborated this tale in one Storyteller event too, how it was dark and spooky, and the Jays bribed the caretaker to let them in after hours. John said, "No lie, a cricket came and landed on my hand!"

In 2001, IMAX did a documentary called *Amazing Caves*, which involved cutting-edge research in microbiology, and the producer decided he wanted the Moody Blues involved in the background music. And they are, from jungle drums, to Gregorian chants. The opening scenes in the head-reeling IMAX theatre were incredible; the stars came out, and the Moodies were all heard singing a "monkish" heavenly chorus. The songs have Latin lyrics: "Nights in White Satin" is de- and re-constructed so many ways before the movie is over, you feel you have gone on a little journey to inner space along with the scientists. It's a fantastic soundtrack and movie, and if you missed it, don't hesitate to see it at your earliest opportunity. I've shown the video many times for science class, and youngsters really like it, too.

John's daughter Emily grew up pretty fast. In 2000 she was part of an "around the world" sailing team (BT challenge), which Moody fans avidly tracked via the Internet. John met her in New Zealand and played golf there! Aren't events like this a strange and wonderful adventure?

Justin was spotted in 2001 at a party of Uri Geller's, chatting with Michael Jackson.

Justin sang with a young Greek performer named Mario Frangoulis in the spring of 2002, in an ancient Greek theatre in Thessaly! That show was videoed for PBS and comes over like a solo version of *A Night at Red Rocks*, shot in an ancient Greek theater, in Macedonia. The Italian versions of "Skimming Stones" and "Nights in White Satin" are beautiful beyond belief.

In June 2002, Justin did a benefit (June 20) at the Rock and Roll Hall of Fame in Cleveland, for Amazonian conservation (which included chefs, and shamans from indigenous South American tribes.) Dr. Mark Plotkin, president of the Amazon Conservation Team, is also an excellent author, and a friend of Justin's. (I recommend his books, very interesting.) Why is it "strange times" for shamans to show up at the Rock and Roll Hall of Fame? About time it happened, I say! Justin did another solo show the next night (June 21), which is commercially available, *An Audience with Justin Hayward* at the Rock and Roll Hall of Fame.

In early 2003: we don't know if it was related to the crash of the *Columbia* but the announcement hit the Internet newsgroups just a few days afterward. Sadly, Ray Thomas had dropped out of the band. The Moodies toured in the late fall of 2003, showcasing several of the songs from *December*. A new flautist (Norda Mullen, from Justin's solo shows in the '90s), with considerable abilities and credentials of her own was added, and the show went on.

In 2003, Graeme responded to the fiery crash of the *Columbia* by putting the poem "Higher and Higher" back into the line-up. (The song was originally written to celebrate our first landing on the Moon.) What a great show it was!

Graeme did this huge "thunder dance" thing, bashing on drums, strobes and stuff, dancing around on the stage. I was lucky enough to be front row more than one night when Graeme did "Higher and Higher," the highlight of my Moody experiences, to dance right along with Graeme, through one of their more rocking songs. I heard several kids at shows say they really liked "that funny guy dancing," and Graeme always gives his drumsticks away to the little guys in the front rows. Lots of fun.

Sept 13, 2003 Cote d'Azure was ravaged by wildfires. Two weeks later, Justin and many other musical celebrities came together under the auspices of Radio Caroline South for a benefit "Night of the Phoenix" for the families of the victims (three firemen were killed, as well as tourists.)

In 2004, the ultimate compiled album, *The Best of the Moody Blues* came out. The Moodies were inducted into the Rock Walk Hall of Fame in Hollywood, California, mushing their hands into cement in a huge ceremony.

April, 2005, the Moody Blues flew to New Zealand for a series of concerts and were greeted by a Maori powhiri. It's a wonderful video, well worth digging for on *youtube*.

Jun 11, 2005 *Live at the Greek Theater* (in Los Angeles) video released, available commercially. They added "One More Time to Live" to the line-up this year, very intense song, and as John says "It's even more true today than it was when I wrote it."

The Moodies also toured Australia this year. 2007, Justin sang a track on *Excalibur II*, done by Alan Simon. The *Excalibur* albums are quite fascinating, Simon is developing a "Celtic Ring" cycle, based on ancient and fragmentary Celtic mythology. In the bardic tradition, the stories are set to song.

Justin has recorded (mostly vocals) with other international producers here and there throughout his career, I may have missed some. Justin also sings with Marty Wilde, live and in concert, this year (2007.)

2008: Justin and Alberto Parodi re-mastered *Octave, Long Distance Voyager,* and *The Present* (ref: Justin's website blog, Sept 2008). Justin told a great story in an interview about how they had a dedicated fan who was hanging around the studio, and how said fan had "virgin" vinyl records that had never been played. They talked him into letting them use the vinyls, and thus were able to take what was on there, and digitally combine that sound with what was left of the original masters.

In 2008, "Nights in White Satin" was used in a "tunnel of love" ride at the Hard Rock Amusement Park in Myrtle Beach; the Moodies donated an old mellotron to the park. The park sadly went bankrupt within the year, which had nothing to do with the Moodies. Several other bands were involved; one attraction was Alice's Restaurant, another was a roller coaster that gave you thrills to the strains of "Whole Lotta Love," by Led Zeppelin.

Press release *The Earth Times* (Las Vegas) Sept 16, 2008 mentions John's art on display at the Mandalay Bay.

Spring 2009: a lovely commercial for a credit card came out, with "Tuesday Afternoon" laid over videos of a psychedelic aquarium. Aquariums really DO look like that now, if you haven't been lately, they light up jellyfish with ultra-violet.

April 17, 2009: John Lodge song "Sunny Sunshine Faces" debuted on Brooklands radio (Swindon) and John followed up the début by getting with the producer Mike Smith and offering to sponsor the local kids soccer team with their Threshold logo on the tees. John is always popping up in benefits for kids.

Early summer 2009, *Isle of Wight: Threshold of a Dream* DVD released, the Moody Blues concert portion from August 1970.

July 5, 2009, Gordon Marshall chatted on-line with fans, and gave backstage tidbits about *The War of the Worlds* tour, which he and Justin were both with at the time. Justin and Gordon both worked on the classical sci-fi stage show with Jeff Wayne, for several years. (Gordon praised the food service, which tells you where his priorities are!) And it continued unto 2010. *The War of the Worlds* (stage musical) was also released, available in PAL at *www.amazon.co.uk*, and in American format as well.

Mike Batt's video with Justin in it, *The Hunting of a Snark*, was released on PAL format (U.K. format) DVD in 2011 (available at *amazon.co.uk*: try *amazon.com* first, it might be out in American format by now.)

December 10, 2011, Justin did a charity Christmas show at Canterbury Cathedral with Ian Anderson. There was no commercial release of the show, but some of the videos have turned up on *youtube*. Those who were there said the show was marvelous, and the two musicians did wonderful music together.

Graeme can be found at home in Florida, watching *Star Trek* and war movies (his favorites), or even more exciting, chasing women!!! He's single, why not? No I won't put out ALL the details (do your own research! He made the cover of the *National Enquirer*, with a retouched photo) but with Graeme being in his '70s, you gotta say *more power to him!* Some fans were upset, the rest of us laughed in amazement and wonder. It sounded like his 20-year-old date for the evening tried to roll him in the back of a limo, then stole his cell phone.

Graeme also posts on Facebook a lot and is quite funny and charming. He's still into natural science and always posts about the critters in his yard.

Ray remarried!! There are now some marvelous photos and "tales from the road" on his website, which his wife has worked very hard to bring to the fan base.

Mike Pinder continues to record with his sons, and they have built their own studio in Roseville, CA.

John and his wife Kirsten work with children and benefits in both the U.K. and in Barbados.

Denny Laine lives in the Las Vegas area, and solo tours occasionally.

Feb 11, 2013: Graeme Edge performed with the Sarasota Pops, conducting the final movement from "Pines of Rome" by Ottorino Respighi. Easily found on *youtube* (a cool musical piece if you've never heard it, was in *Fantasia 2000*.)

Graeme and Gordon have both been bitten by the writing bug and have out books of "tales from the road," and lost poetry. Spring tour 2012 finds Graeme's book of poetry available on Amazon, and at shows. Gordy and Graeme have also done "talking book" versions of their published writing, and last I heard, Gordy has done "gigs" of talking books for other publications as well. Gordy has a really nice speaking voice!

Summer of 2013, a massive box set *Timeless Flight* was released, chock full of lost and collectible music and video. In 2014, another massive box set collection *The Polydor Years* was released, and it really has some great live tracks including Patrick Moraz doing sublime synth. It even has an Easter Egg: check out where Graeme's hand went on the cover.

Four cruises on the waves of the Caribbean happened with the Moody Blues from 2013 to 2018. In 2013, the Moody Blues successfully cruised with 3,000 of their fans to Jamaica and Grand Cayman Island. I was there and it was a great time!!! But by the last day I was ready to debark, for sure. They did two more beyond that, and in January 2018, will do their fourth. In early 2019, John and Justin will take different cruise paths with their own solo bands (John, Alan Hewitt, Norda and Gordy Marshall from the Moodies with *Cruise to the Edge*; Justin, Mike Dawes and Julie Ragins from the Moodies, *On The Blue* cruise.)

Cruises (*yacht rock*) are a lot of fun, and there are a lot of other Boomer music groups along too, but little weird things come up on these cruises. Trying to have a "meet and greet" VIP party with the Moodies turned into a riot on the first cruise, and it wasn't attempted again. It's not until you're in an insane crowd like that, with a band around age 70, that you understand on a visceral level how popular they are. Some of the other bands came out and socialized during the cruise, but Justin stayed in the "no fans" section of the ship, as did most of the Moodies. As I said earlier, Moody fans OVERWHELM.

What Just Happened???--As I update, Fall, 2017: the Moody Blues continue. Many things have happened since I finished the first edition. Personnel changes. Paul Bliss left the band (I shall refrain from repeating the rumors I heard), Gordon Marshall left the band under friendly circumstances, saying "It was time." I was (still am) very fond of Gordon, he's a real class act, and I think he just wanted to spend more time at home with his family (I think he lives in or near Cumbria in the U.K.) Gordon spent over 20 years with the Moody Blues, which is plenty for anyone! Gordon and Paul remained friends outside of all band business and formed their own tribute bands. Gordy has picked up plenty of work in the U.K. stepping into the drummer spot for a long running *Thriller* musical and other rock operas.

When Gordy left, for their second drummer, the Moodies hired Billy Ashbaugh, who is quite good himself, and comes over a bit like a hobbit (very cute!) His drumming style seems a little closer in style to Graeme's and he is not as flamboyant as Gordy but upholds his drumming duties quite well. Alan Hewitt was Paul's replacement and has his own face book and website.*

Inspiration has got to find you working -- Picasso (as quoted by Justin)

Justin claims to be writing and mixing music in his spare time (lots of unreleased stuff on Hayward's shelf); or he spends time walking in the Alpine wilderness near his home in Cote d'Azur. Justin appears (in later years) to be the point man when it comes to re-mastering the Moodies' collective catalog. (As Graeme puts it, *Justin is a work-aholic, and loves being in the studio.*) In March 2012 Justin did a radio interview with Steve Goss (Atlanta WABE) and discussed at length how *Days of Future Passed* was originally produced (on four and two track systems), he found the details fascinating when he re-mastered it for Universal to 5.1 format. He works with Alberto Parodi, and no surprise, Alberto turned up engineering the live *Days of Future Passed* orchestra stage show at the Hollywood Bowl, in 2017.

Between the first and third edition of this book, Justin (2013), issued a solo album called *Spirits of the Western Skies*, has toured for four years (in between Moody tours) with his own pick-up band, including Alan Hewitt and Julie Ragins (back-ups for the Moodies) AND including a wonderfully talented young Englishman named Mike Dawes on guitar. Look him up on *youtube*, oh *WOW*.

On a roll with his company Eagle Rock, Justin also was able to release a live CD and DVD of these tours entitled *Spirits… Live*. Mike Dawes (did his own solo opening act for Justin's tour) also has out two albums VERY worth having. Mike is a leading figure in a guitar method called "finger style," really marvelous stuff. I was able to see many of these shows out in western America, and was blown away not only by the performances, but also by the technical talent on the sound board.

A special note has to be inserted here, on the end of the *Spirits of the Western Skies* album are two "techno" songs, suitable for playing in the rave discos popular with young people these days. A couple of European engineers named Carl Ryden and Peo Haggstrom did a really wild remix called "Out there Somewhere" in which Justin can be heard wailing lines from "I Know You're Out There Somewhere" only he sounds like he's lost down a wormhole!! Really fun (African rhythms!) and good stuff to dance to! Kudos to Justin, staying up with modern music and not getting lost in a hippy-music back-eddy.

After *Spirits of the Western Sky*, Justin did "Wind of Heaven." Justin and David Minasian wrote this lovely song as a theme for a movie by the same name, about an Afghanistan soldier who comes back with shell-shock and finds himself working with horses. The song is a beautiful tear jerker, and everyone (as of this writing) is looking forward to the movie. (*windofheaven.com*) At last report, "Wind of Heaven" has a mention for a Grammy nomination.

Then, Justin released his own double album (sold at a lesser price as a single album) *All the Way* with many obscure cuts on it. The most unusual and lovely turned out to be an alternative version of "Blue Guitar" as first mixed at Strawberry Studios with members of 10cc on the track.

For the new Millennium, John Lodge launched his own wine label, Krisemma Wines, named for both of his children. His daughter Emily is the label's CEO and manages things while her dad tours. Not surprisingly, much of the Moody touring in the western USA goes through California wineries.

Kristian Lodge lives in Florida (last I heard) and manages much of John's on-line business, such as his Facebook. The Lodge Family is close, they all show up for big Moody shows, and many come on the cruises too, unlike some other band family members.

As of 2016, John Lodge has started his own solid solo career (it was there before during the 70s) and has issued a lovely solo album, *10,000 Light Years Ago*. Very nicely done, and I recommend it; it was followed by a DVD filmed live in Birmingham (U.K.) His "John and Friends" band consists of Gordon Marshall, Norda Mullen, Alan Hewitt, and Duffy King. Alan also did a lot of engineering work on the album itself. What I've heard of the show seems very favorable live, so if the show comes near you, go see it. Or travel long distances if you are dedicated.

Days of Future Passed--In June, 2017: the line-up changed (THANK GOODNESS) very welcome to us "regulars" because the old line-up was very stale. Sadly this left out Graeme's clog dance to "Higher and Higher." Graeme was into his 70s and had health issues, which this book will not discuss. BUT it was the 50th anniversary for their 1967 psychedelic album *Days of Future Passed*. The NON-orchestra shows were very odd, and also pretty high tech. I was at the opening night, in Palm Springs, and there were a lot of mistakes, but a lot of beauty too. The first half of the show was a grab bag of "best hits" and favorites for the band.

Then for the second half... a video started with the sound track of the album laid over it. The Overture played, and one by one the band trickled onto the stage, like it was something they "just found" and decided to join. A large screen hung in back of the band, and the viewpoint panned over a night-time Earth, came to rest in England, and then the band played live "Dawn is a Feeling"... and proceeded through the entire album from there, using the original album tracks for the instrumental parts. Justin sang Mike Pinder's songs, and John sang Ray Thomas's songs.

The down side: there were long stretches where there was nothing but canned music with video, but I enjoyed it and thought the video slide show was beautiful. I know some didn't like that (they wanted live music) and I think it bothered some of the band at first. One person found the songs "dated" but while the first night (for example) "The Sunset" was awkward, the second night it was like the band said "F*** it" and really cut loose, the song ROCKED. I saw nine of the shows, all over the west coast, and it was fascinating to see the live performance grow from that first worrisome night, to the full complete show at the Hollywood Bowl.

It's hard to describe the stage show: images, the video, the slideshow, the movie. Having seen the video now (filmed later in the tour in Toronto) some of the slideshow survived the edit. Stars, images of Stonehenge, the Thames River, rainbow colored rail-way tracks, forests and wildflowers. Children dancing. They toured with seven shows up the west coast of America, then bounced back to Los Angeles, Justin did a solo promo show for "Wind of Heaven" at the Grammy museum (14 June 17.) THAT was in the middle of the week, and then that weekend, they did their show with a LIVE orchestra for a benefit at the Hollywood Bowl.

Unless you've been to The Bowl, it's difficult to explain, it's a huge natural bowl and dates WAY back in California history. It was pretty full this night, and the band looked darn small and lost down there on that huge stage. I managed to move closer for the second half of the Moody set (their backdrop screen was absolutely lost in the huge arena.) The full orchestra finally came out (it wasn't the LA Philharmonic, I think it was a grab bag of musicians who performed for the benefit.) The classy Boomer lady with the bull fiddle looked over at the band and smiled broadly... obviously a fan of their music. Out came the handsome conductor, a backward gong bang, and the first notes.... live.... *Days of Future Passed*. This, the first time the album had been done LIVE even though it was a signature album of the '60s. I burst into tears.... it was marvelous.

    The show came together the way it was supposed to. Stars, outer space, and Stonehenge. Rainbow chaser lights all through the seats during "Another Morning" and fireworks at the end during "Question." The spotlights crossed in the sky out front. This was the most perfect Moody Blues show I've ever seen and I've seen just a few! If you ignore the total solar eclipse I saw later that summer (the most fantastic event of my life) the show that night was the second highest point in my life. I spent the next 24 hours stumbling in stunned disbelief, it was that good.

    Later in the year, 2017, the Moody Blues were finally inducted into the Cleveland Rock and Roll Hall of Fame. This is after much screaming lobbying and niggling from east coast American fans. As of this writing, Denny Laine is part of the induction (rightfully so because he was not inducted with Wings), and Mike Pinder will be there as well.

    So far, the Moodies show no signs of stopping touring nor of ceasing to write and record fine musical material. You have to admit (those of us who have seen too many shows!) that band members sometimes seem to be a well-oiled machine on stage, but the music never suffers. And frankly the Moodies never did claim to be a pretty boy act, it's about the music, not the glitz. Tours continue despite the Moodies' obvious aging. We're ALL getting older. The Moodies still sound good. May they rock on forever!

The Final Word--As I type, it is autumn 2017, and it seems like an eternity since I began to write this book, and I've taken more years beyond to polish and revise later editions. I remember being so disappointed when the word went out that the editors of *Higher and Higher* magazine were putting their Moody biography on hold because "It was in the hands of the band." Even today, search on *Amazon.com*, and you will find this biography by Mark Murley "pending." The band, without a doubt, is going to approve of an "official biography" roughly around the time Satan takes up snow-boarding in Hades.

I remember diving into the project and writing until my eyes crossed, and I have been polishing this book ever since. Mark Murley's comment about why he didn't publish is (more or less) the same reason this book will be *unauthorized* when it goes to the publishers. I think the band would have various levels of nervous breakdowns if they had to review all the things that have happened in their collective careers. If Mark indeed gave them a book to look over, my guess is they found a dark, deep hole somewhere to hide it in. Sad too, because Mark is a good writer.

The band has nothing to be ashamed of in this retrospective. The Moodies are ALL wonderful people. "Finding the best that's within us" is what being a Moody is all about! And it was a pleasure to put it together. So much has happened since I started. Let the story never end!

But I have lost track of all Moody events, on radio and on television, at Rainforest benefits, concerts for autism, and for UNICEF. They landed in New Zealand and were greeted by a Maori powhiri; in response, the band launched into "Lovely to See you Again." I don't think they get much rock n' roll action in New Zealand, there was quite a turnout of locals for the event.

So many world events went by as I wrote this. 9/11 happened, and John posted a poem about it on line. Another war started; all the songs about peace, all have been for naught. Would that terrorists could bring some more melody into their lives, and less hatred. Poverty is no excuse for the way our world is today. My uncle grew up a poor man with dirt floors in his home, the family lived off squirrels he shot out of the trees. He didn't make bombs and become a suicide bomber; he constructed a guitar out of cigar boxes and made music!

Tipping the Gaff--"Life can be like December Snow," can't it? November 19, 2005, Las Vegas: I saw the closing show of the Moodies' tour for the year. They looked tired. They did "One More Time to Live." Live, it really hit home, and was kinda scary (in fact it was very scary**) but fit the mood. It was a good show, but everyone still looked their forty years of touring. It wasn't necessarily a bad feeling. Justin did "Nights in White Satin" with a deep look of calm and contentment on his face, just like he was ready for his own couch in front of the telly. You could tell it was personal, and perhaps he was reflecting just how much that song had done for him. The lyrics were born of sadness, but his life was changed by it too, for the better. *Just what you want to be, you will be in the end*.........

The moment was spoiled. As "Nights" came to an end, the front rows, as if on cue, (and perhaps it was, as most of the front rows were "die-hard fans") rushed the stage and crowded down front for the finale. They looked like white corpuscles moving in on a bacterium. Justin immediately reacted: he looked like he had just been splashed with cold water, and if he had been wearing a fur coat, his hackles would have come up a mile!

Ah well. All the Moodies finished the show with style, and waving, smiling and bowing, all vanished off stage, guitars held high. I hadn't seen many of the other fans in recent years, I'd been busy working, with family, and other priorities that took the place of what once was real fanatical fan-mania in my own life. After the show, I went to the Mirage café with some fans. For the life of me, I don't know their names. If I've met them on line, I've blacked it out. Everyone was tired, many had followed the band to other cities on the tour. Many of them were hungry, and digging in (with dedication) to pies, coffee, breakfasts, and late-night snacks. I guess I must be cured of the fanatical fandom. They were nice folks, but I had nothing in common with them, and found myself thinking of the nice, warm bed back in my cheap room. I sipped a glass of water, excused myself, smiled and departed.

At midnight, all the doors look alike. Looking for the exit, I opened one door off to the side in the café. It opened onto Backstage. Wow how about that good security, eh? It was a quite dirty hallway, floored with cheap, chipped linoleum and lined with amps, peopled with bustling, bandanna-wearing roadies. Show biz is funny that way, the show out front can be beautiful, the illusion complete. Take one look backstage and see the real grunge and grubby conditions performers have to put up with, the filthy alleys they have to slink through, and it doesn't look so glamorous.

Not one to pass up an opportunity, I yelled at a roadie standing there, "Hey I have a stupid question!" He was a friendly chap and grinned back at me. "What does the word 'snakes' on the amplifier mean?" That got his attention. "Huhn?" his mind was obviously blown. I explained it, babbling a little. You see, for the past fifteen years I'd been lurking around front rows and backstage at the Moodies shows, before and after, during strike, and peeking into the wings during shows. There is always this same stencil "snakes" on the black cases. I thought maybe Graeme had a weird Freudian sense of humor and had personalized his amp or something.

"NO!!! That means that those are the long cables that go out into the audience, they connect back into the House..." the roadie trailed off. That made sense. It's been a few years, but I've done my time as a theater electrician, and I got it finally. I thanked the nice young man, and went on my way, letting him do his work.

Almost out the café, it finally dawned on me what I had just done (duh, slow moving nerve impulses). I went back, and slunk through the door, and actually stepped into the grubby hallway. It was a heart flutter moment; honestly if I had met a Moody Blue on his way to the loo, I would have slid to the floor, passed out, right there on that ugly tile-work. I did walk (cautiously timidly pussy-foot) a few yards and checked out the walls. They were covered with autographed photos of all the performers who had been there. THEN before I could tip-toe any further, some prissy little control freak manager swished out of an office like a mad barking Pekinese and ran me off. I went quietly. I felt like telling him to put on a frilly apron and mop his filthy floor! It was an interesting experience though, a bit like Alice going through the magic door.

    Writing this book was "going through the magic door." On the other side is a wonderful garden of delights with thorny, fragrant roses, but there are also wicked queens, and flimsy houses made of cards. Yes there ARE snakes in the garden!!! There were goofy games with all manner of wacky creatures, and many a cry of, "Off with her head!" And it was always a lot of weird, dream-like fun. I hope your journey is always as magical as mine has been, and I hope that, since you are obviously a Moody Blue fan, (just like me) that you can always say it with love.

*I HAVE to stop and talk about Alan for a moment. Alan is a blonde "mop top" that seems so popular with Moodies' fans, but that's not all there is to him. He is ALWAYS up beat and pleasant, even when it rains on the band. I've talked with HIM quite a few times, just happenstance bumping into. He is very kind to the fans and always has a word for them at the bus or in hotels. But, he has his own following of groupies and has been cautious at times. For example, the Justin and Friends solo show came through Los Angeles (Alan was not part of the performance that night) and played the Troubadour a few years ago. I spotted Alan in the crowd, going for his tickets at the box office, I just happened to be behind him going to Will Call. I was LA cool and didn't bug him. He waved at ME!!! "How are you?" he yelled most cheerily and actually reached over some people to take my hand! What a sweety! Anyway he was there with a lady (I presume his wife) who was very quiet. Alan asked me with a very tiny note of concern "Did you see any of the others here yet?" by which meaning, one of the "regulars" who follows the band around. It seemed a real solid LA blues crowd frankly, not all that many of the silly ones who attack the band in public. "No" I answered. Our fan base is like that, they stake out certain venues, then all show up to gossip and talk about the band, each other. get drunk, eat, and chase Moodies to their hotel rooms. Anyway, Alan grinned and waved, and I later saw he and his lady up on the balcony watching the show from a healthy distance. Bless him he trusted me! I know who he was worried about showing up, and I'd have been worried to. She didn't. Poor Alan, he gets bugged too. But most importantly, he doesn't let it spoil his life. Alan is also very realistic and another time asked me what the tickets to the cruise had cost me (apparently doing a quick estimate of the total gross of the cruise.) Very personable guy. He and his wife were doggy parents last I heard and keep basset hounds.

**This is one of those places in the book you need to take out the album and play the song. "Confusion, revolution, evolution............" It was closing night. They sounded angry and tired as they sang the words. Live performances have a much more visceral impact than mere album recordings, and it was the first time I had heard it live. The generation that the Moodies and I belong to, the Viet Nam baby boomers, we ALL have tried so hard to bring world peace. But even though we have made SOME headway, the problems still aren't fixed, and all the conflicts and wars still seem so stupid, wasteful. Why don't all the terrorists go plant some trees instead? If future generations read this book, and listen to their music, will it help? Will the message finally reach everyone?

XXIII) Absolute final word

We (my tech team and I) uploaded the ebook version of *Wildest Dreams* on Jan 20, 2018, as the sun went into Aquarius. The paperback "first edition" had been released via Amazon in 2013, in a VERY limited printing; the ebook had several significant updates in the five years it was dormant, and this fourth edition "print on demand" version has even *more* updates.

For those who have never taken on the (99.99% perspiration!!!) task of writing and publishing a book over 500 pages long, be aware of some facts. Right now, the publishing world has so many word processors and different platforms, it's a nightmare when you upload, or transfer to a new media. Typos just merrily insert themselves where they darn well please. Then Word decided it liked a *British* spell checker rather than an *American* spell check. *Blblblbl*

I've watched with some dismay reviews of *Wildest Dreams* as an ebook, as well reviews of *Long Distance Voyagers*. Both glowing and black hearted reviews popped up before anyone could possibly have read and fully processed either book. While yes it's exciting that finally comprehensive biographies are available for those wanting to know the Moody History, the casual music history reader should understand, that the Moody fan base has around 40 to 50 "hard core" fans, and about half that number have some really serious anger issues. Sigh, does this happen in David Bowie's fan base? Probably. It just seems to be part of the fan experience.

The Moodies are very human (flawed as are we all), and after reading the Norman biographies of both Lennon and the Stonies, I vowed to be upbeat with this biography. I tried to leave flaws "between the lines" rather than spread unfounded gossip (as Norman did.) Good readers will find *lots* of Moody character details if you pay attention. Let's leave it there.

Literally as we published (these things take time to coordinate, and I was on the cruise!!!) during the process of final editing, many things happened in the Moody world. The fourth "Moody Cruise" pulled into Miami at 7 am on the 7th of January, 2018. The internet lit up, and we learned to our dismay and sadness, that while the whole Moody world was partying on the high seas, Ray Thomas (original band member and flautist) had passed suddenly with a heart attack on January 4th, just a few days after his 76th birthday. The band knew and were terribly sad at times during cruise shows... but "It's the Moody way" to go on with the show and not let Ray's memory die. Norda is married to a friend of Ray's and she played the flute with unusual beauty all through the cruise, many of her melody lines composed by Ray of course.

What a sad way to start the new year, but we're all going to go on. Ray would want the music to continue. Some fans actually claimed they saw a guy who "looked like Ray" on the ship. Is it "too out there" to think Ray's ghost joined us mid-cruise? Complete strangers told one another in line as we debarked, everyone stunned with disbelief, shaking our heads as we claimed our bags.

RIGHT with this came the announcement of Marc Cushman's first edition of *Long Distance Voyagers*. Plainly with the publishing dates, I've never had time to read this (I'll get around to it someday) and in my humble opinion, you can never have enough information about the Moody Blues. I wish him well, go out and buy THAT book too! Whether I get around to putting that "second volume" *Wildest Dreams Blue Timeline* out is up in the air. Just remember the wise words of John Lodge... "It's out there, all of it, you just have to go find it!"

We look forward right now to the Moodies' induction ceremony into the Cleveland Rock and Roll Hall of Fame and to Justin and Friends touring northern Europe in the same month! Justin's and John's solo shows will be doing more touring and cruises. Vegas in Fall, 2018. Happy Moody trails!

Was that fun???

Get ready, more to come in *Wildest Dreams Vol II: Blue Timeline*

Appendix A: Standing in a Tour Zone: the view from the footlights.

The Gemini Dream — see you somewhere on the road

How do you get out of the spaceship??-- internet question to the Moodies.

"The Dreams that always haunt Moody Blues drummer Graeme Edge the week before a tour begins; not being able to find his way to the stage, and no drumsticks anywhere in sight...."We're a bloody quite bit older, and the consumption of controlled substances has abstained. We're a bit slower and cooler in our music, not quite so frenetic and high paced..." The Colorado Gazette, Oct 26, 2000

Imprisoned lovers wrestle for fun, senior citizens wish they were strung..... Graeme, reciting a poem on his birthday in Las Vegas (mid '90s).

The tour could be (in the words of Dickens), "The best of times, the worst of times."

We never got involved with… throwing TV sets out of the windows … what were you going to do for the rest of the night? John Lodge, *Classic Rock Magazine* Oct 2010

Whilst recording, the trend in later years has been for the "action" to be dominated by John and Justin, but when it comes to touring, that is when the drummer(s) and the flute players really shine. Graeme is possibly the most fun person to watch on tour. In the later years, he was not much for obvious contributions to the albums, but in concert, he is sometimes a one-man circus. Adding Gordon to the show in the '90s only escalated the fun in the drumming section.

You might well ask why fans go over and over to see the Moody Blues. The answer is, they always do something different. The drummers juggle drumsticks. Bias wears wild clothes. Ray wiggles his eyebrows at the ladies. The music plays just a little different each night, and that is all part of the enjoyment of the music. Not to mention, they always do a wonderful job on the lights!

I think the drumstick toss began at the Dallas show in 1993. I can remember at least one instance where the drumstick toss was deleted, and as I was sitting in the orchestra pit, I made motions to Gordon from the front rows to "toss".....he actually shook his head at me in negation, and didn't miss a beat drumming. Ray and John regularly have to dodge the flying drumsticks, and at times, one wonders if Graeme isn't aiming at John on purpose.

I found some really wonderful interviews with Graeme that point up what the touring experience is like for the band. Graeme says in *Modern Drummer* that "the other boys" can't rock properly if there are no real acoustic drums, although he'd rather explore the synthesized world of rhythm.

Or like this great commentary, clipped from a review, October, 2000: *It's great to do those songs once again as a band,* he [Graeme] says. *We can mess around. For instance, during 'Question' I play it a little differently than how it was recorded. The song was recorded with a drum fill, but Justin never liked it because it cut across his vocals so he isn't too fond of it. Every now and again I'll throw that fill in there, and he'll turn around and give me a look and I'll stick my tongue at him. Little things like that keep the band alive.*

Over the years, the band really couldn't change TOO much. In many of the year 2000 interviews, Graeme especially brings up the point that when people go to see classic rock bands, audiences EXPECT to hear the old classics. He used the examples of going to see Bob Dylan, and Elton John himself, and being miffed when they played nothing but their new music. I personally have seen loud mouths in the front rows of Moody concerts, yelling "Play your old stuff!" The Moody Blues have tried to keep their classics in the musical line-up, as the audiences seem to expect it. Wasn't it Ricky Nelson that did that wonderful song, the "Garden Party"? It's so true. People will throw eggs at you if you don't do what is "expected." So the Moody Blues line-up rarely changed in the later years.

Collecting bootlegs might be very illegal, but it allows the fan and researcher to observe an interesting facet of the Moody Blues (and it's all over the Internet now, anyway). While on tour, the band began to do acoustic sets on various radio spots. I think the nicest of these that is bootlegged, turned out to be from a South Africa radio show. They repeated this same mini-show several times at Tower Records, and on other radio shows across America and Europa. Ray and Graeme finally started to join John and Justin on the acoustic radio spots; the unplugged style pointed up the versatility and talent of the band, that they could go from orchestra, to street band, to full-scale rock band. I can't recall another performing group that has done this, nor one that has done it so much, and consistently so well.

Road crew --I picked up some interesting factoids from a *Relix* article dated December, 1993. One of the roadies told the interviewer, "You are a pirate on the road -- you do what you want and leave!" There are twelve racks (bunks) on the bus, mostly for road crew, though the band uses a tour bus when shows are close together. As of this writing, the band and crew travel in different buses of their own.

They have a million dollars in gear, sixteen speaker arrays (and impressive chains holding them up.) The lighting gear has advanced considerably since I studied stage lighting in the 1970s! Instruments are now the size and shape of briefcases and placed in a row on the front apron (or hung overhead on pipes), are then networked into a computer somewhere off stage where the stage manager runs the show. The Moody Blues are alleged to be sparse and economical compared to other pop acts. In the '90s, they had two semi's to haul all their stage gear. As of 2011, they have only one truck.

In the '90s, I captured a cue sheet from Justin's tour, at the Santa Barbara Coach House: anyone who has done technical on a stage show will know what I'm talking about, it tells you when you turn mikes on or off or turn on certain lights. In 2005, I asked a roadie for a cue sheet after their closing show in November. He told me the entire thing was on computer, and there were no tech cue sheets. Just imagine!

There are really good articles on technical matters and stage lighting in *Higher and Higher* #20 and #30. I was able to chat a bit with some road crew after a show at the Schnitzer in Portland (1992) and got a big kick out them. They worked on into the night, after the Moodies had exhausted the good company in the bar back in the Heathman. The roadies were nice folks, and even though they told a few adult jokes, they were actually real gentlemen.

We accidentally set a glass of wine on a roadie's chair once too, and he got really upset! "I'd be fired if I was drinking!" poor guy. So, yes the Moodies and their stage crew are VERY professional.

In 2011, I was able to do a "backstage" tour prior to the show, and the stage manager explained that they could set up a show in two and a half hours and break it down in an hour and a half. The sets were VERY simple that year, and most of the effects were done with lighting and projections. There were three lighting techs, and three sound techs that year. He also said, that lighting, sets and procedures can change not only from year to year, but during the tour as well.

They were six weeks on the road when I saw this tour in Eugene. From reports back through "Elizabeth" (Rene Martinez's lady friend I bumped into at one show, a nice gal), she commented that Rene (the head guitar roadie) was very impressed with Justin's efficient technical attitude. Justin is the kind of guy who leaves sticky pads all over amps and guitars, saying "this needs tuning" or "this has a problem," and so forth, very organized behind the scenes. I also observed when I was backstage once (VIP ticket packages), that Justin's guitar straps were set "just so" lined up, in the racks, but John's guitar straps weren't in any sort of order.

Touring might be fun to some, but those of us who are older, might well wonder how a rock band in their sixties feels about sleeping in a different hotel room each night. A scenario that repeated itself and was indicative of the feel; notes were shoved under the hotel room door "Bags at 10:30, bodies at 11:30." John is frequently mentioned as being the last Moody out of the dressing room, no doubt making sure no one leaves valuable jackets behind (I forget where it was, but he bemoaned, in one interview, leaving a good flight jacket somewhere.) Fans have actually been known to do panty raids on their dressing rooms. Life is never boring on tour.

Even with the way it complicates one's life, touring had its moments of humor for the band. One story was about "How many Moodies can you squeeze into one elevator?" At some hotel, Tracy was the last one, the rest of the band was already stuffed in the lift, and yelled at her, grinning a bit, "Come on!" You'd have to see Tracy to appreciate it, she used to wear mini-skirts just about as short as you can get them, and a couple of the band members I've heard are butt pinchers when drinking. Tracy was the original "good sport" though; as cute as she is, I suspect she handled it well. "Oh all right," she said, and crammed on with them. No wild shrieks went up so I guess they kept it professional.

One of my pen-pals told me she got chased around a hotel room once by Patrick and Graeme. She'd send me a bomb too, if I revealed who it was. Yes those things really happen. Ah well, that was long ago. I've heard worse.

Gordon started doing a tour blog around 2010, he's a good writer! From his book, Gordy seemed to get the biggest kick out of "funny tour stories," he wrote one amusing tale for the fan club newsletter in which they all followed (John I think) through the dressing room of their co-touring band (either Chicago in 1992, or Neverland in 1991), and straight into a broom closet. They thought it was an access door to their own dressing room; talk about red faces!

Another good topic of discussion on tour was "What fake name do I register under?" Yes, in the world of rock n' roll, subterfuge and espionage are always at the top of their minds, in the effort to gain some privacy. I know of fans, the "same old stalkers" that actually will call all the hotels in a given town, trying to nail down where the band was staying. I know of managers who leak fake information about this to fans on the nets, as well. Anyway, they came up with new fake names all the time, and we heard some pretty good ones over the PA system while we were at Tahoe. (Caesar's Tahoe is a good deal of fun to page people in, or to call people in other rooms......never mind, but it was fun for fans too.) Some of the better names (you'll have to say them out loud) are Pete Tool, Edna Bag, Norma Stitz, Rusty Springs, Ian Gee, Roland Butter, and when the puns ran out, they resorted to allusion rather than homonyms, such as paging for Mr. Christian (John) and....Kim Wilde. (I'm sure Kim would have gone under her married name for security, had she really been there!)

The touring is always fun, but at the same time, there are going to be awkward, or rather rude moments to any interaction, even between fan and performer. For example, I can vividly remember Justin checking out his watch toward the end of a show I was rather enjoying. (Gee Justin, sorry to keep you so long!) In Justin's defense, sometimes it's a matter of money if the band goes overtime (depends on the venue.) Or sometimes the fans did strange things like waving a Grover puppet at Graeme in the front rows, in Las Vegas. (Probably the most childish, rude thing I've ever seen done to a live performer.) Sometimes the fans followed the band to the airport and hotels and heckled them there. Thankfully this sort of thing was rare. "Hey it's Rock n' Roll!" to quote Ray.

With the advent of the orchestral tour, the fan pressure escalated to unreal levels. At least one bad thing happened which could have been much worse; a fan got close enough to Justin's prized cherry red Gibson 335 to put a sticker on the case. (I kid you not, someone thought it was the place for bumper stickers.) The disgruntled guitar roadie that caught the sharp side of Justin's Libran tongue over the incident, was later found drowning his sorrows in a Vegas bar, where he vented his woes to a fan. For the next five years, we would see Justin hand-carrying his Gibson to and from the band's van, not trusting it to anyone's hands but his own. He probably started taking it to bed with him! (Only a guitar fanatic will appreciate this.)

A Texas-sized bug landed on Justin's arm. He slapped it with a slap that could be heard even over the microphones! (Moodymania #29)

Justin had a running battle with bugs (perhaps he tastes good!) One crawlin' critter bit him on the tongue in California, during the 1990 tour. And a Japanese beetle crawled in his ear in Wallingford in 1994. He actually stopped the show, screamed in pain (as one friend told me), and asked the classic line, "Is there a doctor in the House?" And a doctor appeared to pull it out for him. (The story went out like lightening over the wires with peals of mirth and Yoko Ono jokes in its wake!) Allegedly Justin and the doctor appeared back on stage, the doctor threw the bug down in triumph and Justin stomped it!

It was a running gag during summer touring, especially when the bugs reached helicopter proportions! With all the outdoor shows during the summer, the bugs gave the entire band a lot of trouble. One thing many fans are not aware of is that by the nature of stage lighting, if you are on stage, sometimes things are not visible until they enter the light, by which time they are about five inches from the performers' noses. This may be why Justin steps out of the lights sometimes too (he can see the crowd then.) Ray had a bad reaction to some bubbles that fans in the front row were blowing at one show. You have to go back to the Moody Blues roots: they've played places in their early days where nastier things than bugs and bubbles came over the footlights! (Tossed Coke bottles in Wolu City, Belgium, summer 1968: I have the documentation. And the Moodies walked off stage too!)

Anyway, after his close encounter with the Japanese beetle, Justin started jumping visibly in mock (or real) terror whenever a moth came after him over the footlights. I saw him do a whole routine about a "collection of bugs in his guitar" and how "the nitty little things get up there" complete with a nose wrinkle. I about fell over laughing, it was 2009 in Eugene. Bugs crawl into guitars, and short out the pick-ups! Not funny at all, to a guitarist. In Florida, Ray spent a good deal of time stomping (unto doing a flamenco) a Palmetto bug on stage. (That's a tropical insect that resembles cockroaches large enough to arm wrestle you, if you don't kill them quickly.) The back-up ladies, frequently wearing sleeveless dresses, finally got the hint, and started carrying bug repellant, spraying the air around them during the show.

Then there was the occasional revolving stage. There aren't too many of these left on tour circuits, as they are high maintenance (i.e. always broken!) The only show I've seen like this would be the Star Circle Theater south of San Francisco, in the early '90s. (I think it's been torn down now.) The first time I saw the Moodies there, the darn stage didn't rotate! Man, were we upset! That is, all the people in the back who got to see a lot of Moody backsides! Again, the Moodies are troupers, and adjusted, John spent a lot of time coming to the back of the stage and waving at us. Thank goodness for remote pick-ups.

A year or so later, the Moodies returned to the same theater. Disgruntled mumbling in the crowd would be an understatement, as most of us had been through this already. The band came out, they struck the first chords of "Lovely to See You Again" and THE STAGE MOVED. Oh my, the shout of joy that went up from the crowd! After about two songs, the moving Moodies finally got into the fun of it, and started pointing out crowd members, saying, "This is really nice to see the fans moving around! Now you're over here……."

I think this was the show that my eight-year-old son encountered a roadie in the restroom. Naturally he was talking to strangers, like he wasn't supposed to do. My son came out, saw the guitar picks that my friend and I had been handed in the crowd (we were feeling quite special, and squealing with delight), and my sweet little child says "He has a whole BAG full of picks!" From the mouths of babes. This roadie was working the crowd and passing out picks with John Lodge emblazoned on them!

For the first of the Red Rocks shows, Graeme recited "Late Lament" from *Days of Future Passed*, but as that got over-used, he switched to "Threshold of a Dream" ("White Eagle of the North.") According to *Moodymania* #15, at a Kalamazoo show, mid '90s, *a voice came from the audience "Speak to us, O wise one," as Graeme recited his poem. Graeme continued to recite, and ever so slowly and subtly lifted the middle finger of his right hand in an age old, unmistakable gesture. The audience roared with approval, Graeme smiled at the guy and the concert kicked off.*

At Red Rocks 1994 the wind came up so strong, (the Moodies look good in a wind, they seem to enjoy playing in it) Ray was trying to blow his flute, and finally gave up, yelling to the skies, "STOP BLOWING!! I'll do it myself!"

Date: Mon, 18 Aug 2003 19:32:34 -0700 (PDT) From: "Carrie Nelson" Subject: The Night the Lights Went Out on the Moodies After reading all the discussion about the power failure, I remembered the night in June '96 when the lights went out at a Moodies show not just once, but twice. The venue was Deer Creek in Indiana. With your kind indulgence I will quote from the account I wrote back then."…. the weather took a bad turn. It had been raining slightly, but now it came down harder. They announced a storm warning, and let the folks on the lawn come under the roof. FLASH! CRASH! And the power went out. The crew scrambled to disconnect equipment. After 15 or 20 minutes everything came back on, and they got ready to start the show…..As the show progressed, the rain got heavier and the wind picked up. Nature added a light show. Bias very carefully covered his keyboard with a towel. Graeme decided what he wanted to protect and wrapped a towel around his head! Finally came the moment we had all been waiting for. 'Work away today, work away tomorrow. Never comes the day for my love' KABOOM! The lightning flashed, the thunder crashed, and the place went dark again! A collective scream went up from the audience. In the lightning I could see Justin jump back, throwing his hand up. As the emergency lights came on I could see him laughing. Roadies scrambled to grab guitars and turn everything off again. The band left the stage saying they would be back in 5 minutes. It was half an hour. What an experience!"

Deer Creek, for at least two summer shows, had outrageously frightening thunderstorms and electrical displays rain out the Moodies. One can only surmise that John Lodge had not done correct Native American homage to the local rain gods. John is rumored to carry an eagle feather with him on tour, just for such moments.

In Tampa, Florida (June 7, 1996), the show was treated to some wonderful lightening displays (at a distance) during "Legend of a Mind" prompting many fans to wonder if Dr. Leary wasn't looking in on his band. June and July of 2017 were also beset with thunderstorms, toad-choker down-pours, you name it. They skipped one encore after playing "Question" and hustled off stage. Funny, they either get lots of bugs, or lots of rain during those summer outdoor tours.

Some of the fans had a thing about saying, "The tour looked like it was laid out with darts!!!" that is, all over the map. Check out the fall tour for 1968, you'll see what I mean. It's rough on fans who follow them from show to show. At the Sept 24, 2011 Storyteller show, Justin discussed one tour where they did Sweden, then hopped a plane to Spain for the next night's show, then back to England to do two shows. (I still haven't figured out what year that was.) Tour management and booking is obviously an art, practiced at varying levels of competence by organizers. As I've said elsewhere, it all seems glamorous until you think about the grueling travel.

What do they do when traveling? Sleep probably! But when the hours get long and tedious, reports are the Moodies play cards, with gusto. Bridge was mentioned in later years, but during the 1973 world tour, Graeme and John said they were doing a long term, on-going "mad poker game" using yen, dollars, pounds, guilders, whatever they had in their pockets. As everyone had forgotten the exchange rate, it was just nuts! (2gb radio, Australia, November, 2011)

Food-- Care and feeding of the Moody Blues What do the Moody Blues eat on the road? Ah gosh, what do they like to eat in real life??? Enquiring minds want to know!

Moody Blues were all apparently curry freaks in the early days (on their bios they mostly list "Indian food" as their favorites.) Graeme Twitters about "Found a great Indian restaurant," Justin talks in the Storyteller shows about "the perfect curry." They like spicy food. As they like a spicy life!

Eating right becomes a challenge on tour, for the performers. Travel and eating don't always mix, it seems to be a fact of nature, for anyone. Just ask all those fans who follow them around on road trips! Health freaks are everywhere in the band; over the years some have confessed to being vegetarian (Mike, Bias, Patrick.) Only two of the Moodies can eat before going on stage (Ray is one of those with cast iron stomach) because they are too keyed up. I heard somewhere that Justin can't eat before shows, then looks around for food like a hungry hound afterwards. Also, rich food and rock music do NOT mix, too visceral; try eating a double cheese burger and onion rings before any rock show, and you'll see what I mean.

Justin is the one who lost his sense of smell some years back; he then got heavily into naturopathic health after he recovered his smeller via zinc treatments. In recent years, the band drinks a "specially brewed" herbal tea (no not THAT herb, probably green, white or black tea) when on tour. Back during the '80s, Justin claimed to drink lime flower tea, which we avid fans have tracked down to health food stores. It's actually pretty good stuff, like a very light jasmine tea. Tea is good for blood pressure and has anti-toxins.

While Justin mentions lime flower tea, Gordon mentions green ginger tea. Justin has mentioned eating (whilst on the road), trail mix, and boiled eggs, hopefully not at the same time. Though you never know, like the Spies told me, "Justin eats weird things." I'm trying to picture Justin's stock of boiled eggs lurking and rolling around in the tour bus refer. Others claim Justin drinks a concoction of beets and honey, fresh from the blender, before a show "for his voice." As Justin is in excellent shape for his age, we should all sit up and take notice.

Gordon has mentioned taking his own portable blender along in his luggage, when on tour! This became a big topic of discussion on one social group, Gordon says he nicks bananas, fruit and yoghurt at the breakfast bar, and takes them back to his room to make smoothies. He's really into health, runs a lot and watches his diet!

Clipped from an article in 2009: *When the Moody Blues played the PAC in 2005, event staffers took orders for Taco Bell, Subway sandwiches and sushi.* Avid fans frequently spot Justin and his family going for rabbit food at the salad bar in Caesar's, when they play there.

Food is a big deal to many people, unto entire books being written on the subject of feeding rock n' roll stars. The Moodies made it into *Backstage Pass* (the best book I've found while researching this), written by some of Los Angeles' finest caters (Crisafulli, Fisher, and Villa). I really recommend it if you are into cooking, a "must have" for recipe collectors. I was impressed that the dishes for the Moody Blues all relied on olive oil, which tells me they are very heart healthy. While other rockers prefer Thai or Italian food, the Moodies seem to prefer fish and veggies. (So far I've tried a variation on the Lime Ginger Shrimp, and it was marvelous!) The other Moody Blues recipes are entitled "Halibut atop Braised Spinach," "Champagne Tarragon

Sauce" (for fish), "Braised Spinach" and a puree of broccoli soup.

Over the years all sorts of recipes have popped up from the Moodies themselves. Recognizing they have a woman-heavy fan base, this makes sense, because many of us fans (once we get over sorting and drooling on our Moody pictures) next turn to *Ladies Home Journal* for a good recipe to cook for the hubby and chillin's. Food is important to Moody fans. With this in mind, I herein present all the "food" data I've been able to glean about the collective band.

Ray Thomas: once in the '90s when fans persisted in writing the fan club secretary Ivy, asking what the Moodies loved to eat, they did indeed respond. Ray's recipe got the most action. He sent us all a recipe for some sort of "liver and onions" delight! (I almost gagged.) Either Ray truly enjoys liver, or he was pulling our legs. In retrospect, and knowing his sense of humor, I'm shocked he didn't send a recipe for Mountain Oysters! Having said all that, Ray HAS been sighted in herbal shops, apparently he prefers his spices fresh. Ray seems a typical Capricorn, and I haven't met a Capricorn male yet that isn't an excellent chef, and master of the grill!

John Lodge: one or possibly two "Frank Sinatra" recipe book (s) included John back in the '80s, and this article made the rounds until it was faded from multi-generational copy machines. It involved some sort of "stuffed pork chop" recipe, laden with cream sauce; that his wife Kirsten was prone to cook and feed the bass player. It is well known that John likes wines; and he bottles, blends and dabbles in his own wine making. There are entire eating cultures based on wine country cuisine, so I would direct your attention there for further study (stinky cheeses and such). I don't think John cooks, his wife is however described as a "very good cook." But, when the Moodies were a young band, starving in Belgium and trying to get started as musicians, John was alleged to be the best at stretching their food budget, he made "egg dips" which we

Americans call French toast. In an article from 2009, John says he is a "yoghurt freak," and a peek into his home refer will show a healthy stock of this delight! John, bless his heart, always has a food and recipe section on his news groups, and they are lots of fun.

Justin Hayward: along with the John Lodge pork chop delight, came a recipe (likewise a faded copy) for Justin's "favorite food," a British delicacy called "bubble and squeak" and I've never figured out what book that came from. After some digging, "bubble and squeak" turns out to be a generic British term for "How to use up the left-over pot roast and veggies." My own family has a "potato pancake" recipe that came down from the British branch of the family, it's a bit like that, only "the real Brits" mush in cooked carrots and cabbage to the mix. Justin recommends Brussels sprouts. Justin finished his commentary on the B&S with, "Goes well with HP sauce." Again this could be tongue-in-cheek, as horseradish puree tends to drown any flavors it touches.

[I got into a weird discussion with Fiona Lane once, who lives in Aberdeen Scotland, over what HP was. I thought it was like A1-sauce. It turns out there is a "brown sauce" in the U.K. that is identical to American A1 sauce, and HP was something entirely different. Odd how two people can speak the same language, and still be confused in communications.]

Reliable reports are that Justin is a very capable cook. In the past he's mentioned "cooking Mexican food" which shows how long he has lived in California! (All Californians can cook Mexican food standing on their heads.) Justin has also reported he and his family enjoy homemade soups, with lots of veggies. I mentioned the entire Hayward family at the salad bars in Caesar's, so that should explain things. All the Haywards are quite trim and watch their weight. Justin is a Libra, and they are usually health freaks. In a March 17, 2011 Q&A for Justin alleges that he enjoys cooking Spaghetti Puttanesca.

Graeme Edge: spring of 2007, Graeme was bemoaning having to do his own cooking, he and his wife had separated. Graeme strikes me as the sort of guy that grabs some junk food or takeout, and heads for the couch to watch *Star Trek*. He has some lady friends taking care of him now, and they "all like expensive wines." (Nice ladies too, one did the cruise with us.) If his Facebook postings are to be believed, Graeme enjoys banana jokes (became a running gag. Gordon went that-away, portable blender in one hand, and bananas in the other!)

Mike Pinder: says he and his whole family have been vegetarians for years. He has been sited in grocery stores buying egg beaters. In the FoMP magazine, Mike published "vegetarian shepard pie" recipe, which sounded pretty good. Yes Mike is a Capricorn and loves to cook! Tara Pinder is recognized as a Master Gardener and has an extensive herb garden that is admired far and wide.

The Backup People: we did spot Bias reading vegetarian Thai cooking once, so we assume he cooks. The other back-ups don't talk much about their private life (which is how they like it I'm sure.) Gordon does mention that his wife is a great cook, and that's a good thing. Paul Bliss has admitted to a sneaking craving for Boston Crème Pies.

Rock n' roll is thirsty work. What does the band want stocked for their cast and crew, iced down in coolers in the back room? I was lucky enough to have a friend named Cheryl who worked the Wolftrap for one show, who sent me a write-up on just this. Then I compared it to *Backstage Pass;* the lists were remarkably similar, with a few minor variations. The essential stocked drinks are: Coke (diet and regular), Beck's beer, Molson beer, Corona beer, 7up, various juices, waters (Spring, Evian and Perrier). Services for coffee, tea, honey, milk, fruit bowls (bananas at the top of the list!) AND a bowl of fresh cut limes (for the Corona). For the crew, twenty-four quarts of GREEN (not purple, blue or pink) Gatorade are essential. Cheryl said the Wolftrap mistakenly got some of the newer colors, and the road crew really got upset! Out went the caterers, to exchange the wrong colored Gatorade. I've seen Graeme with a bottle of green Gatorade at his drum stand. I see it every show now that I know about it!

Water bottles (and Gatorade) are set before the performance, just like props. In addition, some of the Moodies smoke, and some don't (you can tell by who gets in the smoking limo, and it changes from year to year), but those that do smoke have expensive taste in cigarettes. "Silk Cut" and "Rothman's Blues" are mentioned. For the record, Justin says he quit smoking around 1992.

Cheryl said at the Wolftrap, menus for various local restaurants were provided (Chinese, Thai, Italian etc) but she said "I think the Moodies ate before they came in," which makes sense, given an entire city in which to choose restaurants. (I'm trying to visualize the tour bus pulling through the drive-up at Taco Bell.) At big venues in hectic cities like Los Angeles or New York, they probably have caterers that come right to the venue, where there are pleasant set-ups for band dining (the Hollywood Bowl has a nice backstage eating area), but not all venues are so equipped. Certainly the Moodies have done a lot of wineries since the year 2000, possibly for just this reason, the food service is good!

Julie Ragins did make a pithy comment about their "on the road" eating arrangements during one on-line chat, she referred to "Cracker F***ing Barrel" and I have to agree with her on this one. "I think the bus drivers get a kick back for pulling into these" she continued. Possibly this is a "dude" thing, most men like to go in, sit down and get fed a "home cooked meal." While their biscuits-n-gravy is passable breakfast food after you dump a bunch of pepper on it, Cracker Barrel gets a prize for having the most gluten in their meals, IMHO. To each his own, as they say.

For the tour buses, the caterers stocked a case of long-neck Buds, sodas, dips-n-chips, and twelve pizzas. We all know how RV road trips go; the roadies probably grab the good stuff left over backstage, and load that right into the bus too, as they move out. On sold-out nights at the Hollywood Bowl (orchestral tours of the '90s), the writers of *Backstage Pass* claim the Moodies like to have iced-down champagne and caviar waiting for them backstage after the show. So much for the ecology message. Sturgeon (whence comes the finest caviar) is a threatened species.

Human Frailties: Justin especially seems to be most susceptible to illness on tour, though all the band would say over the years they "caught the tour cold." I've seen Graeme pretty sick with colds too, on stage. A band member would show up from parts unknown (Singapore, the French Riviera) bearing "bugs" that everyone else immediately caught, as they all shared dressing rooms, elevators, and space on tour buses. Justin at times took to holding up signs "Not Talking" backstage, in attempts to save his voice, and ward off impending laryngitis. With the onset of flu season, they totally quit shaking hands even at backstage "Meet and Greet" events.

During the 1996 tour, Justin did something to one of his shoulders; the flooded dressing room in rainy Vancouver at the beginning didn't help. He showed up on stage with the whole arm wrapped, and dutifully played on, wincing occasionally. Then he did the same thing in the 2000 tour, skimming stones onto Lake Tahoe. You'd think he'd take it easy with his weight-lifting habits after that!

Graeme seems to be a person of juxtaposition. He on one hand will do really raunchy things, as per fan reports, yet I can say from first-hand experience he's fond of kids and knocks himself out to give them drumsticks after every performance. The band constantly gives things away to those in the front rows; picks, tambourines, drumsticks (not unlike other bands of course). Usually they single out kids in the front rows for this: in Las Vegas, after "Question," Graeme almost broke a leg, giving my nine-year-old son his sticks. We were all in shock. Stephan was asleep and Graeme actually had to tap him on the head to wake him up! My son was overwhelmed.

In Vegas once, Rhonda Conley and I happened to wind up on the same elevator with Graeme. The entire elevator went dead silent when he got on, toting his briefcase. Graeme kinda looked down and muttered something about "Uh! Those glow wands!!" Apparently it's pretty weird- looking from stage, probably looks like a cult movement. He kept looking down. I thought he was shy, but later I finally figured out he was looking at my ankles, and Rhonda's; we were both wearing heels and nylons! Seriously, his eyes were going back and forth. Very funny in retrospect. Whatta lecher! He had recited something really funny on stage, and in the elevator said, "I don't even remember what it was!" Rhonda gave him an awesome painting she had done of the Red Rocks concert (saying "Happy Birthday!"); and he bemusedly tucked it under his arm. I think the other folks in the lift were dumbfounded.

In 1996, something unusual happened at Caesar's Tahoe. The Moody Blues happened to play there during Thanksgiving weekend, and on Saturday they were happy to play a part in lighting the Caesar's Christmas tree. It was all very cool, the Moodies got to ride in the sleigh along with Santa Claus, and parents all brought their little kids out into the cold to see it. There were fireworks and everything.....a very neat weekend.

Things happened on tour, and in shows that never got to bootlegs, fanzines, or TV interviews. This happened in Tahoe, shortly after Moody Blues had appeared on *The Simpsons*. (That was very funny too, the cartoon Moody Blues mugged poor Homer.) Ray came out on stage in Tahoe (spring 1999), and just as he prepared to put his flute to his lips, he said in this deep precise British accent "I want fatty..." I guess sitting right in front of him had something to do with it, but I about fell out of my chair laughing, I could see the facial expressions quite well. Shrieks went up from the audience. Next he licked his lips, raised his flute and said "I didn't write it" in a rather disgusted, sharp tone, which I thought was even funnier. Apparently a lot of the bigger fans, sensitive about the subject, took offense, and wrote the fan club nasty notes. The only thing I have to say is that Ray actually had just lost a good deal of weight himself and looked pretty foxy for a man knocking 60.

Ray wasn't the only one to get laughs on stage in Tahoe: during the '90s, Justin was able to retain notable guitar technician Rene Martinez to handle his axes. For a couple of years, there was a ghost gripe that kept following Justin and his guitars, probably a bad pick-up; he finally went back to hard-wire with his red 335 and gave up on remote. Rene once came out to adjust Justin's remote pick-up (a fanny pack) and Justin actually jumped like he had been goosed, as Rene messed with it. The Moodies are so funny when they do things like that on stage, because they are usually so "straight" and keep that dry British demeanor all the time.

Did I mention all the "hanging around the stage door" stuff? *Oh myyyy*. This is the most fun part of a Moody Blues tour. All the weird behaviors and strange fans congregate there, while the parking lot is slowly emptying. Nice fans too, of course! Fans hold reunions, like old comrades, then separate again for another two years. People whimper for autographs, some hold huge stacks of old vinyls. (Sure, the band is going to stop and sign them all, aren't they?) Some claim to be doing charity auctions, if the Justin or John will just sign the photo? People block the limo door, planting themselves against it. Women are wild-eyed, and stand patiently, a bit like vampires, staring at the stage door, late at night. Did you know the band often uses vans and not limos?

David Hakan, manager of Good Works Ventures (a retail enterprise selling official Moody Blue merchandise), John and Graeme (with wives) all took off in February of 1998 for a celebrity golf cruise in the Bahamas, which was also a "Make a Wish" charity benefit (*OFC magazine*, summer 1998.) Early in the year 2001, the entire band did the same for an IBM executive cruise in the Bahamas. If I stopped to document all the benefits that Graeme and John have done golfing, I would be adding another chapter; so I won't. But it's safe to say, the two of them really love to golf, spend a good deal of their off time doing it, and get up early whilst on tour to squeeze in a few rounds.

All of us, the band, and their life-long fans, are getting older. The crowds are full of baby boomers. At Great Woods 1993, some smart alec with a plane and banner actually buzzed the (aging) crowd advertising health care plans. Our baby boomer generation was and is still a powerful group of people, and many still retain the '60s "values" in the songs of the Moody Blues.

To conclude about the Moody Blues and their touring; they are what Justin Hayward terms a "working band." Graeme puts it another way, saying everyone is a real ham, and none of them can stand to see the others go on without them! I think this says something about the dedication the Moodies do have to their profession. The term "trouper" comes to mind, in the truest theatrical sense. They are getting older, and the flesh is weaker, but they still love to play, and try to stay in shape physically.

Every tour, rumors go out amongst fans that "this is the last tour." I've been involved in the fan club since 1991, and every year, the same rumor comes out over and over again. Twenty years later, they show no sign of retiring. Sadly in spring of 2003, Ray Thomas announced he would no longer tour with the band. But I bet they will probably be wheeling Justin out on stage (like they did Eldon Shamblin in the *Tribute to Bob Wills* concert) and putting a guitar in his hands at age 90. *Vivan los Moody Blues!*

Appendix B: Blue World: the view from the House.

With regard to being a fan...........

If you can keep your head when all around you are losing theirs, you probably haven't had an accurate update of the situation -- spotted on Mike Batt's Twitter

I don't expect that you should follow me -- Justin Hayward

And if we would all do the things we know to be right, gone would be the childish fear of danger in the night. Each of us is fine, for we have all heard the word. But grouped together, Babel's triumph stampedes the thoughtless herd. -- Graeme Edge, 1999.

A fish is not aware of the water -- Tao saying

I wrote and re-wrote this chapter countless times. I'm a fan too, and it can be difficult to be objective. But the data is here and it's important and should be passed along.

We all play our pathologies out for the group --Yalom

Most Moody friends I found WERE "just folks," nice people; but as with all social groups, there's going to be a lunatic fringe. Interacting with other fans on newsgroups was like long-term group therapy, only with no experienced facilitator. (Some groups had good moderators, some did not.) It was often like the Mad Tea Party, all of us happily unbalanced and babbling (and I often felt like I got the dirty saucer.) Projection and transference ran rampant. There was weird stuff around personal boundaries, and pseudo-relationships.

I was shocked in the first few months of reading (pre-Internet) letters from other Moody fans. It seemed everyone had an "inside story" about the band they just had to tell. If what I read was true, the band had no private life, as Justin said in an interview "Whatever privacy you had just goes completely out the window." Some gossip was obvious fantasy, in fact a good friend of mine, Victoria Rivers worked through her OWN fantasies by writing a pretty good bodice-ripper romance novel based on the Moodies, and of course, changed the names. (I wonder if she ever published. I hope so, it was very entertaining, and total fiction.) But sadly some of the fans were like a malicious raccoon you might encounter, out digging through your recycles. (There actually WAS an incident in which Justin got his trash heisted.)

Robert Heinlein wrote a hilarious novel in 1961, entitled *Stranger in a Strange Land*, in it is the only comprehensible essay about "fan mail" I've ever read. If you know the novel, it's right after "the Man from Mars" is on the television. I've often thought Justin would have made a perfect Michael Valentine Smith. I hope someone sent the Moody fan club secretaries a copy, because they probably needed it. (*Where Heinlein got the info I don't know, unless it was from hanging around L. Ron Hubbard too much. The '60s were indeed a weird time to be alive.*)

The science fiction angle brings to mind another (rather sad) story I once read, in Leonard Nimoy's autobiography *I Am Not Spock*. He actually had fans come to him, hoping he could cure their terminally ill friends with his "magic touch." John Lennon mentioned the same thing in interviews. The Moody Blues are, after all, just singers in a rock n' roll band. And they do wonderful work raising money for charities too. *Music is the best medicine*, as Dr. Barriatua says, but "cure me with your music" is a little bit heavy for the average rocker.

With this in mind, I herein present twenty years worth of data I've collected in the Moody Blue fan base.

What the hell drives people to be such ardent fans of a rock n' roll band? What is "weird"? Is one indicative of the other? Are all fans weird? Are all weird people prone to hero worship? Oh, of course not! A lot of dedicated fans are very nice people indeed. One of the best "fan things" that happened that I was able to observe was "Blossomfest," organized by Ken Barnhart. He was a Moody fan who lived near Popular Creek, where the Moodies played every other year. Fans got together and sold Moody collectibles, and hand-made Moody crafts. I have several nice Moody magnets that came from here, Christmas tree ornaments, things like that. Ken is a good guy, well-liked by all in the fan club.

Weird. Now THAT can happen any place, any time! In the early Moody days, with fans "on the fringe," it was weird, male, and aggressive: by the year 2000 it would mutate into weird, female, and *passive*-aggressive. In the early days, the "weird fans" were not always harmless or funny. In an interview in *Circus*, December 1972, is the account of one nut who got backstage, and was ranting. Their then manager, Peter Jackson, walked in and saw Justin, who was pretty shy back then, being shoved across the room by this nut. Said nut was booted unceremoniously out of the backstage area. I have no idea how common this is; I've seen well over 100 shows myself, and only seen ONE person crawl on stage and get forcibly shoved off. Security is DARN uptight about who gets backstage, it's a liability thing.

There is no doubt, that sometime during their early years, the Moodies started getting people coming to them (fans), rappelling down through sky-lights naked, and asking for a blessing. Mike Pinder claimed "She Came in through the Bathroom Window" was about one of these fans, when they toured with the Beatles. Or they'd have fans whisper about a UFO that was ready to take them to *Alpha centauri*, (and would the band like to join the crew? Sixties hippies have good senses of humor if nothing else.)

And the Little Man. This is a cool one: take the album cover to *On The Threshold of a Dream*, and look in the upper right hand corner in their group picture inside. There is a little man standing there. The Moodies said they NEVER figured out who this guy was, but he started following them around, and would pop up in the weirdest places, like something out of the *Twilight Zone*. (He's been trimmed out of later issues of the album. *Too weird*.)

The band didn't know what to say or do about the "strange ones." John describes (*Legend of a Band*) some fellow who jumped off the balcony at a show; John proceeds to calmly give figures on how fast the guy was accelerating when he landed. You can just imagine engineers John and Ray backstage after the show, doing the calcs on this. We all have our coping devices.

In a 1976 radio interview, Mike Pinder summed it all up. He said that the Moody Blues band was "high energy" and of course, the band tried to put out positive energy. But when there is that much energy, it collects the *dark* energy too. The trick was to keep focused on the positive.

Case in point: after being a fan and attending a bit over 80 shows in 20 years, in summer of 2009 I had the displeasure of attending a week of the hottest outdoor Pacific Northwest shows on record. Gordon Marshall said that the fan blowing on him at Chateau Ste. Michelle (east of Seattle) was like a hair dryer. Girls were pulling hair in the front rows. One of our more negative fans proceeded to post on her blog, a large collection of reviews that said "how horrible the Moody show was in Seattle." Hey, I was there (it was an expensive ticket, too) but when I was "handed lemons, I made lemonade." I folded a fan out of my program, and still enjoyed the show. The band worked very hard that night, they were miserable too (especially with the stage lights on them, over 100*F), but the music was still wonderful. I guess those complaining were blaming the Moodies for the weather. People are like that. It really IS all about attitude.

Moody Blue fans, to look at them in the 21st century, are among the most staid and square of people. Those who have attended Grateful Dead, or even Jethro Tull concerts, will understand this. For most vintage '60s and '70s bands, we're not just talking about a few long hairs in tie-dyed t-shirts; we are talking people dancing naked in feathers and capes, in some instances. "Being weird is cool" to the baby boom generation.

Lunatics are truly fascinating, but they probably take up more space in Moody Blues articles than they deserve. (What is a "lunatic"?) The nice thing to remember is, most people who go to see the Moody Blues are mainstream, regular folks, hard-working people on holiday; and they don't give a hoot for fan doings. They are the nicest people to meet at concerts. They are the real fan base of the band.

For the most part, the Moodies and their fans have interacted positively. Graeme especially talked about the fans in *Moodymania* #3, and in *Higher and Higher* #42/43, saying they are the "greatest." Nancy Wilson took a trip to the fan club offices in Cobham and wrote up a very positive report of her visit with Ivy Stewart in *Moodymania* #10. At Moody Christmas parties, some fans even came all the way from the U.A.E. That is serious dedication, to make a trip that far to see your favorite band!

Being children of the '60s, and looking at their audience in Dockers, the Moody Blues perhaps enjoyed the off-beat in the audience at times. Weird is interesting. Sometimes the "Moody Elf" showed up, I saw him several times in the '90s, and maybe you have, too. It was in Vancouver, B.C. at Nat Bailey stadium. The rain had dropped in buckets all day. It finally cleared up just in time for the show and the sun came out. Down the front aisle came this guy with a beard, long hair, flowers in his hair, beads and bells swinging, in a genuine tartan kilt, and dancing and twirling in some sort of Highland fling. He did his thing across the front, then proceeded up the centre aisle, right in front of Justin. Up to this point Justin has kept his usual "poker face," still grumpy about his soggy dressing room, no doubt. But I swear to you, he cracked a grin like the sun coming out at this and gave a hearty chuckle. And then Justin kept right on singing NOW with a smile on his face, while the other band members stared slack-jawed in disbelief. Thank you, Moody Elf, wherever you are, you made it a wonderful show.

I did my Master's thesis in psychology on this subject (fan behavior), so I think I can talk with relative authority here. From what I can tell, people with true mental disorders seem to have no more incidence in the Moody fan base than in the normal population. But when you hang around the fan base for a while, the people with neurosis take the focus. Where it got frightening was when fans used classic projection and transference to dump their issues on the band! Some even did it on computer news groups. It caused cyber riots.

I mentioned elsewhere, the Christmas party in 1990, which was covered in *Moodymania* #4. Some did not appreciate the (slightly twisted) humor of others at their table regarding a portrait of the Blue Jays, sent by an artist fan Stateside who could not make it. Char would report this as "unlady-like behavior." I wasn't there, and could not judge, but I heard stories and I think it would be safe to say some fans over-reacted.

But I have also observed that the more some fans "brush elbows with the rock gods" in this fan club, the more aggressive and jealous they become. Some mouthy blondes who got lucky in Dallas and got backstage come to mind. After their encounter, they thought they were "special friends" of the band, and there was no living with them on line. Some fans who managed to meet the band in person, thought they were on Mt. Olympus with the gods.

The Christmas party of 1996 was even stranger by reports. Justin has this comment he's made in interviews, where he says he "feels like a gunslinger walking into the bar," and this was apparently one of those times. He took his time getting to the 1996 Christmas party, no surprise, because he was stampeded at the 1990 party. It was just as well, because once he got there, the other band members were ignored, and it turned into a massive photo shoot. Ray's date for the night (I've forgotten her name, Ray was single and dated a few fans over those years) was offered by a fan, a photo of Ray. Ray's lady friend replied, "Why do I want photos when I have the real thing any time I want?" Photos became like precious jewels to some fans.

The party got a little ugly when some European fans made snooty comments about the American fans. Americans have a rep for being cheap and pushy. (*I'm not cheap and pushy, I dunno about you, my fellow American.*) So after the reports I've had of fans at the Threshold offices, I'm not surprised Ivy Stewart stopped doing Christmas parties after the '90s. People just can't be PEOPLE. People got snitty, and then out come the cameras, like it's a trip to Disneyland. I still don't get it. Primitive tribes do say that cameras capture your soul. It can't be true, because the Moodies are very well photographed, and still seem to have a lot of soul to go around.*

In Jim Morrison's poetry, he says the camera touches the person it photographs, something metaphorical like that. Maybe the camera is the way the fan touches the star. It's worth pondering.

Moodymania 1990--Enter the fanzine, *Moodymania*. It by no means was or is a perfect group, but they were heading the right direction. They started out as a very sweet, positive grassroots fan magazine. The good news is that it empowered a lot of fans to tribalize and hang together (pre-Internet), essentially forming a women's support group. The entire fan phenomenon is a very maturing, interesting process to be a part of, and many people who have met one another through Moody Blues fan organizations have remained life-long friends. "Reaching out" is indeed what it is all about.

The bad news is that some, thus empowered, would try to correct what they perceived as "problems with the fan club." And in doing so, they sometimes created more social problems than they solved. A fan club can be a good thing, but when it became a group of and for the purpose of the *fans*, and not the *band*, it lost its original meaning. Probably the hardest part of writing this book was wading through the repetitious and subjective reviews of well-meaning fans, in fanzines, on newsgroups, and in personal letters, in order to glean valid band information embedded therein.

Moodymania started as a party at the Tropicana in Atlantic City (1990), which many fans, and the Moody Blues (a couple of them) came to! You can read about it in *Higher and Higher* #13, as well as *Moodymania* #1. It was a positive affair, and it precipitated so much mail for the organizers, Char Kemp and Nancy Dix, that they began their grassroots magazine. Through it, many woman fans were able to network, and began promoting a campaign of "letting the band have their privacy." Remember this was pre-computer news group days. Fans connected by snail mail back then!

Moodymania used to produce about three issues per year; I lost track after *Moodymania* #41. Nancy Dix got married, and eventually moved to North Carolina and started her own quasi-mystical Moody magazine *Eternity Road*; Char Kemp continued to team-build fans from her home in Florida. Both *Eternity Road* and *Moodymania* have some excellent information and are well worth collecting their back issues if you can find them. Char was one of the most instrumental and dedicated fans to spread press releases in the fan club pre-Internet; truly she is an unsung heroine in Moody fandom. There are a lot of good writers and photographers in the Moody fan base; many published in *Moodymania*.

Sadly Char was heckled a good deal by Lesser Fans, for "violating copyright." In 1993, some stinkers made an issue over this; simultaneously I was battling the same thing (with some *very* aggressive people) on the Internet Moody fan groups. They bugged Char, as she habitually copied articles of interest, and sent them around with *Moodymania*. Apparently, these stinkers didn't know *shucks from shinola* about law. Char (a police officer!) dug in and came up with a concept known as "fair use" as a provision. This is pretty well covered in *Moodymania* #12; Char does not clear a profit from *Moodymania* (never did), it was only ever intended to be a thing "between friends."

Char summed it up by saying "I'd rather be sued than not share." To date, no one has sued Char (to the best of my knowledge.) Only fools turn such a small friendly situation into a legal battle, but it happened. I always rather liked Char and her approach (a fair-minded lady), and it was sad to see so many shivs go in her over the years. Go figure where some fans are coming from; the jealousy thing again, perhaps. That green-eyed monster feeds and thrives in fan clubs.

Gifts of the Magi--Some fans, apparently doing Inner Child work, began taking toys and costumes to shows, and doing their own little show in the front rows. In many cases it upstaged the band, which was annoying to other audience members, and I know of no performer who enjoys being upstaged. Some-times it was just right, as when some smart-alec put a walking toy dinosaur on the stage. Sometimes it was weird funk; red glowing cow horns come to mind. Other times it started lovely, as when the entire front row threw flowers on the stage, but then some drunk followed the flowers with a glass of ice and hit a flinching John Lodge.

Band members make frequent eye contact with those in the front rows, which can be a bit unsettling until you get used to it. (No Fourth Wall here!) They always wink at little kids in front, and frequently give picks, tambourines, and drumsticks to kids in the front rows, much to the delight of the recipients. The band occasionally gets even LOOSER; Justin jumped into some girl's lap in the '90s (probably trying to annoy his wife of 25 years, who habitually viewed the show from the light booth.) John, seeing a late fan rushing to their seat in the front rows at another show, pointed to his watch, "tut tutting" the latecomer. I never will get over John Lodge jumping off the stage RIGHT in front of me (I was sitting on the lawn against the stage), at Britt Hill in the summer of 2009. (He's a pretty big guy, YIKE! I'm so glad he didn't trip!! I still have flashbacks of those big black boots going past me.) The band had fun too, at the shows.

> *It was all right to keep anything that came to [him] by parcel post provided that none of it was a) ever paid for b) ever acknowledged c) nor ever returned no matter how marked….. Jubal assumed conclusively that unsolicited [gifts] from strangers always represented efforts to make use of the Man from Mars, and therefore merited no thanks.* --<u>Stranger in a Strange Land</u>

Another odd thing keeps surfacing in the fan world, is that concept of "giving gifts to the band." It's nice in a way. Gift-giving is weird anyway, as anyone going through a Christmas season can attest. How much is "too much"? How much to you spend on Aunt Maudie, whom you see only twice a year? Did they send YOU a gift last year? And so forth. Gift giving is a social bonding thing and has probably been uplifted to the greatest heights by the Pacific Northwest natives, in their potlatch ceremonies. (I don't feel like belaboring the social model here, get a sociology book if this fascinates you.)

Anyway, there was a definite class of Moody fans who enjoyed giving gifts to their heroes. One story comes to mind of a lonely fan, who had inherited major amounts of money, paid scalpers top dollar for front row tickets, and followed the band around, a lot. She mailed some expensive crystal to the fan club one Christmas, for the band member she loved the most. The follow-up was, the fan club secretary never acknowledged the arrival of the expensive crystal, and the fan was livid that her valuable gift "vanished into the Black Hole." The point of this being, did the band, or even the fan club secretary, really owe this woman any feedback? It was a gift allegedly freely given, yet a response was required in the eyes of that fan.

Disappointed by a lack of social bonding with incidents like this one, a lot of fans dropped out of the fan club, when they didn't get "attention" from the band. (Like this was all that made them fans, the band was going to pay attention to them???? *Brrrr…..*) It must have been disappointing for them to not be able to make friends with the Moody Blues by sitting in the front rows for ten straight shows and sending them expensive gifts.

Possibly the silliest instance of this I've seen personally was a fan delivering a big bag of food to the ticket counter "For the band, a little taste of home," she explained it on and on, apparently it had clotted crème and scones in it, with jelly. Home-made too I bet. English cooking does have some pretty good traditional brekkie food.

Now YOU think about it. If you were an entertainer, and some fan sent you food backstage, would it be a good idea to actually eat this? Shucks, we learned THIS lesson when we were little kids doing Trick or Treat! My understanding is they leave this stuff in the Green Room and anyone who is brave enough, can eat it. Some roadies of course will eat anything. Yep food is very important to some. As I watched this fan hand off the huge bag of scone goodies, I commented "That's a very nice thing to do," just being polite. The fan gave me a dirty look, like I had intruded on her *intimate* moment. Go figure.

Take a Picture, It'll Last Longer!--There were huge piles of mail when I first got into the fan club, there they lurked in my mail box. It was overwhelming. I've put some time and distance on those days in 1991, but I can remember the first thing all those people asked for. **Pictures.** "Do you have any photos of the band you would share?" "I have over 400 photos of Justin." "Do you like pictures of Justin in the Old Days, or do you like recent pictures?" Etc. For a while I tried my best to make my new friends happy (remember this was all pre-digital camera, pre-color copier, pre-email attachments and just on the verge of the Internet age) and spent a lot of time and money sorting and filing negatives, making prints to mail out. Sorting photos can take up your whole life if you let it.

I finally wised up. So many of those first pen-pals I haven't heard from for so long; some I only heard from once, long enough for them to get my pictures. Sadly some of them are only into it for the visuals, and they aren't very friendly at all if photography isn't your thing. They arrive at fan gatherings, with huge photo albums of nothing but Moody Blues. It's how they relate socially. Poor things, maybe they don't have families of their own to make photo albums for. Another thought worth pondering.

After the PBS *Night at Red Rocks* show in March of 1993, the photography thing escalated by leaps and bounds. One really neat post surfaced on NVN (chat site) regarding a gal at a SoCal show, with a camera in the front row. The Nazi security guard began to hassle the photographer, and of all people, right before the finale, Justin walked up to the usher, saying "She's with me" of the photographer. (She wasn't with Justin at all, which made it even funnier, to Justin as well as the fans.) Justin enjoyed that; no one likes bullies, and security guards can be horrible.

And the Moody Blues would later say of photography, "Hey we look good, we don't mind!" They probably minded when flash cameras went off in their faces. I saw that happen in the front rows of Caesar's Tahoe once. The guitarists both leaned over, smiling at a gal in the front rows, and she zapped them right in the eyes. The flasher was a mature woman and should have had more sense! Justin and John blinked a few times, and bless them, played on and thankfully didn't fall blinded into the orchestra pit. *Ouch*.

Justin rescued another photographer a few years later at the Melody Tent. The guard was being more disruptive than the fan, and Justin muttered under his breath "I'm just up here trying to do a show!" After the disruption died down, fans booed the cops!

I saw a real scene myself; in Kennewick in 1999; after the guards made some poor, quiet, sweet lady in the front row empty out her film; John would spend a good deal of time that concert, rolling his eyes at security guards, guards with *guns* strapped on them. Kennewick hired the local police to provide security. The Moody Blues haven't been back to Kennewick, either.** John even shot the Peace Sign to the cops.

Then there was the incident at the end of Justin's solo show in San Diego, at 4th and B, the first concert of that tour series. I HAD a front row seat, until the end when a bunch of folks (I don't know who they were) with big bottoms and even bigger telescopic lenses crowded rudely in front of me, like a herd of cattle shoving up to the watering hole. I am not joking, it was a forest of telescopic lenses, all pointed at Justin. He banned "professional cameras" after that for all his shows, and even now at Moody Blues concerts the trend continues: personal cameras only, no flash. I was horrified watching from behind these people. Just imagine what it must have looked like for the performer, who is only up there trying to do a good gig and share his music. The *Bigbutticus telescopicus* is a curious beast, indeed.

    The whole photography and power struggle with venues is probably a psychological phenomenon worthy of more study, but frankly it gets pretty boring after about the 100th roll of film. I still find it amazing that people can go to ANY concert and treat the whole thing like a tourist attraction. They bring along flash cameras, to use in a darkened artistic, theatrical show. I don't know if it's rudeness, or foolishness. Enthusiasm and passion, perhaps. A way of life to some. Yes they are even sold in a grey market to other fans hungry for "the perfect photo."

    As technology has improved, cameras thankfully get smaller and better; but try watching any concert from the balcony. You can't believe the forest of digital lights out there, people recording and photographing.

Security is security.--the Unknown Roadie

    Stalkers--Yes it can be scary at times. There are innocent sorts of "stalking" things, like asking the roadies for John's water bottle after the show. (Ick, sorry, that weirds ME out, don't know about you. *John's lip germ culture, to highest bidder on Ebay!*) That's harmless, you have to agree. Sorta. But some female (I hesitate to use the word "lady") fans, when attending shows, babbled like sailors on liberty, especially over a song called "Deep." (I always thought it was a song about whale dreams and dolphins, myself.) THEN Justin wrote "In Your Blue Eyes" which is metaphorically erotic in places; when he played it, the front row gals would gaze raptly at him (maybe it was just me, but I found it a little creepy.) Justin has said that the adulation of women is easy to handle, but it was men walking up to him and saying how much the music means that got to him and impressed him. (Ed Sciaky, Philadelphia, Feb 23 interview)

Oh yes, the fans got a little out of hand at times. In *Moodymania* #12, there are reports of fans stalking the band on their time off and rocking their van after shows in Florida. (It's nice to be wanted!)

One of the funniest stories *Moodymania* did involved a Moody Blue signing back east (1991?) The band was MOBBED and Justin came up (off the bottom of the heap) rather heavily smeared by lipstick! After that scare, the band became a little more careful in setting a table between themselves, and the raving maenads.***

This is an excellent example of fan behavior from some of the more un-lady-like, as reported to me (Aug, 1997), at the stage door, at a venue on the east coast: *They were drunk and mad because Justin was slipping away without signing a thing! One fan acted as if it was a union meeting, telling us to "STAND YOUR GROUND" when we were asked nicely to leave. I wish the fans would understand that stardom does not give us a license for rudeness. Quite frankly, I was happy he slipped away —not personally (because I wanted to see him), but to show those fans that they don't own this man.*

I saw my own similar "stage door" encounter (one of many). The fans were lurking behind the Circle Star (south San Francisco) after the show (1992?), when a limo pulled up. We crowded around it. One woman, quite determined to get her photo signed (she repeatedly claimed it was for a cancer benefit), literally leaned against the limo door, plastered her formidable butt against the door handle (!) blocking all access unless she was spoken to. She had a funny look in her eye. She clutched her picture with a death grip, setting her jaw firmly. The limo drivers smiled.

As this was playing out, the Moodies were rapidly hopping into vans at another secret door (behind some trash cans.) This woman with her photo, finding she had been outflanked, went ballistic. She glared at me, said something rude when I asked what had happened, and off she flounced into the night, like a furious tsunami.

Imagine having to hire a second limo to decoy the fans. Sadly this sort of thing was necessary but I know the band didn't like it. In the mid-90s, the Moodies came out in Santa hats, outside Caesar's Tahoe. The Moodies were having a great time, they rode in a sleigh with Santa, they helped in lighting up the tree, were smiling at the kids. But as the fireworks went up (everyone oohed and ahhhed), I "looked where I wasn't supposed to." And being hurried out of the crowd and under the stage by security were the Moodies. Ray had one of the most pained looks I've ever seen on a man, almost paralysed disgust on his face. It got to him. But it WAS a big crowd, and you couldn't argue with it.

I wonder if fan adulation will ever become safe for celebrities. Though John, Justin and Graeme at various times have been positive toward fan adulation, Ray managed to hide a good deal during the 1990s, as did Paul Bliss. Various band members have been questioned about all the "fan adulation" over the years, and they often reply, "We'd be worried if they DIDN'T come up and ask for signatures!" Good point.

In the early '90s, Justin's daughter was an extension student at UCLA, the premier university of Southern California, a school you do NOT get into unless you have the grades to do it. She was there a year, and then did a year's worth of internship at VH1 in video production. For the two years she lived in Southern California, the house she shared with roommates was apparently the subject of cruise-bys from Moody Blues fans, especially when her dad was in town. I heard this from numerous independent sources, so I have to assume it was true. If so, those fans know who they are, and should be ashamed of themselves, as they scared these young women out of their wits. It's not funny; stalking is definitely a criminal activity in California. Having said that, I'm sure it was just excessive zeal on the part of the fans, and I doubt that any female Moody fan could be a serious threat. There is always a first time, of course.

Nights in Casinos --Parallel to the concert series in the '90s, the Moody Blues kept returning to the casinos at Caesar's for some more cabaret punishment. Some very funny stories filtered back through the grapevine over the years about the Vegas show weekends. The band rarely interacted with the fans in bars, but occasionally a Moody would escape for a drink or to visit with their own friends. For the most part, the fans respected their privacy. But some fans would wait lurking in halls for the Moodies to go to limos and vans, immune to all glares (John, Kirsten, Justin and Marie can really turn on the *stink eye* when they want) so they could waylay them for more signatures.

Really, how many signatures does a person need? They just wanted to talk to them. Without a doubt, the band members are very aware of their fans, and in their own way, interact. On their own terms.

When fans started meeting each other at the Hard Rock Cafe in Las Vegas, unbeknownst to all, Emily [Lodge] began to attend incognito, taking the time to try and figure out what the whole fan thing is all about. Her cover was blown eventually, but I did meet her once in Vegas before that, and she looked just as concerned and overwhelmed as I felt. Casino shows tended to bring out the more enthusiastic fans.

My fave casino story of all time: Rhonda Conley is a noted artist in the Moody fan club. She said she was at Vegas once, and had her sketch pad at the pool. She has a thing about feet (you'd appreciate this if you ever meet Rhonda, it's just like her.) Anyway, she was poolside minding her own business, trying to sketch Justin's feet, as there they were, laying bare on a chaise lounge. So as she started sketching, the realized that Justin was staring BACK at her. Flustered, she gave up. (This isn't that uncommon for artists to sketch people sleeping in public, I've done it myself to total strangers. Much different than stalking.) If you have sharp eyes, you'll see she eventually got The Feet onto a Christmas cover she did for the OFC newsletter. There is Justin with bare tootsies.

Justin and John (and the back-up singers), not being shy, spent a good deal of time at the casino pool working on their tans, and it got the fans all stirred up. Once some girls in Vegas got a raft, and floated on it in the pool, getting as close as they dared get to the sun-tanning Moodies, hoping to get good photographs. It wouldn't be my idea of good treatment for my camera!

Another time, a disgruntled (kinda sleezy looking) hotel manager at Caesar's Vegas, who habitually spread rumors about "band members having affairs," walked past me and a friend. And deliberately said that (about affairs) within our earshot, loudly, for our benefit. Obviously, the man needed to get a life. Another hilarious story circulated about a woman at a bar in Vegas showing everyone pictures of two little towheads and claiming them to be her children "by John and Justin." No kidding. Even creepier, other fans took her seriously.

Other incidents with fans illustrate how comedic the entire thing could turn. In 1992, I met a lot of other fans during a Moody weekend for the first time at Lake Tahoe's Caesar's Palace, and to say we partied hearty would be an understatement. Friday night after the show (there were to be two more shows the next night), I got word that some of my friends were up "waiting for the Moodies" on the top floor. So I took the elevator up, the doors swung open, and there were four of my friends sitting on a little bench by the elevator. One of them was lying on the rug, writhing trying to crack her back. I cautiously poked my head out of the elevator. "Can I bring you a sleeping bag?" I asked politely.

"Hey, John just popped out of his room, wearing a fluffy white bathrobe! He saw us and popped right back in!" The poor Moodies were essentially trapped in their rooms, unable to get to the soda or ice machine, without encountering fans. On one level, they really should have just gone to the machines, carrying a cricket bat to whack offenders. It really wasn't right of my friends, and I was shocked that John was so nice and DIDN'T call security.

I'm proud to say I didn't stay long; at various intervals during the night, I rode the elevator back up, and continued to urge them to decamp. I think it was later that same weekend on Sunday, that one of that group actually DID corner Justin at the soda machine. And (finally fed up) he called security on her. Served her right. The same fan later tried to forge backstage passes too, and really annoyed a rather hot-headed John O'Keefe, then security manager. She was bribing the maids to let her look in their rooms. A nice gal to chat with, a friend of mine, HARMLESS and a good mother; but she was also very horny, and determined to have "relations" with a Moody.****

Another humorous incident comes to mind about the same group of gals, during a Tahoe concert weekend in the early '90s. We were standing in the lobby near the elevators, one morning after a show, and most of my friends (being hung-over) were standing limply, wondering what to do next. We knew the band was leaving soon 'cause we saw the golf clubs being loaded into the limo; several fans were, of course, wanting signatures. A shout went up from one, "There he goes!" I swear to you, about five of us pelted down the hall like a pack of she-wolves, to the limos after the rapidly fleeing Justin. I was at the back of the pack; and I assure you, it was one of the most ridiculous things I've ever seen or done; you should try laughing hysterically and running at the same time! Justin had legged it to the limo by the time I got to the glass doors. All I saw was flying blonde hair, a tennis shoe (white Nikes), and a white satin jacket!

Several of my friends were being held back by a very burley, angry female security guard. I stayed well clear; for women at age 40, behaving like groupies reaches surreal levels. You could probably write a fantastic comedy if you could only video the happenings in that limo hall at Caesar's Tahoe.

I think while we were all chasing Justin, the rest of the band strolled calmly to the limos out another door.

The Moodies probably quit doing the casinos for a reason: some of the fans took it upon themselves to spread blue glitter in front of Justin's hotel door once it was found out. Poor Justin had to change rooms several times. That could get really annoying.

Another fun incident was during a weekend in 1996 when my friend Cindy and I were at Tahoe. (I swear this is a true story.) It was after the show, and time to prowl. She opened the evening with a story about a certain '60s crooner (who used to perform with the Moodies) insisting on a bowl of fresh grapes in his dressing room before performances, as part of his costuming needs. (I'm still not sure I believe that one, Cindy.) Finding the bars boring, we got a wild hair to play "Elevator Operator" and see what got on the lift with us. (Gordon did, and we leered at him, he leered back, kinda fun. We were having a hard time keeping a straight face after the fresh grapes story.)

Anyway, after we let Gordon out on the ground floor, we went back up, punching each floor button on the way. I explained to Cindy that, "Whatever floor the fans were roosting on, that would be the floor with the Moody Blues," like it was a new game. We stayed in the elevator, stopped at each floor, peeked out, spotted no one, went down and strolled past the security guards at the desk. And we overheard the guards' walky-talkies say, "Trouble with fans on the 10th floor."

Aha! We did an about-face, and went up to the 10th floor, peeking out of (but not leaving) the elevator. There, where not a minute before there had been no one, sat two good-sized female fans, who literally outweighed Graeme and Paul. I would have called security too, in terror; Graeme tells stories about almost being strangled by fans back in the Beatles days. By the time we went BACK down the elevators (cackling hysterically) we passed (going UP) what Cindy called, "The House Dick, and he didn't look happy."

He looked like a regular person to me, wearing a nice suit. Cindy has a talent for these things.

We did another walk-through the casino, saw no one we knew, and about a half-hour later, decided we would go back to the room for wine coolers (we brought our own stuff). Who should get on the elevator with us, but those two stalkers! This time, they were prepared to settle in, and were bearing foot-longs from Subway (about twice what I could gag down, especially approaching midnight as it was.) They punched the button for the 10th floor. "Oh, you ladies have rooms on the 10th floor?" I said with a straight face. They nodded vigorously, smiling greasily. When they got off, Cindy again went into hysterics (imagine two women in evening dress, falling around in the elevator shrieking), and I grimly punched the button for the lobby. This was the safety of the band we're talking about. I'm ashamed to say we narked on them to the House Dick who was standing at the bottom, and he went back up there, a bit angry. We distanced ourselves from the elevators after that.

Thankfully, that was the last we saw of the "ladies" (they out-weighed us too, and we were scared!) But it does point out that some fans really have no class when it comes to allowing the band a little bit of privacy in their off time. And some fans are pretty damn persistent and aggressive.

I think it was later that same night that we overheard security laughing at a particularly good story. A well-dressed woman had arrived at the security desk at Caesar's Tahoe, saying she was the wife of a band member, had forgotten her key, and wanted to call her husband to let her in. Security called the room and the real wife answered the phone!

Cindy and I were very cruel that weekend. There was a Brit gal (flew in just to see the band) roaming the halls of Caesar's, who claimed to have been "John's caddy." I personally saw her waylay Justin on his way to the gym; Justin gave her a decided brush and cold shoulder. I was very impressed. Anyway, every time Cindy and I saw this gal, we took to yelling "foooOOOOREE!!" with visions of the

19th hole dancing through our heads. It was a lot of "wicked gal friend" fun.

The Internet Thang--As of Mar 23, 1992, Bias Boshell was still on Prodigy and posted from Caesar's Vegas, as a member of the first Moody Blues newsgroup online. He got off publicly after that, as people started putting some rather personal stuff about him online.

After that, it was a long time before a Moody Blue would interact openly on any of the newsgroups, but we finally coaxed some into chat rooms. John did it a lot, and his chats turned out rather nice. When Justin got on chat, it was predictably riot conditions. In fact, Justin said he has logged on under a fake name, and immediately got flamed!

They do cyber-interviews, but most don't participate openly in the numerous cyber-newsgroups. It's a jungle out there, a shark tank. On Prodigy when I started getting flamed (my humor wasn't appreciated by the more "sensitive"), I was emailed privately by many sympathetic people saying, "These people weren't on here a month ago." Online interaction has come a long way since then, but there are still some imperfections on Moody news-and-chat sites. Many fans have gone away because of this, and most Moody on-line fan action is currently on Facebook.

The Ann Arbor News would review the Moody Blues June 12, 1992 and quote the Moodies thus: "The whole yuppie instant gratification period had come to an abrupt end and we wanted to reflect that." Spoke too soon, no it didn't, it was just the beginning. "Instant gratification" needs were going to leap "higher and higher" with the oncoming juggernaut called the Internet. The Internet community was just beginning to sprout when I got online in January of 1993, with the first major Moody Blues online group on Prodigy. It quickly became apparent that there were a lot of people sitting at home, chatting in cyberspace, who thought it was ok to be rude to others if one didn't have to see them face-to-face. Passive-aggressive fans took jokes the wrong way.

The Moody Blues fan base would explode on-line with the March 1993 PBS showing of *A Night At Red Rocks*, and on-line chaos from computer savvy fans was the result. Things mellowed out after a decade, but there are still people online who are lonely, who don't have anything better to do except natter, people who do weird or rude things (or imagine situations that don't exist); people drunk and saying things they would not say face-to-face. There are also deliberate troublemakers online too, who think "evil is cute." And there are still normal people, serious fans, trying to sort out real information.

Above all there are some really nice Moody fans out there to meet and talk with. It's not just the Moody Blues, it's every fan phenomenon, all across the Internet. It was and is also an excellent opportunity for social scientists to research, which many have. The Moodies have a HUGE fan base on and off line. Log onto any Internet search engine, and you'll find the Moody Blues have a healthy showing for websites; indeed they seem to be more organized than other rock fan bases.

Moody fans have lots to say, that's for sure! The nice thing is that sometimes you can meet and socialize with people you have made friends with through discussing the Moody Blues online. The bad thing is that sometimes you meet those you have run across discussing the Moody Blues online. I have been yelled at in elevators (at Caesar's on Moody weekends) by pushy Internet Moody fans, been grabbed too; I still don't know who the creepy gal was that grabbed me in Kennewick, but it scared the hell out of me (I almost belted her.) I've had notebooks stolen by Moody fans I barely have encountered online, but who think they have the right to violate my boundaries. Being flamed for no good reason has become a norm. I've resorted to fake names and wearing disguises when the paranoia got to me. I'm just another fan. I can't imagine what trouble these people might cause for the actual band members and technical crew.

The band has more or less moved into the 21st century on line. Most have chat sites, Twitters, Facebooks. They all have their own websites: *mikepinder.com, johnlodge.com, raythomas.me, graemeedge.com* and *justinhayward.com.* Some "band" Facebooks are fake-out fan sites, beware.

The good news is cyber Moody fans continue to be critical of news sources, which is as it should be in any journalism. For better or worse, the Internet is journalism, at the growth rate of a cancerous cell. It lends a whole new level to "freedom of the press." ANYONE with an agenda can publish. The old saw, "Do you believe everything that is in print?" comes up over and over again.

Just about anyone can and does post reviews of the shows they have seen, and every review is avidly tracked by Moody fans, every tour. Most fans are Moody Blues fans, because they like their music. But intermixed into this group, one must assume there are "fans" who are drawn to those other human cravings: money, sex and (social) power. Now, of course, all of us like money. It buys nice things. But I think perhaps the ugliest comment ever heard uttered by a fan, casually overheard in the halls of Caesar's Tahoe would be (and I quote): "They should come out and give us some signatures before they leave and talk to us. They are paid well enough for it!" *Fans like that I can do without.*

I'm afraid to get too far into the social power thing (enough data for another book) but of serious note; there was one (married) dude who anointed himself the "point man" for the fan club. He apparently was using his social suaveness to contact various promoters and side-men and get inside information. He then used his social power to hit on lonely chicks in the fan club. He tried it on ME; and as he resembled the hero of Sir Betjamin's "Slough," I almost hurled. Some of his targets were adult but physically vulnerable; this is downright *predatory.* Watching people suck-up to the guy on cyber newsgroups (thinking he was a source of backstage info) was gross and surreal. Thank God he was a very rare critter in our fan base. And further, I had a roadie tell me this guy was kicked out of backstage, just like any other intrusive fan. Yes indeed, the band knew who the fans were, and kept their eye on them. *Security is security.*

When the winds of change blow, some people build walls, and others build windmills -- Chinese proverb

The Master's Thesis--Did I say I got into the Moody Blues fan base the very same month I got into my master's program in psychology? It's not important now, but it seemed so at the time. Things were changing in my life (which has nothing to do with this book), but I did do a master's thesis on the fan club and the fans. FYI, I'll put in the following information to illuminate the fan phenomenon, and also to help anyone struggling with this "fan addiction." I'm here to cure the negative energy, if I can, with the light of information.

One day, in the years before the Internet, there arrived in my mail a paper entitled "The Existential Angst of Justin Hayward." In fairness, I later heard that the author of this paper (also in counseling school) was mortified that the paper was "on the loose" in the fan club. Someone actually sent it to Ivy Stewart, the fan club secretary. Not me!!! It was not intended for publication! I'd agree: it was not very clinical I'm afraid. The author cherry-picked the songs that fit the "personality profile" she had dreamed up for Justin in a fit of counter-transference (which all counselors suffer from occasionally) and tried to analyse him. Yike how invasive!!

I guess you could call it the "Justin myth." It conveniently left out songs like "Top Rank Suite" which (in my humble opinion) is pretty sarcastic and not "full of angst" at all. Like other fans, she was working out fantasies that Justin is some drippy, sad, emotional wreck. And of course, he isn't; he comes over as a well-adjusted, intelligent guy after you've met him, or have been around the club for a while. He has a great sense of humor too, they ALL do. You can't tour and survive in the music world like Justin has, and be an emotional wreck at the same time. Not possible. I think most of this mythology is a "projection and transference thing" from the fans. Yes, songs often get written in an angsty moment I'm sure, but in the morning, things look better; and you have a pretty song in your hands, born in the pain of late night maunderings. Don't we all maunder once in a while? It's the poet's job to maunder!!! And it's the stage performer's job to look beautiful on stage.

My findings (and I'm being as objective as I can here): When I wrote my thesis, I came up with an interesting model for female latency in the fan base. [*Latency* as a concern has been rendered moot as per any APA standards after the DSM-IV, in case such things still concern you.] Beyond latency, I think, pure and simple, there are deeper issues of intimacy in women (and a few men) who "fall in love with a perfect man at a distance." Which perfectly describes the more heavy-duty of any celebrity fan base. I also established (with limited data, but certainly more than thirty samples) that the Moody fan base is a normal population, skewed a bit toward the social sciences professionally. And of course, Moody fans are primarily a female group.

More intense fans (1-2% perhaps?) show clinical signs of schizophrenia, sub-type erotomania (as per DSM-IV) in that some fans feel the need to "protect" Justin. (See above about the perceived "angst.") And not just Justin, John's #1 fan also got pretty vocal in her "defense" of John. (I avoided her, it got repetitious, thankfully she was otherwise harmless.) This is pretty common with fan phenomenon.

There was a smattering of OCD and bulimia, some "grandiose" types. (See earlier comments, "social power" and "hob-knobbing with the rock gods.") The good news about erotomania (if you can call it that, see the DSM-III to get my meaning) is as far as I could tell, all of these were women.

My views aren't real welcome by that small 1-2% of those in dire need of meds. I hide at concerts, and smile a lot, I'm never sure how they will react when they meet me.

Many fans and their families understand there is some dysfunction around the fan thing. I asked a husband of a Moody friend (who was madly in love with the lead singer) once how he felt about his wife going to "all these concerts." Said husband told me she could be "running the streets" and considered it all a harmless fantasy, a "girl's night out."

Another very beautiful fan (whom I liked, but she was just using me for information) told me "I want to have an affair with [her favorite Moody] and then go back to my husband." I know there were death threats aimed at the lead singer (from jealous husbands) and at the lead's wife (from jealous fans!) so there is indeed a dark side to any fan phenomenon. Thankfully these things were rarely obvious at the shows.

I Spy--So last but not least I'll record for posterity the Great Moody Spy Tale. It started in 1994, when, living in Hayward, California, and being on the mailing list for pen-pals in the Moody Blues fan club magazine; I suddenly found myself overwhelmed with letters. Everyone apparently wanted my postmark. I was contacted by a person, a Mrs. G, who said she "knew the Moody Blues" personally, as friends! Yeah right, and I'm the Queen of England. I enlisted the help of a very good friend in Portland, my first pen pal, Carol Hubbard. I bundled up a bunch of letters (including Mrs. G), asked her if she would be so kind as to write some of these guys. And bless her heart, she did.

After about a year of corresponding with other Moody fans, I started my own "underground" fanzine (for the same reason Char Kemp and Nancy Wilson-Dix did, to keep up with all the letters!) That turned out to be a nightmare I'd rather forget; chalk it up to unexpected "mission creep." But, eventually Carol convinced me that Mrs. G was "legit," as was her close friend Mrs. D. These two gals used PO boxes in Sacramento, and Mrs. D's husband, Mr. D, was alleged to be the son of a music promoter. A fourth friend, Ms. H eventually joined the group (alleged to be another concert promoter on the west coast), and she even used to post on Moody Blues websites.

I corresponded with these people (or possibly one multiple personality) for around five years. I'm ashamed to say that I ever believed any of them, and there have been times that they really had me stirred up far too much over Moody rumors. Some of their stupid tales I actually reprinted in my underground "fanzine," but I assure you, what reached print was small potatoes compared to the REST of the wild information they fed me.

One of them claimed to have daughters who were roommates with one of the band member's daughters. Mrs. G claimed to be the spouse of a musician who was originally part of the Brum Beat thing. Another was allegedly a real estate agent, and apparently able to access records pertaining to Mike Pinder. One claimed to have played golf with Graeme. One claimed to be the former fan club secretary for Creedence Clearwater Revival. Another allegedly rented to Justin's daughter while she was living in Los Angeles. One claimed to have affiliation with Coombe Hill Country Club, where most of the Moodies were members, along with their spouses, and of course, where rumors off the golf course flew thick and fast.

Is it just me, or does all this sound just a little fishy? While some "inside scoop" was silly and mundane (*Justin likes to eat weird things.* Does a rumor like this mean he eats his green beans with blue cheese dip? Nori-flavored ice cream? Beer milkshakes? Or *What*???) some was not. The rumors that came from these people concerning ALL the Moody Blues reached the proportion of large glowing mushroom clouds in their toxic content, and surreal aspects. Some of the information turned out to be legitimate, just enough to make it interesting, but for the most part, even if the rumors *had* started out as real, some were so twisted in perspective, that it amounted to character assassination. Especially targeted by these guys were John and Justin, as well as their families. (They got in a few zingers on Ivy Stewart, the fan club secretary as well.)

In researching for publication, it has been VERY difficult to sort out reality from fantasy, with some of the borderline truths these guys passed to me. I still don't know what these peoples' real names are, or if they really WERE "friends of the Moody Blues" as they claimed. My attitude became after a while, *with friends like that, who needs enemies???* I tried to pump them for information for a while, but they eventually dried up as they ran out of lies to tell. They were so crude, that even after writing each other for five years as more-or-less friends, they would not meet me for a drink at Tahoe on Moody weekends, lending even further suspicion to their true motives.

As with ALL documents regarding ANY subject, a serious researcher must always be alert for yellow dog journalism, bogus stories and just plain old false information. Take my word for it, it's rampant in ANY fan club. These same "spies" operated for over ten years that I know of, in the Moody Blues fan club. They have interacted with several fans as pen pals, especially if they are high profile. I have my suspicions that these "spies" are promoters of some kind, but there is no way to tell. They seemed very well organized. Spreading rumors about a band is an old promotional trick, it worked for the Stonies. Promoters are REAL WEIRD. I met some baseball promoters at a wedding once and found them very unsettling. Like Graeme said in one interview, *it's a dirty dirty business.*

Even after the character attacks that these people spread (one rumor was a doozie, supposedly Justin was driving down a road in Tahoe, on a cell phone, looking for his long lost-love who allegedly lived on a golf resort in North Shore Tahoe. *Sure.*); even after the peeps into their private lives that any fan eventually gets after hanging around a fan club long enough; the Moody Blues are all still very likable people. I hope that any reader who wonders about what the Moody Blues are in real life will understand that they are very humanistic people; and for the most part are true gentlemen. (Well I take that back about Graeme, and that is all just a matter of personal taste on the part of the ladies he asked to perform the naughty act; and besides he was drunk at the time. And Graeme has a very warped sense of humor, too.)

My Conclusion?-- The Moody Blues are ALL very intelligent men. Even Graeme, whose exploits and occasional raunchy behavior are legendary, even the drummer is capable of thoughtful reflection, good humor, and intelligent conversation. They are polite until pushed by pushy fans. I have NEVER had a bad encounter with any of the band members (weird, but not bad), and I have been a serious fan since 1991. They most certainly get MY vote as "good guys," or I wouldn't have bothered to write this book.

And for the most part, fans are nice, too. These are only the worst-case scenarios, "pick of the litter" vignettes if you will. Mostly, you go to see Moody Blues' shows, and absolutely nothing strange happens. It's all nice, good happy entertainment and everyone goes home singing under the stars. The fans with real intense behavior tend to fade away after a few years. It's just that even nice people CAN turn into a mob, and mob action can be swayed by a few stinkers. When you join a fan club, be sure you have good manners, and be sure you aren't one of the stinkers! Or stalkers. Don't "bite the bait" when the High Mach types go trolling.

I'll bet it's the same in Paul McCartney's fan club. Or in any other fan club you could mention. Ray Thomas really unloaded about "weird fans" in an article in *Classic Rock*, June 2013. The stories even shook ME up, so if you think the stories you just read HERE are weird, go get the article and read it. It has very good information about the core seven years.

While putting together this chapter, I was struck by nostalgia; how much I miss my Moody friends I haven't heard from in years. Most Moody fans are all wonderful, normal, everyday people who love the music of the Moody Blues, just as you and I do. Moody fans ARE the greatest.

*This sort of history is probably why on the 2013 cruise, the VIP party was more a controlled "pep talk" with security guards; rather than a true "meet and greet," where the band mingled with the fans at a cocktail party. Moody fans are very enthusiastic, and the band has had bad experiences, sadly. I was at the VIP party in 2013, it was a visceral experience and very frightening, unto chaotic.

**Someone told me that, after the Kennewick show, the Moodies were almost mobbed, and of course by then, security was nowhere to be found, and of absolutely no use. What turkeys, the fuzz showed up all bad ass, packin' heat for the free show, and then were no use when really needed!

***If you have a flair for movie history, you can flash here on a movie called *What A Way to Go*, in which Gene Kelly is stampeded by ravenous fans. It's one of the funniest views of "fans" ever put on screen, especially the look on Kelly's face right before he is trampled.

****I'm embarrassed to say I let this friend talk me into stalking Justin at the gym once (early '90s), and we actually found him! Who would have thought that gym would be where Justin actually went to get away from the casino and work out a little? The details make me squirm to remember, and I've never done such a rude thing again, it was just plain geeky. But on the way home to Lodi, my friend whispered, "We should have gotten his towel." I almost wrecked the car. THAT is what it's like to be a fan!

Appendix C: Who Are You Now???

Have you had a good life? Is it enough to make a movie of? —James Morrison

Sometimes it's very much like taking a journey. Sometimes the journey seems to be too heavy. But you have rays of sunshine that hit you as you go along. And suddenly you realize all the problems you've encountered along the way were only clouds. But the sunshine keeps popping through. Then you follow your dreams -- John Lodge, interview *Moodymania* #9

The threads of so many lives have intersected those of the Moody Blues. It's been impossible to weave them all into the warp and weft of this story, so all I can do is add the information on at the end. Last but not least, here are a few final tidbits I couldn't fit in!

Tony Clarke:
Tony was born Aug 21, 1941. He had his own recording studio on board his yacht, *The Tao Princess*. His crew was his wife Helen, and her daughters. He worked with Rick Wakeman on occasion. He was producing the Dave Terry Band in 1995. He worked with Russian recording artist Tania Black in the fall of 1996. In spring of 1998, he and Mike Pinder were reported to be working together on a project. In 2005, Tony was merrily answering questions on *www.mikepinder.com;* his thread-forum was up for a long time, a nice guy and he was full of history. As of March 2007, he was collaborating with Mike Pinder again, in 2008 he was working on another album "with stuff he set aside,"

Tony was continually working on something. In chat (Sept 23, 2007) Tony came forth with a lot of interesting biographical things. He was networked to the Hubble telescope, he was working on a multi-media production called ARC (has to do with Pioneer I and the message put on it, traveling to the cosmos). He was involved with bands with the names Spock's Beard, and Porcupine

Tree. He worked with Rick Wakeman after parting from the Moodies.

Interesting note: Tony claimed he was given a tour (when they still were based in England) of a science museum in London by Arthur C. Clarke himself! If you were alive in the '60s, you know what a big deal this was! A.C. Clarke was super popular. Wow what an honor! Tony Clarke passed away Jan 4, 2010. Those wishing more information should use the power of Google or contact Mike and Tara Pinder. They were very close.

Graeme Edge:

Robin Lumley of Loud, Confident and Rung (Wrong?): last word was from his hilarious portrayal of the Edge household first thing in the morning, as seen from his bed on the living room couch. (OFC newsletter, summer 1995). In Robin's writing, Graeme's long-time companion and wife is referred to as "Commander Amander." Robin characterizes Graeme as a WWII war movie freak (especially aviation movies) and into "Hun Bashing." Graeme is also a *Star Trek* fanatic, so if you want to visualize him laughing his butt off at scenes of Dr. Bashir and CPO O'Brien fresh from the holodeck in flight jackets, please do. Loud, Confident and Rung (Wrong?) was a side band Graeme put together, which also included Gary Brooker of Procol Harum.

Son Matthew Edge (nicknamed "Medge") has his degree in physics. Various fans have chatted with Graeme in bars over the years, and report that Graeme's view toward physics is a "step into the Twilight Zone." Graeme in general likes sci-fi and mystical things; I had a friend threaten to beat me up if I revealed Graeme's gypsy fortune-telling habits.

Graeme refers to himself as a "mongrel intellectual." *Doomsday Clock (Domesday Clock*???) is another album that Graeme allegedly has played on. [side note, the *Domesday Book* is a survey of England done in 1086: the Doomsday Clock allegedly tells us all how close we are to the end of the world.] I have yet to track this down, but would like to, as *Kick off Your Muddy Boots* is VERY good, and I'd like to hear more solo stuff by Graeme and his friends. This is a tidbit from *Higher and Higher* #24; there are notes about Graeme sitting in for an injured drummer with Fairfield Parlour: Ray did the flute part, and Elton John did high vocals for "Just Another Day." I could not nail down the date on this, but it sure sounded interesting!

Graeme lives in a Spanish villa that was built in Florida in 1922. In 2002 Graeme lent his money and backing to a project in Bradenton, Florida to convert a run-down section of the town to an arts center, with landscaped lakes and shops. I think Graeme later sued the developer, but it hasn't been high on the radar; hope it all came out ok. Interesting to note, Graeme has spoken of seeing music as "hills and valleys" [fascinating] and has referred to written music scores as "tadpoles on wash lines."

Graeme can vanish quickly. Don't Blink! -- Moodymania #23

Graeme is alleged to have written a poem "Cocoanut Christmas," which they were thinking of putting on the *December* album, but he said it was "too depressing." I sure hope someday Graeme rounds up all his unpublished poetry and publishes it. I bet he has lots of poems that never made it on an album. Now Graeme and Gordon are both doing books, chock-full of stories about touring.

As of early 2007, Graeme split up with Amanda, which is very sad. I rode the elevators with Amanda once in Tahoe, and she seemed like a very neat, funny person. In one early interview, Graeme claimed, "The only reason I wear clothing is that I would be arrested if I didn't." (!) Summer of 2009, both of Graeme's solo albums are destined to be released under the Esoteric Records label. Graeme has the ultimate claim to fame in the band. He can safely say, with total certainty, that he has made EVERY Moody Blues performance since they first were formed in 1964.

Justin Hayward

Hugh Fielder (in an interview): *Would you ever have sold your soul to the devil if the terms were right?*
Justin: *How do you know I haven't?*

I found the best description of Justin yet from his band-mate (and former roommate) Graeme (Columbia, Maryland, 6 July 1981, during the Moody Blues' *Long Distance Voyager* tour): *... you mustn't look upon Justin really as a lead guitarist. He's a songwriter and a six-string guitarist, and he plays lead guitar, but he just hasn't got that biting edge of ego that an improvisational guitarist needs; he's too gentle. That guitar is a beautiful woman to him; it's not a dirty whore. He caresses it; he don't screw it. That's his attitude, and so he feels happy and comfortable working out the lovely melodic lines he does—and it seems to work.*

Like many great performers who use their hands to earn their living, Justin used to wear certain rings, and this is (was) an avidly tracked detail for many Moody Blues fans. Ring details are in *Higher and Higher* #19, pg 19. In the late the '90s one of his rings disappeared (the pinkie ring) with no explanations. (Were they really needed?) The signet ring was reported as "rather cheap up close" by a friend of mine who asked Justin about it in an elevator. (Just reporting what I heard, I wouldn't have the courage to ask!) Justin says he got it in France when young and "wears it for sentiment," and that it actually throws off playing style when absent, due to weight. Last I looked, the signet ring had vanished too. I also think Justin's fret speed has picked up since the rings disappeared. (I've seen a lot of live shows over the past two decades.)

Justin says he likes sci-fi novels but is usually seen reading mystery and thriller novels when the band is at Las Vegas. One writer Justin has mentioned enjoying is Nigel Barley; quite a good author, go look him up at the library! He is also friends with writer-researcher Dr. Mark Plotkin. Justin reads a LOT, in fact ALL the Moodies seem to be readers.

Justin belongs to an organization called SODS (Society of Distinguished Songwriters.) I can't even begin to sort out the awards and honors that the Moodies have all received over the years, but they have been plentiful. I clipped this just since 2000 online somewhere: *ASCAP held its annual PRS Awards in October at London's Grosvenor House Hotel Ballroom. A highlight of the event was the presentation of the ASCAP Golden Note Award to Justin Hayward, the longtime guitarist, singer and songwriter of the Moody Blues.* I would encourage those interested in Moody honors to consult their favorite search engine on the Internet: John has some ASCAPs as well. John and Justin list their awards on their websites.

Justin mentioned in an interview, calling up Lonnie Donegan over some benefit using "Nights in White Satin" in just the last few years before Donegan's death, so apparently they were still on speaking terms. Donegan passed away while I was writing this book. The copyrights to all songs Justin wrote prior to 1974 belong to Donegan's estate. I presume this excludes anything written prior to Justin's contract with Donegan. Donegan's partner David Platts inherited Tyler Music after Donegan passed away.

Justin seems to have tons of friends, and contributes to various productions, books etc. I have a note about him contributing to *Bittersweet: The Clifford T. Ward Story* (possibly only in the first printing, left out of later editions) and he also did a forward to Vic Flick's biography *Guitar Man.*

Justin's daughter, Doremi, after getting her degree in American studies and doing an Internship on VH1, was working as a TV announcer for a while. She lives in the U.K. with her family (Justin and his wife Marie live in the Monaco area.) Doremi got married in 2005, and the happy couple left the wedding riding on a haywain (a country wedding, I'm sure it was clean straw!) Doremi was at one time working as a manager for a fabric company in the U.K. (Remember, her Grandma was a home economics teacher, so I suspect Doremi is handy with a needle.) Doremi now has her own practice in physical therapy. Justin became a grandfather in early 2008 when she had her son Cassius.

    Many rumors surround Marie Hayward (Justin's wife); she is alleged be French, and to have grown up in the Liverpool area, was part of that music scene. She was alleged to have dated a musician by the name of Leapy Lee prior to dating and marrying Justin. She probably met and dated a few rockers at the Bag o' Nails, due to working there as a hat check girl. I wouldn't normally mention this (I can find no documentation, just hearsay), but the name Leapy Lee really struck me as worth a giggle, and a Google (an interesting musician.) Marie also dated George Harrison (ref: *Magical Mystery Tours* by Tony Bramwell) no surprise, the Bag o' Nails was a Beatles hang out. Marie and Carol (Edge) were like all the other young people in the London rock movement, trying to make a life for themselves; and like all young people of the '60s, partying hearty. The Bag o' Nails in Soho was apparently the place to be doing it in 1967.

    "Hay" means "fence" in an old Celtic language; (Hay Ward means "fence keeper," not "guardian of the grass"!)

    Justin is alleged to have collected model trains at one time. He also likes to walk (especially under starlit skies) and mentions this as a stress reliever and source of inspiration. He is documented as being a walking stick collector. One of his favorite books he has mentioned in various biographies is *The Songlines* by Bruce Chatwin. It's a VERY cool book, about Australia and the Aborigines, and "walking the songlines." Justin claims to have a bit of an archaeologist bug under his saddle.

    Justin wears (or used to wear) Tiffany "Declaration" as aftershave, he uses a Mac-based PC for musical and computer needs. (Many musicians do use Mac platforms.) He drives a Smart Car around the narrow roads of Monaco and drives an older Mercedes for long trips. Interesting side note: Justin claims he was able to sneak into Shepperton Studios during the '60s and check out the stage set to *Dr. Strangelove*. Without a doubt the funniest movie of the Cold

War era, Justin claims it is his favorite Kubrick movie, though it is overshadowed by the more spacey *2001: A Space Odyssey*, in the minds of many Moodies fans.

Justin's home town of Swindon is a sort of crossroads suburb community in the west country. It was also home to Gilbert and Sullivan, Desmond Morris (wrote *The Naked Ape*), and is the final resting place of Nicky James.

Denny Laine:

Denny of course, joined Wings (Paul McCartney); considerable history followed McCartney and Laine both through this time period, which falls outside the scope of this book. Denny said he must have played on the soundtrack to *The Magic Christian*, but wasn't even certain of this in his *Higher and Higher* interview. He co-wrote many songs with McCartney. When Paul McCartney got busted for weed coming into Japan, and they lost their tour there, Denny bailed out of Wings, too. Sir Paul wasn't pleased about that, but in Denny's words, "It was time." Denny has shifted around a lot but seems to think it was "the right thing to do at the time," and seems to bear no ill will to anyone. Denny has his own nightclub, he picks up odd gigs here and there, and tours. More can be read about him in his interview with *Higher and Higher*, as well as on his websites. Use the power of Google for current tour information.

Denny and Tony Visconti worked for Denny Cordell (soon after Laine left the Moodies, and Tony had arrived from Brooklyn.) For a time Laine had a group called The Electric String Band. Cordell was the producer for *The Magnificent Moodies*, their first album. Sometime after Denny Laine left the Moodies, he joined with Trevor Burton (from The Move) and formed a band called Balls. In December 1969 his drummer was Alan White, who eventually went on to be in the band Yes. Denny is alleged to live in Las Vegas now, according to Tony Clarke. There are (were) pictures of Tony's boat on Denny's website. People in Moody fan groups online post about Denny occasionally, so he stays active, tours quite a bit. In 2008 he played in Bahrain,

U.A.E. Denny has more than one website. I like the music he has had up here and there, quite good stuff. An excellent composer.

Dr. Tim Leary:
The definitive biography of Dr. Timothy Leary is out, written by Robert Greenfield, and published by Harcourt. I haven't had a chance to read it, but if "the Sixties" turn you on, go for it. There are several mentions of Leary in *The Electric Kool-Aid Acid Test* as well. The American '60s won't make sense until you understand the social movement around Leary and the Viet Nam War. Dr. Leary passed away on Memorial Day, and after having being decapitated on film (his head was cryogenically frozen, and possibly was the inspiration for an early episode of *Futurama*), he was cremated and his ashes were sent into outer space. *Bon Voyage*, Herr Doktar!

Leary loved the concept of quantum mechanics, and the Uncertainty Principle, "creating your own realities." Be ready for a trip to the twilight zone, if you read his books.* The latest news is that Leonardo DiCaprio is cast to play Leary in a movie biography of his life. *What a long strange trip it's been.*

John Lodge:
Higher and Higher #11/12 "The Story in His Eyes" is an extremely well written John biography, having to do with the thought and philosophy behind John's approach to music and life. And it's footnoted!

John's original stage name of "Johnny C. Storme" was possibly a "steal" from Marvel Comics, as research has shown the *Fantastic Four* debuted in November, 1961. Hopefully Stan Lee forgives John.

John seems to be one of those guys who loves risk-taking sports, he snow skis and also water skis. There is a story on the Brooklands interview that is unbelievable, about landing in a sand castle through a bad motorboat move! He's the one who broke an arm during the recording of

Octave, so he's a real active guy! John and his wife Kirsten have lived in Spain for years. I don't know when he moved there, or if he's still there; in later interviews he refers to his wife Kirsten and he, as "gypsies" moving all over the world to various homes and locales.

He likes his Burgundy and Spanish wines (*hear hear*!!!); he has been referred to as a *chevalier du vin*. This is an avid wine collector and connoisseur; he's actually a Knight of Burgundy! (Brooklands interview, April 27, 2009.) You have to think in terms of Hemmingway, Picasso and Spanish caravans to get a grip on where John is coming from. John has been trying his hand at MAKING wine, and blending it, no easy task!! His wife is very tolerant if this is going on in her kitchen. John has also picked up a paint brush and tried his hand at some very acceptable portraiture, which has been auctioned for charity. John had a winter home in Barbados but I think he has moved to Florida in later years, and he often gets involved in charity golf events there, playing golf with other celebrities, such as Alice Cooper. John has had a hand in in funding the Sunshine Center for early childhood development, at the Barbados Sunshine Village; he is involved in autism charity, which I find really awesome. Many of his charity events were written up extensively in *Moodymania* #11.

Did I say that John claims to have written songs for both Elvis and for Gene Vincent? But said artists sadly never got a chance to record them.

Emily Lodge has been working as an accountant, and handles Krisemma wines, which is the family wine business. (Quite a way to come for someone who started out as a lullaby on her daddy's guitar!) Along with her brother Kristian (who shows some talent as a video producer and studied at UCLA's cinematography school) they did a backstage video entitled *All Areas Access*, associated with the Royal Albert Hall orchestral show, May 1, 2000.

John is alleged to be on the special edition of Wayne's *The War of the Worlds*, doing "Thunderchild."

According to documents on *The War of the Worlds* website, John was supposed to be the original performer of this song.

According to Graeme (A. Thor interview, 2/3/2004) John has delved into the "Antediluvian World" (like Donovan) and has an interest in Egyptology and Atlantis myths. In 2009, John was reading a book called *1421*, about the Chinese "discovering" America (a VERY good book, I recommend it too!!!) He's also read *Pilgrim's Progress*, so his reading tastes are rather impressive.

John is also a "Brother Rat," a benevolent fraternal order in the U.K. I would urge those interested to read John's website, he has lots of nice stuff on it. I'm pretty sure his son Kristian runs all of John's on-line feeds, and those are all great sources of information.

The Pinders:

Over the years of research, I contacted Tara Pinder several times. (She won't remember it as I've used many names.) I can safely say, she is a LOVELY person; Mike showed great intelligence and wisdom in hanging onto her all these years!

Ray Thomas:

Ray's original flute (from the early hippy days) has been mentioned as being a (black?) Conrad Mullenheimer "he got in Frankfurt." Ray has also been sited throwing defective flutes over his shoulder when they don't work on stage, so he may not be fussy about which flute he uses, of late. Apparently, the magic black flute was broken when Ray dropped through a black hole on stage. He also broke some toes in the incident. Ray claimed that "Sheila" (the black flute) was repaired, and the current owner is Emily Lodge!!!!

A 1972 Official Fan Club newsletter notes Ray is "having a showing of *Seven Brides for Seven Brothers* in his loft," so that will give you some idea of Ray's inner workings. Ray was a gardening freak as of 1971, and presumably still is. He has been sighted in herbal shops in the U.K. getting fresh spices for his cooking. One Christmas, he was spotted online (2011?) sending around his homemade orange marmalade (with his cute little dragon logo) to various friends.

Ray used a "C" flute, an alto flute, and a bass flute, depending on the song. "Driftwood" takes a very low, big bass flute, while "Never Comes the Day" takes a harmonica. In 2005, the new flautist Norda Mullen, picked up a little "lady" harmonica, and ripped off a very acceptable riff during "Never Comes the Day." Ray and Norda apparently are friendly off-stage, and I think Norda married a guy who is a friend of Ray's.

Ray settled down with a musical American gal he met through the fan club (a redhead named Lee) and seems very happy since his retirement from the band. Notes from him and about him pop up on Moody Blues newsgroups periodically. Last heard of, he was doing some recording with Bias Boshell, and as of summer of 2009, he was noodling and fishing with Mike Pinder (and Tony Clarke) somewhere in darkest Wales. His CD box set (re-release of his two solo albums, *Hopes Wishes and Dreams*, and *From Mighty Oaks)* was released Sept 24, 2010 at a gala signing at Threshold Records.

Ray has three children, Adam, Nannie and Zoe. Adam is an exact clone of Ray, I sat at a table with him in Vegas in the mid '90s. Between his children, Ray is a proud grandfather of seven grandchildren. Ray and his wife Lee are active in environmental issues in Wales, as well as animal rescue.

Clint Warwick:

Clint socialized a bit online with Moody fans, stayed in touch with other Brummie band people, passed away May 15, 2004.

Sidemen

They've been through a total of eight keyboardists, each of them very talented. Madonia, Boshell, Bliss, Pinder, Alan Hewitt, Julie Ragins, Bernie Barlow, and Moraz (a bit like *Spinal Tap* and the imploding keyboardist!) They first added a female keyboardist (Bernie Barlow) after Bias and Tracy departed. In 2006, Bernie departed to have a baby, and was replaced by Julie Ragins in 2007. Paul Bliss was dropped from the 2010 American tour, Alan Hewitt added. All have their own websites to follow up on, with far better biographical notes than I have. Some are even on Facebook!

I haven't kept up on Patrick Moraz: I clipped this off his website: *After 11 years as a member of the Moody Blues, Patrick's 1991 disassociation from the group left a hole which no single performer has yet been able to fill.* Go figure. There was one interview Justin did in 2001 or so, where he mentioned Patrick had "terrific mood swings" whilst with their band. From the court tapes of Dec 1992, Patrick certainly seemed a very sensitive person. He too has his story, he stays busy, and is truly a very imaginative and talented person, with a real flair for sci-fi.

Two articles surfaced in the late writing of this book. In Patrick's interview dated December 2000 (*Let It Rock*) he discusses being dropped from Yes just prior to being picked up by the Moodies, and I don't think he was real pleased with his unwilling departure from Yes. In that article he side-stepped discussing the Moodies. In *Classic Rock Magazine* (Oct 2010) Patrick even back-peddled a bit and said his years with the Moodies had been good ones. So, bottom line, no matter how gifted you think you are, the life of a musician is never easy. Take care of your contacts and contracts!!!

Bias Boshell: has been, not only with Procol Harum, but with a band called Trees, with David Costa of Wherefore Art? David Costa does a VERY good interview in *Eternity Road,* Oct 1994, on rock n' roll, in general. Bias has a biographical interview in *Higher and Higher.*

Paul Bliss: a very talented session musician! He has played with Celine Dion, Annie Haslam, and did keyboards (and songwriting? six tracks?) for the 1983 Hollies reunion album *What Goes Around.* (Justin's original band backed up the Hollies when young, so there is a connection.) Paul worked with the Hollies in 1989, 1983, and 1990. I rather like his solo album *The Edge of Coincidence*, there is a very funny song on there, "No One's Going to Find us Here in Rio," (about The Great Train Robbery, check it on Wiki.) He's also the composer for the theme to *Star Fleet Academy*, a sci-fi show in the U.K. which never made it to the States; it's a REALLY nice piece of music. Oddly he claims he can't read music but says Gordon has been trying to teach him.

He has his own media studio, builds websites, and is as of this writing, embarked on freelance business online, *http://blissmediaworks.com*. Paul is born under the sign of Cancer and shows it because he's always worried about money! As of fall, 2011, Paul and Gordon Marshall are starting a band called "Reflections of a Rock and Roll Band," easily found on the nets. The information might be erroneous out there, Paul and Peter Bliss are not related, though both turn up in Moody notes.

Maddy Bell: sang a bit with the Moody Blues in the '80s. Maddy couldn't tour due to personal issues. She sings backup on Gordon's solo album.

Gordon Marshall has started a website, *www.playdrumswithgordymarshall.com*, on which he has a blog, photos, and a chance to take drum lessons from the man himself! Gordon is a very talented musician, not just a basher, a no-nonsense sort of guy, and a real anchor-point to the band here in the New Millennium. He also Tweets and Facebooks! Gordon did a very good chat on July 5, 2009 and talked about how he now has a "brain" for his drum set, which is the end product of what Graeme was trying to develop back in the late '70s with his electronics. It's like fly-by-wire, only it's play-by-wire. Always in tune! He said he recorded his online lessons in Paul Bliss' studio, which worked out well for both of them. He's been involved in the stage shows *Thriller*, and *The War of the Worlds* in the U.K. Gordy also dropped out of the Moodies around 2015, under friendly circumstances (replaced by Billy Ashbaugh), and now plays with the John Lodge band when they tour.

In the late '90s and on into 2001, Gordon, Tracy Graham, and Doremi Hayward grouped up and were sighted running together at nightclubs, on and off tour. Frequently Gordon's wife and Tracy's fiancé were with them. Tracy has her own band and her fiancé plays drums; this all as per *Moodymania* #12, and as per *www.johnlodge.com* March 1, 2001. Tracy was dropped from the Moodies in 2001, but she will do fine wherever she goes I have no doubt. She was last heard of with the Chicago Blues Brothers, *www.chicagobluesbrothers.com*. The Moodies dropped Bias and Tracy with their first boat show, May/June 2001. Bias showed up on a Moodies biographical DVD and looked quite happy.

Other People, Places and Things

Ginger Baker: was last online at his website, and previous to that, seen living in Spain on a horse farm with polo ponies. Ginger is a popular guy! He was once with Crème. He turns up a lot in rocker history.

The Beatles: Just another band from Liverpool, but something tells me a few of them spent a lot of time after hours hanging out at the Bag o' Nails during the recording of *Sergeant Pepper's Lonely Hearts Club Band* (1967). Justin turned up in a Beatles documentary DVD *Beatles Stories* (2012).

Lionel Bart: Is the composer/co-composer for the '60s James Bond theme music. Oddly, Justin used to throw a bit of the "Bond" theme into the jam section of "I'm Just a Singer in a Rock and Roll Band" (as per bootlegs.) Justin hung out a LOT at Bart's house during the initial "Bond" blitz in the '60s, one can't help but wonder if Justin was involved in the composition of the theme. Vic Flick was involved in the Bond theme as well, but this goes outside the scope of my research.

Larry Baird: I lost count of the number of orchestral shows he did with the Moodies. (Remember, no bean counting here.) Larry is no longer with the Colorado Symphony. I can tell you from the shows I saw, it was as fascinating to watch Larry conduct as it was to watch the rock band. He's VERY good. In addition to working with the Moodies, Larry has worked with Kansas (Always Never the Same), Michael Bolton, Three Dog Night, Al Jarreau, and Alan Parsons.

Mike Batt: what a wonderful man he is from his website! He had a cute kid's story about a slug named Ergo on it, with some darling sketches and I hope he finds time to produce or publish it. "It's about a slug who wants to play the piano, but who has no hands, and wants to marry a fairy." Summer of 2009, I started subscribing to Mike Batt on Twitter, and doesn't HE have a good time on there!

Ray Coleman: originally slotted to do the official Moody Blues biography, passed away in late 1996. What notes he had started on this project are unknown. It's a shame, as he was a good writer, from the various articles he has done on the band.

Dave and Ray Davies of the Kinks are uncles to Phil Palmer; they have a big active family; "Something to Believe In" is a for real song after the brief Kinks research I did. Phil Palmer produced *The View from the Hill*. Of course, the Moodies toured with the Kinks back in the mid '60s. Phil Palmer defines himself as "a session musician," and has played with Dire Straits, rumored to be Doremi Hayward's fave band at one time. Phil Palmer also worked with Bob Dylan, Sting, Roger Daltrey, Eric Clapton, was also part of the Bliss Band, with Paul Bliss. His *Phil Palmer Project* is very good. I can only research so much and the Kinks are a very worthy band, but outside the scope of this book.

James Driscoll: friend of Justin's, he wrote the theme for *Shoe People*. Driscoll started as a DJ, did some road work. Then he did *Shoe People* and made considerable money off it with illustrator-artist Rob Lee. Driscoll has gone on to become quite an investor in U.K. animation.

Mickey Feat: as per Paul Bliss in chat, is "now a shrink, will shrink your head right off!" As of 2011, he's joined with Phil Palmer to form a band Straits. Feat has worked as a session musician (bass) with Art Garfunkel, Van

Morrison and Tina Turner. I love his voice, he sings "Hot Wheels" on the *Phil Palmer Project*. There is more of his biography in *Higher and Higher*.

Mario Frangoulis: out there somewhere on *youtube.com*, there is a link to Mario singing "Nights in White Satin" in Italian with Justin (a few years ago), it was done in the ancient ruins near Thessaly. Nice stuff, Mario has done several albums, one of which is *Sometimes I Dream*, lovely music. Mario F. is a tireless supporter of charities, and quite well-known in the Mediterranean area, more so than the States. Justin did a couple of gigs with him, at the Royal Albert Hall, and in Athens.

Mel Galley: formerly of Whitesnake and Trapeze (and some other Moody evolutions) passed away summer of 2008, of cancer.

Adrian Gurvitz: (co-artist on Graeme's solo works) has worked with Billie Davis, the Gun, Three Man Army, Baker-Gurvitz Army, and Toto.

Jimi Hendrix: Both Mike Pinder and Graeme Edge (*Indystar*, Aug 28, 2009) claimed to be friendly with Hendrix back in the early days. Mike said he and Hendrix enjoyed talking about UFOs together; I'll refer you back to *Alien Rock* for that one!!! <insert *Twilight Zone* theme song> Graeme claims to have been one of the first people outside the studio to hear "Electric Ladyland," when Hendrix showed up at his house at 4 am with the tape. How fun!!! Graeme says he first met Jimi at The Scotch of St. James (a nightclub in London.) Graeme, Jack Bruce, Eric Clapton were all jamming one night; when in came Hendrix with (his manager) Chas Chandler. While Eric and Jimi jammed, everyone sat with mouths hanging open. I wonder if this isn't where Graeme made contact with Hendrix's management and thus the Moodies converted to WEG.

Peter Jackson: to the best of my knowledge, is not the same fellow who directed *Lord of the Rings*. This one went from bodyguard and roadie to management in the '70s sometime. No word from him lately.

Nicky James: was on the *Classic Artists* DVD about the Moodies (2006) and in 2007 passed away with a brain tumor. He played with many Brummies, and seemed to be a nice fellow, will be sorely missed. An album called *Thunderthroat* by Nicky James also has various Moody Blues on it; it shows up for sale on *www.Amazon.co.uk* as a vinyl. Nicky James, born Michael Nicholls, passed away on Oct 8, 2007, services held in Swindon.

Tom Jones: was WELL known to audiences of the '60s and '70s: "It's Not Unusual" was his signature hit song. I personally wasn't a huge fan, but he did give the Moodies quite a boost when they became his intro band in France in 1967. In February, 2004, I spotted him on the Ellen Degeneres show, and he sounded pretty good! (He had a new album out, *Tom Jones Reloaded*.) He also did a star spot on a very funny camp movie *Mars Attacks*. He appeared in Queen Elizabeth's Diamond Jubilee (2012) and looked (and sounded) pretty good!

Mike Keyes no longer works with the Moodies (worked for Eric Clapton for a while), and was heard to be very ill in 2008 (from a roadie). Keys was the permanent stage manager, and mostly ran the business along with Ivy Stewart in the '90s.

I have a very weird note about a *Peter Knight* leading a skiffle group called Moonshines and The Phantoms in 1956? It's in *Brum Rocked*, pg 43, and I wonder if it's the same person who did the orchestrations for *Days of Future Passed?* (Wow) Peter Knight helped the Moodies orchestrate many things over the years, including "I Dreamed Last Night" and selections on *Moving Mountains*.

Sir Edward Lewis: head of Decca, according to Justin and John (Nov 14, 2009 BBC interview), Decca owned many American holdings until after WWII when they had to sell them. Moodies and Stonies both owe their success to his support.

McIlroy's: in Swindon, site of many early rocker gigs (particularly Justin and his various bands), is now known as The Apartment.

The Maharishi: is someone the Moodies got interested in during their second album, *In Search of the Lost Chord*. The Maharishi started transcendental meditation in 1955, brought his technique to America in 1959, and really got big when the Beatles gave him publicity in 1968. His side of the story is Lennon and he had a falling out when he caught the Beatles using drugs at his retreat in the Himalayas. He passed away in Feb 2008 at the age of 91. "Maharishi" means "great seer" in Hindi. John Densmore put good notes about "The Rishi" as the Doors called him, in his band memoir *Riders on the Storm*, so the Rishi must have gotten his start in California. No surprise there!

Hugh Mendl: (who helped get *Days of Future Passsed* going) passed away July 12, 2008

The Mellotron: more good notes about the subject in the documentary *Mellodrama*, Mike contributed to it (I think some Yes bandmembers did, too.) The mellotron was referred to as "The Beast." It has a major documentary with Pinder in *The Isle of Wight: Threshold of a Dream* video released in 2009. Who else used the Mellotron? Beatles, King Crimson, Genesis, Cheap Trick, The Beach Boys, and Goblin.

Murray the K: worth researching if you are into musical history, but again, it falls outside the scope of this book. I did turn up a document saying that Murray the K was off the air by Feb 27, 1965, and that predates the arrival of the Mach I Moodies to do their gigs over the Dec 1965 holidays. No I don't get it either. Murray the K (the man, not the show) was a pioneer in the Fillmore style of party pits, converting an airplane hangar and putting bands in there, charging admission, etc.

Providence: *www.gallopaway.com*. Tim and Tom Tompkins are obviously brothers. Tim's wife got into the recording act, check out their song "San Juan Chickens," and Tim's song "The Commuter," there are samples on their website, as well as news about him and links about Jim Cockey and Andy Guzie. As per Cecile's TER interview (Dec 2007) Tom Tompkins says he played with the Red

Rocks tour, as part of the orchestra. He also claimed that members of Providence were tapped for Justin's potential *Songwriter* tour, but it never happened (Justin was struggling with production finances, as I recall the article of the time.) Tom mentioned a Providence bootleg "Heavenly Harmonies" which he didn't like. Bartholomew (lead singer) passed away Oct 19, 2009. Tom Tompkins has been part of a band called Onomatopoeia for years. Google *Ever Sense the Dawn* or check on all social media, also there are samples on *youtube.com*. Incredible, wonderful album produced by Tony Clarke.

Mike Read: producer, composer of *Poetry in Motion*, as of Nov 2007 was DJ on the Big L Radio. He was involved in confectionary art of all things! (Chocolate art!)

David Rohl: who did the laser (IR?) photography on the inside cover of *A Question of Balance*, appears to be a true Renaissance man. He later produced the album *Eye of Wendor*, which Justin was part of (along with Barclay James Harvest and members of 10cc). A good interview about his time as a semi-official photographer on tour for the Moody Blues can be read in *Higher and Higher* #33. David Rohl has since become a serious Egyptologist and was an advocate for Tibetan independence. A man worth researching.

After the Move and the Moodies parted company with him, *Tony Secunda* promoted several Birmingham bands, including T. Rex. He passed away in 1995 at a fairly young age.

Ivy Stewart: fan club secretary from 1991 to 2010, passed away suddenly Dec 27, 2010. Threshold Music, the store under the office Ivy operated out of, closed shop Feb 28, 2011.

Timon: is now known as Tymon Dogg http://www.tymondogg.net

Derek Varnals: mentioned repeatedly by band and technicians as being a genius sound engineer who created their audio stereo "picture" we all enjoy on Core Seven albums. Last I heard, he lives in Australia.

Sue Vickers: singer backed by the Moody Blues as Threshold Records in the very early '70s. If my research is accurate, she was married to one of the Manfred Mann rock group (may have been involved singing and writing), and she died April 19, 2007. What a lovely voice! Check for her on *youtube.com*

Tony Visconti: continues to do some very good work producing various musical artists. Last we heard, he and his wife May Pang, who have two kids between them, were separated (*People Magazine*, c. Dec 2000), May turned up backstage with the Moodies during their summer 2014 tour. At least one record Tony produced post-Moody is *Seahorses*, which I only know about as some fool on the Moody news groups insisted on posting over and over about it. Apparently it was a LOT different from Moody Blues music, which is a good indication that Tony and the Moodies were probably correct to go separate ways. Tony also has a biography out; his mention of the Moodies was not very kind (he put some downright tacky and probably truthful Moody stories in it), but then again they DID fire him in 1991. These things happen. Justin still speaks well of Tony in later interviews. Tony is an American citizen, I have notes that he was born in Brooklyn, NY, and didn't show up in London until 1967, where he rapidly enmeshed himself into the rock scene.

Date: Thu, 9 Sep 2004 From: "Angela ****" Subject: Tony Visconti: For you Tony Visconti fans, check out the Sept 20, 2004 issue of Forbes. In the first few ad pages, you'll find a two page spread for a company called Capgemini and there's a great shot of Tony on a rooftop doing I believe T'ai Chi. Way cool.

I haven't heard from *Laura Vitez's* sister for a long time; she was dumping Justin as a love object, and becoming a fan of Sam Neill, last I heard. From her report, the entire footage Laura shot for *The Other Side of Red Rocks*, was something like nine hours, not unusual for any documentary. Due to time constraints, and issues with copyright (I think some orchestra members didn't waive rights to be filmed for a commercial documentary), it was cut back to a one-hour tape. I know that Laura was able to tour a bit with the band, and video other shows besides Red Rocks.

Jeff Wayne and *The War of the Worlds*: as of 2013, Jeff put together a "Next Generation" of performers for the stage show. Justin was not in the show, he dropped out due to conflicts with Moody touring. I found notes, Justin says he did some of the original guitar work on the original album, and of course, we found out that John did guitar work on "Thunder Child." The show goes on!

The Whispers: one of Justin's very early bands with high school buddies, consisting of Chris Richardson, Mike Greenland, and Nigel Norman. More info at *www.swindonmusicscene.co.uk*.

Marty Wilde: (Reg Smith) is also mentioned in *Brum Rocked,* on pg. 39. Marty seems to have taken a quiet approach to rock n' roll, and as of 2006 looked and sounded pretty good still. His daughter Kim Wilde was a popular singer in her own right. Marty is one of the few people you will find that stands TALLER than Justin Hayward; Justin is six foot two. Joyce, Marty's wife, was the other third of the Wilde Three, and she came from the Vernon Girls, who performed in '62/'63 in the U.K.

Pip Williams: produced *The Present, Long Distance Voyager.* As of 2002 Pip was working with a British band Mostly Autumn, *www.mostly-autumn.com*. Hopefully he's still fishing, too.

Other Stuff

I am really not a guitar monster, but I do occasionally get interested, such as in the case of Fender guitars. Justin and John both have Fenders of various collectable varieties. I can't keep up with John's axes, but in Justin's case, the white Fender he sometimes plays is apparently a "fake" Stratocaster Squier. I've seen him play a brown Telecaster too, for "Ride My See-Saw." Justin claims that is what "Ride My See-Saw" was first recorded with; it looks like the same model Buddy Holly played on Ed Sullivan.

An interesting note on Fenders: in the 1960s when Justin bought his first, they were not so expensive. They were made in a place called Fullerton, California, a small, mildly cruddy town full of orange groves which coincidently is where your author grew up in the 1960s; my childhood library is now the Fender Museum. My only other connection is that my Dad got his vintage stereo (with tubes) repaired at Fender Radio once (and it was a very dusty shop too.)

Today, a LOT of "Fender-like" guitars are actually cheap imitations made South of the Border. This is no shock, as Fullerton people run down to Mexico all the time, and back. The designs are not exactly top secret; a friend of mine went dumpster-diving once in the bin out back of the factory and came up with a complete set of schematics for Fender amplifiers. Having said all that, some of the "fake" Fenders apparently sound just as good as the real thing. I have no idea if the story about Justin's brown Fender guitar is true; it allegedly is one he has had since the early days. I've heard many conflicting stories about it; chalk it up to "Moody Mythology."

From an interview in 2001 on his site, Justin says his white Strat is "made in Japan" (not Fullerton) in the '80s. I talked to a young guitar player once, who had a bend for this sort of thing, and he said Fenders were "deadly cheap" in the '60s, and they sound really good, too. Imagine what a Telecaster bought in 1965 might be worth today if you took good care of it.

The Moodies have toured Japan, South Africa, England, Scotland, Europe, Australia and New Zealand, Canada, and America, but never Israel, South America, or the Middle East, though Justin has mentioned vacationing in the lovely warm Gulf country of the UAE (Dubai, "The Emirates.") According to vague reports, the Moodies were supposed to tour the Middle East, but it fell apart due to security issues.

The Lost Chord: Herein for the record is the story to "The Lost Chord." Mike Pinder apparently found the concept when Jimmy Durante sang a comic ditty, "I am the man who found the Lost Chord." After reading this blurb, I think you'll understand the whole thing. *Sir Arthur Sullivan (of Gilbert and Sullivan) wrote the song while sitting at his dying brother's bedside. It has spawned innumerable parodies (see Jimmy Durante). It has gone somewhat out of fashion, but in the era of 78rpm records it was recorded by almost every tenor imaginable, including Enrico Caruso. The song begins with a simple recitative on one note, builds tension gradually through the four verses, and ends grandly with a cataclysmic cadence for the organ (the instrument for which the accompaniment was originally written). "The Lost Chord" came to be particularly associated with Sullivan's mistress, Mrs. Fanny Ronalds, who made a name for herself as a capable amateur singer, with this song. Sullivan bequeathed her the manuscript, and on her request, it was buried with her.*

As a youngster with a mum who lived to hear Caruso, this song occasionally was played on the piano at our house. In fact my mum made me stand at the piano and sing it, until I got too old to intimidate and RAN. The original song is familiar, but it wasn't until I got into the Moody Blues fan base that I heard about the satire Jimmy Durante did.

The Fillmore East is now a condo unit in New York. The Fillmore West is still there, on Fillmore Street in San Francisco, and there is a big photo of Janis Joplin hanging over the stairwell, a great place to visit if you are ever in The City. They still smoke dope during the show too, right there on the ballroom floor. Some old hippies have told me that the Fillmore Ballroom is NOT the original Fillmore West. That research is just beyond my scope as a Moody Blues researcher, but it bears investigation.

The original Bag o' Nails was called "The Club" for a while, now has original name back, and is a vintage sort of place in a basement.

As of 2012, the baby score is: Graeme's daughter Sam has two daughters (one named Tiger, total 7 grand kids for Graeme); Gordon has two daughters with wife Susan, Paul Bliss has kids, Alan Hewitt and his wife raise Basset hounds! Ray's daughter Zoe has a little boy who was the inspiration for "My Little Lovely." When Mike Pinder did the Border's tours, the Pinders had a young woman in tow with them, who was also wagging a baby. Justin and John are also granddaddies. So the Moody family has continued to grow.

The Moody Blues and everyone associated with them appear to be very much bookworms (it's a good thing on long tours.) Indeed, when the Moodies were granted their wish by their godfather, Sir Edward Lewis, to "have every musical instrument ever made" put in their studio, they found they could not play several of them. So they would "get a book and learn how." John frequently mentions *Pilgrim's Progress* in early interviews; Justin reads anything with a mythic theme and has mentioned C.S. Lewis. Doremi's book appetites were already mentioned. Bias too seems to enjoy reading, as I ran into him in the bookstore at Tahoe once. Very interesting, seeing Bias Boshell sitting cross-legged on the floor (in shorts), avidly perusing a book, and all the "regular" fans trying to look nonchalant and watch him.

Melodies from *The Zodiac* (the album that inspired the Moodies) surfaced in the theme to *In Like Flint* (starring James Coburn), of all places! (For those who missed that movie, it was a spy spoof from the '60s, an "ancestor" to *Austin Powers*.) The "Flint" theme was composed by Jerry Goldsmith. *The Zodiac* continues to be popular in an underground way with younger generations, I heard a teen playing it on his MP3 player in August, 2007 and about dropped my teeth! .

About their coffee table they used to sit around and brainstorm? The "table" is *confined to our museum of past articles* -- John Lodge, KTAR Phoenix *Moodymania* #14. Justin claims to have their mellotron in storage too. One of their many mellotron's was given to the Hard Rock Park in Myrtle Beach, which went bankrupt less than a year after it opened. The mellotron was rescued, and it's back in storage again; on the 2018 cruise, the Moodies said they might give it to the Rock and Roll Hall of Fame. Justin gave his sitar to a rock museum in London. So this stuff has been sent around to good homes. The 12-string guitar Justin wrote "Nights in White Satin" on was reclaimed by Lonnie Donegan, then Justin got it back, NOW latest word is Justin plans to present it to the RRHOF.

Was "Strange Times" written when the comets Hyakutake or Hale-Bopp were in the sky? If you look at the dates, I think it was. Hale-Bopp was beautiful and deserved a song!

Various rumors about "mangled lyrics" have surfaced over the years in the fan club, and many of these "fractured lyrics" pop up online on various websites. The funniest is alleged to be the Moodies themselves singing lyrics that begin "Aren't our wives strange?" I clipped this online somewhere. *A version of "I Know You're Out There Somewhere" that has to be seen to be believed. They were fooling around during rehearsal and crossed it with Devo or the Talking Heads. It was surreal with the new lyric "my arms close around your brain."* The very best of all poets of mangled lyrics is Steve of Kentucky, who penned the infamous "Say It With Suds."

Someone, somewhere is hoarding a lot of tapes and masters from Threshold and other Moody recordings after that. Copyright issues are likely holding some from release.

>"London is Behind Me" has been done hillbilly style with Donegan and Justin (*Puttin' on the Style*). Also it's done as a bootleg under a fake name and the entire band obviously on the backing track, it's on *youtube*.

>The masters to *Ever Sense the Dawn* have never surfaced, although the CD exists as an import from Japan.

>Tapes done by Justin and Lionel Bart for *Gulliver* were finally released on *The Genius of Lionel Bart*, and yes Justin sings on two tracks, and they are wonderful.

>"Forever to Be Alone" so called that by *Higher and Higher*, exists as a bootleg, but has never been released, and it's a very nice song. On *youtube*.

>Some songs from the ill-fated "eighth Core 7" album, recorded between 1972 and 1974, are also alleged to be in

Justin's hands. (Graeme claims they were erased.) "Justin #1" as "Island" was first called, has been released on the SACD *Seventh Sojourn*, but "Pinder #1" an un-named song that was left off of *Question of Balance*, surfaced on *youtube.com*. "The Dreamer" (released in 2005 on an enhanced version of *Every Good Boy Deserves Favor*) sounds like something from an H.P. Lovecraft story, which may be why it was held back, too weird for normal "Moody music." But it would go nicely with the cover to *Threshold of a Dream*.

>Live recordings of the Moody Blues on the BBC have been found, re-mastered and released in 2005. More were found and released with the *Days of Future Passed* 50th anniversary issue.

>"Wrong Time, Right Place" was released on Justin's re-mastered *Songwriter* CD.

>Justin has unreleased tracks he and 10cc did together in the '70s

>According to Dennis Lambert (producer), a song entitled "Get It Right" by Justin was slotted for *The View from the Hill* album, but it has never been released.

>*Timeless Flight*, a massive box set, released 2013, had some unreleased material, such as the live recording of the *Blue Jays* tour. Justin's double solo release *All the Way* also has a different mix of "Blue Guitar" and other tidbits.

>A song "Beautiful Dream" (John Lodge) surfaced in a live performance (*you tube*) by the Moodies, dated July 13, 1968. It was probably lost for a reason, the copy on *youtube.com* is VERY rough.

General reasons cited for not releasing (when the Moodies are cornered on this) are that the song is stale, "sounds too much like," "not finished," and in some cases, "NO PROMOTION." Some Moodies come right out and say, "There are no more songs" contrary to other reliable reports. Justin has muttered about "keeping mum" about songs he is hoarding, and along with Tony Clarke, "not leaving a trail of unreleased recordings behind them." If the artist is not comfortable with the release, there is no reason to release it, and I see no reason to heckle them about it.

Recorded music is like any other art form, sometimes it needs rest and thought before release. A good example: "Road to Love" was held for many years before surfacing in 2013 on Justin's "Spirits" album.

In the 2008-2009 timeframe, "six lost songs" written by Justin and apparently recorded by the Whispers (?) in his pre-Moody days, escaped to the Internet. They are darn good songs too, though very raggedy to listen to. Hopefully Justin will get around to cleaning them up or redoing them, they are a lot of fun. Even as a youngster, Justin showed major skill in constructing melody and rhythm. Justin claims to have a lot of bits and pieces of poetry and songs that have "fallen by the wayside" as he tends to concentrate on what is immediate and pertinent to his life at that given time. Graeme also writes a lot of poetry we have never been able to read. Every artist is like this: one hides (burns) what they consider the "iffy," and only releases what one thinks is really beautiful.

The band has a thing about catching the "official tour cold" when they go on the road; in fact, Graeme passed a nasty virus to several ladies he was smooching with in a bar one tour during the '90s, a bit of *schadenfreude* there. Much of the "regular fan base" came down with the bug as they were following the band from show to show. Yes being that close in the front rows can pass all sorts of germs, some band members skip shaking hands after shows for this reason. In fact I think they even stopped shaking hands at their "official meet and greets" a few times for this very reason. *Swine flu angst.........*

The Moody Blues are alleged to be the basis for the movie *This is Spinal Tap*, right down to the keyboardist who keeps mysteriously vanishing! When Groening did *Spinal Tap* on *The Simpsons*, sure enough they did a song called "Dust of Future Passed." (*Moodymania* #8)

This book has been a long time coming. Since I started writing it, Nicky James, Clint Warwick and George Harrison have passed away with cancer. Tony Clarke went with emphysema. They were smokers and grew up in the once toxic pits of Birmingham and Liverpool. It's always sad when a musician dies, some of the light goes out of the world.

    Say it with love.

* My final reader is also a physics major, and regarding quantum mechanics, commented in the margins "a popular misnomer." I have to agree. Our Moody Blues newsgroups are often invaded by fans, who are firmly convinced that they can alter their own reality with sheer mind power. Some of their "proof" essays are quite long and involved, always subjective and referring to Quantum Reality. And of course, never referring to the stats and math behind quantum mechanics. I would refer all readers back to field experiences with LSD and various hallucinogens. Dr. Leary always said the music can get you high by just listening to it. THAT I agree with. Remember, Dr. Leary was a psychologist, not a physicist!

Appendix D: Moody Art

A culture is only as great at its dreams and its dreams are dreamed by artists. -- Robert A. Heinlein

Fine art and beautiful pictures have been the byword for Moody Blues album covers and posters since they began with *Days of Future Passed*. There is a great article on album cover art in *Higher and Higher* #18/19, which is a major area of Moody interest I've barely gotten into with this book. While researching, I turned up a few more interesting notes.

According to the cover, David Anstey did the art for *Days of Future Passed*. I do find it interesting that Justin appears to be looking at a book with the phases of the Moon, and that turns up on the album cover. It's very typical of art in that era. Sometimes a group of us hippies would put a huge piece of paper on a table, then everyone who came along would add their sketch-n-doodle to it. It reminds me of that.

Covers to *In Search of the Lost Chord*, *To Our Children's Children's Children*, and *Seventh Sojourn* are all done by Phil Travers, who worked for Decca as a cover artist. The Core Seven covers are pretty much up to the interpretation of the individual. The Moodies used to invite Phil into the studio, and play the songs for him, so he could get inspired to do the covers. Phil Travers ALSO designed the Threshold logo, visible on old vinyl albums, it looks like a desert ghostie, a big rushing face out of a cloud.

With *A Question of Balance*, the Moody Blues took a different direction with the album design and did it sideways! For the cover of QOB, Travers intended the cover to show "impending storm clouds" boiling up on the horizon. Everyone on the beach enjoying the day didn't get the hint that dark times were coming. Again, art is subjective; I personally saw distant storm clouds that might or might not ever reach the beach, but which are lovely, and fully worthy of the audience on the beach, watching them boil and roll. Storms out on the ocean at a distance are very beautiful indeed. Then, you have the front cover with this scary, horrible "God" figure reaching out of a cloud with a huge cigar in his hand. Tony Clarke laughed, and said, "That really DID have a model behind it, the producers at Decca wanting the next album!!!" And you have the juggling act of the Moodies and all their wives, trying to balance on the blue car in the corner, very much what was going on in their lives. It's a great album cover.

They were actually sued by the guy whose face was used in the safari portrait, apparently it was pulled from a newspaper photo. They had to put black rectangles over the eyes, adding to the whole concept. (See *Higher and Higher* #33.) Justin has, hanging in his front room, the original oil by Phil of the *Question of Balance* album. (Justin IS a Libra, he'd like that about "the Balance.") In the 2007 tours, the lighting techs took this cover, and turned it into a twirling tunnel, pretty nice for a light show!

On the Threshold of a Dream: the cover looks like they've ALL been reading too much H.P. Lovecraft! Done by Phil Travers.

Every Good Boy Deserves Favor-- also done by Phil Travers, but in this case he snitched a little bit from a German print called "Der Krystal." It's not uncommon for album cover designers to snitch a little bit from fine art (like songwriters snitch from William Blake sometimes). Joni Mitchell used the closed volute of the Flemish era *The Garden of Delights* (Hieronymus Bosch) on one of her albums, and everyone thought it was great psychedelic art! (This was before she started doing such nice paintings of her own.) The picture on the inside of *Every Good Boy Deserves Favor* reminds one of the Panathenaic Frieze, and indeed looking closely one easily picks out band members, and sometimes even their wives.

Solo years, 1974 thru 1977

Kick off Your Muddy Boots (Graeme Edge, Adrian Gurvitz) design is by "Shoot that Tiger." (I had to check this as it really looks like Phil Travers again.) The same designers stayed with Gurvitz and did other album covers for him.

Blue Jays cover was done by Phil Travers. Again, Phil possibly (probably) dug into history and snitched just a little bit of art from William Blake.

Paradise Ballroom: the "Playboy cover" and one of the prettiest in all Moodydom. The centerfold contains a very space-age picture of Graeme, flanked on either side by the Gurvitz brothers. J Peragno (as best I can make out) did the design for this album. Graeme, ever the bold one, branched out from "the official Moody cover designer" with excellent results!

Hopes Wishes and Dreams, From Mighty Oaks (Ray Thomas solos): both covers are done by Phil Travers. They are "very Ray" both lovely pictures of the English countryside, with family themes.

Natural Avenue (John Lodge solo): I found a weird thing once, a refrigerator magnet that has this cover painting on it, only it's reversed! Peter Max used to call those stones on the cover "floating zooples" they were popular in psychedelic art. John got bold and also branched out, this design is done by Martyn and Roger Dean of Dragons Way, LTD.

Songwriter (Justin's first solo): cut and paste, but with style! "Shoot that Tiger" did the work, so Justin was still on speaking terms with Graeme. Computer graphics was JUST coming into being by 1977 when this cover was done, so remember this was cutting-edge graphics at the time. The first Apple PC was barely on the market this year, and the Commodore/Amiga was right behind it with graphics. (Bill Gates was still trying to get DOS to work in 1977.)

The Promise (Mike Pinder solo): really pretty much a cut and paste but the photos are great. Again, the graphics are cutting-edge for 1977.

The Second Octave

Octave, The Other Side of Life, Keys of the Kingdom, A Night At Red Rocks, and *Strange Times* all look like they are very well done cut-and-paste graphics with photos. Nothing wrong with that of course, but they aren't ART in the same sense Phil Travers' work was.

When *Strange Times* was issued, they took the design a little further. This was the first Moody studio album to be TOTALLY CD, that is no vinyl was cut; the CD itself has lovely little sea shells on the disc.

The Other Side of Life has floating frames that remind me of the Richard Donner version of *Superman*. (General Zod ran off with Graeme's first wife, remember?)

December is also very cut and paste, they clipped the little boy right off the *Long Distance Voyager* cover. Justin says they left off a wonderful swooshing star on the original artwork, because it wouldn't fit on the CD cover. Bummer.

The Present is snatched right off a very famous Maxfield Parrish painting called "Dawn." The artist re-did the classical art piece to a flashy disco electric color scheme, and added in the little *Voyager* satellite, also in the sky above the crowd on the cover of LDV. Maxfield Parrish is a noted artist from the *art deco* era, 1920s, and his pastoral glowing artwork (popular with hippies in the late '60s) has also been used in Enya's videos, and Sally Duvall's costumes in *Storybook Theater*. There was once a Nestle's chocolate commercial using Parrish's piece "Ecstasy." Parrish is an artist who inspired graphics in the movie *Lord of the Rings*, as well as Tim Burton's *Alice in Wonderland*.

When *Sur la Mer* came around, Justin (? well he lives near there) apparently dragged in a painting from the south of France, *Le Fort d'Antibes*, by Nicolas De Stael. It's a neat painting, those of us who lived in the '50s immediately recognize the color combinations; it was painted in 1955.

On the cover of his *The View from the Hill*, Justin bought a sketch of himself from a Moody fan, Monique Trempe.

I didn't bother with most of the "Best of" reissue albums, most being cut-and-paste. The "Live at the BBC" album released in 2007 has a really neat "hippy doodle art" piece on the front. Hey what a shock, real art after decades of cut and paste!

Posters

Three posters of note should be mentioned here:

The Kinks Poster (green-yellow-magenta reprint). As far as any of us can tell, this is a made-up "fake out" poster, which has been published to make money off the "60s collectibles" trend. The dates don't fit into any Moody tour dates and reading Chapter One will fill you in there. It's nice for decorating but has absolutely no validity when it comes to band history or reality.

Wear your Dreams: this one I bought off the Moody Spies because I thought it was so pretty, and it is totally bogus. What we think happened is this poster was done when a promoter began putting together a rock concert that never happened. It's a "dream" poster. It has a Midsummer and "Titania" fairy theme. I do like it, it's worth having to decorate with. The Moody Blues are in very small writing at the bottom; a lot of big name bands from the time are on it too. The Moody Blues are also listed on the original Woodstock poster, but it's a well-known fact that the band didn't make it there.

I have problems with collectors putting these up for sale out there, when they are not even "real event" posters. So *caveat emptor*, those who collect old vintage posters.

The Tale of the Water-Stained Posters: When I first joined the fan club in 1991, I had my name put on the pen pal list, and sure enough like clockwork, here came ads from Mike Pinder! (So he was getting the OFC newsletter.) As per this ad, he was selling some old Moody Blues posters for $350 to $400 dollars apiece, and he signed them! It wasn't much to look at, just a black, spacey, melty sort of picture of a bearded hippy, black ink on white, "Nights in White Satin." Pretty art, but I was under whelmed at the time, and besides, that was a pretty steep price for 1991. What really turned me off was the comment, "Some have minor water stains." *Ick*. There's nothing more gross than an old mildewy poster. I passed.

Eventually my friend Nida showed me the poster she bravely bought and framed, indeed it was numbered and signed. And it WAS stained, rather unsightly. But it was ok framed there under glass and signed, and she enjoyed it, and that is what matters. Poster collectors told me that these posters were originally printed up by the band, and they went around hand-delivering them as promotional items in the late '60s or early '70s. Later research says the art was done by Ray!

Some fans back east tracked Justin down to sign this poster (trying to collect all the Moody signatures), and Justin claimed (after refusing to even touch it, he probably dislikes mold as much as I do) "A bunch of posters just like that are in the basement at Threshold" in Cobham. I was a fan club member at the time, paid my dues too! After hearing this bit of *hear-say*, I wrote Threshold saying that since the posters were languishing in the (damp?) basement, could they please dig them out and sell them anyway, no matter what shape they were in? I never heard back. If you have been following along, you might come to some very weird conclusions. That is all I plan to say on the matter. The poster was re-issued to go with the 50th anniversary release of *Days of Future Passed*.

VCR

The Beggar's Opera Meets the Veteran Cosmic Rocker, or *who the heck is Hogarth?* Herein, an argument for Hogarth on the cover of *Long Distance Voyager*. [Note to the reader: You will have to get out your own copy of the *Long Distance Voyager* album cover to make sense of this essay, and/or find references on Hogarth.]

June 3, 2011 (Storyteller show, Portland OR), John mentioned the original lithograph for this album cover, saying "It was huge!!!" and after saying "What a neat thing it had that little spaceship in the sky." Obviously John was storytelling a bit. THEN Justin said "It is a well-known picture." The Jays have yet to clarify the title and artist of this piece. I've LOOKED HARD, and it ISN'T out there in the art world. No one ever said musicians were strictly honest!

Tales about *where* the lithograph came from continue to be garbled; on cruise, John said he found it in a junk store and got it cheap. It allegedly hangs framed now, in some family member's house. *Higher and Higher* did full coverage of *Long Distance Voyager* in issue #31. Editor Mark Murley discusses where the Moodies found the cover, allegedly Justin Hayward spotted the old, faded print in a photography shop somewhere in England, when they were doing their promotion photo series for the album. "It was perfect," he said, the picture had bits and pieces from all their songs and themes in the album. The only thing they added was the blue tint, and the cute little spaceship hanging in the sky.

There's a story out there that they found it at the Arts Union Glasgow. Those of us who have been around formal and classical art recognize it for what it is, an old masterpiece by someone who probably had architectural training. The trees are incredibly detailed (standard for draftsmen in those days), and there are formal vanishing points.

After what Mark said (or didn't say) about the original artist of the piece, I got interested. It was a mystery, and art history was always my strong point in college; besides I wanted to see more of the guy's work, whomever he was! First, I turned to an art history book, and started flipping casually and quickly through it, looking for the same style. All artists have a style, sometimes they can be "nailed" that way, but you can only tell it if you look out of the corner of your eye, which I did.

One photo stopped me. It was "The Shrimp Girl" by an artist unknown to me, Hogarth. And Hogarth was an English artist. We're on the right track! Then I looked at the dates. Hogarth died in 1764, he was noted for his comic ribaldry, in fact he was one of the first political cartoonists to be printed in newspapers. Most of his work is connected to the early 18th century, but he didn't stop drawing until he died, so we could be talking about LATER than the *Beggar's Opera* or *Marriage a la Mode* (two of his most famous art series). The 18th century was a time of the "common man" coming forth politically, a human evolution reflected by both the American and French revolutions that same century. Think *Moll Flanders*. What we Americans went through politically with Mother England was happening on the home soil as well; King George wasn't real popular with the common man at all.

I then started picking apart the album cover for costume details. When doing clothing history, you have to be sharply aware of a few realities. There was NO photography back in the 18th century. The only records we have of "what people wore" comes from 1) the old clothes themselves 2) FORMAL portraitures, which may or may not bear resemblance to what the "common man" was wearing at the time; and remember 3) fashions are dynamic, not frozen in time. Those of us who lived through the '60s and '70s understand this, and it's why we cringe and LAUGH when we see retro-movies like *Austin Powers*.

This is what makes Hogarth so important to costumers, he painted the common man, not just the rich and wealthy. Hogarth enjoyed rubbing peoples' collective noses in Realism.

Another important point: what was fashionable in any given century was often tied to a particular city that was the "trend setter" of the time. In the case of the 18th century, that would have been Paris, France. If this is Hogarth, then we are talking about ENGLAND (not Paris). In the case of this painting, we might be looking at a "day in the countryside" in England, with folks that are just dressed for everyday life, not for formal portraits. Mark Murley, being a guy, spotted the One Man Band wearing the stove pipe hat. He placed the date of the picture as Civil War, which makes it 1861.

Before you jump to conclusions, check out the stove pipe hat. It slants in just a bit toward the top, doesn't it? That means it's earlier than Abe Lincoln, take my word for it. Pilgrims in New England wore hats slanted like that, and they were high-crowned too. I looked at the women in the picture, since they tend to be more "trendy" than guys. I was a costumer in a former life, and (if not precise with the dates) with a quick surface glance, I placed it at least a century earlier than Mark's guess.

With Hogarth as my clue, I began to look for details that would match the people in the portrait with early to mid-18th century. Check the sleeves on the men's clothing. The shoulders are dropped, loose and almost "mutton chop." This would put them more toward the end of the 18th century, but then again the clothing "cut" might be something local. Fashion moguls of the time had a habit of taking "what the peasants were wearing" and modifying those styles for fashionable wear. Several of the boys in the picture are obviously apprentices, and are wearing smocks, which are also looser fitting.

The turbans. The boy in the foreground and a guy in the back with a tray (of bread?) on his head are both wearing turbans. These were trendy for common wear throughout the 18th century all over Europe (I'm not sure why, but I know that people both White and Red were wearing turbans in southeastern U.S. up until the War of 1812, and it was African influence there.) They also wear turbans in the movie *Amadeus*, so think of those fashions; it's the same time period.

The guy by the gate, maybe he's not just "a coachman," maybe he is the owner of the property, the landowner who has come to listen to the music. He's probably dressed in the "proper" formal clothing of the era. There is another clue, check the old guy with the funny gathered hat in the crowd, leaning on the staff. He is wearing knickers too, look VERY closely.

The boys and the middle-class men are wearing something new. If this was truly Hogarth doing the art, it would fit with his style, as he was always into "changing times," they are wearing full-length pants. Full-length pants come about in later 18th century according to Lucy Barton, but why wouldn't they have already begun in the countryside, where people went for practical clothing, not knickers?

I found a Hogarth exhibition, went and talked with a curator of the prints. She seemed to think Hogarth was more "in your face" with his art and wasn't sure the LDV cover really was a match for the artist. But I disagree. Look at some of the details. The dog is right off several of Hogarth's paintings (and the dog is always stealing something.) A boy almost dead center in the crowd is turning his head almost the same way "The Shrimp Girl" is, something about them looks the same. The Hogarth collection I saw had many studies of children's faces, round and cherubic, as are many of the children's faces in the crowd. In fact, Hogarth's studies reminded me of Da Vinci, and some of the faces in this do too. Da Vinci has been studied by many artists since his time of course. And better yet, the old guy in the back is a dead ringer for what Hogarth probably looked like as he got older, unto even wearing the same sort of hat he wore, and his turned-up nose. I think he painted himself into the tableau.

Want some more? Look at the woman to the far left. She looks annoyed, like she has been traveling somewhere, and had to stop while her family went to listen to the Veteran Cosmic Rocker. She is holding her infant, and would really like to keep traveling, don't you think? Even though her two small children are also watching the musician. She is young, and she has a large bonnet. Her over-dress looks heavy, she looks hot; contrast this to the young woman in front in the light dress with peasant sleeves. All the other women, who are older, and more provincial, are wearing smaller bonnets. The well-dressed young matron could be "styling," that is keeping up with the trend of bigger bonnets on the Merveilleuse ladies, whose bonnets reached outrageous sizes during the Empire or she could be wearing a traveling bonnet.

The other young matron toward the front of the crowd at first glance DOESN'T match up with the Lucy Barton vision of 1760, but I did a little digging. For one, Hogarth himself was a trendsetter in English society (he designed sets and costumes for the stage), and he favored a looser, more "shepherdess" look in his costumes. With digging, some of the styles during this period indeed show a looser sleeve, rather than a ubiquitous severe straight sleeve on over-gowns. This is summer perhaps (the trees are all leafed out!) and these are country folk. The "peasant blouse" with the easy-to-make puffy sleeves are very popular in any era; indeed I was thrilled to find the same sleeve and line on the girls in the classical movie *Brigadoon*, set in 1754.

The woman holding the baby in the front is very young, barely out of her childhood herself, and that might be what Hogarth was saying, that she hadn't quite started wearing women's fashions. The looser muslin puffed sleeve was what girls mostly wore. The waistlines and over-skirts are exactly right for the mid-18th century, in a few years they would go higher during the Empire period. They aren't tight ENOUGH for the Crinoline Era, which would be the American Civil War era.

The stove pipe hats are another sticky point. I dug and found evidence of that general shape of hat as early as 1781. When DID the classical beaver skin top hat come about? We don't know, because the FORMAL pictures don't show anything near it until 1781. Remember, these are English peasants, not rich people. They might be wearing all sorts of oddball things, which is exactly what Hogarth perhaps wanted to capture with his costumer's eye.

Hogarth was the sort of fellow who tried to paint life "as it really was," a bit like Rembrandt (only more snide.) Life is NOT clean and simple, it's very complicated, like the picture. He always told a story when he drew his characters. The Moodies spotted the print for a reason, there are stories all over it, and in the corners.

Overall it's wonderful art, that keeps me looking at it over and over, trying to puzzle out what it means (rather like Moody Blues music.) I have concluded one of two things 1) that it was started by Hogarth, and then possibly finished by a student of his when he died in 1764, thus the apparent disparity in period styles or 2) this is the real thing. Hogarth did it with his photographic eye, saying "This is a transitional time. Look at what musicians can do. Look at what people look like right now in 1762."

And Hogarth was also saying how much he enjoyed music, and lovely days in the countryside. He was the same as the Moody Blues. It excites me that the Moodies might have found a "lost" Hogarth. This is not far-fetched; Hogarth had many of his pieces done as lithographs (the 18th century version of posters, yes quite large); and this is what the Moodies found in that photography shop, forgotten and fading on the wall. It's a fact that Hogarth's House is between Bayswater, and Kingston-on-Thames, two locales where Justin has lived. I suspect the "castle-like" building in the background is very familiar to Londoners.

As I researched for this paper, I found myself laughing with Hogarth, and enjoying his "snap-shot pictures" and what he had to say with his images. Hogarth was really a funny guy,* the sort of fellow you would have enjoyed quaffing a pint with. Decide for yourself, and then go find out about this wonderful English artist, whom I hope never gets lost in the mists of time.

My final reader pointed out that Gainsborough is from this same time period. Comparing Hogarth and Gainsborough, they're VERY similar, but Hogarth has more action in his work. Gainsborough was stiff and more portrait oriented.

Annotated Bibliography:

Barton, Lucy Historic *Costume for the Stage*. Boston: Walter H Baker Co: 1935. This is the "costumer's Bible" in theater, but can be supplemented by any source, so long as you research carefully and honestly.

Gorsline, Douglas *What People Wore*. New York: Bonanza Books, 1957.

Kohler, Carl *A History of Costume*. New York: Dover Publications, 1963.

Laver, James *Costume Through the Ages*. New York:

---

* I found this quote on a daily calendar of all things! "A wealthy collector commissioned a painting to be called 'Destruction of the Pharaoh's Host in the Red Sea' from the artist William Hogarth. But he wouldn't agree to pay the artist's asking price. Hogarth dreamed up an artist's revenge, and turned in a canvas that was solid red. When the collector complained he wasn't getting what he'd asked for, Hogarth explained that "the Israelites had all passed through the Red Sea, and the Egyptians were all drowned in it." I'm also shocked to report that Hogarth was a noted pornographic artist of the 18th century, but that tidbit does not come into the scope of this research. YEEP.

Appendix E: Say Again? Odd phrases and words

I believe it was Winston Churchill who referred to the English and Americans as "two peoples divided by a common language." Writing this book certainly has educated me to our British cousins' dialects, and I still can't understand them when they mutter. I'm sure Americans, especially old hippies, confuse the British just as much. (Mike Batt once said, "Arguing with an American is like being in the movies!") For a true vision of slang pertinent to this book, please refer to *Hippie Dictionary* (McCleary). Not only did I use a lot of slang and outdated words in this book, but there are also a lot of "coded" words in the fan club at large; if you plan to get online with this bunch, you will have to know the lingo to survive.

Addy: address. Brits are a real kick with their slang: I was blown away when Ivy Stewart first wrote me asking for my "expiry" on my VISA card, meaning of course the "expiration date." Mike Batt twittered me that a "mozzie" is a mosquito!!! The "ee" phonetic ending winds up on the end of a lot of British slang, such as Glasgow being pronounced "Glasgee" by the locals. It's probably a hang-over from the Gaelic tongues of the U.K.

Albion: very old term for England. "Albus" is "white" in Latin, the name probably came from Julius Caesar and his first view of the white cliffs.

Angel: in a theatrical sense, this is the person who backs you financially.

Anoraks: one of those bulky jacket hoodies (with fur) favored by people in the FAR north. In a musical context, these are people who used to jump in boats and go land on (and pester) the pirate radio boats off-shore in the U.K. In a broader sense, mildly derogatory term for persistent band followers (as in *what the heck are they doing this for, are they nuts???*)

ASCAP: Association of professional songwriters [a bit like AIA: American Institute of Architects]. Justin Hayward and John Lodge both belong, along with Mike Batt, Marty Wilde, and too many others to list. ASCAP will come get you and fine you if you play recorded songs in your coffee house without permission, so they are a bit like a union (or a guild) as well. They protect song copyrights.

Asgard: home of the Nordic gods, also the name of a rock band backed by the Moody Blues as Threshold Records, in the very early '70s. It's a fairly interesting album *In the Realm of Asgard* for the discerning Moody collector (or Gothic nut), and has been reprinted on CD.

Baby Boomers: (for short, "Boomers") this is a well-known population phenomenon (an unstable r-strategy population, for the biologists out there.) Basically this is every person born for the next 10 years, right after WWII in Europe or America, beginning in 1946. Much of the Northern Hemisphere was plunged into a heavy war during the early years of the '40s, many people were killed, and when the war was over, everyone did their best to replace those who had died. A lot of children were born at the same time, and all grew up together. In America, it manifested as a lack of jobs, and high enrollment in colleges in the '60s. Sadly, it also manifested as having too many young men with no jobs, who went to war, and in turn were killed themselves in Viet Nam. The Baby Boom generation is now in their sixties, and still is driving society. In the '60s as teens, we created rock 'n roll; now we are all becoming senior citizens together and will soon place a burden on the medical care systems of Europe and America.

Bag o' Nails: '60s pub/nightclub in the Soho district of London. The Moody Blues were allegedly a House Band in

1967, until they started touring America and making the big bucks. It was quite the hang-out for young London folks, and for those who were recording in Soho, (Denmark and Dean Street) which is a theatre district in London (very Bohemian in the '60s.) Despite it gaining a rep for being a "Beatles' hangout," the B o' N was apparently a pretty rough place. Tony Clarke (chat, 9-23-07) says he got caught there, in some fisticuffs crossfire and knocked out cold on the floor whilst pub hopping with the Moodies (would have been early 1967.) Tony was a really meek guy, how horrible for him! Bag o' Nails refers to some "working man" theme, nails for carpenters, that sort of thing. There is another Bag o' Nails pub just south of Buckingham Palace but is not the place the Moodies played.

Beatnik: "The Beats," counter-culturalists from the late '50s or very early '60s. They were really into poetry, art, and experimental home decorating. "Cool people." White people who adopted cultural details from African-Americans. These are what Bohemians eventually turned into. Beatniks in turn became the hippy movement (in France, the anarchist movement).

Bed-sitter: this is a very, very small apartment (or flat), with no more room than for a bed to flop out of the wall or let down out of the ceiling. You literally have nothing but a bed to sit on. Gypsy Rose Lee told a horrible story about a pet poodle of hers who got squashed in one of these beds that fold up, so they are apparently not very pleasant or conducive to nice living.

Bigsby tailpiece: I'm sure there are other names for it, but in Moody Blues lore, this is an attachment on Justin's 335 Gibson (which happens to be red.) I've heard the term "whammy bar" used for this (?) Justin's is not the only 335 with a Bigsby, I personally spotted one that was "custom made" in Emerald City Guitars, Seattle in 2009.

Birds: in the U.K. a term used by young men to refer to young women. If you have ever heard a group of young British women talking together, they tend to resemble a flock of twittering songbirds, or cooing doves. This term has not taken on over in America as the young women tend to shriek more here, and are louder than their Brit cousins. (Germans too, are much quieter than Americans overall.) Rather like "chicks" is short for "chickens" here in the States.

Bloody: this is a really nasty word to use around Brits, the sort that gentlemen don't utter around ladies. (No kidding, I had a Brit apologize to me for using this word when I was overseas.) To us Americans, the word "bloody" just means something is bleeding, like your toe. When a Brit uses it, it's an extreme oath.

Blue Meanie: turned up in *Yellow Submarine* (the movie) but I had an old Deadhead tell me that this was the term for security that worked for Bill Graham when the rock bands first got going. They wore blue overalls. Cops wear blue too, of course.

Bohemian: see Beatnik, Hippy, Moulin Rouge

Boo: hippy term for marijuana, or the stash of marijuana. *Cannabis americanus* went by many terms in the '60s, including weed, grass, herb, dope, smoke, pot, Mary Jane, bud, and yes colitas. "Reefer" was the slang used in the '40s and '50s: in the '60s we used the term "joint." As it got down to the butt, it was called the "roach" and the very small glowing end was called the "cherry." This was something you were careful not to suck down your windpipe if you were the last guy to get passed the roach, clutched firmly in the roach clip (usually hemostats or alligator clips with bright feathers tied on the end.) Ruder words like "the shit" were usually reserved for more destructive drugs, such as heroin.

Boots: short for "bootlegs," that is, illegal "field" recordings of concerts, music or interviews. This seems to be pretty ubiquitous in all rock fan clubs. The vast majority of boots are of material that is impossible to get in any other way, other than through an underground source. Most bootlegs are traded among friends; a minority of crooks and greedy people sell these openly on Ebay and in *Goldmine* magazine, with no royalty going to the artist. The volume of trade is such that the FBI and the artists (and ASCAP) are unable to stem the tide. In modern slang, a "booty" is the *gluteus maximus,* and to pirates, it was treasure. Go figure, a popular flexible word!!! "Boot This!!!" -- Mac Davis, *Legends and Lyrics,* Feb 2009 (as in "boot the computer.") Much stuff that used to be traded as Moody boots on tape are now all over the Internet, and *youtube,* or in *Timeless Flight.*

Brotherhood of Eternal Love: group of idealistic young people supported initially by Dr. Leary in the '60s, who smuggled much cannibus over the Border and essentially supplied all of Southern California with inexpensive weed. They established themselves as a legitimate religion. As Dr. Leary put it "For a brief moment in the mid '60s, utopian ideals flourished." Eventually the BEL turned into a cartel of dope smugglers, in it only for the money. Owsley at the same time was supplying much of the Bay Area with LSD. "Real Hippies" were ok with marijuana, mushrooms and LSD, but didn't encourage the use of heroin, meth, amphetamines, etc.

Brum: this is short for "Birmingham" that is, the town by that name in the United Kingdom (or the U.K.) Yes there is a Birmingham in Alabama too, but it has nothing to do with the story.

Brum Rocked: and *Brum Rocked On* by Hornsby (referred to as BRO.) I did find two typos regarding Moody Blues in this book, one is that Denny Laine formed a band called the Electric String Band, not Incredible String Band.

(Research of the Incredible String Band has not turned up Denny's name, a much different band; Celtic, and sounded a bit like the Strawbs.) Also the Krew Kats are erroneously called the Krew Kuts (the band with Mike Pinder and Ray Thomas, did German cabaret.) BRO is a good book, but like the first book *Brum Rocked*, it rambled a bit, and probably would only be deeply interesting to another resident of Birmingham. Information about the Moody Blues, and even sometimes about the Beatles and Led Zeppelin, are sprinkled throughout the book rather like raisins in rice pudding (delectable when you find them.) I skimmed it rapidly (back to front) in about two hours the night I got it, and will list pertinent pages for the Moody Blues, El Riot, The Avengers and so forth. There is quite a bit of Moody information in it for the avid collector, and photos, but about 80% of it I found (prior to reading the book) elsewhere in my research. It's well indexed, the avid researcher is encouraged to find it, it's out of print and quite pricy second hand.

Some pages of note in BRO: Pg 59, 68, pg 44 (very sweet story about Ringo Starr at the top of the page), pg 77 (great photo Clint), p 128, p 78, pg 89 (Carpetbaggers), pg 95-96, p 106 (very early photo Mach I Moodies), pg 112, pg 137, pg 146-147 (details about "Everyday" and photo), pg 159 (wonderful photo of The Move), pg 178 (John Bull Breed), pg 185 (Wilde Three), pg 190-191, pg 208-209, pg 218, pg 230, pg 254 (ref Mel Galley who later played on Moody solo albums), pg 284-285

Bubblegum, Bubblegummer: generally, a derogatory slang for something a little immature, like 6th grade girls with teen idols on their notebooks. (We can all agree there is a market that targets this population; my friends all found the Beatles in 6th grade, all very innocent at the time.) A bubble gummer would be like a teeny-bopper, that is a girl in 7th or 8th grade, in worst-case scenario, those with not very nice, adult behavior. Girls busy losing their innocence.

Carnaby Street: in London, was noted for their progressive fashions, known far and wide, even unto America in the '60s. John Lodge referred to a place called "King's Row" which also had the real flashy wardrobe stores.

Cavern Club: nasty old basement club (actually an old wine cellar, and those can be quite ancient and manky in Europe) in Liverpool wherein the Beatles got their start. John Lennon was alleged to do skiffle there in the very late '50s. I haven't reliably tracked the Moody Blues to this club, but I would presume the Mark I Moodies played there as a Beatles opening act at some point in their travels. According to reliable sources, the original Cavern Club was filled in, and the current Cavern Club is a rebuilt replica.

Chick: see "birds"

Cold War: the "battle between Communism and Capitalism". The Cold War is something we "children of the '60s" grew up with, and still don't perfectly understand. For me it became real when my Mum showed me photos in Life magazine of people being shot going over the Berlin Wall; and with me learning to dive under desks in 1st grade (in case of atomic attack.) DUCK AND COVER!

My father was in Viet Nam working with military intelligence sometime between President Kennedy being shot, and the LBJ re-election and subsequent escalation. So it would have been 1963 or 1964. Dad also worked with a freedom fighter from Czechoslovakia, so the Cold War was not just something America manufactured to promote their own Imperialism. It was real to a lot of people in Eastern Europe, in that they didn't like the Communist government, and couldn't do anything about it. My Dad was a pretty sharp cookie, and saw the Viet Nam build-up, and also supported Goldwater's campaign in 1964, not trusting LBJ. He also saw to it my brothers were in the Navy! They graduated from public school in the years 1966 and 1968 and were subject to the Draft. My family all swims well and we don't like paddy water.

Even John Steinbeck (a pacifist) was aligned with LBJ against "the threat of Communism" because of the heavy-handed way the Communist party had behaved during the Depression in America, and that would take another book to outline. However, looking back now, it seems LBJ built up Viet Nam because he had a sagging economy, and a huge ego. It can be argued that the "shootin' match" in Iraq was generated the same way. The major difference is that there was a draft in the '60s, and there is NONE with the Middle East conflicts. All conflicts were driven by oil. Shell Oil was a MAJOR player in Viet Nam, our troops protected their interests.

Tie-in to Moody history: in Czechoslovakia, the Russian Communist tanks rolled in August 21, 1968, and the Moodies were there doing shows. When they got home (hitched a flight home with the Red Crescent), they started getting more interested, and eventually became part of the anti-war movement (along with most of American youth.) They also played at a Communist rally in France the same weekend as Woodstock. After what they learned and experienced, to this day they mostly remain publicly "non-political." Justin has been known to speak up about ecological matters, and didn't care for Maggie Thatcher. Ray is the only one to come out and say he doesn't dig left-wing social systems (see his website, *www.raythomas.me*, the story is on there.) Graeme has said he is "liberal socially, conservative fiscally." Should this "Cold War" chapter in history intrigue you, I highly recommend *The Complete Idiot's Guide to the Viet Nam War*. It's not an idiotic book at all. I also recommend looking up "Prague Spring" on the Internet, as it applies to the Moody story.

Core Seven: this term is used pretty exclusively in the Moody fan club, it refers to the first seven albums released by the band, *Days of Future Passed, On the Threshold of a Dream,*

In Search of the Lost Chord, To Our Children's Children's Children, Every Good Boy Deserves Favor, Question of Balance, and *Seventh Sojourn*. Tony Clarke and Mike Pinder called it the "Core Blimey." Many a Moody Blues fan has shown up in the front rows hollering "Play your old stuff!" and by this, they are referring to songs from this set of '60s classics. The fan club is pretty evenly divided as to whether the music is really any different on the rest of the albums. The Moody Blues have issued a total of 15 studio albums with original work (if you count the Brum Beat Moodies, they have released 16), and I refuse to count the "compiled" and "best of" albums. This is not including all the "live" and solo albums, which are just as good as the group albums, all a matter of taste.

DOFP: *Days of Future Passed*, title of the Moody Blues' first "concept" album, and the first album with the second line-up containing talented members John Lodge and Justin Hayward.

Dormobile or transit van: British version of the infamous VW bus enjoyed by American hippies. This movement started possibly in Southern California where the baby boomer population was highly mobile. My brothers had an old Helm's bread truck ('55 Chevy panel) which they painted blue and drove around picking up girls and such. Also, the surfers had "woodies" or panel trucks they drove in the late '50s and early '60s. Woody, microbus, dormobile, all the same idea. The Moodies had a dormobile they drove around in too, and they put airplane seats in it.

Dosh: British slang, for money. Cash.

Deadhead: a log that floats about just under the surface of the water, a dead flower on the top of a plant stalk, and a follower of the Grateful Dead music group. Broader definition: an old worn-out hippy who still smokes dope and drops hot ashes and stale bong water on the carpet. I hope no one is offended by that statement, but if the shoe fits, wear it proudly.

Denmark Street: "Tin Pan Alley," London. Soho District. The actual street is very small, and the location of famous nightclubs (the UFO club), music shops, sci-fi bookstores (Forbidden Planet) and lots of activity involving the recording industry. Google was there at one time I understand. Some of the architecture there dates to the 17th century! (from Wikipedia.) Justin mentioned Dean Street also as being part of the recording district (just a few streets over from Denmark Street.) *The Other Side of Life* (album, song and video) was done in Soho.

EGBDF: Every Good Boy Does Fine, Every Good Boy Deserves Favor (the album is named the same), Every Good Boy Deserves Flogging, Every Good Boy Deserves Fudge. All are mnemonics for the lines in the treble clef in music.

EMF: electro-magnetic force. Basically electricity causes magnetism, and *visa versa* (you shoulda paid attention in 8th grade science.) If you don't understand electricity, you are welcome to call this "magic."

EMP: I noticed I used this in the book. It has two meanings, the second being a play on the first. 1) Electro Magnetic Pulse. This is something that comes from massive radiation, such as Intruders (jets), or atomic attacks. It is a burst of radiation that totally fries any electronics in the area. Some blackouts along the western coast of America have been caused by pilots leaving on the wrong switch in their Intruders. (Not many thankfully, and they will never admit to it.) Scott Carpenter used it as a plot device in his wonderful adventure novel *Steel Albatross*. And 2) Experience Music Project. This is Seattle's version of a rock n' roll Hall of Fame, mostly dedicated to Jimi Hendrix, underground bands, and those local to Seattle. Parts are interactive, and it's great for school field trips too. *Never underestimate a story* *from Seattle*. It is a very cool place and LOOKS like an Electro Magnetic Pulse from the outside, too. Check out the website, *www.emp.org*

EOAP: Excessive Obsession Around Photos. This is a serious issue with fans, some go into debt bidding on photos of the band on Ebay. The photos are out there, one just has to be patient.

Equalarian: term possibly invented by Robert Heinlein, reference to someone who wants (in the name of "fairness and equality") money and resources for no effort. They think they deserve what others have earned and worked hard for.

ET or ER: *Eternity Road* fanzine. Nancy Wilson started out working with Char Kemp in Florida, back in 1989 or 1990, they had a fan get together which the Moody Blues actually showed up at. They got so many fan letters, asking them for photos and information back, that they started their own grassroots magazine, which I think sold for like $5 per issue (covered costs.) Nancy moved, got married, and for a while published her own more "mystical" *Eternity Road*. Some of her stuff was pretty interesting, she was into ley lines and poetry.

Extra songs: Most recording artists DO have a few goodies that didn't quite make it on the original album, for whatever reason. Since 2000, Justin has been taking a hand in digging these out and putting them on SACD's of the Core 7. "Wrong Time Right Place," "The Dreamer," "Island," are but a few titles. If you make friends with other Moody fans, they will send you all sorts of interesting "unknown" extra songs as well, most music fan clubs pass these around. Lots extra songs are on *youtube.com*. One good example would be a "lost" Ray song "Burning Gas, Smoking Grass" apparently only out there on private bootlegs.

Fag: British term for a cigarette. In America, derogatory term for a gay man. Old English, "faggot," a burning (flaming) stick of wood. If a Brit asks you if they can "pinch a fag," it means literally to "steal a cigarette," i.e. borrow a smoke. My brother heard this in the U.K. during the late '60s and almost belted the guy!

Feng Shui: I think I mentioned this in regard to the garden "arranged to tap the energies of the cosmos" in the garden of Threshold Records, as related to me (second hand) by one of their interns, "Christine." Another fan claims there are stone circles in their garden. English gardening is a VERY obscure (but lovely) corner of the Moody world. Should this interest you, try looking up *Old Farmer's Almanac* for 2012 ("Create an Astronomical Garden"); or better yet, *Feng Shui in your Garden* by Roni Jay.

FoMPer's: Friends of Mike Pinder

Football: be aware that if I mention "football" being played in the U.K. it is SOCCER. In the U.K. "football" as American's know it is called "Gridiron." Gridiron football is an outgrowth of rugby, which is a very wicked game indeed, they play it without pads or helmets, and it looks quite dangerous. Soccer football is a worldwide passion for many people, especially for the British. Justin refers to American football in one article as "a war game of chess played by freaks, like basketball." Last I heard, Justin was a fan of the Welsh Red Dragons, possibly Ray is as well.

Fuzz box: I wish I knew more about it, but it's a favorite of '60s bands. Justin has mentioned using one, and the Doors used one too, a lot. (I'm thinking of a piece on *Waiting for the Sun*, "Hello I Love You" has a great very gnarly fuzz effect at the end.) Justin used it on "Nice to Be Here" in a sorta hilly-billy song written by Ray (EGBDF.) Justin calls it a "Marshall Fuzz box, mains powered into a Vox AC 30.1" (on his website, dated 10-22-2000.)

GE: shorthand for Graeme Edge

Gig: pretty common expression for "a show" for musicians. It's also a term for killing small animals (as in "his eyes popped out like a gigged frog"); and I believe a "gig" is a sailing/nautical term, something about a small boat. A "gig bag," of course is what you put your guitar or instrument in.

Gizmo: device developed by Justin and Lol Creme, along with other members of 10cc. It has whirling wheels that touch the strings of the guitar in certain ways for certain sounds. I *think* I saw an application of the technology on the guitar sculpture in the EMP in Seattle. There are gizmos all over the thing, and they make a lovely buzzing abstract melody.

Gobbledigoop: I picked this word up, not as an insult, but as something John Lennon used to describe songs like "I am the Walrus." In the '60s, there was some "fake out" stuff going on in the art world. You must remember that all these people were commercial artists, trying to create and keep a cash flow. A lot of stoners were impressed by abstract art: the weirder the better. John Lennon was quite up front about doing this sort of thing (Picasso did it too, at times), and so long as it sold, who was to mind? It's a bit like a Rorschach blot; you "see what you want to see" and that is perfectly fine sometimes. "I am The Walrus" is the Beatles' nod to this art form, and IMHO I think "Say What You Mean" is much the same, on the Moodies' *Keys of the Kingdom*. If there IS meaning, it's very hidden behind obscure symbolism.

Gredge: one of Graeme's nicknames

Grouch bag: this is an old theater term. Back in the days of Vaudeville, performers kept their money in a small chamois bag around their neck, while on stage, so that other hungry performers didn't steal it. This is not funny, I saw a make-up room stripped once during a performance, the actors were too naive to lock their stuff up! Groucho Marx got his name from this. In general terms: a bag that a performer keeps his/her live cash in.

GWV: Good Works Ventures, rumored to be run by a friend of Justin's, handled merchandise for a while, and had some questionable habits with charge cards. I heard more complaint than praise and had my own bad experiences with them. Now there are always nice tees and goodies at merchandize stands at the concerts but be prepared to pay through the nose. Not sure of the name of their merchandise company as of this typing. Moody merchandise can be purchased through *www.moodybluestoday.com*

Gypsies: word that Justin uses a lot to describe traveling musicians who work independently and hire out in the recording industry. Specifically refers to string players. "Gypsy violins."

H&H: *Higher and Higher* magazine. Professionally produced fan magazine for the Moody Blues. Went away in 2007 after publishing fifty lovely issues.

High Mach: I noticed I used this word. It's a common term in social psychology, means "High Machiavellian" that is, people who follow the principles of Machiavelli. People who will lie, steal cheat (etc.) to achieve their desired end. A personality type which can be determined by tests. Everyone lies a little, these people do it as a way of life.

Hippy: alt Hippie: a counter-culturalist from the late '60s and early '70s. A "hip" person. Another name tried to get going at the same time "Diggers" i.e. "people who dig it" or borrowed from the Digger Indians. I think Diggers used to pounce on cockroaches and eat them, an odd splinter group in the Haight. Mostly these late '60s counter-culturalists were "Merry Pranksters" who enjoyed playing mischievous jokes on other, more "square" people. Running up to strangers in cars at stop-lights and making faces would qualify as this sort of stunt. You can't believe how much average people were frightened by youngsters dressed in weird clothing. For the true definition, I would refer you to *The Electric Kool Aid Acid Test* by Thomas Wolfe.

HoF: Hall of Fame, that is Rock and Roll Hall of Fame (RRHOF) in Cleveland Ohio. The Moody Blues are not in this as of this writing. A LOT of really talented musicians aren't in the HOF in Cleveland. I haven't lost any sleep over it yet. LATE NOTE Dec 13, 2017 the Moody Blues were announced as inductees.

Hosed: messed up (peculiar '60s term in Southern California?) An extension would be "hoser," describes a jerk who hosed you (screwed you over), but lately has come into usage by gay men to refer to folks "with a hose," as anatomy becomes a flexible state of being in the gay communities.

Hootch: slang for hard liquor, booze (probably Scots in origin.) I spotted an interesting British cultural thing. Apparently in England when you get rich, you keep one person in the staff to be in charge of liquor, always keeping "what you like" available, as well as keeping your good friends in supply when they drop by for a snort (i.e. Queen Elizabeth had a trusted staff member like this who also took care of feeding the Corgis.) They show up with a drink for you after a hard day's work. I don't know if there is a formal title for this job position. "Mother" was the Moody roadie who did this for the Moodies in the '80s. The French term is "sommelier," they take care of the wine stock.

Hotlegs: band backed by Justin Hayward, he eventually recorded "Blue Guitar" with them. They turned into 10cc but toured with the Moodies prior to 1974 as Hotlegs. Nickname "Legs"

IKYOTS: I know you're out there somewhere (song)

IYWD: "In Your Wildest Dreams", a song on TOSOL

Jays or Blue Jays: short-hand for John Lodge and Justin Hayward, the guitarists who frequently play acoustic radio sets together, or sit in with other artists. Justin is sometimes called "JH" and John is "JL." I tried to eliminate the initials in my writing, but some might have gotten past me.

King Crimson: their first album, *Court of the Crimson King* was pretty much a cloned Moody Blues album. Tony Clarke did some of their producing on that first album, and at one time Tony, Graeme and Mike Pinder were talking to them about joining Threshold (*Higher and Higher* newsletter, Jan 11, 2002).

KISS principle: KISS is a band first sponsored under the Threshold umbrella, they of course broke off and became a legend in their own time. It may come from the acronym *Keep It Simple, Stupid*

KotK: *Keys of the Kingdom*, album and also a verse from *The Bible*

le Kremlin-Bicetre: commune in southern Paris (France) a bit like the Haight in the same time period. Location of the mental hospital where Marquis de Sade was treated. The Moodies played this hippy infested area several times during the late '60s, lived there in Paris a few months, had girlfriends there.
http://www.youtube.com/watch?v=NnOLztkIuJU&NR=1

Loo: Aussie slang term for "the bathroom" or the toilet (rest-room, potty, WC, water closet etc.) Apparently used in England as well and gaining in popularity in the U.S. Lends new meaning to the old hoe-down song "Skip to m'loo, my dahlin.'"

LC: stands for *Lost Chords* (newsgroup on line)

Liddypoole: slang for Liverpool, home of the Beatles; a tough town, shipping port in the U.K.

LOAM: "Legend of a Mind," song written by Ray Thomas in tribute to Dr. Timothy Leary.

LOAB: *Legend of a Band*, videotape released by the Moody Blues c. 1990, telling some of their history and having some of their videos. Nice video.

MBs: stands for Mitchell and Butlers, Mercedes Benz, Milwaukee Brewers, Marx Brothers, Marvin Berry, but for the purposes of our tale, it stands for the Moody Blues, the band and road show.

MBA: *Moody Blues Attitude*, newsgroup online which concentrates on a cyber Moody Blues museum. Very nice, lots of good data.

MBT: *Moodybluestoday.com* The alleged official website for the band. The home page works pretty well, often you can check there for the latest in articles, shopping, or tour information. However, if you click on "community" you are in for a rude surprise, as the community message posting area has gone "feral" that is maenads, jerks, trolls, ad bots, and even a few porno posts in Spanish have taken over. No one supervises. It is highly recommended to find other newsgroups to socialize (many to choose from on Facebook.) My understanding is the band cruises the nets just like the rest of us, and often communicate under fake handles. The last place Moody fans check for news is MBT.

Maenads: I love this word, it perfectly describes female rock fans. Graeme occasionally talks about his own bad encounter with lady fans back in the Beatle days. Where Maenads come from is this: there is a Greek myth about Orpheus who has lost his wife (look it up, a great story.) He is the ancient Greek version of a rock star, only he plays a lyre, so well that the gods themselves were moved to tears. Anyway Orpheus is moping about the hills one day, playing a sad song about his dead wife, and meets some Maenads. These were women who drank themselves silly, dressed in animal skins (if anything) and ran around the hills in a frenzy. Possibly this is an allegory about menopause, come to think of it. Maenads are the Ancient Greek version of Red Hatters. They captured small defenseless animals and pulled them apart and ate them. When Orpheus dissed these wild women, they pulled him to pieces too, and presumably ate him on the spot. After that graphic image, be glad that Boomer women have finally gotten through the menopause. The '90s were pretty lively for the Moody fan base. Jim Morrison was the first modern poet to get this concept. Rick Riordan wrote a cute story about modern maenads too.

Mach I Moody Blues: Denny Laine (lead guitar, vocals), Ray Thomas (vocals), Graeme Edge (drums), Mike Pinder (keyboards, songwriting), Clint Warwick (bass). Originally dubbed the R&B Preachers and pulled together from Birmingham groups such as the Diplomats, the Avengers, and the Krew Cats. Disbanded sometime in mid-1966 (i.e. the guitarists left). **Mach II Moody Blues** would be the band of the late '60s, Justin Hayward (lead vocals, guitar, songwriting), John Lodge (bass) replacing Clint and Denny. Eventually ALL the band members took turns at songwriting and singing.

Moodies: used in the fan club as a term of affection for the Moody Blues. Notice the change of the ending; it is not spelled "Moodys" it's "Moodies." Spell checkers sure don't like the shift in spelling!

Moody, doing a: putting one over on someone, such as calling in sick when you are really going fishing. A hustle?

Moody Nation: term coined by a lady who was teaching what is in this book, academically. I've lost the article, but she claimed to be writing the biography as of 2002. Alas, another work in process.

Moodymania: grassroots magazine, mostly run by Char Kemp (who works as an officer of the peace somewhere in Florida.) It's very scrap-bookie, something she does as a hobby. See "Eternity Road." Char got some exclusive interviews with the band over the years, so her magazine is worth having back issues of. I've turned up three questionable references from *Moodymania* in the writing of this book, so while I think the editor's heart is in the right place, take that publication with a grain of salt. We are only as good as our sources. As of 2008, Char is on hiatus from her publications, or just sharing with very close friends.

Moody spies: I covered these guys in chapter "Blue World" but then used the term more in the rest of the book, so they warrant an entry. Basically Moody Spies are anyone who claims to "have an In" with the band, and who dribbles out info to fans lower down the food chain. Their information is often suspect and non-verifiable, but "plausible." The group (or one person with multiple identities) I corresponded with allegedly lived in the Sacramento area and were loosely attached to Tower Records. I never figured out what their agenda was, but various theories include 1) promoters for the Moodies 2) bored real estate agents 3) fired previous members or 4) the band (or band family/friends) themselves with "drop" post office boxes. Spreading rumors about a band is an old promotional trick and a sleazy one, too. Whomever the guys were I corresponded with, they impressed me as being a little snotty, and prone to name dropping. I only include their information if I can align it with other reports. I understand as of 2015 there is another "Moody Spy" who operates out of Monaco and is in Justin's social circle.

Mum: a flower, a way to be quiet, and British slang for "mother."

Nark: (var. "narc" as in *Bored of the Rings*), originally used as a noun, it refers to someone who is a narcotics officer, usually undercover. These folks dressed like hippies, were really undercover police, and turned in those who were trafficking large amounts of drugs. Later used as a verb, "to nark" on someone is to tattle, or turn them in. There was a really bad incident during the '60s, in Southern California where a free press newspaper listed a bunch of "narks" who allegedly were out in society, watching and turning in others. A lot of these guys turned up DEAD. And many on the list weren't narks at all. Another example of bad journalism.

OFC: Official Fan Club. This wasn't running for awhile, started again in Jan 2006 (see MBT.) It stopped for a while because Ivy Stewart, the fan club secretary hired in 1991, wasn't into sorting photos anymore. Ivy turned into the office manager for Threshold, and at-home band manager, worked with Mike Keyes, stage manager. The band has had a multitude of tour managers, who handle things like hotels and limos, they seem to change about every two to five years. John usually works with management on the road and helped with the OFC when it was operational. Anyway, Ivy got tired of dealing with the mountains of photographs that were forwarded to her every tour, and gladly turned over fan club matters to the MBT website. The OFC is no more, just MBT now. Splinter fan groups form occasionally, but break up just as quickly, usually when the "followers" get tired of the self-aggrandizing "leaders." We went years without word from Ray and Graeme; we used to get dribbles of info with the OFC newsletter. With the advent of Internet, Ray finally got a site, and Graeme does Twitter and Facebook just fine as of this writing. Justin and John post stuff to their own websites all the time, as do Mike Pinder and Denny Laine.

Oz, Land of: world created by L. Frank Baum, but also applied to the continent of Australia: also "Aussies" or "Ozzies" the people who live there, interchangeable spellings.

PAC: Performing Arts Center

Patter: the stories that musicians sometimes tell in between songs. Also the chat that a magician keeps up while he's trying to draw your attention away from his hands. Vaudeville term and concept.

Pigs: derogatory hippy term for police. In a broader sense, anyone who tries to shove their weight around, or acts in a piggy, greedy, selfish fashion. See George Orwell's *Animal Farm* for origins. I've known several police officers over the years who think the term is funny; one even had a wristwatch with a uniform-wearing pig on it.

Pinched: pretty common slang in England for stealing something. "Swiped" in '60s Los Angeles slang. "Kipped" or "kyped" also, same meaning.

Pindy: nick name for Mike Pinder

Posh: "Port Out Starboard Home" expression used to describe the "best room" originally on ocean-going liners headed to India from England. It was the shady side of the ship. Could be taken two ways, if you think about it.

QoB: *Question of Balance*, album

Quid: slang for a unit of money in the U.K. I think it's 1 pound (£).

R&B: Rhythm and Blues

RAB: Royal Academy of Ballet

RAH: The Royal Albert Hall

Red wine nights: Gordon used this delightful expression in a chat (7-7-12) and you can understand it perfectly. One of those nights you stay up late drinking cheap wine (with friends and/or family) and discussing how the Universe is put together.

RT: Ray Thomas shorthand

RS: *Rolling Stone Magazine*

Roehampton House: I have no idea where Roehampton is, but this refers to the house the Moody Blues (first incarnation) lived in together, and the site of many legendary parties. They were called "raves" in those days, and I understand the term has made a come-back. According to Denny Laine (*Democrat news*, 9-21-17) George Harrison lived near this house, and there was much coming and going between the Moodies and the Beatles in those days.

Rubber: in England this is an eraser, and never mind what we Americans use the word for. I was just seeing if you were awake or not.

SACD: Super Audio CDs (and hybrids). The early Moody masters were apparently taken back to the studio by Justin and cleaned up a lot, so that more sound is discernible in the background. EGDBF and *Seventh Sojourn* both have extra songs tacked on. "The Dreamer" (EGBDF) *really* rocks and makes it well worth getting the SACD version of the album. After reading numerous interviews from year 2000 onward, it became clear that Justin was REALLY unhappy with the initial transfer of Moody master tapes to CD format, so he went back to the earliest generation of "masters" and redid it himself. I'm with Justin, TOCCC really suffered from "flat-itess" losing the highs and lows in the early digital processing. It gets very involved with digital signals, waveforms and so forth. Before he tackled the Core Seven masters, Justin worked on the remasters of his OWN solo albums, *Songwriter* and *Night Flight*. While he was at it, he added on extra songs to those as well, so the serious Justin fan will want to find these. He also added on different takes of various songs, such as "Wrong Time Right Place" on *Songwriter*. See *Higher and Higher* #50.

Skiffle: a form of music that comes from being poor and having a lack of instruments. It involves banging on trash cans, rocks stones etc. to get the sound or the music. Irish spoon whacking is a form of this. "Trashin' the Camp" in Disney's cartoon version of *Tarzan* is pretty close to skiffle. Mac Davis called it "Hambone" on his *Songpainter* album, and he was slapping his thigh to get the sound. So it has some roots in Irish music and back-country American music too, not to mention the African and Native American drumming roots. Good music comes from EVERYWHERE doesn't it?

SLM: *Sur le Mer*--title of the 12th Moody Blue album, and also French for "from the Sea". *La Mer* is the title of a very beautiful symphony by Claude Debussy.

SIWL: "Say It With Love" a sign-off amongst Moody fans, also a song on *Keys of the Kingdom*.

Skimming Stones: song written by Phil Palmer, sung by Justin Hayward on *The Phil Palmer Project* (sound track for *Three Men and a Leg*).

SODS: Society of Distinguished Songwriters, apparently a stag club of some kind in the UK, which Justin and Mike Batt belong to, as well as Marty Wilde and David Arnold (music for *Voyage of the Dawn Treader*). They get together for

Christmas parties, and "roast" each other, that sort of thing. A "sod" is slang for a dirty old man in the U.K. as in "sodden old guy" also used in Nadsat (*A Clockwork Orange*.)

ST: *Strange Times*. 14th album, or the 15th if you count the first Brum Beat album.

Starkers: British slang: insane or crazy, as in "stark raving mad." Picture if you will, King Lear, nutty as a fruitcake and galloping about the forest with no clothing. Mental.

Stash bag: same as a grouch bag, only you keep drugs in it. As the '60s progressed, the stash bag was simply the place you kept your most valued possessions, usually a cute little drawstring bag, worn on the belt loop, or under your clothing. Nice stash bags were leather and had fringe or beading on them.

Stoners: people who do drugs a lot. Someone who drinks for their high is a "juicer."

Stonies: slang for "the Rolling Stones" band (Mick Jagger et al). The Stonies were embracing a "raunch and roll" perspective of the same music the Beatles were performing, only the Beatles cleaned up better. 1964 saw the Stonies invading America right behind the Beatles. The Stonies and the early Moodies did "My Little Red Rooster," which is an American R&B song, and apparently the Doors in Los Angeles also picked up that song for their act, enjoying the implications in the lyrics. The Beatles recorded with Capitol Records, and the Stonies with Decca. *Sergeant Pepper* (Capitol), *Days of Future Passed* (Decca), and *the doors* (Elecktra) [first album] all came out in 1967, and all were hits, "must haves" of any self-respecting hippy music lover of the time.

    The Stones' biography is (no shock) entitled *The Stone*s by Philip Norman. While I recommend the book for the history of the time (as well as Norman's biography of

John Lennon), I thought he was a little too focused on the negative. While Norman claims Jagger clashed with Sir Edward Lewis for example, my research on the Moodies showed that Jagger and Hayward both thought a lot of Sir Lewis (obviously an English gentlemen's club.) David Cousins of the Strawbs said the same of Lewis, during THEIR storyteller on the 2013 Moodies cruise. All praised Lewis's handling of Decca and their respective bands.

What is certain, is that while the Stones struggled with various drug busts during 1968, simultaneously the Moody Blues were rising Decca stars, and wisely kept their noses clean (somehow), which must have endeared them even further to Decca management (after *Days of Future Passed* became an unexpected hit.) I know the Moodies partied with the Stonies, they must have slithered out the back window while the cops were busting in the front door (ditto on the Beatles, they never got caught either.) Also, one will find more information about John Lennon's El Fenebre (limo) in chapter 7 of Norman's book *The Stones*.

'strine: slang for "Australian"

Tabs: Tabloids (newspapers). In the U.K. this is a bigger problem apparently, in the U.S. this would be the sort of thing you see at the grocery check-out stand, which everyone laughs at, and you never see anyone buying. Noted for their fake and embarrassing stories about celebrities. In America, "to keep tabs" on someone or something is to keep track of them, further confusing the issue. Tabs are also short for "tabulations" which are an alternate version of sheet music for guitars, banjos, ukuleles, and mandolins.

TER: *Travelling Eternity Road*, free fan bulletin board online. Very similar to a previous incarnation of the same sort, *Blue World*. The same fans surface over and over again on Internet discussion sites, and have since 1990, when *Lost Chords* first began as a cyber-mailing list. *NVN* and *Prodigy* were other active chat sites, also now defunct. The basic concept is, at any given time there are about three to ten Moody news groups, and the "action" travels from one to another. Some degenerate into idle chit-chat, and the really good ones have previews, reviews and news about the next tour, or new DVD/CD releases. Facebook has many rock band groups, and probably around twenty devoted to Moody Blues.

Teeny bopper: The (young) age of most '60s Beatle fans (they scream a lot.) See *Bubble-gum*

Timeless Flight: HUGE Moodie boxed set, costs around $300, has old videos and live performances, LOTS of them. Issued spring 2013.

Tin Pan Alley: generic term for an area where musicians and performing artists congregate and swap ideas, connect, record, etc. See Denmark Street. In America this is in Nashville (Tin Pan South), and the original "Tin Pan Alley" is somewhere in New York. I have in mind the musical movement right after WWII with Leadbelly and Woody Guthrie; Bob Dylan also came out of this. George Gershwin worked there as a song tester. According to my sources, Tin Pan Alley in New York is "off-off-Broadway," and has existed since the 1900s. It's "a place where you try out your music in the little nightclubs." Some say it gets the name from the "tinkling" sound coming out of all the windows, back in the early 20th century, from all the song testers on pianos.

Tipping the Gaff: carnie expression, means to "spoil the illusion."

TOCCC: *To Our Children's Children's Children* album. Dustin Hoffman got to use this expression in the movie *Hook*, and it pops up here and there poetically. It is also the dedication to *Fern Gully* (cartoon movie).

Tomo: Ray's nickname, coined by Graeme's first wife.

"Threshold" company the Moody Blues founded (like the Beatles' company "Apple Records"), or the album *On the Threshold of a Dream.* The Moody Blues' music store in Cobham, Surrey on High Street. Closed as of February, 2011.

TOSOL: *The Other Side of Life,* both the album and a song by that same name. The band actually calls this "tossle." This song is a great fan favorite, and some of the "regulars" used to put on red flashing horns during this, rather like the Dolly Parton song "Halos and Horns." (You're right, I can't figure it out either, and neither can the band, from what I've heard.) Some of the less kind fans have referred to this group as "The Red Horned Cows." As of 2007, the RHCs are a thing of the past, but the blue glow sticks go onward. The video to this is one of the funniest the band has done to date, a bit "grunge." Justin and John do a "stoic" dance to this in concert. Dropped from line up about 2010.

Vaudeville: ties into ALL early rock n' roll. In the pre-movie era, the "common man" had little in the way of entertainment, except traveling road shows such as the circus and vaudeville. One of the earliest literary references to this in America would be from *Huckleberry Finn* (the Royal Nonesuch, which if you have never read it, is a "must.") In England, they called this "Music Hall," and it was favorably regarded there. In America, these performers were considered just one step up from pond scum.

With the onset of movies, vaudeville took a serious dive in profits, and performers had to find other ways to keep eating. In America, it became Burlesque or *Burly-Q* as me mum called it. (I refer you to the collected writings of Gypsy Rose Lee, what a marvelous lady!) Burlesque was "underground," but tolerated in the backwaters of America; peelers like Gypsy Rose Lee and her sister June Havoc became respected artists in their own right. The Marx

Brothers were also in vaudeville but were able to cross over to the "talkie" movies. Some stars crossed over, some didn't. Jimmie Durante was for example, a "top banana" in Burley-Q before making it in movies.

England seems to have been different; since Elizabeth the First's reign, England has had a strong "legitimate" live theatrical tradition, as per Shakespearian theatre. Blue laws drove the more risqué acts to "German cabaret" (Amsterdam, Hamburg) and at this point I'd refer you to the movie *Cabaret*. If British gentlemen wanted to see naked ladies, they had to board the ferry and cross the Channel. It's probable that Hitler used this "decadent" cabaret culture as part of his climb to power, denouncing vile living, and preaching to the German people the values of "Kitchen, Kirk und Kinder."

Into this comes Graeme Edge's family history. His father, grandfather and GREAT-grandfather apparently had a routine similar to the Marx Brothers' Uncle Sheen, who had a vaudeville act called "Gallagher and Sheen," (hugely popular in America.) The format was simple, two men would stand on stage, trading jokes and singing songs. One I can remember from Gallagher and Sheen (a very grainy film clip) involved them standing there in pith helmets and shorts and singing *"All the girls along the Nile they wear nothing but a smile, that's why I'm here Mr. Gallagher, that's why I'm here Mr. Sheen!"* You get the picture. Graeme tells stories about his paternal ancestors, standing on stage in tam o'shanters doing a similar routine. I have the suspicion that Gallagher and Sheen snitched the concept from English Music Hall, but who knows WHO came first! One of the Edge (Graeme recited this on the cruise, spring of 2013) ditties went thus: *Oh the divets flew and the curse words too, About the man that I am after, Is the rotten little Scot that invented this plot, To rob the world of laughter!* (obviously about golf, Graeme loves golf)

As you can tell, those who have read this book, and know the history of the Beatles; rock 'n roll in England had roots in both German Cabaret and English Music Hall (John Lennon's father was an Irish tenor who sang on stage.) In the meantime over in America, rock n' roll came out of southern honky-tonks (see *The Buddy Holly Story* as well as *The Color Purple*.) Entertainment changes from generation to generation, but the fundamental things apply: good music, lots of traveling to find an audience, and a little comedy.

Viet Nam War: see "Cold War." Alt spelling "Vietnam" both are valid.

Wigan Hall: (Barnes) I run across this in Moody notes occasionally, the story being that they rehearsed out of here for a month or so in 1967. On the Moodies cruise, a quick comment by Justin popped out "I took it to rehearsals where we were at Wigan Hall," regarding the new "Nights in White Satin" song he had just written. Wigan Hall is apparently near Manchester.

Annotated Bibliography

Bramwell, Tony *Magical Mystery Tours*. New York: Thomas Dunne Books, St. Martin's Press, 2005.

Childs, M.S. and March, J (ed) *Echoes of the Sixties*. New York: 1999 "Moody Blues"/"Mike Pinder"

Clayson, Alan *The Best Of Rock:* Moody Blues San Francisco, CA.

Clayson, Alan *Beat Merchants*. London: Blanford, 1995.

Demain, Bill *Behind The Muse* Cranberry Township, PA: 2001

Denver, John *Take Me Home* Delta Music, 1995

DiLello, Richard *The Longest Cocktail Party* Chicago: 1972 (Beatles book mentions 1965 tour dates with Moodies)

Flick, Vic *Guitarman*. UK: Bear Manor Media, 2008. Very enjoyable book about the music industry, London's "Tin Pan Alley" and my edition has an introduction by Justin Hayward.

Frame, Peter *Rock Family Trees* "Birmingham Beatsters" London: Omnibus Press, 1979, 1983, 1993 Excellent source for not only Moody history, but also for Gene Vincent & the Blue Caps.

Goldberg, Danny *Bumping Into Geniuses*. New York: Gotham Books, 2008. Moody Blues only mentioned for three pages, mostly on rock in general.

Greenfield, Robert *Timothy Leary*. New York: Harcourt, Inc. 2006. Well researched, leans heavily on Leary's autobiography and the *Playboy* interview.

Hall and Clark *A World Bold As Love* New York: 1970 (various quotes throughout book by Moodies)

Henke, James (ed) *I Want To Take You Higher*. San Francisco: Chronicle Books, 1997. Various mentions throughout the book, excellent material on the Psychedelic Era.

Hornsby, Laurie *Brum Rocked*. UK: TGM Ltd, 1999 AND Brum Rocked On. UK: TGM Ltd, 2007
http://brumrocked.tripod.com

Larkin, Colin Guinness *Encyclopedia of Popular Music* New York: 1995 "Moody Blues"

Leary, Timothy *High Priest* Berkeley: Ronin Publishing, 1968. It rambles a bit, but it is a source document for information on Leary.

Leary, Tim *Flashbacks* New York: GP Putnam's Sons, 1983. Autobiography: also rambles, and has difficulty staying to a time line, but also has a good list of Leary's collected works. He was quite a prolific writer.

McCleary, John B. *Hippy Dictionary*. Berkeley: Ten Speed Press, 2002. I found this a little bit unnecessarily filthy-mouthed, not all hippies lived in the gutter, but it's fun if you weren't there, I suppose.

McCormick, Adele <u>Notes</u>. I gratefully acknowledge her perspective of her father's time with the band, sent to me via email

Maga, Tim (PhD) *The Complete Idiot's Guide to the Viet Nam War* Wiley Publishing, Inc. 2000

Murrells, Joseph *The Book Of Golden Discs* UK: (sections on Moodies)

Norman, Philip *John Lennon, the Life* New York: HarperCollins, 2008

Norman, Philip *The Stones* London: Penguin Books 1983. A bit raunchy, but EXCELLENT source on the development of English R&B

Ochs, Michael *Classic Rock Covers* Italy: 2001. O'Donnell, J. The Rock Book 1975 (?) (section on Moody Blues)

Pang, May *Instamatic Karma* (reprint) New York: St. Martin's Press; 2008

Partridge, Elizabeth *John Lennon: All I Want Is the Truth*. New York: Viking Press, 2005

Rivers, Victoria <u>Collected works</u>. Victoria was a pen pal of mine for a while and wrote a wonderful total fantasy "bodice ripper" novel about the Moody Blues, totally changing names and so forth, but they were quite entertaining. As of this writing I've lost contact with her, but would love to publish her books, a lot of fun.

Roxon, Lillian *Rock Encyclopedia*. New York: 1969, 1977. (Moodies section)

Ruddick, TR <u>Familias</u> Fan generated document showing relationship between all the bands the Moody Blues were associated with over the years, and also their own personal families.

Rust, Victor *The Moody Blues Encyclopedia*, Vol I/II. UK: Victor Rust Publications. *http://stores.lulu.com/victorrust* This book was not used in my research, and I have no idea what it is like, included for those wishing to follow up on information.

Samagaio, Frank *The Mellotron Book* Vallejo CA: 2002 (forward by Pinder, sections on Pinder and Visconti)

Sugarman and Hopkins *No One Here Gets Out Alive* New York: Warner Brothers Books. 1980. General notes on the times, biography of Jim Morrison.

Tobler, John (et al) (US) *Rock And Roll Years*, "The Moodies On The Threshold" and "Moody Mania In The States " (retrospective) 1990.

Trubo, R. and Cole, R. *Stairway To Heaven* New York: 1992 (Led Zeppelin book mentions Moodies)

Visconti, Tony *Tony Visconti: The Autobiography*: Bowie, Bolan and the Brooklyn Boy. UK: HarperCollins, 2008 (reprint)

Weintraub, Jerry *When I Stop Talking, You'll Know I'm Dead*. New York: Hachette Book Group, 2010. An entire listing of bands and acts handled by Weintraub and Associates, is to be found in his autobiography, I think I recognized every band, a respectable group indeed. As a side note to rock history, Weintraub claims, that it was handling Elvis that allowed his management approach to restructure the "rip off" management practices of the time. Elvis was such a monster act, no one would argue with him. It's fascinating reading, Weintraub explains the music management industry as being a bit like a protection racket, lots of middle men scooping off their cut. The Weintraub approach put more money in the pockets of the artist, and cut out the middle man, thereby attracting MORE business to them. A win-win for everyone doing the real work.

Wincentsen, Edward *The Moody Blues Companion*. Pickens, SC: Wynn Publishing, 2000.

Wolfe, Thomas *The Electric Kool-Aid Acid Test* (reprint) Picador Books, 2008.

Recipe Books with Moody goodies in them

Crisafulli, Fisher, and Villa *Backstage Pass* Nashville, TN: Cumberland House Publishing, 1998. Delightful book, the Moody Blues catering details are in here, as well as some yummy recipes!!!

Edge, Graeme: Facebook posting (July 2012). I erroneously mentioned earlier that Graeme didn't cook, but during a chat with Gordon, 7-7-12, Gordy mentioned a bacon and tomato delight Graeme cooked for him. Many Americans are familiar with the famous "BLT" sandwich, this seemed a new British twist, so I posted on Gray's FB requesting the recipe. He answered! *christie, you do not want to avoid mushy. start the toms frying and when they start to go soft place the bacon (old style canadian is best) on top and cover with lid leave to poach until toms are reduced and bacon cooked but not crisp, eat on sourdough toast with salted butter and enjoy*

The Backstage Gourmet Cookbook: *http://www.backstagegourmet.com/* this is an obscure reference I pulled out of Mike's FoMP newsletter. Has Mike Pinder's recipe for vegetarian Shepard's Pie.

Sinatra, Frank (ed) *The Frank Sinatra Celebrity Cookbook* There appear to be two different editions of this, and likewise two entries for John Lodge recipes.

Encyclopedias (of Rock) There seem to be a lot of these, and many are poorly documented as to press details. The Moody Blues make it into most of them. Entries tend to repeat in content.

Clifford, Mike Harmony *Illustrated Encyclopedia Of Rock* New York: 1992 (section on Moody Blues)

George-Warren and Romanowski (Editors) *Rolling Stone Encyclopedia Of Rock and Roll* New York: 2005 "Moody Blues"

Logan and Woffinden Illustrated *Encyclopedia of Rock* New York: 1977. (Moodies section)

Pascall, Jeremy Illustrated *History Of Rock* New York: 1978. (photo and section under "The Age of Rock")

Rees, D and Crampton, L (ed) *VH1 Encyclopedia of Rock Stars*. New York: DK Publishing, 1996, 1999. "The Moody Blues". This is a massive tome, fun to read, and a lot of data, so no surprise, there ARE some inaccuracies in the Moody history in this.

Rees, D and Crampton, L. (ed) *Rock Movers And Shakers* 1991 (?) (section on Moodies)

Stambler, Irwin *Encyclopedia of Pop, Rock & Soul* USA: 1974 (Moodies section)

York, William *Who's Who In Rock Music* Seattle, WA: (section on Moodies) (ed unknown) Planet (Fillmore Collector's Edition) (page on Moodies)

(unknown) *The Encyclopedia of Pop, Rock & Soul*. USA: (section on Moody Blues History)
(Unknown)*The Illustrated Rock Almanac* USA: (section on Moodies)

Biographical and performance DVDs

Rime of the Ancient Sampler 1993
   http://www.gordonreid.co.uk/catalogue/rime/rime.html
Batt, Mike *The Hunting of the Snark*. UK: Dramatico/Sony/ATV Music Publishing LTD. 1987.
Dilworth, Dianne (director) *Mellodrama: the Mellotron Movie* Bazillion Points: DVD release January 19, 2010. I haven't had a chance to see this, but it has good reviews and seems to cover all technical details of the Mellotron and the Chamberlain synthesizer.
Eagle Rock Productions/PBS *Days of Future Passed*. Live video of orchestrated album (50 year anniversary), filmed in Toronto Canada, June 2017.
Hayward, *Justin Live in San Juan Capistrano*. Nightswood Productions, 1998.
Hayward, Justin *An Audience with Justin Hayward*, at the RRHOF Cleveland: Nightswood, 2004. Justin sings and "story tells"
Hayward, Justin *Spirits….Live* Eagle Rock productions, 2014 (includes documentary well worth watching for information)
Lerner, Murray *Message to Love, Isle of Wight* 1970. New York: SMV (Sony Music Video), 1997.
Lerner, Murray *The Moody Blues Threshold of a Dream* (Isle of Wight 1970) Eagle Vision, 2009.
The Moody Blues *The Lost Performance Live in Paris*, '70 SRO Entertainment, 2004.
Moody Blues *The Best of the Moody Blues* (20th Century Masters series) New York: Universal UMG/Polydor, 2004. Has videos to Your Wildest Dreams, I Know You're Out there Somewhere, The Other Side of Life, Running out of Love, No More Lies.
The Moody Blues Videobiography. Ragnarock Films, LTD 2003 (?) Catalog #CRP2418. Unauthorized biography, interviews with various Brum rockers, and Tony Clarke. Worth tracking down (it's very nice to have some of these folks on tape indeed.) The "Go Now" video on here is a sort

of Bo Diddley/Soupy Shuffle performance, Ray and Denny are quite entertaining. The first incarnation of the band had a lot to offer!

Moody Blues, *Legend of a Band* London: Polygram, 1990. Interviews and videos, nicely done, should be commercially available on disc.

The Moody Blues *Purple Box*. Cobham: Official Fan Club Press, musical videos of Silverbird, Street Café, Nightflight, Steppin' in a Slidezone, "Cover Story" (interview) Your Wildest Dreams, The Other Side of Life, Running out of Love

The Moody Blues in South Africa. Cobham: Threshold Record Co, LTD. 1995. A fun video put out by the official fan club of their small tour in that year to South Africa. Has a blue guitar on the front of it. Lots of "home movie" sorts of things.

The Moody Blues *Rock Art* (Fractal Animation) Aeon Home Video, 1990.

The Moody Blues *Classic Artists The Moody Blues* (DVD) Chatsworth, CA: Image Entertainment, 2006. Worth having, interviews.

Moody Blues *A Night at Red Rocks*. London: PolyGram Video, 1992

Moody Blues, *Live at Montreux* 1991. USA Eagle Rock, 2005. eaglerockent.com

Swirsky, Seth *Beatles Stories* 2011. DVD Julukesy Films. VERY GOOD.

Vitez, Laura *The Other Side of Red Rocks*. New York: Television Inc/Good Works Ventures, 1995.

Wayne, Jeff (producer) *The War of the Worlds*. London: Universal, 2006

Periodicals

Murley, Mark, and Salas, Randy. *Higher and Higher* Magazine, Florida: issues 1-50.

Kemp, Char *Moodymania*. Florida: collected works years 1990 through 2008.

Wilson, Nancy *Eternity Road*. issues 1-4

There are over 500 articles from various magazines over the years that are not listed herein. I hope to compile these eventually as a supplemental *Blue Timeline*. I do refer the reader to *Moody Blues Attitude* On-line for a comprehensive library of all Moody Blues data bits from the past 50 years.

Writing by the band

Edge, Graeme *The Written Works of Graeme Edge* (audio, written, Kindle) Gordon and Graeme released books of their own. Graeme's audio is said to be quite "earthy" so enjoy tracking them down.

Hayward, Justin: On line blog, *justinhayward.com/notes* Taken together, Justin's long, thoughtful blogs constitute a book in their own right.

Marshall, Gordon *Postcards from a Rock and Roll Tour*. Gordon posted some of these on line, while he was actually touring, and they were very entertaining.

Pinder, Mike *Pinderings* on line blog, *www.mikepinder.com*. Mike's writing tends to be more "news blurb" in nature, but occasionally he writes just to pass along his thoughts or history. Very enjoyable.

Write ups found in album liners:

Liner notes from *Trapeze* and *Medusa* (both bands and albums produced by Threshold Records.) MANY reissued CD's have good history notes in the liner write-ups.

Powell, Mark *Timeless Flight* Box Set Universal 2013. Respectable book included with Moody Blue biography. I think I found two mistakes in it, but overall it's very well done.

Tracy and Schinder *Time Traveler* (liner notes). Polygram, A&M Records. 1994.

Albums involved in this book (besides the solo works):

Bart, Lionel *The Genius of Lionel Bart*: London, Sepia Records, 2012

Garson, Mort *The Zodiac*. Los Angeles: Elektra, 1967. Paul Beaver did the synthesizer work in this, and Cyrus Faryan did the vocals.

Lennon, John and Yoko *Imagine,* London: Apple Records, 1971.

Songbooks and sheet music (note: most publishing rights to Moody Blues music are currently held by Universal Music)

Blue Jays Songbook. UK: Justunes/John Songs 1975. Leeds Music, Croydon. Photos. Songs included: I Dreamed Last Night, Remember Me, My Friend, This Morning, Nights, Winters, Years, Maybe, When You Wake Up, Who Are You Now, You, Saved By the Music, My Brother

Hayward, Justin "London Is Behind Me". London/New York: Essex Music/Tyler Music, 1966, 1982.

Hayward, Justin "Day Must Come" London/New York: Essex Music/Tyler Music, 1966, 1982.

Hayward, Justin "I'll Be Here Tomorrow" London/New York. Tyler Music /Essex Music, 1982

Hayward, Justin "Tuesday Afternoon" (Forever Afternoon) London/New York: Essex Music/Tyler Music, 1968, 1970

Hayward, Justin "The Story in Your Eyes" Tyler Music London/Cheshire Music, NY 1971

Hayward, Justin "Blue Guitar" Bright Music, 1975 WB Music Group

Hayward, Justin "Driftwood" Bright Music/Warner Brothers Music, 1978

Hayward and Lodge "Highway" Ilfaend LTD/Johnsongs/WB Music Corp. Warner Brothers (FL) 1991

Lodge, John "House of Four Doors I/II" London: Palace Music Co. LTD 1968, 1969, 1972

Lodge, John "Gimme A Little Somethin;" New York: Natural Avenue Music, LTD 1977

Moody Blues *The Greatest Moods of the Moody Blues* Plymouth Music Co Inc (Ft Lauderdale, FL) Songbook includes: Cities, Leave This Man Alone, I can't Face the world without You, Fly Me High, Day Must Come, I'll Be Here Tomorrow, London Is Behind Me, Long Summer Days, King and Queen, What Am I Doing Here?, Overture, Morning Glory, Another Morning, Peak Hour, Tuesday Afternoon, Time to Get Away, Twilight Time, Nights in White Satin, Late Lament, Resolvement, Legend of a Mind, Voices in the Sky, Visions of Paradise, The Actor, Lovely to See You, Are You Sitting Comfortably, Never Comes the Day, Gypsy, I Never Thought I'd live to Be 100/A Million, Question, It's Up To You, Dawning is the Day, Procession, The Story In Your Eyes, You Can Never Go Home

Moody Blues *Question of Balance Songbook*. MCA Music, NY 1970 Liner notes by Graeme Edge, comments and photos from all the band members. Music included: Question, How Is It We Are Here, And the Time Rushes In, Don't You Feel Small, Tortoise and the Hare, Minstrel's Song, Melancholy Man, The Balance, Higher and Higher, Eyes of a Child, Floating, Beyond, Out and in, Eternity Road, Candle of Life, Watching and Waiting, Nights in White Satin, Ride My See-Saw

Moody Blues *Songbook* (brown cover) MCA Music, NY 1973. Liner notes by Keith Altham. Music included: After You Came, Emily's Song, For My Lady, I'm Just a Singer in a Rock and Roll Band, Land of Make Believe, Isn't Life Strange, Lost in a Lost World, New Horizons, Nice to be Here, One More Time to Live, Our Guessing Game, My Song, Procession, You and Me, When You're a Free Man

Moody Blues *Long Distance Voyager Songbook* MCA Music (NY) Warner Brothers 1981. Songs included Gemini Dream, In My World, Meanwhile, Nervous, Painted Smile, Reflective Smile, Talking out of Turn, 22,000 Days, Veteran Cosmic Rocker, The Voice.

Moody Blues *The Present Songbook* MCA Music, NY 1983 Songs included: Blue World, Meet Me Halfway, Sitting At the Wheel, Under My Feet, Hole in the World, I Am, It's Cold Outside of Your Heart, Going Nowhere, Sorry, Running Water

Moody Blues, *The Other Side of Life Songbook* Warner Brothers Publications, 1987 Songs included: I Just Don't Care, It May Be a Fire, The Other Side of Life, Rock n' Roll over You, Running out of Love, Slings and Arrows, The Spirit, Talkin' Talkin', Your Wildest Dreams

Moody Blues *Sur la Mer Songbook*. Suffolk, UK: Panda Press, 1988. Warner/Chappell (London) Songs included: I Know You're out there Somewhere, Want to Be With You, River of Endless Love, No More Lies, Here Comes the Weekend, Vintage Wine, Breaking Point, Miracle, Love is on the Run, Deep

Moody Blues *Keys of the Kingdom Songbook*. International Music Publications, 1991. Songs included: Say it With Love, Bless the Wings, Is This Heaven, Say What you Mean

I/II, Lean On Me, Hope and Pray, Shadows on the Wall, Once is Enough, Celtic Sonant, Magic, Never Blame the Rainbows for the Rain

Pinder, Mike "So Deep Within You," "Have You Heard? I/II, " "The Voyage," "Sun Is Still Shining," "Om" The Sparta Florida Music Group, LTD London, 1969, 1972.

Pinder, Mike "Dawn is a Feeling," "The Sunset," "The Best Way to Travel," The Sparta Florida Music Group, LTD London, 1968, 1972.

Pinder, Mike "Please Think About It" The Sparta Florida Music Group, LTD London 1977.

Pinder and Laine "This is My House," "Boulevard de la Madeleine" The Sparta Florida Music Group, LTD London, 1966, 1974.

Thomas, Ray "Dr. Livingston, I Presume" London, Palace Music Co. LTD 1968, 1969, 1972.

Wayne, Vigrass, Osborne "Forever Autumn" Duchess Music Corporation (NY) 1972.

Legal Sources

Pinder v Decca Records Co, LTD, and Another. May 15, 1981. Unknown if this was filed in London or Los Angeles (Decca had offices in both places).

Moody Blues v. Moraz, December 1991; County of Los Angeles. Televised on Court TV, January 1992

Pinder v. Moody Blues January 11, 1994; County of Los Angeles. Complaint was filed, but never went to trial, settled out of court.

Band Protection: What's in a Name? Published to the Internet, February 14, 2012. Author did not identify himself. (ref: *http://travellingeternityroad.yuku.com/topic/10906/Pinder-vs-Decca-moraz-mentioned-as-well#.UsR5PrSWRdd*

Are You Sitting Comfortably? Part II (A Manifesto)

[Author note: this postscript was written before 2013 when *Wildest Dreams* was first published and released. Since then, we have had another biography published, which is not "official" either. I have no idea what is in it, but I did read an interview (Jan 2018) with the author on *Moodybluesattitude,* and I felt like I was reading my own words.]

Let Merlin cast his spell........

"If you make an outright statement in a song, the only people who are going to listen to you are the people who agree with you. whereas if you just try to start the thoughts in motion..." ... John Lodge
"I only hope that people criticizing the Moodies do it with some humor.

You either like us or you don't. There's no halfway"-Justin Hayward, in a Ray Coleman interview, *Daily Telegraph* Dec 1993
  "The Who's?"
  "The Moody Blues," I answer. "They're a '60s band"
  "Oh." The young man at the ticket counter dutifully types in the name to the computer, sometimes asking me to spell it. So sad. I wonder why the younger generation never knows who I am talking about. On the other hand, sometimes there is no hesitation; the ticket sales personnel immediately recognize the name. Usually it's an older woman my age when that spark of recognition occurs. I never could understand why they are not universally acknowledged as the greatest band to ever pick up an electric guitar. Then again.......... Yes, I'm a fan. A real dedicated one. You either love 'em, or you have a huge vacuum in your life where they ought to be.

It would be awful to have an empty diary -- Justin Hayward

This sends me back to the very beginning, and the very reason why I got into music in the first place... it changes people's lives, it makes you feel

less lonely, it makes you feel less crazy, and it makes you feel that you've got a friend out there -- Graham Nash, Ravina, 6/3/2010

Why (write it)?--You know, you really don't have to read this; after all, you're here for the Moody Blues Story, aren't you? I just had a couple of things I wanted to get straight.

You write the thing when the lack of writing it becomes something you can no longer do -- Gustav Holst

I don't know why I wrote it. I'm just a confused psychologist that fell off the counseling wagon and wound up a little obsessed about the Moody Blues. *Heavens*. How many people have tried to write "the Moody biography", and not quite finished up? Or have gone off, chasing down some sort of (as Mike Pinder puts it) "mad rabbit hole"? Their music is such terribly personal stuff, and you want to do it right! The Moody Blues get so far under your skin, it's damn difficult to be objective about them. Mark Murley (editor-in-chief for *Higher and Higher* magazine) already made an attempt to write this biography; the last I heard from Mark, the "Moodies were supposed to finish it" whatever that means. His note to me was dated Jan 4, 2003.

Rumors of the *official* Moody Blue biography? It was originally supposed to be done by Ray Coleman. Marc is alleged to have a lot of pictures in his. (*What good is a book without pictures?* as Alice said.) Victor Rust has written and published a *Moody Blues Encyclopedia*. There's a lovely coffee-table book in the *Timeless Flight* box set, full of (yes you know it) photos. I tried to go a different direction; I hope this reads like a novel, something you can curl up in a comfortable chair with and read on a quiet night with a cup of hot cocoa in hand. I bet a lot of fanatics will say "But she left THIS out," "She left THAT out!" EGAD. They await me with buzz-saws. You have to leave SOME mystery, something a little more to discover! And the Moodies are a band still "in process" still growing.

When asked about "a band biography" in one interview, John said, "It's all right there!" Yeah, large wheelbarrows full of it!!!!!!!! The Moody data is overwhelming. (My computer kept on muttering to me "I have miles and miles of files, pretty files.......... and a hoard of pretty miserable photocopies!") The information NOT in this book, is spread out virtually all over the Internet, and in countless hobby-hoards of uncounted Moody Blues fans, and posted on multiple newsgroups. This is a good reason to make friends and share the information. There is always new Moody information to find out there!

(My mind occasionally flashes back to a Moody friend I once had, who got angry with me on line, and haughtily demanded I never use her name in my Moody research, so I haven't. But when I mentioned I had some articles about the Moody Blues, and which did she want, she said "Just send copies of them all." I looked sadly at my two file boxes full, and this was after I had been in the fan club only a year. At last count I have five file boxes, and that doesn't include what I've kept as cyber files in my computer.)

I found a wonderful quote in a Moody review, fall of 2002 written by Nancy Stetson for the Bradenton Herald, in Florida. She says *The Moody Blues developed what was to be their signature sound, sweeping orchestration punctuated with rock chords and lyrics inspired by the space age, spiritual awareness and medieval folklore. Listening to the Moody's music is like taking a trip on an astral plane with Geoffrey Chaucer on one arm, and Jimi Hendrix on the other, with Timothy Leary providing commentary.* Whew. What could I add to that? Late note: did you hear the induction speech Ann Wilson did for the Moody Blues on April 14, 2018 at the Rock and Roll Hall of Fame? *Yea.* What she said!!!

Yes the '60s were a wonderful time, there were spacemen and hobbits running through our stereo sets, televisions and bookcases. But there were occasional demons running through our cosmos, too: Viet Nam, and out-of-control parties and mind-altering potions, to turn the head and sear the heart. They were the best and the worst of times; all of us who lived through them should take the time to write down what we experienced. This book isn't just about the Moody Blues. It's about everyone who lived through the '60s. Remember. Don't forget. And as John Lodge puts it, "Well done, you've made it THIS far!"

This was the kind of arty rock that had rougher, tougher bands and hipper-than-thou critics cussing, spluttering, and spitting for years to come, while the Moody Blues calmly counted their royalty checks. -- Philip Dodd

View from the Worm's Eye (Vibrations from the Underground)--I tried to keep my opinions down (opinions are like the anatomical *cloaca*: everybody has one.) The reader is probably quite capable of deciding whether they like the music or can come up with their own interpretations of lyrics. I may have overstepped my bounds in discussing which books the lyrics come from, but that falls into the "mythology" arena; "Tuesday Afternoon" for example, has several stories as to its origin. I guess you could say it was seeking an expansion on the mythic nature of the songs.

Days of Future Passed was the first album I owned, in 1968 when I was thirteen. Part of the reason for putting in historical events, from my worm's perspective, is to reflect WHY the Moodies wrote what they wrote, an eyewitness account from someone who was there. I was there when the Moodies were first releasing their music; it's what they're all about; poetry, bluebirds, and wonderful sunny days with white, windy-fluffy clouds. That's what it was about when I grew up in the '60s in Orange County, happy beautiful things.

I heard a neo-hippy band on the telly doing "California Dreaming" (Mamas and Papas) the other day, and got tears in my eyes. Those years are GONE. But it seems the '60s memories still continue to trail us around like a lost puppy and just won't go away. In the lifetime of the Boomer generation, we have seen the Berlin Wall go up.

(This was impressive as a small child, to see pictures in *Life Magazine* of people being shot, going over a wall in Europe.) And then my generation saw that same wall COME DOWN. What a social shift to see from beginning to end!

One of the most important factors of our generation is the enlightenment and attitude change we created, things like "Radio Free Europe," and the open exchange of music and ideas. The Moody Blues were there to hold the mirror up to the world and show us all what was going on. It helps to know the history of the times. The Moody Blues were at the very core of radical changes, along with their fellow musicians. From Hendrix to Donovan, all have all been important players in this game.

The concept I followed in writing this book is "to tell a story." Part of the stress of meeting other fans is that (in order to be polite) you must look through their photo album of Moodies. I feel there is a large audience that wants something other than photos, wants to know what the Moody Blues are like as people, their hopes, wishes, and dreams, and how they have lived through what is a very tangled web of music, money, and fame. The Moody Blues are people to be admired, intelligent survivors in the very ruthless business of pop music. None of them have overdosed, they don't get convicted of drunk driving, haven't had liver transplants, haven't apparently been in jail, all have raised children and have families, all seem to be normal people in many ways, which is their true charm and attraction.

One of my original ideas, in planning this book was to insert at the appropriate spots a "cue" for a certain album, writing it like a screenplay, with asides and stage directions. Then it seemed contrived and cheesy, so I dropped the idea. But you might try it on your own; when you see an album mentioned, cue up that old vinyl! Wouldn't it be nice to include a CD with a lot of the "lost" Moody music on it, with this book? We can dream… and besides, as of the early 21st century, Justin Hayward has already taken on that task, saying "I have a responsibility to the Past." See *Timeless Flight!*

We hang our memories on sounds -- Mike Pinder at Border's Books, Tigard, OR

What is a musical risk?? -- Justin Hayward, *Prodigy* Jan 20, 1995

What Makes It Really Good music?--Ray said somewhere in an interview that "The Moody Blues can't be pigeon-holed." They defy definition so well, that the FANS can't even think of a label for THEM-selves. There are Parrot Heads, Dead Heads, and so forth, but Moody Heads? No...... The labels just don't fit. Justin once described Moodies music as "Rock bass end, funk in the middle, and classical icing on the cake." -- (*The Moody Blues Story,* 1981). What I like is the way the band has integrated the blues, and a country western steel guitar sound with an orchestra. I talked about "What is rock n' roll" in the first chapter of the book. Think about it, "My Baby Does the Hanky Panky" and "Little Red Rooster" are same song and chord progression, but one is the blues, and the other is rock n' roll, due to some funky bass and a fine tail piece. No pigeon holes please. Can you really define it?

Some of the Moody Blue sound has to do with "three or more of us on the mikes at the same time," as Justin put it. A live performance, taped at La Taverne de L'Olympia (Paris, 1970) and released in 2004, shows the musical power that they started with. Four male voices and cutting-edge music synthesizing, all done on a stage closer to a coffee house than any other sort of theatre. They were and are an other-worldly group, taking us to other places and other lands.

Many Moody fans insist on including other bands in the equation. King Crimson hit the charts in very late '60s (flute music plus rock pre-Jethro Tull, and initially produced by Tony Clarke), they were popular with the Moody Blue crowd. Procul Harum, Barclay James Harvest, Al Stewart,

and the Strawbs (an excellent Decca band produced by Tony
Visconti, sounding more like the Incredible String Band than
the Moodies) are other groups mentioned in the fan club as
"being like the Moody Blues." Historically, the Moody Blues
are "at the beginning" as classical rock artists, right along
with the Doors and the Beatles. But the Moodies are the
first in their sound. The mellotron and the flute gave them
the orchestral sound live, on stage, before they could afford
to hire the orchestra. And they did it all with just five guys.

They've been going in and out of style, but they're guaranteed to raise a smile---Lennon and McCartney

The biggest problem is that our own biggest competitor is our own back catalog. -- Justin in *The Star Tonight* (South Africa) June 8, 1995

Lodge says he came to understand the group's stature while looking out of a window during a train ride through the English countryside in the 1970s. "Somebody said to me: 'Do you realize the amount of albums you've sold? As we passed these homes, every one in ten houses has an album of the Moody Blues.' And I thought that was a staggering thing to think about." -- Las *Vegas Review-Journal* Oct 27, 2000

Why (were they in the right place at the right time)?—A certain phrase leaps to mind: *To boldly go where no one has gone before*. The '60s audience was also suddenly discovering the romance of outer space in reality as WELL as in shows like *Star Trek*. They cancelled *Star Trek* after only 3 seasons; look what it went on to become. The Moodies responded and were responded to by that same audience. People WANT to explore and find new, intelligent, thoughtful, "way out" themes in their lives. Popular media was opening all these new doors, thus making that human need to explore a reality.

Before *Sputnik* even went into orbit, there were (of course) already great pop singers. I am not the sort of person that thinks Elvis or the Beatles were "gods" of any sort, nor did they invent rock n' roll (though of course, they put out fine music and wonderful blues.) But over the years, so many good musicians have been forced to live in the shadows of super-stars, and one is driven to ask if this perhaps was the best way to make good music. The creative process should be original and fresh, or there is no reason to be doing it. The Moodies stepped into a cutting edge, musical niche of the Electronic Age. It wasn't until they did their own original stuff and added the synthesized flourishes, that they started to make it big.

The music must continue -- Justin Hayward, shortly after Ray Thomas retired in 2003

The Moody Blues have pride in workmanship. They do the best that's within us and follow the credo "to do what is right," which has really helped them to survive as recording artists for four decades. The Moodies enjoy what they are doing, therefore they continue. They are authentic.

Picasso once said "You mustn't always believe what I say. Questions tempt you to tell lies, particularly when there is no answer." I copped that one off Justin's website.

You contemplate the grotesqueness of old men playing young music but never apply that to yourself. Justin in *New York Daily News*, weekend 4-9-95

Heard You Had a Story to Tell--The Moodies have always been a gentleman band, not riddled with scandal, not posing naked on magazines, not found crawling through hotel rooms drunk, or in car accidents with underage minors. Downright boring to most salacious reporters, aren't they? Then again, with rock 'n roll, a bit of smut never hurt audience ratings. Take the Rolling Stones, who were cronies of the Moodies in the '60s and (I think) shared a house or apartment building with them at one time. If it's a naughty act, then the rumor has followed Mick Jagger, true or not.

But who cares? The Stones have one of the finest acts onstage since the '60s and there is no denying their mass appeal.

There's the money. OOOhh. *Yeah.* So many fans I've talked to really focus on this. (If you were a rich man and all an acquaintance could talk about was money, how would YOU take it?) In 1966, the band went through financial problems that various band members either chalk up to THEFT (Graeme), shift in musical trends (Ray), or to over-spending (Denny Laine.) I leave it to the reader to figure it out, but the fact is, it was honesty, sweat, work, persistence, talent and LUCK that pulled the band out of their financial slump in 1967. The Beatles had Brian Epstein as their guru who looked after and promoted them; the Moodies merely developed a suspicious attitude and plugged onward.

Even to this day they consider themselves a "working band." And they are. As John Lodge put it, "Where was *you* when we were pooling our money on the bed, wondering who was going to eat that night?" I could say that to a couple of Moody Blues managers from those early days, who dropped them like hot potatoes when they had a slump. The Moodies have been in several other slumps since 1967, and they always pull out of it, because they ARE good.

No, we never experimented with drugs. We were experts! -- Graeme Edge (chat, March 31, 2004)

Then there's the drugs. Again, speaking as a baby boomer and child of the '60s ...... *don't be silly*! On repeated occasions ALL the band members (excepting John, who was a Boy Scout) have talked about cocaine (ever listen carefully to the lyrics of their Coca-Cola commercial?) peyote, marijuana, and furthermore, were cronies of Dr. Tim Leary in the '60s. In fact, one of the band members referred to Dr. Leary as "a chemist who found this substance," which tells me what context the Moodies met him in, cooking up something over a Bunsen burner in the kitchen! Dr. Leary held his doctorate in psychology, not chemistry! Even Dr. Leary recognized at some point the mistakes he was making in the interest of expanding the human mind and tried to clean up his act. *(The Electric Kool-aid Acid Test,* by Thomas Wolfe)

I digress. The point is, if you find only titillation about the "evil '60s" in the lyrics to "Legend of a Mind," and you don't find the humor, you are probably missing the point. As Justin says, "We were just all a bunch of baby boomers, having a good time," and it's as simple as that. John Lennon talked about the Beatles at "Fellini orgies" in his interviews. Wild living was everywhere, at least on the west coast, from about 1967-1972 (and into the '70s if you were in the right spots!) American kids were (rightfully) angry about the draft and the Viet Nam war, and tired of seeing friends come home in body bags; so it all got crazy at times, for many reasons. But for the most part, hippies were peaceful and harmless when smoking weed. Like the bumper sticker says, *Dope is dangerous: want a cookie?*

Then there are REALLY personal matters. I tried to handle it in this fashion: I don't know if this Moody "factoid" is true or tab, but would I want it to be in a biography about ME? If that was the case (and the answer was NO), I left it out. Fan clubs are breeding grounds for veritable schools of red herrings. The Moodies, like many celebrities with fan clubs, have fan gossip of illicit affairs, gayness (is this bad?), and drunkenness following them. It just seems to be part of the fan phenomenon.

Of course, in reality, these things are part of life for all of us. Rock stars are not superhuman, and they rebelled against the post-WWII "Beaver Cleaver" lifestyle wholeheartedly, as did we all in 1967. If you want to discuss salacious rumors, my suggestion would be to check your own neighbors, or for that matter, start a soap opera based on a local college dormitory. From what I can tell about the Moodies, they are utterly normal in their personal lives, with about the same rate of "life events" as the rest of us (marriage, divorce, birth, death). They ALL think highly of their families, and are not only protective, but proud of their children, and no one is a wife beater.

Muddy Boots--There are rather nasty notes about bootlegged tapes of the band in the Moody Blues' Official Fan Club newsletter, spring 1995, and fall, 1997. If I may quote Lennon and McCartney: "Fixing a hole in the ocean." It's now all over the Internet and *youtube.com* for the taking. In massive amounts.

The object of the exercise is to share. -- Justin Hayward, in many interviews

Justin said, "I hate that sort of thing" about bootlegs on Prodigy, Jan 20, 1995. The entire bootleg situation with vintage AND modern rock n' roll bands has grown into very weird shapes-n-sizes. In the early years of researching for this book, I used to habituate a fellow named "Hey Joe" in Portland (OR), a charming Boomer a little older than me ('60s relic.) He had an old house, converted to a small shop; he and his family lived upstairs. Below, he had a LOT of boots, mostly of the Grateful Dead (some Donovan and Hendrix too), and other goodies left over from the '60s, a sort of a resale shop. I found some wonderful used Moody Blues things there, notably *Starlight Sojourn*, which was released on a German label, and I'm sure the Moody Blues didn't get a cent off the thing. BUT IT'S A GREAT CD!!!!

"Hey Joe" finally had to close his shop for fear of being busted by the FBI, and I miss visiting him. He was fun to talk to. Dead Heads who collect field recordings mostly did this as a social thing, from what I can tell. Some Moody fans are totally over-center about collecting live Moody performances, odd, as the lineup so seldom changes. The Dead usually did a different show each night, each show a unique improvisation. Thus there is commercial worth to trading boots in the case of the Dead. But sharing taped interviews is best in our fan club; the Moody Blues say cool things and are worth listening to on the radio. They are entertaining conversationalists, especially when they discuss their collective history, or do one of their songs acoustically on a radio show. Oh, someday someone will collect all those acoustic songs and print them as a CD. How wonderful it would be.

Not just audio, but video bootlegs are part of the Moody Blues legacy. At Radio City Music Hall in '93, one bold fan with a camcorder managed to capture the Moodies coming out of rehearsals. Graeme snarled at the camera, Ray and John smiled good-naturedly, Marie looked secretly pleased and smiled for the camera. Kirsten showed she has brains, by dashing rapidly (and unnoticed) past the camera.

Most amusing of all, Justin and Paul came out deep in discussion, looking like two nuclear scientists talking in calculus codes. They totally ignored the camera. This bit of pirate camera work was only to be topped by "tree Tad" as we came to call him, hanging in a tree outside their venue in Vancouver (1994) and recording with his palm-cam the rehearsals of "Gypsy." As you might expect, the camera bobbles a good deal, and there are branches in the way. It's not so much the thrill of seeing the rehearsals, it's the fact that someone had the *cajones* to do this stuff that makes boots so fun.

The point being, if there weren't bootlegs (from the pre-podcast world), there is no way I could have written this biography. The legitimacy of bootlegs is rendered moot with modern technology. I sat in the balcony of the Ryman in 2008 and looked down on a literal sea of digital cameras, all busily recording the Moody Blues' show. One spin through *www.youtube.com* looking for Moody Blues live performances illustrates the situation fully.

The danger of inner discovery is a danger to the Establishment -- Dr. Leary speaking about LSD.

What (Gets under Your Skin)???--A search for intimacy scares people. It's like trying to take the mask off the Lone Ranger! Poets and artists have such personal interest and intimacy wrapped up in their work, it might be impossible to explain it, or might be too painful to talk about with strangers.

If it's pretentious, then every time you really open up your emotions, there are going to be people who are a bit embarrassed that somebody is actually brave enough to stand there and expose their own emotions, which is like what a lot of these recordings are. They are just stripped bare, some very personal feelings went into them. I can see how that would embarrass a number of people who would never do that, who have such an act around them. -- Justin Hayward, *Street Magazine*, February (year unknown)

In interviews, Justin frequently says, "You have to be open with your feelings," that is the only way to be "truthful" with your music, and your creations. And if you are authentic, then you will be successful in selling your creations. "The purpose of life is to make it a better place," is a good example of a Justin quote, regarding his compositions.

You just pick a song out of the air, there are a lot of them floating around out there --Willie Nelson (paraphrased) "The Big Six-Oh" concert.

To be matter of fact about the world is to blunder into fantasy--and a dull fantasy at that, as the real world is strange and wonderful. -- Robert A. Heinlein

The Spirit World, the world that exists behind this one, where there is nothing but the spirits of all things -- *The Life and Death of Crazy Horse*, by R. Freedman

Dreamtime--Justin always says that music "Opened a whole world of fantasy and wonder for him." Like music opens spiritual doors of awareness for many in religious services, Justin claims his music is about making the world a better place through intangible emotions. He also has mentioned writing songs about waking dreams. There is a world that we visit in our dreams, psychologists call it the subconscious, or the collective unconscious (Jung); the Aborigines of Australia call it Dreamtime. In many aboriginal religions, "shamanism" is involved in tapping Dreamtime in order to bring those intangible feelings and symbols into the realm of reality. So in a broad sense, the Moody Blues are all shamans, as are all artists who can go to the realm of the invisible, and bring "meaning" back for the rest of us in a tangible form.

If you like, you can call the search and need for Dreamtime, spirituality. This rich, lively world of our sleeping dreams and waking fantasies is the realm of Moody Blues songs and lyrics. It seems odd, that during a computer listening party, a girl named Fiona, at her computer in Aberdeen, Scotland, and I in San Francisco at MY computer, would both visualize the white cliffs of Dover during the song "Visions of Paradise," but we did! And that's the "proof" if you will. The music appeals universally to different people in different places and taps the same symbols in the collective unconscious. The Moody Blues can take us on a journey to the intangible land of make-believe, to Dreamtime, with their wonderful magical music.

Being openly in touch with that nebulous world is frightening to some, and I suspect that is the source of attacks and negative reviews about "pretentiousness." Some always wants to deny their dreams. Moody Blues fans have almost a religious reverence for Moody Blues music. It's probably a basic human need, that we seek out Dreamtime adventures. Even so, the Moody Blues are reluctant gurus, and have never claimed to be anything more than musicians.

Another theme that crops up in Moody interviews is the desire to "do a stage show," to "take the audience on a little journey," "to do a musical," to "live in the land of make-believe." You must remember, they first wrote during a time when students in the streets of Berkeley discussed Jungian archetypes with drug addicts in the gutters. It was the time Joseph Campbell wrote most of his lecture notes. There were gurus on every street corner back in the '60s!

*Some of the weirder chords I got by playing a D chord over open tuning-*Justin talking about songwriting

How Do You Feel?--Whilst researching, I found a review in *Guitar Magazine,* May 1995. Said article goes on at length about how Moody Blues music is structured, analysing *ad infinitum.* The average musician who picks up an instrument (and plays what sounds good or plays the sounds that describe the emotions they might be feeling at the time), will skid off this sort of article like a greasy banana. I suppose there are people who study music academically and can say "the x-y-z chord sequence will evoke feelings of pity" or some such thing. But the vast majority of music lovers aren't interested. Analysis is not needed to pick up a guitar and play it.

When I first started this project, I was academically researching the effects of music on emotions. I can safely say, it's a VERY nebulous field. During our cognitive research in the early '90s (Klapp et al, CSUH), our data showed a trend toward at least half of a normal human population not even being able to distinguish one musical rhythm from the other. (You can guess which half the critics of the Moody Blues belong to.)

The purpose of music should be for fun and enjoyment, and I hope everyone reading agrees. It's like looking at a rainbow: don't get out the physics books and look for the frequency of that spectrum of light. Just enjoy it!

There IS an odd effect I have noticed with Moody Blues music. Small children go quietly to sleep in the front rows of their concerts, when their parents have obviously dragged them along "to see the rock icons." Perhaps you yourself have noticed your cats and dogs go soundly to sleep when you play your favorite Moody Blues album. (My cat sure does.) The point is that Moody Blues music is soothing, and just about everyone with a good ear for music likes it. Moody fans are a "silent majority" as one casual acquaintance once expressed it; they are people who like good music, and don't care if it's popular.

Great music can happen when you realize it's not about you and it's not about me. "We are merely vessels in which, if we are skilled enough, and work hard enough, great music may pass" -- unknown, it just jumped into my notes.

What (Makes It Good Orchestral Music)?--Not being an "expert," I wouldn't want to say for certain why the Moody Blues orchestrate better than other rock n' roll stars. And I'm not just trying to single out the Moody Blues here either; I think Bob Wills, and the Beatles orchestrate well too, among many other pop musicians. Nilsson orchestrates well. But as a guitar player (with opinions)(everyone has them); I'll say it has something to do with their songs having more than three chords to them.

Take for example, Dylan's song "Girl from the North Country Fair." It's very typical Dylan, pretty folk music, the melody is easy to learn (only three chords), the poetry is sublime. But an orchestration of it would be boring. It really sounds good with Dylan and Johnny Cash singing though, doesn't it? Or take the honky-tonk classic "Irene Goodnight," which Arlo Guthrie presented in concert (PBS) with a full orchestra. It was repetitious after two verses; but it's such a lovely folk classic, they layered on the violins and got away with it.

Then take a song like "New Horizons" or "Strange Times" by the Moody Blues. The turns and twists in the melody are sophisticated, intricate, and FAR more than the three simple chords in folk music. Even a beginner can pick out folk music on a guitar. Try picking out "New Horizons" sometime by ear, with no sheet music or tablature. See what I'm saying?

In many of his early compositions, Justin does a very insidious chord shift from C to Bb which is unexpected, but really euphonious and bluesy. In "Strange Times" and "Broken Dream," Justin does a complete key shift at the end. The meter changes in "The Swallow," and "Blue Guitar", mid-melody; and in "I Dreamed Last Night" too, on *Blue Jays*. It's that level of intricacy, in my humble amateur musician's opinion, that makes the Moody Blues great classical composers. Their music integrates musical textures and shades of tonal color. They are flexible and adventurous in their broad use of musical instruments. They experiment, and switch with ease from sitars to bongos, from orchestral to folk, from didgeridoos to breathy wheezy mellotrons, to rip 'er up rock n' roll. The ongoing juxtaposition of electric vs. folk/ballad is the continuous conflict of the "Moody sound," but that conflict sets the stage for more variety and creativity. Their musical elocution is a whole new language of musical melody.

After all that babbling; there is nothing like sitting in in the audience in front of Justin while he sings "Nights in White Satin." Who cares what the meter is?

Find a wise man and follow him -- Justin Hayward

To whom among the jealous throng of maids dost thou inscribe thy song?-- Pushkin, *Eugene Onegin*

Why (follow them around)?--I admit it. I've made a fool of myself, and been a crazed fan, I've chased the Moodies to their limos and run after them for autographs; Justin is a very fast runner. I think Graeme just hyper-warps. I've written (very) dopey letters to their fan club secretary. I plead insanity for some of my actions in the fan club, without a doubt. But it WAS fun, the fan club offered a way to find an identity group, to tribalize, and to reach out to others.

Beyond being a fan, I love the music. It's so frustrating to see fans who collect pictures of the Moodies, as if they are Barbie dolls, with the incredible body of philosophy and art around the band. We went through a bad time when the Internet first started, with some fans analysing lyrics with subjective "interpretations." Like the saying goes, "You see what you want to see, and hear what you want to hear." People got angry about "the meaning of lyrics" and then argued on line! Just because you have good taste in music, it does not mean you are a nice person to visit with.

One of my Moody friends wrote me and said of Atlantic City (after she had been to the same Moody show at a casino there, six years in a row), "It's like growing up in grade school with the same kids, seeing the same faces and how they change year after year. They even bribe the *maitre d'* for the same seats year after year!"

So is fan adulation like this "over-center weird"??? If you have never been a fan of a celebrity, you are missing out on one of the most passionate, FUN pastimes a person can have. There's a dark side, too. Writing this has been necessary therapy.

Fans are the greatest for collecting neat tidbits about the band, and there is no way I could have written this book without the wonderful network of fellow fans I have contacted, written and talked to over the twenty years I've been involved. But, at times it has been very difficult to maintain a positive outlook, and not lapse into negative cynicism. Perhaps Justin's words say it best. "Our music means a lot to a lot of people," simple as that.

A lot of the "crazy fan" stuff can be chalked up to people having a good time partying at concerts! Overall, I think too much press has been given to "weird fans." Everyone was weird in the Sixties, and some of those people are still Moody Blues fans. The music of the Moody Blues is inseparable from the times: they wrote and still write about things that happened around ALL of us in the Sixties.

Nuts and Bolts--It's been a very interesting process collecting and synthesizing all the zillions of articles, reviews, interviews BUT (tear my hair out) the information keeps slipping away in the process of telling the story!

There has never been a comprehensive biography of the Moodies. Part of the problem is, as in any fan club, there is so much scurrilous misinformation and rumor-spreading, some of it honest mistakes and some is wishful thinking. It's incredible how much disparity I found in many articles during this research. One of the band members is prone to tell outrageous "stretchers," a sweet man, but doggone him, it's messed up the research! Disparity even surfaced between *Moodymania* and *Higher and Higher*, and for a fact, I know that the editors of those publications mean nothing but good toward fans and the band alike.

Justin actually said in his website journals January 2003; none of the band members remember things the same way. There are so many little details, and different set lists, different nights with orchestras, and so many variables, that it's impossible to keep track of all of them. After a long night of note taking, and flipping through files, I would suddenly realize I had forgotten to write the reference on something John said twenty years ago, something he will have forgotten he babbled to the press. They have been interviewed so much, they sometimes say the same thing over and over during a "release" period for an album; then five years later might contradict themselves. Honest mistakes are made, and indeed the band themselves, like normal people, are subject to faulty memories, or tell stories just to get interviewers off their backs about what might be touchy subjects.

If it's difficult for the artists to remember fifty plus years of musical career, think of how it is for the researcher to sort out fact from fiction. Just because it's in print doesn't mean it's accurate. Some articles were reprinted in different magazines, and while researching, I would find myself re-reading the same thing over and over. Many of the articles, especially from U.K. tabloids, are suspect; we always have reporters out there who write anything for a buck. There are some pretty questionable stories and butchered documents that keep circulating through the fan club. You do what you can.

Some of their songs that have won awards are not the best the Moodies can do, in my humble opinion. "Popular" might not be "best." I have no numbers on CDs sold, but I do know they have a lot of platinum records to their credit. Though it's wonderful to have awards, I suspect the Moody Blues are truly just as proud of the soccer awards they earned in the '60s, when they played for charity events.

Some fans keep pressing for the Moodies to be inducted into the Cleveland Rock and Roll Hall of Fame. WHY? No one made the Lords of Cleveland experts in rock n' roll. There are many other musical Hall of Fame sites in America and the U.K., notably the Experience Music Project of Seattle, and the Rock Walk Hall of Fame in Hollywood; the Moodies are in this last one. Late edit: Dec 13, 2017 Moody Blues inducted to the Cleveland RRHOF. General reaction on line: **It's about time.**

I glossed over the accounting, because this is not a book about bean-counting and money, it's a book about people and music. I did find a note, the Moodies have sold 58 million records worldwide; that interview from May, 2002. There, some bean counting for you. That's a lot of beans. I don't even know what the gross take of the Red Rocks tour has been and don't see that it matters; when one sees the "gross", one never sees the other side of the ledger, where the paychecks of the Union musicians and the electric bills are listed.

Likewise, I don't talk much about ASCAP and other awards that the Moodies have received. For one, I'm too lazy to keep track of this, for two, this information is readily available to anyone who cares to do a search online. I hate regurgitating what others have already written so well. Suffice to say the honorariums go on and on for the Moody Blues, and especially for Justin; he claims four ASCAPs on his website. The ASCAPs seem to be Justin's most prized possessions, as that is recognition from his peers, for musical talent and effort. So if I leave out some of the "fame" stuff and the statistics, I hope I will be forgiven.

Dates are all given in American "notation" that is, month first, then day (not day first then month). If I've written 11-12-11, that's Nov 12, 2011, not December 11, 2011.

My final reader had a *fit* about some of my spelling! After careful research, I found that *Vietnam* can also be spelled *Viet Nam* (depends on how old the reference is, I learned the word in the early '60s when my father was over there.) *Hippie* can also be spelled *hippy*; I was around when the word was invented, and both spellings are valid; my reader is a few years younger than me. *Moody* is sometimes spelled Moodie, this is a fan thing, we refer to the band as "the Moodies." *Liverpool* was in olden times spelled as *Liverpoole*, some dictionaries list this spelling as "archaic." I probably picked up the "e" ending from an old map. Insult added to injury, my spell checker magically (fiendishly) shifted to British spelling at the end, and I write in American English. Everyone will just have to get over it!!!

So many individuals are involved in the origins and careers of the Moody Blues; I'm sorry if I missed any deserving souls. I have no idea of the names of each and every manager, nor the histories of the side-folk and technicians, nor ALL the names and faces of all the true helpers along the road the Moody Blues have traveled.

In writing this book, I stand on the shoulders of many Moodies fans who have done their own massive footwork in keeping fans informed. Notably I must bow to the talented Mark Murley and his associates at *Higher and Higher,* who worked hard ferreting out the lives and pursuits of the many side men (and ladies) with the Moody Blues, Bias Boshell, Paul Bliss, Gordon Marshall, Sue Shattock, Tracy Graham, June Boyce, Patrick Moraz, Bernie Barlow, Norda Muellen, Alan Hewitt, Billy Ashbaugh, and Julie Ragins. Every one of these performers is a very talented person in their own right, especially Tracy, who has a voice that gives me the chills. Their biographies can be read in *Higher and Higher.* There is too much material to include them in this book, and I hope they will forgive me. Use the power of Google, many of them have their own websites. And I bow as well, to the mistress of the grassroots fanzine, *Moodymania*, the bold and courageous Char Kemp. Hey Mark and Char, publish those darn magazines in one volume, already!

    Sure and it's true I tend to write a little too academically at times, but after all, this is supposed to be a quasi-historical book! I've tried to stay with the KISS principle; that is, I try to do what a good communicator should do, get to the point and keep it simple. Having said that, I'm also a teacher, and sometimes throw in a big word or two, just to keep your brain (and my brain too!) awake. If I use a "big word," take a moment and get friendly with your dictionary. You should learn something new every day, or you quit growing and turn into a slug!

    Above all, I deeply hope the readers will forgive my occasional skewed humor! I saw Weird Al on Donny and Marie Osmond's show once. When they asked him why he had written lyrics making fun of their act, his eyes got big and round, and he replied (in the most disarming way), "Well, I said it with love!"

    Said with love, Christie Grayson

Finis

If you have an eagle eye for editing and you spot something wrong, will you please email me where it is? Thanks, and it will be corrected.
josiec5150@gmail.com

Printed in Great Britain
by Amazon